LONGITUDINAL MULTIVARIATE PSYCHOLOGY

This volume presents a collection of chapters focused on the study of multivariate change. As people develop and change, multivariate measurement of that change and analysis of those measures can illuminate the regularities in the trajectories of individual development, as well as time-dependent changes in population averages. As longitudinal data have recently become much more prevalent in psychology and the social sciences, models of change have become increasingly important. This collection focuses on methodological, statistical, and modeling aspects of multivariate change, as well as applications of longitudinal models to the study of psychological processes.

The volume is divided into three major sections: Extension of latent change models, Measurement and testing issues in longitudinal modeling, and Novel applications of multivariate longitudinal methodology. It is intended for advanced students and researchers interested in learning about state-of-the-art techniques for longitudinal data analysis, as well as understanding the history and development of such techniques.

Emilio Ferrer is Professor in the Department of Psychology at the University of California, Davis, US, and a member of the Graduate Groups in Biostatistics, Education, and Human Development. His research interests include methods to examine multivariate change and developmental processes.

Steven M. Boker is Professor of Quantitative Psychology at the University of Virginia, US, Director of the Human Dynamics Lab, Speaker-Director of the LIFE Academy, and Director of the Center for Dynamics of Healthy Development. His research concerns dynamical systems modeling, interpersonal communication, and methods for the study of development over the lifespan.

Kevin J. Grimm is Professor of Psychology at Arizona State University, US, and head of the Quantitative Research Methods PhD program. His research interests include longitudinal data analysis and data mining.

Multivariate Applications Series

Sponsored by the Society of Multivariate Experimental Psychology, the goal of this series is to apply statistical methods to significant social or behavioral issues, in such a way so as to be accessible to a nontechnical-oriented readership (e.g., non-methodological researchers, teachers, students, government personnel, practitioners, and other professionals). Applications from a variety of disciplines such as psychology, public health, sociology, education, and business are welcome. Books can be single- or multiple-authored or edited volumes that: (1) demonstrate the application of a variety of multivariate methods to a single, major area of research; (2) describe a multivariate procedure or framework that could be applied to a number of research areas; or (3) present a variety of perspectives on a topic of interest to applied multivariate researchers.

Anyone wishing to submit a book proposal should send the following: (1) author/title; (2) timeline including completion date; (3) brief overview of the book's focus, including table of contents and, ideally, a sample chapter (or chapters); (4) a brief description of competing publications; and (5) targeted audiences.

For more information, please contact the series editor, Lisa Harlow, at Department of Psychology, University of Rhode Island, 10 Chafee Road, Suite 8, Kingston, RI 02881-0808; phone (401) 874-4242; fax (401) 874-5562; or e-mail LHarlow@uri.edu.

- *Cognitive Assessment: An Introduction to the Rule Space Method*, written by Kikumi K. Tatsuoka (2009)
- *Structural Equation Modeling with AMOS: Basic Concepts, Applications, and Programming, Second Edition* written by Barbara M. Byrne (2010)
- *Handbook of Ethics in Quantitative Methodology*, co-edited by Abigail T. Panter & Sonya K. Sterba (2011)
- *Longitudinal Data Analysis: A Practical Guide for Researchers in Aging, Health, and Social Sciences*, co-edited by Jason T. Newsom, Richard N. Jones, and Scott M. Hofer (2011)
- *Structural Equation Modeling with MPlus: Basic Concepts, Applications, and Programming* written by Barbara M. Byrne (2012)
- *Understanding the New Statistics: Effect Sizes, Confidence Intervals, and Meta-Analysis* written by Geoff Cumming (2012)
- *Frontiers of Test Validity Theory: Measurement, Causation and Meaning* written by Keith A. Markus and Denny Borsboom (2013)
- *The Essence of Multivariate Thinking: Basic Themes and Methods, Second Edition* written by Lisa L. Harlow (2014)
- *Longitudinal Analysis: Modeling Within-Person Fluctuation and Change* written by Lesa Hoffman (2015)
- *Handbook of Item Response Theory Modeling: Applications to Typical Performance Assessment* co-edited by Steven P. Reise & Dennis Revicki (2015)
- *Longitudinal Structural Equation Modeling: A Comprehensive Introduction* written by Jason T. Newsom (2015)
- *Higher-Order Growth Curves and Mixture Modeling with Mplus: A Practical Guide* by Kandauda A. S. Wickrama, Tae Kyoung Lee, Catherine Walker O'Neal, & Frederick O. Lorenz (2016)
- *What If There Were No Significance Tests?: Classic Edition* by Lisa L. Harlow, Stanley A. Mulaik, James H. Steiger (2016)

LONGITUDINAL MULTIVARIATE PSYCHOLOGY

Edited by Emilio Ferrer, Steven M. Boker, and Kevin J. Grimm

Routledge
Taylor & Francis Group

NEW YORK AND LONDON

First published 2019
by Routledge
711 Third Avenue, New York, NY 10017

and by Routledge
2 Park Square, Milton Park, Abingdon, Oxon, OX14 4RN

Routledge is an imprint of the Taylor & Francis Group, an informa business

© 2019 Taylor & Francis

The right of Emilio Ferrer, Steven M. Boker, and Kevin J. Grimm to be identified as the authors of the editorial material, and of the authors for their individual chapters, has been asserted in accordance with sections 77 and 78 of the Copyright, Designs and Patents Act 1988.

Library of Congress Cataloging-in-Publication Data
Names: Ferrer, Emilio, author. | Boker, Steven M., author. | Grimm, Kevin J., author.
Title: Longitudinal multivariate psychology / Emilio Ferrer, Steven M. Boker, Kevin J. Grimm.
Description: New York, NY : Routledge, 2019. | Series: Multivariate applications series | Includes bibliographical references and index.
Identifiers: LCCN 2018014758 | ISBN 9781138064225 (hardback) | ISBN 9781138064232 (pbk.)
Subjects: LCSH: Psychology–Statistical methods. | Psychology–Research–Longitudinal studies. | Multivariate analysis.
Classification: LCC BF39 .F47 2019 | DDC 150.1/519535–dc23
LC record available at https://lccn.loc.gov/2018014758

ISBN: 978-1-138-06422-5 (hbk)
ISBN: 978-1-138-06423-2 (pbk)
ISBN: 978-1-315-16054-2 (ebk)

Typeset in Bembo
by Out of House Publishing

Printed and bound in Great Britain by
TJ International Ltd, Padstow, Cornwall

CONTENTS

FOREWORD

John R. Nesselroade

I am deeply honored to write this foreword to Jack McArdle's festschrift, primarily for two reasons. First, Jack is truly deserving of the recognition this volume affords. Second, in addition to his prolific scholarship, innovative science, and highly valued collegiality, Jack has been an "old school" mentor to a large number of researchers now outstanding in their own right. By virtue of both their association with Jack and their own contributions, these scholars have earned the right to speak about Jack's science and their own. And herein, by dint of their thoughtful and lasting contributions, they do so emphatically. This volume will stand for a long time as a marker for an outstanding scientist who forged a great career while pursuing his ambitious goals for the field. These chapters make it abundantly clear that the case for obtaining and analyzing longitudinal data that has been so vigorously prosecuted by Jack McArdle remains in good hands for the foreseeable future.

Through most of the 1970s, I served as Secretary-Treasurer of the Society of Multivariate Experimental Psychology (SMEP). In that capacity, I received a letter one day from a young graduate student at Hofstra University asking how he could become a member of SMEP. I carefully explained to the young man that SMEP was a small scientific society, membership in which could only be obtained through a process of nomination and voting by the active members of the society. I encouraged him to complete his PhD, get an academic job, and be productive in multivariate behavioral research and some day he could aspire to membership in SMEP. My response probably sounded platitudinous, but it was meant to be helpful.

Over the next decade or so, I had several occasions to connect with that young scientist who had hoped to become a SMEP member. It was clear that his research career was progressing in a most impressive fashion. He wanted psychology to become a more rigorous science and he was both innovative and enthusiastic in the way he went about doing what he thought would make it happen. When he had the opportunity to apply for a faculty position in the Psychology Department at the University of Virginia, I was delighted to write a letter of recommendation on his behalf. Parenthetically, he returned the favor 15 years later when I was under consideration for a position at UVA. Over the years we have collaborated on a large number of papers, chapters, and a book. As our collaboration grew, so did our friendship. For decades now, I have been richly blessed to have him as both dear friend and esteemed colleague.

As the reader has likely guessed by now, that young SMEP aspirant was Jack McArdle. In the course of building his brilliant scientific career, Jack's early hope was realized precisely and he was indeed elected to membership in SMEP. In fact, Jack has served SMEP as its president. Yes, Jack made it and made it big! His enduring legacy, aimed at helping to make psychology "a quantitative, rational science," is attested to by the present outstanding volume. The editors and authors have done a great mentor proud!

John R. Nesselroade
March, 2017

CONTRIBUTORS

Naleen N. Andrade, Department of Psychiatry, University of Hawai'i at Mānoa, USA

Steven M. Boker, Department of Psychology, The University of Virginia, USA

Ryan P. Bowles, Department of Human Development and Family Studies, Michigan State University, USA

Sy-Miin Chow, Department of Human Development and Family Studies, Pennsylvania State University, USA

Ryne Estabrook, Department of Medical Social Sciences, Northwestern University, USA

Emilio Ferrer, Department of Psychology, University of California, Davis, USA

Deborah A. Goebert, Department of Psychiatry, University of Hawai'i at Mānoa, USA

Kevin J. Grimm, Department of Psychology, Arizona State University, USA

Fumiaki Hamagami, Longitudinal Research Institutes, USA

Timothy Hayes, Department of Psychology, Florida International University, USA

Earl S. Hishinuma, Department of Psychiatry, University of Hawai'i at Mānoa, USA

Ross Jacobucci, Department of Psychology, University of Notre Dame, USA

Linying Ji, Department of Human Development and Family Studies, Pennsylvania State University, USA

Haiyan Liu, Department of Psychology, University of Notre Dame, USA

John J. McArdle, Longitudinal Research Institutes, USA

Michael C. Neale, Virginia Institute for Psychiatric and Behavioral Genetics, Virginia Commonwealth University, USA

John R. Nesselroade, Department of Psychology, University of Virginia, USA

Stephanie T. Nishimura, Department of Psychiatry, University of Hawai'i at Mānoa, USA

Jane M. M. Onoye, Department of Psychiatry, University of Hawai'i at Mānoa, USA

Thomas S. Paskus, National Collegiate Athletic Association, USA

Todd A. Petr, National Collegiate Athletic Association, USA

Nilam Ram, Department of Human Development and Family Studies, Pennsylvania State University, USA

Sarfaraz Serang, Department of Psychology, University of Southern California, USA

Jeanelle J. Sugimoto-Matsuda, Department of Psychiatry, University of Hawai'i at Mānoa, USA

Junji Takeshita, Department of Psychiatry, University of Hawai'i at Mānoa, USA

Lijuan Wang, Department of Psychology, University of Notre Dame, USA

Miao Yang, Department of Psychology, University of Notre Dame, USA

Xiao Yang, Department of Human Development and Family Studies, Pennsylvania State University, USA

Zhiyong Zhang, Department of Psychology, University of Notre Dame, USA

INTRODUCTION AND SECTION OVERVIEW

Emilio Ferrer, Steven M. Boker, & Kevin J. Grimm

Most phenomena in psychology and the behavioral and social sciences involve multiple processes that unfold over time. As such, much of this research is focused on questions related to how and why constructs change over time. Addressing these questions requires models that can capture changes and interrelations amongst constructs, as well as potential mechanisms underlying such dynamics. This is not an easy task, and is a pursuit that has kept quantitative methodologists on their toes for many years. One of the most influential leaders in this quest for the last three decades has been John J. (Jack) McArdle. McArdle's work has opened the path to models for studying longitudinal measurement, growth, and change, and set the stage for novel approaches to examine multivariate interrelations and dynamics.

In this volume, a number of his former students, colleagues, and friends pay a tribute to McArdle's work, attesting to his creative thinking, his innovative methodological advantages, and the lasting legacy of his work. In particular, the volume presents a collection of chapters focused on the study of multivariate change. As people develop and change, multivariate measurement of that change and analysis of those measures can illuminate the regularities in the trajectories of individual development as well as time dependent changes in population averages. As longitudinal data have recently become much more prevalent in psychology and the social sciences, models of change have become increasingly important to provide a deep understanding of mechanisms underlying development. The chapters focus on methodological, statistical, and modeling aspects of multivariate change, as well as applications of longitudinal models to the study of psychological processes.

The volume is divided into three major sections, each of them dealing with a set of methodological issues.

Section I: Extensions of Latent Change Score Models

Latent Change Score (LCS) models are a class of structural equation models for examining change and dynamics. They are based on latent variables that represent changes in a process and focus on such changes and their mechanisms over time. LCS models constitute a general modeling approach that can accommodate multiple specifications, including one or several variables, determinants of those changes, multiple groups, factor structures with various measures, and unobserved classes, among others. This framework to study multivariate change, developed by McArdle, is the main theme of this section.

The chapter by Linying Ji and Sy-Miin Chow discusses two important extensions of the LCS for bivariate processes. The first extension includes the use of alternative specifications of the initial conditions in the modeled trajectory. Findings from their simulation study indicate that misspecifying initial conditions of means and covariance matrix in a bivariate LCS model does not have a strong effect on other model parameters. This is the case when the specified initial conditions are wide enough to cover the true initial conditions distribution. Moreover, the effect of the potential misspecification is reduced with the availability of more time points. The second extension of the LCS model discussed in Ji and Chow's chapter features the use of stochasticity in the form of process noise and measurement error. Their simulation results indicate that, although most of the model parameters can be recovered with few time points under correct model specification with as few as three time points, process noise cannot be reliably distinguished from measurement error. This issue is magnified when initial conditions are misspecified. Ji and Chow implement all models using their own *R* statistical package *dynr*.

Ferrer presents an implementation of LCS modeling to study the development of fluid reasoning and the contribution of brain structure maturation to such development across childhood and adolescence. He uses an LCS model that includes a measurement structure, thus, defining fluid reasoning as a latent factor. Using data from a cohort-sequential design, he examines whether the fluid reasoning factor is equivalent across measurement occasions and age through factorial invariance analyses. He then specifies an LCS model across measurement occasions and, with the use of discrete age bins, across age in a semi-continuous fashion. Results from this latter model indicate that white matter volume and structural integrity from the entire brain at any given age are related to improvements in fluid reasoning the following year, throughout childhood and adolescence.

The chapter by Grimm and Jacobucci discusses the implementation of LCS models using a nonlinear mixed-effects modeling framework, where participants can be measured at unique points in time. LCS models are typically specified using discrete measurement occasions, which only take on a few unique values. If interested in a continuous time metric such as age, researchers commonly discretize the time scales, thus relying on the assumption that any time-lag is constant within and across participants, when this is not the case. Grimm and Jacobucci propose using PROC NLMIXED in SAS and JAGS to estimate LCS models. Unlike standard structural equation modeling software, these programs allow the specification of any number of time points, thus giving researchers a more fine-grained metric.

Hamagami and McArdle's chapter presents an extension of LCS models based on additive curvilinear effects. These effects are specified in the model together with dynamic feedback and coupling parameters. A typical LCS specification involves an additive latent component that is constant over time, while allowing variation across individuals. In their chapter, Hamagami and McArdle extend this specification by including an additive constant as a nonlinear function form, and allowing the value of this latent constant to be time-dependent. For this, they use a quadratic functional form. By incorporating the additive curvilinear effect, the new LCS model can be used to examine dynamics in data that follow a wide variety of nonlinear curves.

The chapter by Jacobucci and Grimm proposes regularized estimation for examining a range of multivariate LCS models. Typically, determining the most plausible LCS model amongst several alternative specifications involves fitting each of the models separately and evaluating the corresponding fit statistics. Jacobucci and Grimm's proposed approach is a simultaneous evaluation of models based on regularization using both maximum likelihood and Bayesian estimation. In addition to simplifying model selection, this approach allows additional parameterizations of the model, and increases the propensity of selecting the optimal model.

Boker's chapter traces the history of path analysis and structural equation modeling leading up to the so-called Reticular Action Model (RAM), one of McArdle's most influential methodological achievements. The RAM notation allowed specifying structural equation models using three matrices only, instead of the multiple matrices involved in standard programs at the time. This model was implemented in software packages that allowed fitting models in a simplified and parsimonious manner, and is still at the core of some of the most advanced SEM programs. Boker's chapter describes how several important technical difficulties were solved in order to arrive at the RAM model. The chapter concludes by discussing the evolution of structural equation modeling over the past 40 years.

Section II: Measurement and Testing Issues in Longitudinal Modeling

In this section, a collection of chapters addresses issues related to measurement and testing in longitudinal models. These issues cover a wide variety of topics, including statistical fit criteria, sample size, design of measurement occasions, incomplete data, and alternative ways to model change in multivariate data.

The chapter by Serang examines the performance of corrections implemented to fit criteria when using LCS models with small samples. Using a simulation study, Serang shows that the commonly used corrections tend to reduce the test statistic too much, leading to type I error rates below the nominal level, as well as to a decrease in power. With the use of empirical data, the chapter illustrates how such effects can yield spurious and even conflicting conclusions when fitting equivalent models to the same data.

Wang and Yang's chapter investigates the effects of over-simplifying random components on the estimation of fixed effects in linear growth curves. Wang and Yang use derivation work to demonstrate that, when both the random intercept and the random slope are omitted from the specification, the standard errors of the fixed-effects intercept and slope estimates can be biased. The authors replicate their derivation findings using empirical data. The chapter concludes with recommendations for researchers interested in fitting growth curves.

The chapter by Zhang and Liu deals with important design features for studies that involve LCS models. Zhang and Liu carry out simulation work to determine optimal sample size and number of measurement occasions for both univariate and bivariate LCS models. They propose a method that allows researchers to calculate the power for estimating individual model parameters using their own R statistical package *RAMpath*.

Hayes's chapter reports analyses examining the performance of two strategies for dealing with missing data in longitudinal studies. Hayes compares CART (classification and regression trees) and random forest analyses when such techniques are applied to multiple imputation and when they are used to model the probability of dropout through the creation of inverse probability weights. These two approaches are evaluated under incomplete data due to "missing not at random" (MNAR) mechanisms with small sample sizes. Hayes's findings include that, in small samples, CART and weighting methods outperform multiple imputation, indicating that these approaches can help to deal with missing data problems in empirical research.

In his chapter, Estabrook proposes a longitudinal perspective for measurement evaluation, suggesting an extension of a measurement model based on derivatives. This proposed approach builds on McArdle's factor of curves (FOCUS) model, in which the intercepts and slopes corresponding to growth curves of multiple observed variables (or items) repeated over time are factor analyzed, yielding a factor of the intercepts and a factor of the slopes. Estabrook's proposed approach provides a useful framework to address issues related to measurement evaluation over time. This framework facilitates the integration of within-person change and intra-individual processes into behavioral research.

Section III: Novel Applications of Multivariate Longitudinal Methodology

The last section of this volume includes chapters highlighting the many contributions by McArdle to developmental methodology and multivariate longitudinal modeling at large. The chapters in this section cover topics such as measurement and validity, growth and dynamics, and provide examples of current research on which McArdle has left his indelibly mark, such as behavioral genetics, research in collegiate athletics, and studies of minorities.

The chapter by Bowles focuses on measurement in developmental longitudinal modeling. Bowles demonstrates how longitudinal studies are sensitive to violations of interval level measurement, arguing that such violations have important implications regarding validity. Bowles describes three approaches to provide evidence of interval scaling: mechanistic modeling, latent variable modeling, and Rasch measurement. After discussing the strengths and limitations of each approach, the chapter concludes with recommendations for empirical research.

Ram and Yang continue the theme of developmental methodology. In their chapter, they focus on models for examining dynamics in developmental studies, for which they use techniques implemented in fisheries management. At the core of their proposal is the integration of inter-individual differences with intra-individual change. For this, they argue for a switch from the integrated mathematical forms commonly used in growth modeling to differential equations. Such equations, Ram and Yang maintain, allow a richer theoretical description of the model and provide a more cogent articulation of the actual processes underlying the change.

The chapter by Neale traces important developments in the genetic studies of growth and development. Neale emphasizes the contributions to this research by McArdle, including early developments in the psychometric and biometric models, and more recent work encompassing multivariate latent growth curves for twin data. In addition to reviewing these methodological developments, the chapter describes potential extensions and applications of such models.

Petr and Paskus's chapter depicts McArdle's work for the National Collegiate Athletic Association (NCAA). They narrate how, over 25 years, McArdle's work set the stage for high-level research at the NCAA that focused on how schools can predict and promote the academic and life successes of college athletes. Petr and Paskus describe how this work has changed, not just the research conducted at the NCAA, but the very landscape of college athletics.

The final chapter in the volume, by Hishinuma and colleagues, illustrates another important contribution by McArdle to current research, namely his work on multivariate statistics as applied to research on minorities. Hishinuma and colleagues describe McArdle's interactions with the personnel at the University of Hawai'i at Mānoa and emphasize the profound impact of such interactions, not only on the team but on the research area at large. The chapter includes personal notes depicting McArdle's rare combination of skills that allows him to blend into and become part of an organization's culture. These contributions, Hishinuma and colleagues tell us, have been invaluable and have set the foundation for all future endeavors of the research team.

In sum, we are pleased to present *Longitudinal Multivariate Psychology*. As its title indicates, this volume is intended to offer a window into state-of-the-art longitudinal methodology for studying multivariate processes. It is our desire that the volume fulfills our goal of providing researchers with templates for ideas on how to examine change and dynamics. It is also our hope that this collection of chapters honors and does justice to the creative, plentiful, and influential work by Jack McArdle.

Emilio Ferrer
Steven M. Boker
Kevin J. Grimm

Extensions of Latent Change Score Models

1

METHODOLOGICAL ISSUES AND EXTENSIONS TO THE LATENT DIFFERENCE SCORE FRAMEWORK[1]

Linying Ji & Sy-Miin Chow

Few topics in the social and behavioral sciences are as fundamental and as riddled with controversies as the study of change. From the questions of whether and how intervention programs impact the targeted behaviors of interest, to studies of lifespan developmental changes, the pursuit of change arises in a variety of contexts and brings its own fair share of methodological challenges. Particularly well-known in the history of studying change are the various disputes surrounding the analysis of observed difference scores (see e.g., Bereiter, 1963; Cattell, 1966; Cronbach & Furby, 1970; Harris, 1963; Lord, 1956, 1958; Nesselroade & Cable, 1974), such as the low reliability of observed difference scores, and difficulties in interpreting results from factor analyzing such scores. One of the key contributions of McArdle to the fields of psychometrics and lifespan development resides in his proposal to formalize modeling of change scores at the latent variable level. Among the latent difference models proposed by McArdle and colleagues, is the univariate dual change score model, which allows researchers to examine data manifesting nonlinear (specifically, sigmoid-shaped) curves as latent difference score (LDS) models with linear change functions (McArdle & Hamagami, 2001).

LDS models allow researchers to capture change at the latent level, which remedies the low reliability of change scores related directly to the measurement errors of the testing tools. In addition, formulating change hypotheses within a latent variable modeling framework also expands the ways in which researchers may examine the determinants or pathways of intraindividual change and complex interdependencies among multiple change processes – some of the rationales for conducting longitudinal research proposed by Baltes and Nesselroade (1979). Such work builds on the extensive literature on dynamic models in the form of differential or difference equations.

Differential equations are used to represent a system of variables that evolve continuously over time, whereas difference equation model are designed for processes whose changes can be captured meaningfully in discrete time units. In his work with colleagues, students, and collaborators, McArdle presented a latent variable framework that reformulates differential equations measured at discrete, equal time intervals into the form of structural equation models with latent change components (Collins & Horn, 1991; Ferrer, McArdle, Shaywitz, Holahan, Marchione, & Shaywitz, 2007; Humphreys, 1996; McArdle & Hamagami, 2001; McArdle, 2001; McArdle & Hamagami, 2003a; Williams & Zimmerman, 1996). The resultant, discretized (in terms of time) models of latent change are referred to herein as latent difference equation models.

Many phenomena of change can be expressed mathematically as difference equation models. In the last two decades, difference equation models have been steadily gaining traction as a modeling tool in the social and behavioral sciences. For instance, time series models with autoregressive and/or moving average relations (Hamilton, 1994) can be readily formulated as special cases of difference equation models. Models with such elements have been broadly utilized, for instance, within the contexts of cross-lag panel models (Rogosa, 1978), longitudinal mediation models (Cole & Maxwell, 2003), and dynamic factor analysis models (Browne & Nesselroade, 2005; Chow, Nesselroade, Shifren, & McArdle, 2004).

Beyond time series models, Cooney and Troyer (1994) proposed a nonlinear associative memory model in the form of a difference equation as a way to represent individual and age differences in performance on the Sternberg memory task. Another difference equation model that has evidenced a far-reaching impact on models in the social and behavioral sciences is the logistic model. May (1974) evaluated the logistic equation, also known as the Verhulst equation in continuous form (Kaplan & Glass, 1995; Van Geert, 1993), in a difference equation framework. He demonstrated that the logistic model can lead to a rich repertoire of behaviors – a stable fixed point, limit cycle, and even chaotic behavior – but only in the case of difference equations (for a review see: Hale & Koçak, 1991; Kaplan & Glass, 1995). The logistic model has been used to capture changes in ecological systems for decades. For example, Van Geert (1998) applied the discrete logistic model and different variations of it to the context of language development. In Newtson's (1993) call for a greater synthesis between dynamical systems concepts and research in mainstream social psychology, he also used the logistic model as a proxy for representing human action and dyadic interactions.

In continuous form, the Verhulst equation has a known solution and only leads to stable, fixed point behavior: that is, the process would always approach an asymptote level (an equilibrium) exponentially and subsequently settle into this equilibrium. The solution of the Verhulst equation yields a trajectory that is similar in shape to other learning functions more familiar to psychologists, such as the Gompertz curve. The Gompertz curve and other similar nonlinear growth curve variations have been broadly studied and applied as plausible representations of dynamic processes (Ram & Grimm, 2015). However, when nonlinearities are present in the model, special linearization or other related procedures would have to be incorporated into the estimation routines to handle such nonlinearities (see e.g., Browne & du Toit, 1991; Collins & Horn, 1991; Cudeck, 2002).

The dual change score (DCS) model is one of the latent difference equation models proposed by McArdle and colleagues that could generate nonlinear curves similar in form to the Gompertz curve — but as a linear difference equation model without the need to utilize additional linearization procedures (McArdle, 2001; McArdle & Hamagami, 2001). Doing so opens up new possibilities for representing growth and decline processes at the latent level without incurring excessive computational burden. The bivariate dual change score (BDCS) model is a bivariate extension of the dual change score model designed to represent two parallel growth processes. Methodological evaluations and extensions of the BDCS model have been considered by multiple researchers (Bollen & Curran, 2006; Duncan, Duncan, & Strycker, 2013; Ferrer, McArdle, Shaywitz, Holahan, Marchione, & Shaywitz, 2007; McArdle, 2009; Singer & Willett, 2003). The BDCS has also been used to represent myriad empirical constructs, including the growth and decline of fluid and crystallized intelligence across the life-span (McArdle, Hamagami, Meredith, & Bradway, 2000), the relation between anti-social behaviors and reading achievement in adolescence (McArdle & Hamagami, 2001a),and the biometric genetic process in twin studies (McArdle & Hamagami, 2003b), among other applications.

In this chapter, we discuss two extensions to the BDCS model, including: (1) alternative specifications of the initial conditions (ICs) in the BDCS model, and how different IC specifications affect parameter estimation and interpretations of the change processes under study; and (2) the feasibility of incorporating stochasticity at both the latent change as well as the measurement level. We refer to stochasticity in the latent changes as stochasticity due to *process noises*. After that, we evaluate the performance of the BDCS model when the model has both misspecified IC and stochasticity in the latent changes. We demonstrate the implementation of the stochastic BDCS model with the use of different ICs using the longitudinal data of reading and arithmetic performance scores from the Early Childhood Longitudinal Study, Kindergarten Class of 1998 (ECLS-K) study. Estimation results from different variations of the stochastic BDCS model are compared and the substantive implications are discussed. All model fitting procedures in this chapter were performed using an R package, *dynr* (abbreviated from Dynamic Modeling in R; Ou et al., 2017), for fitting linear and nonlinear dynamic models with linear, Gaussian measurement models. R scripts for model fitting can be found in the Appendix.

The Bivariate Dual Change Score (BDCS) Model

Let $y_{1,it}$ and $y_{2,it}$ be two observed variables for person i ($i = 1,\ldots,N$) at time t ($t = 1,\ldots T$), linked to their associated latent true scores, denoted as $\eta_{1,it}$ and $\eta_{2,it}$, through a time-invariant measurement model. Let $\boldsymbol{y}_{it} = [y_{1,it}\ y_{2,it}]'$ and

$\eta_{it} = [\eta_{1,it} \; \eta_{2,it}]'$. This measurement model can be expressed as

$$y_{it} = \eta_{it} + \epsilon_{it}, \qquad \epsilon_{it} \sim \mathcal{N}\left(0, \mathrm{diag}[\omega_{11}, \omega_{22}]\right) \tag{1.1}$$

where ϵ_{it} is a 2×1 vector of measurement errors for the two observed variables.

The BDCS model, just like many other longitudinal and dynamic models whose components at any particular time point show dependencies on previous components from one or more earlier time points, requires the specification of the IC of the latent variables at time 1. The IC specification in the conventional BDCS model will be discussed shortly. For now, we assume that beginning from time $t = 2$, (for $t = 2, \ldots, T$), the true scores for person i at time t are a function of the person's true scores at time t-1 plus latent changes as:

$$\eta_{it} = \eta_{i,t-1} + \Delta\eta_{it}, \tag{1.2}$$

The latent change vector, $\Delta\eta_{it}$, in turn, is assumed to conform to a dynamic model as:

$$\Delta\eta_{it} = \eta_{s,i} + \beta\eta_{i,t-1}, \text{ where} \tag{1.3}$$

$$\beta = \begin{bmatrix} \beta_1 & \gamma_1 \\ \gamma_2 & \beta_2 \end{bmatrix},$$

in which β_1 and β_2 represent the self-feedback effect of the values of $\eta_{1,i}$ and $\eta_{2,i}$ at the previous time point on their values at the current time point respectively; γ_1 and γ_2 are the coupling parameters, representing the effects of $\eta_{1,it-1}$ on $\eta_{2,it}$ and of $\eta_{2,it-1}$ on $\eta_{1,it}$, respectively. $\eta_{s,i} = [\eta_{s1,i} \; \eta_{s2,i}]'$ is a vector of constant (i.e., time-invariant) slopes, or additive components of change, that capture person i's constant amounts of change in the two variables of interest from one time point to the next. If β is equal to a null matrix, then Equation 1.3 dictates that the two processes show linear change trajectories throughout with constant but person-specific amounts of change, captured by $\eta_{s1,i}$ and $\eta_{s2,i}$, in successive time points.

The dynamic model for η_{it} can also be written in a one-step-ahead form as (Chow, Ho, Hamaker, & Dolan, 2010):

$$\begin{bmatrix} \eta_{1,it} \\ \eta_{2,it} \\ \eta_{s1,it} \\ \eta_{s2,it} \end{bmatrix} = \begin{bmatrix} 1+\beta_1 & \gamma_1 & 1 & 0 \\ \gamma_2 & 1+\beta_2 & 0 & 1 \\ 0 & 0 & 1 & 0 \\ 0 & 0 & 0 & 1 \end{bmatrix} \begin{bmatrix} \eta_{1,it-1} \\ \eta_{2,it-1} \\ \eta_{s1,it-1} \\ \eta_{s2,it-1} \end{bmatrix}, \tag{1.4}$$

where $\eta_{s1,it}$ and $\eta_{s2,it}$ are the constant slopes of the two processes at time t, now explicitly constrained to be invariant over time to reflect the person-specific but time-invariant nature of $\eta_{s,i}$. In the conventional BDCS model, the values of $\eta_{s1,it}$ and $\eta_{s2,it}$ are constrained to be invariant over time. Incorporating these elements as part of a latent variable vector, $\eta_{it}^* = \begin{bmatrix} \eta_{1,it} & \eta_{2,it} & \eta_{s1,it} & \eta_{s2,it} \end{bmatrix}'$ as in Equation (1.4) opens up the possibility for these constant slopes to vary over time. Equation 1.4

may be regarded as a special case of the state-space model, or a vector autoregressive model with person-specific intercepts. Here, $1 + \beta_1$ and $1 + \beta_2$ are equivalent to what are traditionally referred to as the lag-1 autoregression parameters in the time series literature.

IC Specifications in the BDCS

Since the BDCS model is a longitudinal model involving lagged dependencies among successive measurement occasions, the specification of IC, namely, the statistical properties of the data at the first available time point, is an important issue. With assumptions of Gaussian distributed measurement processes, the IC of the BDCS essentially includes specification of the mean and covariance structures of the expanded latent variable vector, $\boldsymbol{\eta}_{i1}^*$, at the first available observed occasion, $t = 1$. At $t = 1$, McArdle and colleagues' (2001b; 2001) original BDCS model specifies that the initial structure of $\boldsymbol{\eta}_{i1}^*$, takes on the form of:

$$\boldsymbol{\eta}_{i1}^* = \boldsymbol{\mu}_1 + \boldsymbol{\zeta}_i, \quad \boldsymbol{\zeta}_i \sim N(\mathbf{0}, \boldsymbol{\Psi}_1), \text{ with}$$

$$\boldsymbol{\mu}_1 = \begin{bmatrix} \mu_{\eta_1} & \mu_{\eta_2} & \mu_{\eta_{s1}} & \mu_{\eta_{s2}} \end{bmatrix}', \boldsymbol{\zeta}_i = \begin{bmatrix} \zeta_{\eta_1,i} & \zeta_{\eta_2,i} & \zeta_{\eta_{s1},i} & \zeta_{\eta_{s2},i} \end{bmatrix}', \text{ and}$$

$$\Sigma_{\eta_1^*} = \begin{bmatrix} \psi_{11} & & & \\ \psi_{21} & \psi_{22} & & \\ \psi_{31} & \psi_{32} & \psi_{33} & \\ \psi_{41} & \psi_{42} & \psi_{43} & \psi_{44} \end{bmatrix}, \tag{1.5}$$

where $\boldsymbol{\eta}_{i1}^* = \begin{bmatrix} \eta_{1,i1} & \eta_{2,i1} & \eta_{s1,i1} & \eta_{s2,i1} \end{bmatrix}'$, in which $\eta_{1,i1}$ and $\eta_{2,i1}$ are the initial levels of the two latent processes of interest at time 1; whereas $\eta_{s1,i1}$ and $\eta_{s2,i1}$ are constant slopes for the two processes. Note that at least two time points are needed to define a slope so it may be counterintuitive to impose an initial condition for the slopes at the first time point. However, because of Equation 1.4, which dictates the invariance of these constant slopes over time, these constant latent slopes are defined by the changes across all time points, as opposed to information from just the first time point. This specific form of IC, with all unique elements of the mean vector and covariance matrix specified as freely estimated parameters, is similar to the IC specification used in standard growth curve models (McArdle & Epstein, 1987; Ram & Grimm, 2015). This IC specification coincides with the so-called "free-parameter" approach considered by du Toit and Browne (2007) in fitting SEM-based time series models and by other researchers in fitting state-space models (Harvey & Souza, 1987). As in the original BDCS model, the free-parameter approach also has the characteristic that all unknown parameters in the initial condition distribution of the latent variables are specified to be freely estimated parameters and as such, this approach allows the change processes under study to be non-stationary (du Toit & Browne, 2007).

In addition to the "free-parameter" approach, another IC specification proposed in the state-space framework, and further evaluated within the SEM framework by several researchers (du Toit & Browne, 2007; Hamaker, 2005), is the "model-implied" approach for partially stable processes. This approach assumes stability[2] in the portion of a modeled process that shows lagged dependencies, which, in turn, requires all associated modeling parameters to be time invariant. Imposing such assumptions then enables researchers to use the unconditional mean and covariance matrix implied by the model to specify the initial distribution on the latent variables at the first observed time point. du Toit and Browne (2007) showed that if the true underlying processes do in fact conform to a partially stable structure and are well described by the "model implied" approach, the IC structure can be recovered well using the "free-parameter" approach. We thus do not discuss the "model-implied" approach further here.

Another IC specification commonly adopted in the state-space literature is a diffuse IC specification in which the initial mean vector of the latent variables, $\boldsymbol{\mu}_1$, is set to a vector of zeros; and the corresponding initial latent variable covariance matrix, $\boldsymbol{\Psi}_1$, is specified to be a diagonal matrix with variance entries fixed at arbitrarily large values (e.g., De Jong, 1991; Harvey, 2001; Harvey & Phillips, 1979; Schweppe, 1973). Larger values of variances reflect greater uncertainties in the structure of the IC. This IC specification assumes that limited information is available to specify the IC structure with high precision. Thus, the means of the initial latent variables are all set to zero – a predicted value that is relatively reasonable for many stable, time-intensive longitudinal processes (i.e., time series processes) frequently considered in the econometric literature in which the diffuse IC specification is adopted. With the large numbers of time points typically available from those studies, such misspecification of IC has relatively trivial consequences. This is not the case, however, when panel data with a limited number of occasions is involved (Chow et al., 2016; Losardo, 2012; Oud et al., 1990; Ou et al., 2016).

Indeed, the issue of IC specification has received considerable attention in the state-space framework (De Jong, 1991; Harvey, 2001) and much can be learned from some of the issues, problems, and solutions proposed in that literature. Previous studies have investigated the consequences of misspecification of IC in the context of a vector autoregressive process with moving average residuals (du Toit & Browne, 2007), an autoregressive latent trajectory model (Ou, Chow, Ji, & Molenaar, 2016),and with both stable and unstable processes (Losardo, 2012). However, the effects of IC misspecification have not been evaluated within the context of the BDCS model. Our emphasis in this chapter is to evaluate whether and to what extent misspecification in IC may interact with features of the difference equations implicated in the BDCS model. In particular, we examine whether the BDCS model can reliably distinguish among variations due to interindividual differences in IC, measurement errors, and process noises when model estimation is performed using panel data with limited information.

As an initial demonstration of the consequences of IC misspecification in the BDCS model in the absence of process noise, we simulated a set of data using the BDCS model in Equations 1.1, 1.4, and 1.5; with $N = 500$ and two configurations of total number of time points ($T = 5$ and $T = 10$). We then fit the

BDCS model with the correctly specified IC structure, and the diffuse IC specification with all variance terms in Ψ_1 set to a sequence of possible values: .01, 1, 10, and 100. Table 1.1 summarizes the true values of the parameters used for data generation purposes, as well as key simulation results based on fitting variations of the BDCS model with freely estimated IC (the correctly specified IC), and misspecified IC specifications with different levels of "diffuseness." We also show in Table 1.1: (1) the total bias of the parameter estimates (over nine possible parameters), defined as the sum of the difference between each parameter's estimated and true values across all modeling parameters; and (2) the root mean squared error (RMSE), defined as the square root of the mean of the squared differences between the true and estimated values across all modeling parameters. In addition, we also report the Akaiki Information Criterion (AIC) and Bayesian Information Criteria (BIC) as model selection measures. We found that differences among the conditions where the variances in Ψ_1 were set to 1, 10, and 100 were minimal. Thus, we only included results from the condition with IC variances fixed at 10 due to space constraints.

As shown in Table 1.1, with $T = 5$ and the correctly specified IC, all of the model parameters were recovered very well, with a small total bias and RMSE. Both the AIC and the BIC selected the correctly specified IC structure over the other IC structures. Of the conditions with diffuse IC specification, when the IC covariance matrix was set to $\Psi_1 = 10 \times \mathbf{I}_4$, only a slight increase in total bias was observed. However, there was a five-fold increase in RMSE. When the number of time points was increased from 5 to 10, all parameter estimates were very close to their true values. The total bias and RMSE from the diffuse IC with $\Psi_1 = 10 \times \mathbf{I}_4$ and $T = 10$ were close to those observed in the correctly specified IC. Also, as expected, with larger T, smaller values of standard error estimates were observed.

The level of diffuseness of the IC also affected the quality of the point estimates. In general, if the variances of the IC were specified to be large enough for the misspecified IC distribution to show a reasonable amount of overlap with the true IC distribution, estimation results were minimally affected. On the contrary, if the variances of the IC were specified to be too restrictive – for instance, when some of the interindividual variance terms were incorrectly fixed at 0, considerable decrements in point estimates are noted. As an example, when we decreased the IC variances to .01, all parameter estimates showed substantial biases and RMSEs, even with 10 measurement occasions (see Table 1.1). The AIC and the BIC, again, preferred models with more diffuse (e.g., $\Psi_1 = 10 \times \mathbf{I}_4$) than the model with the least diffuse but misspecified IC ($\Psi_1 = 0.01 \times \mathbf{I}_4$).

It should be noted that a sheer increase in the number of time points, per se, may not always be adequate in overcoming issues pertaining to the misspecification of the IC. For instance, when the absolute values of the self-feedback parameters (i.e., the βs) are large, the changes in the latent processes (differences in the latent processes between successive time points) would be larger and the processes would reach their asymptotic levels faster. As shown in Figure 1.1, when $\beta_1 = -.3$ (the two plots in the top panel), the latent processes do not reach their

TABLE 1.1 Parameter estimates obtained from fitting the BDCS model with diffused IC.

Parameters	True θ	$T=5$ correct IC				$T=5$ $\Psi_1 = 10\times\mathbf{I}_4$	$T=10$ $\Psi_1 = 10\times\mathbf{I}_4$	$T=10$ $\Psi_1 = 0.01\times\mathbf{I}_4$
				Estimates (SE)				
β_1	$-.30$	$-.27\ (.02)$				$-.43\ (.02)$	$-.31\ (.002)$	$-.42\ (.006)$
β_2	$-.20$	$-.17\ (.02)$				$-.32\ (.02)$	$-.23\ (.005)$	$-.03\ (.006)$
γ_1	$.30$	$.28\ (.02)$				$.43\ (.02)$	$.32\ (.005)$	$1.09\ (.014)$
γ_2	$-.20$	$-.24\ (.02)$				$-.07\ (.02)$	$-.19\ (.002)$	$-.18\ (.003)$
ω_{11}	$.02$	$.02\ (.000)$				$.02\ (.001)$	$.02\ (.000)$	$.04\ (.002)$
ω_{22}	$.02$	$.02\ (.000)$				$.02\ (.001)$	$.02\ (.000)$	$.04\ (.001)$
bias	—	$.005$				$.004$	$.004$	$-.90$
RMSE	—	$.02$				$.10$	$.015$	$.33$
Ψ_1	$\begin{bmatrix} .13 \\ .01 & .01 \\ .08 & 0 & .09 \\ 0 & 0 & .01 & .01 \end{bmatrix}$	$\begin{bmatrix} .12(.009) \\ .01(.003) & .01(.001) \\ .09(.007) & .002(.002) & .09(.006) \\ .002(.003) & .001(.001) & .01(.002) & .01(.001) \end{bmatrix}$				$\text{Diag}\left(\begin{bmatrix} 10 \\ 10 \\ 10 \\ 10 \end{bmatrix}\right)$	$\text{Diag}\left(\begin{bmatrix} 10 \\ 10 \\ 10 \\ 10 \end{bmatrix}\right)$	$\text{Diag}\left(\begin{bmatrix} .01 \\ .01 \\ .01 \\ .01 \end{bmatrix}\right)$
AIC		-1678.98				8106.77	4406.53	15230.43
BIC		-1562.50				8141.71	4445.64	15269.54

Note: True θ = true value of a parameter; bias = total bias $= \sum_{k=1}^{9}(\theta_k - \hat{\theta}_k)$; RMSE $= \sqrt{\sum\sum_{k=1}^{9}(\hat{\theta}_k - \theta_k)^2}$; AIC Akaiki Information Criterion; BIC Bayesian Information Criteria.

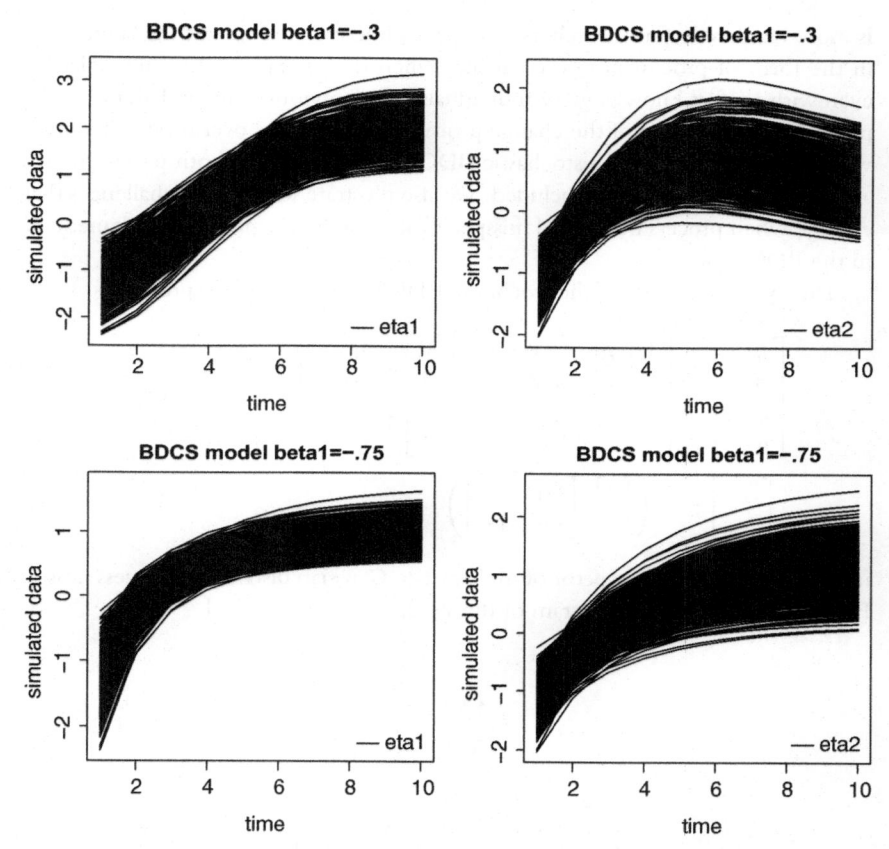

FIGURE 1.1 Simulated trajectories of $\eta_{1,it}$ and $\eta_{2,it}$ with high and low β_1 values. eta1 $= \eta_{1,it}$; eta2 $= \eta_{2,it}$. The true values of other parameters used for data generation are summarized in Table 1.1.

asymptotes until after approximately ten measurement time points. However, with a larger magnitude of $\beta_1 = -.75$ (see the plots in the bottom panel), both latent processes reach their asymptotes after approximately six measurement time points. Since observations collected after the processes have already reached their asymptotes do not provide sufficient information concerning changes to aid estimation, having a greater number of time points after the asymptotes does not help to improve the estimation results.

Stochastic BDCS Model

The original BDCS model assumes that the underlying latent dynamic processes are deterministic or do not show within-person uncertainties at the latent level. In empirical applications, however, this assumption does not always hold. Rather, it is more reasonable for researchers to expect some uncertainties at the latent level in the form of process noises, especially when the unexplained — unexplained even with perfect knowledge of individuals' true previous states and all modeling parameters — portion of the change processes accumulates over time. Therefore, we consider properties of a stochastic BDCS model, wherein both process noises and measurement errors are included. We also illustrate some of the challenges that emerge when process noises and misspecification in IC are present simultaneously in the BDCS model.

The dynamic model of the stochastic BDCS model can be expressed as:

$$
\begin{bmatrix} \eta_{1,it} \\ \eta_{2,it} \\ \eta_{s1,it} \\ \eta_{s2,it} \end{bmatrix} = \begin{bmatrix} 1+\beta_1 & \gamma_1 & 1 & 0 \\ \gamma_2 & 1+\beta_2 & 0 & 1 \\ 0 & 0 & 1 & 0 \\ 0 & 0 & 0 & 1 \end{bmatrix} \begin{bmatrix} \eta_{1,it-1} \\ \eta_{2,it-1} \\ \eta_{s1,it-1} \\ \eta_{s2,it-1} \end{bmatrix} + \begin{bmatrix} \xi_{\eta1,i} \\ \xi_{\eta2,i} \\ 0 \\ 0 \end{bmatrix}, \text{ where}
$$

$$
\begin{bmatrix} \xi_{\eta1,i} \\ \xi_{\eta2,i} \end{bmatrix} \sim \mathrm{N}\left(\begin{bmatrix} 0 \\ 0 \end{bmatrix}, \begin{bmatrix} \nu_{11} & \\ \nu_{21} & \nu_{22} \end{bmatrix} \right), \tag{1.6}
$$

in which $[\xi_{\eta1,i}\ \xi_{\eta2,i}]'$ is a vector of multivariate Gaussian distributed process noises. Figure 1.2 shows a path diagram of the stochastic BDCS model.

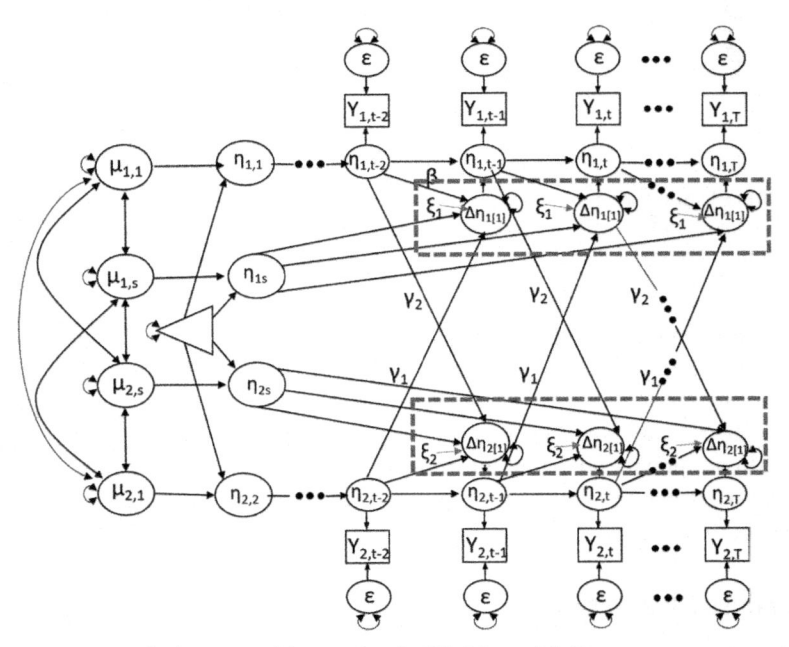

FIGURE 1.2 A path diagram of the stochastic BDCS model. Due to space constraints, process noises variances at latent level were not explicit depicted in the path diagram. We use two-headed arrows to represent the stochasticity of the latent processes.

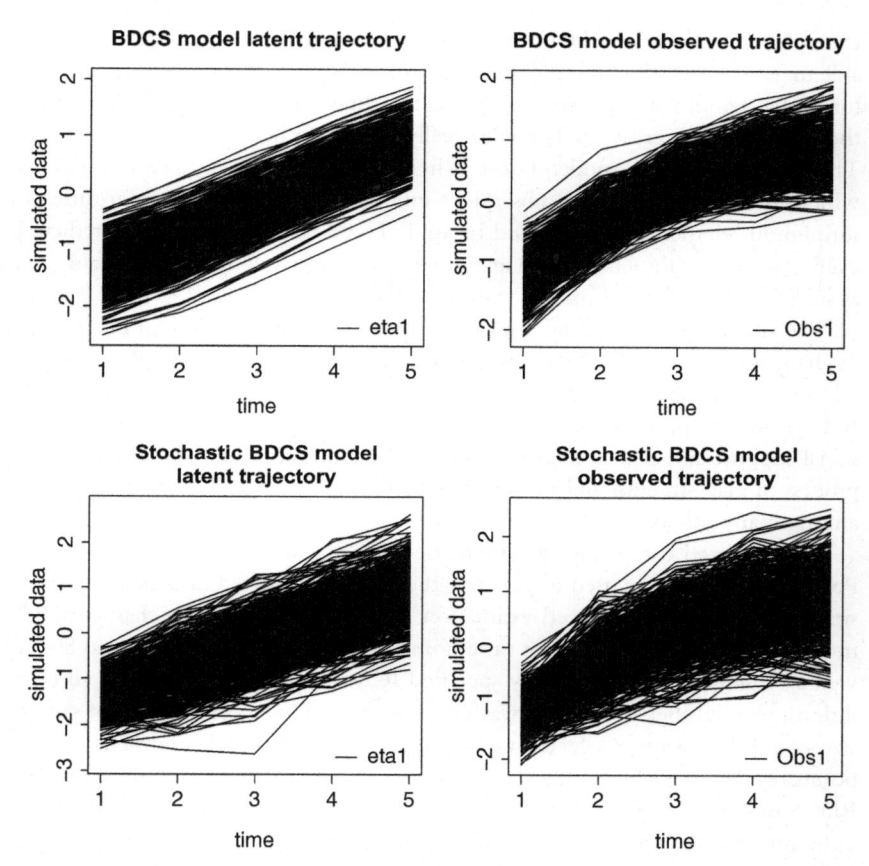

FIGURE 1.3 A comparison of latent trajectories and observed trajectories generated using the deterministic BDCS model and stochastic BDCS model. The true values of the parameters used for data generation are summarized in Table 1.2.

Figure 1.3 shows a sample of simulated trajectories generated using the BDCS model with and without process noises. In the top panel are the simulated latent trajectories of $\eta_{1,it}$ and the corresponding observed measurements, $y_{1,it}$, generated using a deterministic BDCS model. Comparison trajectories generated using the stochastic BDCS model are shown in the bottom panel. It can be seen that the latent trajectories associated with the deterministic model are very smooth, whereas those associated with the stochastic model are characterized by more nuanced fluctuations from one measurement occasion to the next. As distinct from measurement errors, the variations instilled through process noises remain from one occasion to the next at the latent true score level. In turn, these "within-person" deviations/stochasticity in change give rise to greater intra- as well as inter-individual differences in patterns of change at the observed level. As an example, consider the arithmetic learning trajectory of a first-grader. It is reasonable to assume that the "typical" trajectory of such a learning process takes on the form of a sigmoid-shaped curve. Suppose that after transitioning to second grade, the child meets a great teacher who really motivates her to learn mathematics. The child may show a sudden boost in her arithmetic score in the second grade, which, in turn, elevates her subsequent interest and performance in arithmetics throughout elementary school and beyond. These changes cannot be predicted, even if we know the child's true arithmetic score perfectly in the first grade and as such, are regarded as a source of uncertainty at the latent level.

The added flexibility of the stochastic BDCS model in allowing for uncertainty in change processes at the latent level may be helpful in representing psychological and biobehavioral processes such as the changes in growth hormones (GH and IGH.I) around puberty (Loesch et al., 1995), the relations between perceived social support and academic achievement (Mackinnon, 2012), and the declining process of grip strength and nonverbal reasoning in old age (Deary et al., 2011), among many others.

We simulated data using the stochastic BDCS as the data generation model. Population parameters used to generate the data are displayed in Table 1.2. Using simulated data, we compared estimation performance of the stochastic BDCS model with different number of time points conditions ($T =3, 5, 10$, and 50), as well as conditions with correctly specified IC and misspecified IC. For all conditions, the number of subjects was set to be 500. This specific range of sample size configurations was selected to help establish the minimum number of time points needed to enable satisfactory recovery of the parameters from the stochastic BDCS model. Theoretically, a minimum of three time points was needed to provide sufficient degrees of freedom to estimate all the parameters in the stochastic BDCS model, and to begin to distinguish process noises from measurement errors. The quality of the parameter point estimates was, again, assessed with biases and RMSEs, whereas the AIC and BIC were used to compare the fit of the correctly specified IC stochastic BDCS model and the misspecified IC stochastic BDCS model. Because the AIC and BIC were not comparable for models with different T configurations, the extent to which these information criterion measures were able to select the correctly specified model from the models considered was evaluated within the condition where $T = 5$. Simulation results are summarized in Table 1.2.

Results from model fitting indicated that even with $N = 500$, five measurement occasions appeared to be the minimum T needed to obtain good point estimation results and sufficient power to reliably distinguish process from measurement noises under the correctly specified IC structure. With only three time points, even when $N = 500$, the biases for some of the parameters, such as those associated with γ_2 and the measurement error variances, were relatively high (e.g., bias for $\gamma_2 = 0.13$), and were not detected to be significantly different from zero. Particularly worth noting was that the measurement error variances, ω_{11} and ω_{22},

TABLE 1.2 Parameter estimates obtained from fitting the stochastic BDCS model.

		Estimates (SE)			
Parameters	*True θ*	*$T=3$, correct IC*	*$T=5$, correct IC*	*$T=5$, $\Psi_1=10$*	*$T=50$, $\Psi_1=10$*
β_1	$-.30$	$-.31$ (.23)	$-.30$ (.02)	$-.65$ (.03)	$-.31$ (.003)
β_2	$-.20$	$-.26$ (.03)	$-.23$ (.03)	$-.38$ (.02)	$-.21$ (.005)
γ_1	.30	.32 (.11)	.31 (.02)	.59 (.02)	.32 (.004)
γ_2	$-.20$	$-.07$(.05)	$-.17$ (.03)	$-.05$ (.02)	$-.21$ (.003)
ω_{11}	.02	0 (0)	.01 (.004)	0 (0)	.02 (.001
ω_{22}	.02	0 (.005)	.003 (.004)	.02 (.007)	.02 (.001)
v_{11}	.1	.14 (.03)	.13 (.008)	.12 (.006)	.1 (.002)
v_{22}	.1	.14 (.01)	.13 (.008)	.09 (.01)	.1 (.002)
v_{12}	.01	.01 (.006)	.02 (.004)	.02 (.005)	.01 (.001)
bias	–	$-.12$	$-.05$	.09	.01
RMSE	–	.05	.02	.17	.008
Ψ_1	$\begin{bmatrix} .13 & & & \\ .01 & .01 & & \\ .08 & 0 & .09 & \\ 0 & 0 & .01 & .01 \end{bmatrix}$	$\begin{bmatrix} .12(.008) & & & \\ .01(.03) & .01(.05) & & \\ .08(.006) & 0(.01) & .09(.008) & \\ -.007(.008) & -.006(.01) & .01(.006) & .01(.006) \end{bmatrix}$	$\begin{bmatrix} .12(.009) & & & \\ .01(.004) & .003(.002) & & \\ .09(.006) & 0(.003) & .09(.007) & \\ -.001(.004) & -.004(.002) & .01(.003) & .01(.004) \end{bmatrix}$	$\mathrm{Diag}\left(\begin{bmatrix} 10 \\ 10 \\ 10 \\ 10 \end{bmatrix}\right)$	$\mathrm{Diag}\left(\begin{bmatrix} 10 \\ 10 \\ 10 \\ 10 \end{bmatrix}\right)$
AIC	–	1970.74	3792.14	12060.99	50783.91
BIC	–	2092.94	3926.10	12136.70	50889.56

Note: True θ = true value of a parameter; bias = total bias = $\sum_{k=1}^{9}(\theta_k - \hat{\theta}_k)$; RMSE = $\sqrt{\sum\sum_{k=1}^{9}(\hat{\theta}_k - \theta_k)^2}$; AIC Akaiki Information Criterion; BIC Bayesian Information Criteria.

were not estimated to be reliably different from zero when $T = 3$, thus suggesting that three time points were insufficiently powered to distinguish measurement errors from latent process noises.

When the IC structure was misspecified (i.e. fixed with a diagonal matrix with 10), even more measurement occasions were needed for the stochastic BDCS model to produce reasonable estimation results. Table 1.2 shows that with $T = 5$, the estimates were highly biased and were characterized by high RMSEs. The AIC and BIC values were also much larger with the misspecified IC model than those associated with the freely estimated IC model, which confirmed that the fit of the misspecified IC model was much worse than that of the correctly specified IC model. Increasing the number of time points to 50 significantly improved the estimation results, yielding small biases and RMSEs. Although not shown in Table 1.2, increasing T to 10 still yielded less than satisfactory estimation results. These results underscore the importance of selecting the correct IC specifications in fitting stochastic BDCS models, and their relative sensitivity to misspecifications in the IC structure — issues that were much less salient and critical in the context of deterministic BDCS models. In addition, the utility of the AIC and BIC in detecting the misspecification in the IC structure was validated with T that was as small as 5, thus suggesting the plausibility of using these information criterion measures to facilitate the selection of IC structure in empirical studies.

To further evaluate the quality of the parameter estimates, we ran a targeted Monte Carlo stimulation study involving four selected conditions. Two of them were with correctly specified IC ($T = 3$ and 5), and two of them were with diffused IC, where $\Psi_1 = 10$ ($T = 5$ and 50). A total of 500 Monte Carlo replications were run for each condition. We computed two measures to assess the precision of the point estimates: root-mean-squared errors (RMSEs), which were defined for the hth parameter as the square root of the average squared difference between estimates for that parameter ($\hat{\theta}_h$) and the true parameter value (true θ) across Monte Carlo runs (RMSE $= \sqrt{\frac{1}{H} \sum_{h=1}^{H} (\hat{\theta}_h - \text{true } \theta)^2}$), and biases, which were defined as the average difference between estimates of the hth parameter and the true parameter value across Monte Carlo runs (Bias $= \frac{1}{H} \sum_{h}^{H} (\hat{\theta}_h - \text{true } \theta)$). Power (an index of positive detection rates) and coverage rates (an overall measure of the quality of both the point and the SE estimates) were also used as indicators of overall quality of parameter estimates. Power was defined as the proportion of 95% confidence intervals that did not contain 0 across the Monte Carlo replications. Coverage rates were defined as the percentages of replications whose 95% confidence intervals for the parameters included the true parameter values.

Simulation results are summarized in Figure 1.4 (a)–(d). Consistent with previous findings, we need longer time series to obtain reasonable point estimates when diffused IC was used, as indicated by RMSEs and biases. To be specific, for dynamic parameters, we obtained very low RMSEs, close to zero biases, and high power when we had five time points with correctly specified IC and 50 time points with diffused IC. In the condition characterized by limited observations

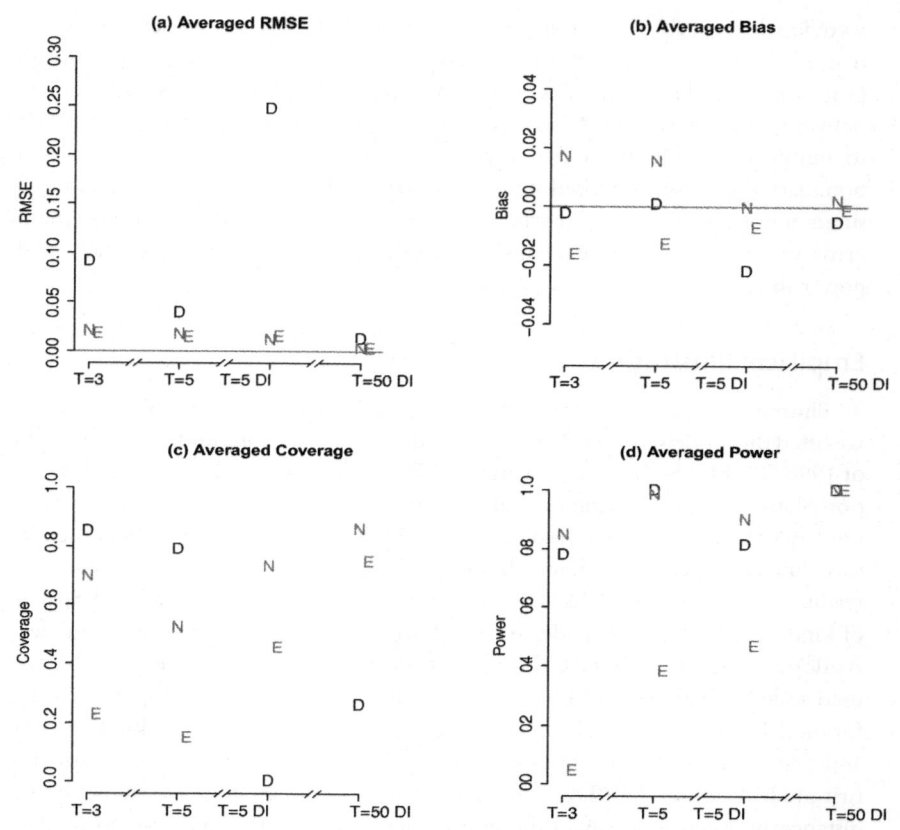

FIGURE 1.4 A comparison of the accuracy of point estimates: (a) RMSEs for three types of parameters on average, including dynamic (denoted as "D"), process noise variance (denoted as "P"), and measurement error variance (denoted as "E") parameters; (b) biases for the three sets of parameters on average. A comparison of the overall quality of parameter estimates: (c) coverage rates for the three sets of parameters on average; and (d) power for the three sets of parameters on average. IC was correctly specified for $T = 3$ and $T = 5$. DI represents diffused initial condition, which was further paired with $T = 5$ and $T = 50$.

($T = 5$) and incorrectly specified IC (diffused IC), the dynamic parameter estimates were the most problematic. We can see from the plot (c) that due to biases in parameter point estimates, coverage rates of the dynamic parameter estimates, on average, were close to zero when we had diffused IC and $T = 5$. The coverage rates increased when the time points increased to 50, but still relative low due to the fact that with longer time series, the standard errors of the parameter estimates became very small.

Even though the RMSEs and biases for the process noise and measurement error variances were relatively small (below 0.02 in absolute value) under all conditions, we found the coverage rates and power for measurement error estimates were low, except for the condition where we had 50 time points. This indicated that longer time series would be necessary for the model to correctly estimate process noise and measurement error variance-covariance parameters. In this particular simulation, measurement error variances were set to a very low value (0.02) to mimic the results from the empirical example. Because of software-related boundary conditions imposed within *dynr* to avoid a non-positive definite measurement error covariance matrix, the near-zero true value of the measurement error variances might have contributed directly to the low coverage rates and power in this specific case.

Empirical Illustration

To illustrate the implementation of the proposed extensions of the BDCS model, we fitted the models to the data from the Early Childhood Longitudinal Study, Class of 1998/99 (ECLS-K; US Department of Education, National Center for Education Statistics, 2010), a longitudinal study on children's school performance from kindergarten years through middle school. A subsample of $n = 2369$ was used in this illustration from the original data set with over 21,000 students. Each student's reading and arithmetic skills were measured across seven waves: Fall and Spring of kindergarten and first grade, and the Spring of third, fifth, and eighth grades. As done elsewhere (Chow, Grimm, Guillaume, Dolan, & McArdle, 2013b), we used scaled reading and arithmetic ability estimates from an item response model for model fitting purposes. We averaged the Fall and Spring scores of kindergarten and first grade to obtain only one score for kindergarten and one score for the first grade. Because the BDCS model is a discrete-time model that assumes equal distance between successive time points, the scores for the unmeasured grades, i.e. second, forth, six, and seven grades, were inserted as missing occasions in the data set for model-fitting purposes. This yielded a total of nine measurement time points for model fitting, five of which were non-missing. The IRT-scaled ability estimates of 50 randomly selected students are plotted in Figure 1.5.

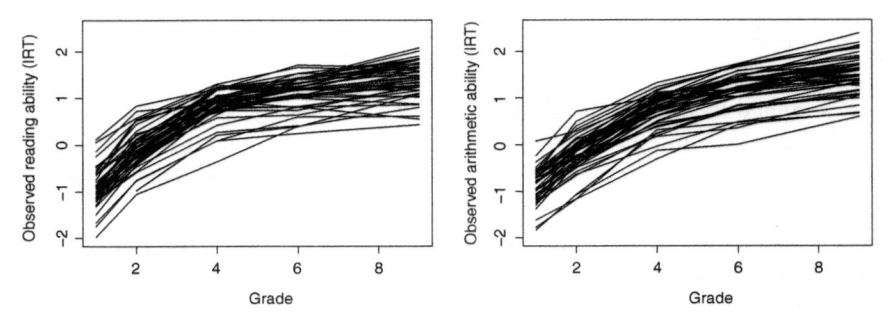

FIGURE 1.5 A plot of 50 randomly selected participants' IRT-scaled ability scores on the reading and arithmetic tasks from the ECLS-K study.

We were interested in examining the processes through which students acquire and enhance their reading and arithmetic skills from kindergarten through eighth grade. With the BDCS model, we were able to consider the two growth processes simultaneously. We sought to examine how each process was influencing itself through the self-feedback relation implicated in the BDCS models (through the parameters, β_1 and β_2), as well as the reciprocal influences between the two learning processes as reflected through the coupling parameters, γ_1 and γ_2.

We compared the results and fit from several BDCS models with different IC and process noises specifications. In particular, we first considered the original BDCS model with a freely estimated IC. Then, we evaluated the sensitivity of the modeling results to changes in the IC structure by fixing the IC means and varying the IC variances. Even though freely estimating parameters in the IC means and covariance structures adds relatively little computational costs in this particular empirical illustrations, it may not always be feasible to freely estimate all IC-related parameters when more than two endogenous processes are involved. There are many other possibilities for other sources of misspecification in IC (e.g., omitted covariates, unmodeled covariations among elements in the IC and other components in the model). Thus, sensitivity analysis can be insightful in revealing the robustness of modeling results to such minor changes in model specification. Next, we compared the results from the deterministic BDCS model with freely estimated IC to a stochastic variation of the model. We considered the stochastic BDCS model because the inspection of the over-time fluctuations in the two observed process (see Figure 1.5) suggested some continuity in stochasticity that may not be well captured by a deterministic model. Across all models, the AIC and BIC measures were used for model selection purpose. Empirical results are summarized in Table 1.3.

Both the AIC and the BIC indicated that the stochastic BDCS model with freely estimated IC structure had the best fit among all four of the models considered. The improved fit of this model compared to the deterministic BDCS model with freely estimated IC structure confirmed the need to allow for process noises for the two learning processes at the latent level. Both of the models with diffuse IC specifications – with the initial variances of the levels and slopes of reading and arithmetic fixed to .01 or 1, and covariances of the initial latent variables all fixed to zero – were characterized by notable decrements in fit. Of the two "diffuse" IC models, the IC structure with greater initial variances ($\psi_{11} - \psi_{44} = 1$) showed better fit than the model with more restrictive initial IC variances ($\psi_{11} - \psi_{44} = .01$). Increasing the IC variances further to 10 and 100 did not alter the conclusions in any way. The results are thus not included in Table 1.3 due to space constraints.

We plotted the trajectories of the estimated latent reading and arithmetic scores for one randomly selected participant obtained using the different BDCS models in Figure 1.6. These estimates are essentially smoothed estimates obtained using the fixed interval smoother or equivalently, factor score estimates using the regression method (Chow et al., 2010; Dolan & Molenaar, 1991). The observed

TABLE 1.3 Empirical results obtained from fitting variations of the BDCS model to the ECLS-K data.

Parameters	Meanings	Estimates (SE)			
		IC freed	$\Psi_1 = .01$	$\Psi_1 = 1$	Stochastic with IC freed
$\mu_{\eta_{Reading}}$	Initial mean for reading	−1.05 (.01)	=0	=0	−1.04 (.01)
$\mu_{\eta_{Arithmetic}}$	Initial mean for arithmetic	−.95 (.01)	=0	=0	−.93 (.01)
$\mu_{\alpha_{Reading}}$	Constant slope for reading	.47 (.003)	=0	=0	.48 (.003)
$\mu_{\alpha_{Arithmetic}}$	Constant slope for arithmetic	.46 (.003)	=0	=0	.46 (.003)
β_1	Reading self-feedback parameter	−.56 (.02)	2.25 (.05)	−.99 (.01)	−.39 (.01)
β_2	Arithmetic self-feedback parameter	.15 (.03)	−3.17 (.06)	−.39 (.01)	−.16 (.01)
γ_1	Arithmetic → reading coupling parameter	.21 (.02)	−2.05 (.05	.68 (.01)	.04 (.01)
γ_2	Reading → arithmetic coupling parameter	−.45 (.03)	3.57 (.07)	.1 (.01)	−.13 (.01)
ω_{11}	Measurement error variance for reading scores	.02 (.001)	.24 (.003)	.05 (.001)	.02 (.001)
ω_{22}	Measurement error variance for arithmetic scores	.03 (.000)	.21 (.003)	.05 (.001)	.01 (.000)
ν_{11}	Process noise variance for reading scores	=0	=0	=0	.02 (.001)
ν_{22}	Process noise variance for arithmetic scores	=0	=0	=0	.02 (.001)
ν_{12}	Process noise covariance for reading and arithmetic scores	=0	=0	=0	.01 (.000)
ψ_{11}	Variance in initial level, reading	.22 (.01)	.01	1	.22 (.008)
ψ_{22}	Variance in constant slope, reading	.01 (.000)	.01	1	.01 (.000)
ψ_{33}	Variance in initial level, arithmetic	.19 (.007)	.01	1	.19 (.006)
ψ_{44}	Variance in constant slope,arithmetic	.01 (.000)	.01	1	.01 (.001)
ψ_{21}	Cov(initial level reading, constant slope reading)	.03 (.001)	=0	=0	.03 (.001)
ψ_{31}	Cov(initial level arithmetic, initial level reading)	.19 (.007)	=0	=0	.17 (.006)
ψ_{32}	Cov(initial level arithmetic, constant slope reading)	.03 (.001)	=0	=0	.03 (.001)
ψ_{41}	Cov(initial level reading, constant slope arithmetic)	.03 (.001)	=0	=0	.03 (.001)
ψ_{42}	Cov(constant slope reading, constant slope arithmetic)	.01 (.000)	=0	=0	.01 (.000)
ψ_{43}	Cov(initial level arithmetic, constant slope arithmetic)	.03 (.001)	=0	=0	.03 (.001)
AIC		−1266.27	42536.4	28284.34	−2149.78
BIC		−1106.92	42584.2	28332.14	−1966.52

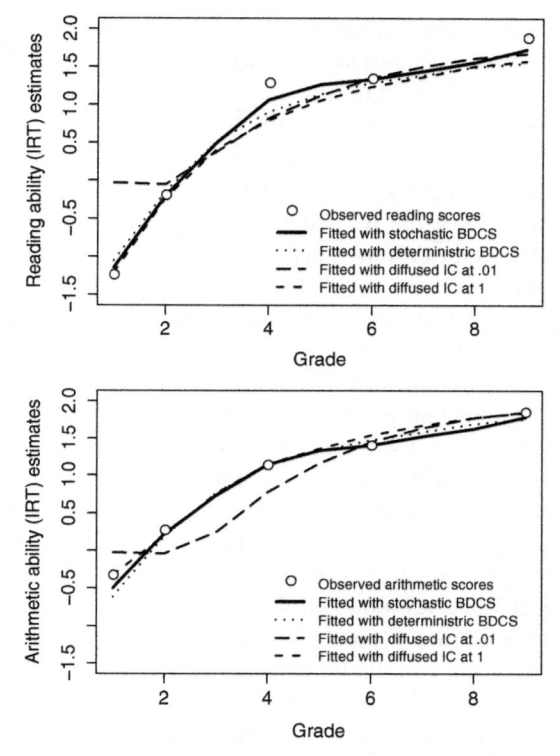

FIGURE 1.6 Plots of one randomly selected participant's estimated true reading and arithmetic scores using the four BDCS models considered. The observed data are depicted as circles in the plots.

data are depicted in the plots as circles. Inspection of the plots revealed some of the ways in which the stochastic BDCS model was able to capture some of the individual-specific, nuanced variations in latent reading and arithmetic abilities across measurement occasions compared to the deterministic BDCS model. For the one participant shown in Figure 1.6, for example, the transition from the second to the fourth grade was characterized by a larger-than-expected rise in latent reading ability score – a rise not predicted by the deterministic BDCS model. The corresponding trajectories generated using the stochastic and deterministic BDCS models for the same participant's arithmetic scores did not show as much differentiation from each other. The BDCS model, at the latent level, assumes monotonic changes in individuals' trajectories – in other words, individuals' latent reading and arithmetic abilities are posited not to regress, but rather to continue to improve or at least stay the same from occasion to occasion. The uncharacteristically large improvement in reading score manifested by the participant in fourth grade was in line with the notion of learning as posited in the BDCS model, and the improvement also persisted beyond just one occasion. As such, it was regarded as driven by process as opposed to measurement noise in the stochastic BDCS model. Figure 1.6 also demonstrated that with limited number of observations, misspecification of IC may lead to serious model misfit, whereas the influence of misspecified IC might be minor when the IC was very diffused. We could see from the plot that when the variances of IC were set at a very small value at .01, the estimated initial condition deviated a lot from the observed data, resulting in severe misfit. However, if the IC is diffused enough (e.g. with variances set at 1), the estimated trajectories were much closer to the conditions where ICs were correctly specified.

Substantially worse fit was observed from the models with misspecified, diffuse IC specification. Here, the term "diffuse" is a misnomer because the two choices of IC variances we considered for illustration purposes actually gave rise to relatively restrictive IC distributions. In fact, with an initial mean vector of zeros and IC variances of .01, such an IC specification was both biased and projected a much more restrictive initial distribution of scores for the participants than that implied under the estimates obtained using the free IC approach. Setting the IC variances to 1.0 imposed a less restrictive IC structure; however, substantial misspecifications were still present in the IC mean structure.

Examination of Table 1.3 indicated that dynamic parameters such as the self-feedback parameters (β_1 and β_2) and the coupling parameters (γ_1 and γ_2) were all highly sensitive to changes in the IC structure as well as process noises structure. For instance, with the stochastic BDCS model, the self-feedback parameter for the arithmetic task was estimated to be -0.16, thus implying a learning curve that would reach an asymptote at some point. In contrast, a positive value of 0.15 was estimated for the arithmetic self-feedback parameter using the deterministic BDCS model, which suggests that individuals' learning curve on the arithmetic task continued to show increasing trends as opposed to converging toward an asymptote – at least over the course of the observed time span. Such notion of monotonically increasing arithmetic skills from kindergarten through middle school is not completely implausible, but may be less intuitive compared to the results inferred from the stochastic BDCS model.

The coupling parameters, γ_1 and γ_2, represented the reciprocal influences of the two learning processes on each other. In the stochastic BDCS model with freely estimated IC structure, a positive coupling coefficient was observed from arithmetic ability to reading ability, indicating that students with higher arithmetic ability at one time point were predicted to have a positive change in reading on the next measurement occasion. In contrast, an "antagonistic" influence was observed from individuals' reading to their subsequent changes in arithmetic scores, suggesting that higher reading scores on one occasion were associated with smaller increase in arithmetic scores on the next occasion. The magnitudes of these parameters were also sensitive to changes in either the IC structure or the process noise structure. When the IC structures were fixed at arbitrary values, the coupling coefficients were observed to vary considerably with variations in IC structure. With freely estimated IC structure, even though the coupling coefficients were estimated to have the same sign in both the stochastic and the deterministic BDCS models, these estimates were much smaller in magnitude in the stochastic BDCS model as compared with the original deterministic BDCS model. This suggested that the reciprocal influences of the reading and arithmetic learning processes were greatly attenuated when processes noises were taken into consideration in the modeling procedures. Such differences in results have important empirical implications and repercussions, such as in the design of intervention efforts to strengthen students' reading and arithmetic skills. For instance, the reduction in coupling strengths may suggest that we could not rely on improvements in one domain (e.g., children's reading skills) to facilitate subsequent improvements in the other domain (e.g., arithmetic skills). Therefore, intervention may need to be conducted simultaneously for these two processes in order to see improvements in both. This underscores the importance of allowing for process noises at the latent level to avoid such over-estimation of the reciprocal linkages between the two learning processes.

Discussion

In this chapter, we considered two variations of the original BDCS model, namely the BDCS model with "diffuse" IC structure and the stochastic BDCS model. We illustrated the implementation and assessed the performance of these models using simulated data sets. A longitudinal data set with measures of children's reading and arithmetic skills from kindergarten years through middle school was used to demonstrate the use of these BDCS models and corresponding differences in inferential results.

We found that when the IC means and covariance matrix are fixed at misspecified values – as was the case in the various diffuse IC conditions considered in this chapter – results pertaining to other modeling parameters were not overly sensitive to such misspecifications. provided that the specified IC structure is diffuse enough to cover the true IC distribution. In the conditions considered in our simulations, for instance, fixing the variances at unity or other larger values (e.g., 10, 100) yielded reasonably satisfactory results in deterministic BDCS models. The effects of having misspecified but overly restrictive IC structure do lessen with the availability of more time points. In the conditions considered in our simulation, for instance, ten measurement time points were enough to attain reasonably good parameter estimates for deterministic BDCS models. More time points were needed (e.g., 50) when stochastic BDCS models were involved and the IC structures were diffuse. The empirical example illustrated the importance of testing the sensitivity of the modeling results to changes in process noise specification in modeling involving variations of the BDCS model. In cases where part of the variances go to the process noise variances when the stochastic BDCS model is fitted, the deterministic BDCS model may not be a good fit to explain all variances in the data, and researchers should explore modeling variation of the BDCS model.

Stochastic extensions of the latent difference score model have been considered previously. For instance, McArdle (2009) alluded to the possibility of accommodating residuals at the latent level but did not discuss the consequences of doing so from an estimation standpoint. Voelkle and Oud (2015) considered a univariate latent difference score model (specifically, the dual change score model) – a univariate special case of the BDCS that can be obtained by setting the coupling parameters to 0 with stochastic process noise but no measurement error. Ferrer, McArdle, Shaywitz, Holahan, Marchione, & Shaywitz (2007) incorporated process noises, which were not explained by the dynamic model and compounded over time, in an application of the BDCS model examining longitudinal developmental dynamic between reading and cognition. In this chapter, we extended the BDCS model to include both process noises and measurement errors, and evaluated the estimation quality of the stochastic BDCS model, especially when coupled with different degrees of misspecification in the IC structure. Our simulation results showed that when the IC was correctly specified, most dynamic parameters could be recovered with as few as only five time points. However, measurement error and process noise variances could not be reliably distinguished under the specific simulation setting we considered. Even more measurement occasions were needed when the IC structure in the stochastic BDCS model was misspecified (e.g. 50 time points in our simulation).

The "free parameter" approach to IC specification provides a relatively general and straightforward way of initializing the BDCS model. This approach has clear appeal in situations where its use is viable. However, in other scenarios, such as those involving more than two latent processes, the corresponding number of free parameters to be estimated may become unwieldy. In such scenarios, other heuristic approaches may be used to improve the specification of the IC compared to the naive, diffuse approach illustrated in this chapter. The diffuse IC approach considered in the present chapter essentially entails fixing the IC variances at arbitrary but sufficiently large values. There are ways to improve model fitting via more "informative" IC specifications. For instance, Oud et al. (1999) proposed to use the cross-sectional Bartlett estimator or the cross-sectional regression estimator as the initial estimator. A related heuristic approach is to first fit a particular BDCS model with diffuse IC to the data, and then using properties of the factor score estimates from this initial model to specify the IC structure of the model in subsequent model fitting.

We only considered two variations/extensions of the original BDCS model, namely the BDCS model with diffuse IC and the stochastic BDCS model. Other extensions are, of course possible. For instance, Chow, Grimm, Filteau, Dolan, & McArdle, (2013a) proposed a regime-switching BDCS model, which allowed for within-person transitions between a coupled regime and a decouple regime, with coupling coefficients freely estimated and fixed at zero, respectively. This model is helpful for representing processes that undergo phases (i.e., regimes) with distinct dynamic properties at unknown but estimable time points. Another interesting extension to the BDCS model is to include fixed and random effects of dynamic parameters such as the self-feedback and coupling parameters. For instance, in the context of children's reading and arithmetic learning curves, the self-feedback parameters may be predicted by person-specific covariates such as the pre-school vocabulary size, children's IQ scores, and children's self-regulation skills. Multi-level extensions of the BDCS model to accommodate hierarchical data – students nested within classrooms within schools, ecological momentary assessment data nested within multiple measurement bursts (or waves) nested within the same individuals, etc. – would also be valuable.

Lastly, the BDCS models assume the presence of a discrete and fixed time interval across measurement occasions (Ferrer & McArdle, 2003). This discrete-time assumption does not always hold. In cases involving unequal intervals between occasions, phantom variables need to be created to account for the differences in time intervals (Rindskopf, 1984) – an approach that is essentially equivalent to our approach of inserting missingness in the data to yield a set of equally spaced data for model fitting. However, this method of creating phantom variables can be cumbersome with more measurement occasions and different numbers of measurement occasions for different participants. To this end, continuous time extensions of the BDCS model provide a viable alternative. A univariate special case of such continuous time models was considered by Voelkle and Oud (2015). Generalizations of the proposed continuous time formulation to the BDCS model and related variations involving higher dimension are a natural next step to the work of Voelkle and Oud (2015), and the modeling work presented in this chapter.

Limitations

The present work has several limitations, some of which we highlight briefly here. First, the conclusions drawn from the Monte Carlo simulations are restricted to the specific simulation setting we considered and may not apply to other settings. For instance, the sample size used in our current simulation ($N = 500$) was, admittedly, relatively large compared to the sample sizes considered in other applications of the BDCS model (e.g., with 100 to 200 participants; McArdle, Hamagami, Meredith, & Bradway, 2000; McArdle, Hamagami, Jones, Jolesz Kikinis, Spiro, & Albert, 2004). Another caveat we brought up earlier is that in cases where the processes reach their asymptotes too quickly, data from the observations after the asymptotes have been reached do not provide sufficient information to facilitate the estimation of most of the dynamic parameters in the model. Thus, a denser number of time points is likely needed during the earlier phases of the study to ensure satisfactory estimation of the change dynamics. Overall, to establish more rigorous guidelines concerning the use of the BDCS models, a more comprehensive simulation study is needed to evaluate the estimation quality associated with BDCS models under different combinations of N and T, different choices of true parameter values, and with different modeling properties.

We also acknowledge that IC misspecification and incorrect omission of process noises are not the only sources of model misspecification that may contribute to estimation biases. When mild misspecification is present, researchers can resort to diagnostic procedures and statistics, such as model modification index and the standardized expected parameter change, to aid in the process of identifying model misspecification and improving the model (Saris, Satorra, & van der Veld, 2009; Whittaker, 2012). These approaches may not work when more severe sources of misspecification are present. Such issues are out of the scope of the chapter and thus not covered.

Closing Remarks

We have attempted, within the space allotted in this chapter, to demonstrate some extensions and "next steps" to McArdle's latent difference score framework proposed almost two decades ago. Our brief simulations have not even begun to scratch the surface of McArdle's numerous impactful contributions to the fields of psychometrics and lifespan development. We chose to focus on discussing the latent difference framework because in our view, it epitomizes some of McArdle's unique and unprecedented qualities as a scholar and a researcher: to develop and enhance methodologies for answering real-world problems in ways that resonate with applied researchers, practitioners, and policy makers. Even though latent difference score models such as the BDCS models can be written in the one-step ahead form shown in Equation 1.4, writing it in the form originally proposed by McArdle and Hamagami (2001b; 2001a) highlights very concretely its links to traditional change score analysis. Such a formulation calls attention to the need to formalize one's conceptualizations of the mechanisms and determinisms of change. This is in addition to some of the more nuanced methodological strengths of the univariate dual change score and BDCS models in providing ways to capture nonlinear growth trajectories by means of a set of latent linear difference equations. Such thoughtful and insightful integration of methods and empirical considerations has and will likely continue to inspire many students, researchers, scholars, and practitioners in years to come.

Notes

1 Funding for this study was provided by NSF grant SES-1357666 and NIH grant R01GM105004 awarded to Sy-Miin Chow. The two authors contributed equally to this chapter.
2 Stability as defined by Lütkepohl (2005), which includes stationarity – namely, invariance in the statistical properties of a process over time.

References

Baltes, P. B. & Nesselroade, J. R. (1979). History and rationale of longitudinal research. In Nesselroade, J. R. & Baltes, P. B. (Eds.) *Longitudinal research in the study of behavior and development* (pp. 1–39). New York: Academic Press, Inc.

Bereiter, C. (1963). Some persisting dilemmas in the measurement of change. In Harris, C. W. (Ed.) *Problems in measuring change* (pp. 3–20). Madison, WI: University of Wisconsin Press.

Bollen, K. A. & Curran, P. J. (2006). *Latent curve models: A structural equation perspective*, volume 467. Hoboken, NJ: John Wiley & Sons.

Browne, M. W. & du Toit, H. C. (1991). Models for learning data. In Collins, L. M. & Horn, J. L. (Eds.) *Best methods for the analysis of change: Recent advances, unanswered questions, future directions* (pp. 47–68). Washington DC: American Psychological Association.

Browne, M. W. & Nesselroade, J. R. (2005). Representing psychological processes with dynamic factor models: Some promising uses and extensions of autoregressive moving average time series models. In Maydeu-Olivares, A. & McArdle, J. J. (Eds.) *Contemporary psychometrics: A Festschrift for Roderick P. McDonald* (pp. 415–452). Mahwah, NJ: Erlbaum.

Cattell, R. B. (1966). Patterns of change: Measurement in relation to state dimension, trait change, lability, and process concepts. In Cattell, R. B. (Ed.) *Handbook of multivariate experimental psychology* (pp. 355–402). Chicago, IL: Rand McNally. 1st edition.

Chow, S.-M., Grimm, K. J., Filteau, G., Dolan, C. V., & McArdle, J. J. (2013a). Regime-switching bivariate dual change score model. *Multivariate Behavioral Research*, *48*(4), 463–502.

Chow, S.-M., Grimm, K. J., Guillaume, F., Dolan, C. V., & McArdle, J. J. (2013b). Regime-switching bivariate dual change score model. *Multivariate Behavioral Research*, *48*(4), 463–502.

Chow, S.-M., Ho, M.-h. R., Hamaker, E. L., & Dolan, C. V. (2010). Equivalence and differences between structural equation modeling and state-space modeling techniques. *Structural Equation Modeling*, *17*(2), 303–332.

Chow, S.-M., Lu, Z., Sherwood, A., & Zhu, H. (2016). Fitting nonlinear ordinary differential equation models with random effects and unknown initial conditions using the Stochastic Approximation Expectation Maximization (SAEM) algorithm. *Psychometrika*, *81*, 102–134.

Chow, S.-M., Nesselroade, J. R., Shifren, K., & McArdle, J. J. (2004). Dynamic structure of emotions among individuals with Parkinson's disease. *Structural Equation Modeling*, *11*, 560–582.

Cole, D. & Maxwell, S. E. (2003). Testing mediational models with longitudinal data: questions and tips in the use of structural equation modeling. *Journal of Abnormal Psychology*, *112*(4), 558–577.

Collins, L. M. & Horn, J. L. (Eds.) (1991). *Best methods for the analyis of change*. Washington DC: American Psychological Association.

Cooney, J. B. & Troyer, R. (1994). A dynamic model of reaction in a short-term memory task. *Journal of Experimental Child Psychology*, *58*, 200–226.

Cronbach, L. J. & Furby, L. (1970). How should we measure "change" – or should we? *Psychological Bulletin*, *74*(1), 68–80.

Cudeck, R. (2002). Mixed-effects models in the study of individual differences with repeated measures data. *Multivariate Behavioral Research*, *31*(3), 371–403.

De Jong, P. (1991). The diffuse kalman filter. *The Annals of Statistics*, *19*(2), 1073–1083.

Deary, I. J., Johnson, W., Gow, A. J., Pattie, A., Brett, C. E., Bates, T. C., & Starr, J. M. (2011). Losing one's grip: a bivariate growth curve model of grip strength and nonverbal reasoning from age 79 to 87 years in the lothian birth cohort 1921. *The Journals of Gerontology Series B: Psychological Sciences and Social Sciences*, *66*(6), 699–707.

Dolan, C. V. & Molenaar, P. C. M. (1991). A note on the calculation of latent trajectories in the quasi Markov simplex model by means of regression method and the discrete Kalman filter. *Kwantitatieve Methoden*, *38*, 29–44.

du Toit, S. H. & Browne, M. W. (2007). Structural equation modeling of multivariate time series. *Multivariate Behavioral Research, 42*(1), 67–101.

du Toit, S. H. C. & Browne, M. W. (2007). Structural equation modeling of multivariate time series. *Multivariate Behavioral Research, 42,* 67–101.

Duncan, T. E., Duncan, S. C., & Strycker, L. A. (2013). *An introduction to latent variable growth curve modeling: Concepts, issues, and application.* New York: Psychology Press.

Ferrer, E. & McArdle, J. J. (2003). Alternative structural models for multivariate longitudinal data analysis. *Structural Equation Modeling, 10*(4), 493–524.

Ferrer, E., McArdle, J. J., Shaywitz, B. A., Holahan, J. M., Marchione, K., & Shaywitz, S. E. (2007). Longitudinal models of developmental dynamics between reading and cognition from childhood and adolescence. *Developmental Psychology, 43*(6), 1460–1473.

Hale, J. K. & Koçak, H. (1991). *Dynamics and bifurcation.* New York: Springer-Verlag.

Hamaker, E. L. (2005). Conditions for the equivalence of the autoregressive latent trajectory model and a latent growth curve model with autoregressive disturbances. *Sociological Methos & Research, 33*(3), 404–416.

Hamilton, J. D. (1994). *Time series analysis.* Princeton, NJ: Princeton University Press.

Harris, C. W. (Ed.) (1963). *Problems in measuring change.* Madison, WI: University of Wisconsin Press.

Harvey, A. C. (2001). *Forecasting, structural time series models and the Kalman filter.* Cambridge UK: Cambridge University Press.

Harvey, A. C. & Phillips, G. D. (1979). Maximum likelihood estimation of regression models with autoregressive-moving average disturbances. *Biometrika, 66*(1), 49–58.

Harvey, A. C. & Souza, R. C. (1987). Assessing and modelling the cyclical behaviour of rainfall in northeast Brazil. *Journal of Climate and Applied Meteorology, 26,* 1317–1322.

Humphreys, L. G. (1996). Linear dependence of gain scores on their components imposes constraints on their use and interpretation: Comment on "Are simple gain scores obsolete?". *Applied Psychological Measurement, 20,* 293–294.

Kaplan, D. & Glass, L. (1995). *Understanding nonlinear dynamics.* New York: Springer-Verlag.

Loesch, D. Z., Hopper, J. L., Rogucka, E., & Huggins, R. M. (1995). Timing and genetic rapport between growth in skeletal maturity and height around puberty: similarities and differences between girls and boys. *American Journal of Human Genetics, 56*(3), 753.

Lord, F. M. (1956). The measurement of growth. *Educational and Psychological Measurement, 16,* 421–437.

Lord, F. M. (1958). Further problems in the measurement of growth. *Educational and Psychological Measurement, 18*(3), 437–451.

Losardo, D. (2012). *An examination of initial condition specification in the structural equations modeling framework.* PhD thesis.

Lütkepohl, H. (2005). *New introduction to multiple time series analysis.* Berlin: Springer verlag. [u.a.].

Mackinnon, S. P. (2012). Perceived social support and academic achievement: Cross-lagged panel and bivariate growth curve analyses. *Journal of Youth and Adolescence, 41*(4), 474–485.

May, R. (1974). *Stability and complexity in model ecosystems.* Princeton, NJ: Princeton University Press.

McArdle, J. J. (2001). A latent difference score approach to longitudinal dynamic structural analyses. In Cudeck, R., du Toit, S., & Sörbom, D. (Eds.) *Structural equation modeling: Present and future* (pp. 342–380). Lincolnwood, IL: Scientific Software International.

McArdle, J. J. (2009). Latent variable modeling of differences and changes with longitudinal data. *Annual Review of Psychology, 60,* 577–605.

McArdle, J. J. (2009). Latent variable Modeling of differences and changes with longitudinal data. *Annual Review of Psychology, 60*(1), 577–605.

McArdle, J. J. & Epstein, D. B. (1987). Latent growth curves within developmental structural equation models. *Child Development, 58*(1), 110–133.

McArdle, J. J. & Hamagami, F. (2001). Latent difference score structural models for linear dynamic analysis with incomplete longitudinal data. In Collins, L. & Sayer, A. (Eds.) *New methods for the analysis of change* (pp. 139–175). Washington, DC: American Psychological Association.

McArdle, J. J. & Hamagami, F. (2003a). Structural equation models for evaluating dynamic concepts within longitudinal twin analyses. *Behavioral Genetics, 33*(2), 137–159.

McArdle, J. J. & Hamagami, F. (2003b). Structural equation models for evaluating dynamic concepts within longitudinal twin analyses. *Behavioral Genetics, 33*(2), 137–159.

McArdle, J. J., Hamagami, F., Meredith, W., & Bradway, K. P. (2000). Modeling the dynamic hypotheses of gf–gc theory using longitudinal life-span data. *Learning and Individual Differences, 12*(1), 53–79.

McArdle, J. J., Hamgami, F., Jones, K., Jolesz, F., Kikinis, R., Spiro, A., & Albert, M. S. (2004). Structural modeling of dynamic changes in memory and brain structure using longitudinal data from the normative aging study. *The Journals of Gerontology Series B: Psychological Sciences and Social Sciences, 59*(6), 294–304.

Nesselroade, J. R. & Cable, D. G. (1974). "Sometimes, it's okay to factor difference scores" – the separation of state and trait anxiety. *Multivariate Behavioral Research, 9*, 273–282.

Newtson, D. (1993). The dynamics of action and interaction. In Smith, L. B. & Thelen, E. (Eds.) *A dynamic systems approach to development: Applications* (pp. 241–264). Cambridge, MA MIT Press.

Ou, L., Chow, S.-M., Ji, L., & Molenaar, P. C. (2016). (Re)evaluating the implications of the autoregressive latent trajectory model through likelihood ratio tests of its initial conditions. *Multivariate Behavioral Research*, pp. 1–22.

Ou, L., Hunter, M. D., & Chow, S.-M. (2017). *dynr: Dynamic Modeling in R.* R package version 0.1.11–2.

Oud, J. H., Jansen, R. A., Van Leeuwe, J. F., Aarnoutse, C. A., & Voeten, M. J. (1999). Monitoring pupil development by means of the kalman filter and smoother based upon sem state space modeling. *Learning and Individual Differences, 11*(2), 121–136.

Oud, J. H. L., van den Bercken, J. H., & Essers, R. J. (1990). Longitudinal factor score estimation using the Kalman filter. *Applied Psychological Measurement, 14*, 395–418.

Ram, N. & Grimm, K. (2015). Growth curve modeling and longitudinal factor analysis. In Overton, W. F. & Molenaar, P. C. M. (Eds.) *Handbook of child psychology and developmental science* (pp. 758–788). Hoboken, NJ: Wiley. 7th edition.

Rindskopf, D. (1984). Using phantom and imaginary latent variables to parameterize constraints in linear structural models. *Psychometrika, 49*(1), 37–47.

Rogosa, D. (1978). Causal models in longitudinal research: Rationale, formulation, and interpretation. In Nesselroade, J. R. & Baltes, P. B. (Eds.) *Longitudinal research in human development: Design and analysis* (pp. 263–302). New York: Academic Press.

Saris, W. E., Satorra, A., & van der Veld, W. M. (2009). Testing structural equation models or detection of misspecifications? *Structural Equation Modeling: A Multidisciplinary Journal, 16*(4), 561–582.

Schweppe, F. C. (1973). *Uncertain dynamic systems.* Upper Saddle River, NJ: Prentice Hall.

Singer, J. D. & Willett, J. B. (2003). *Applied longitudinal data analysis: Modeling change and event occurrence.* New York: Oxford University Press, Oxford, UK.

Van Geert, P. (1993). A dynamic systems model of cognitive growth: Competition and support under limited resource conditions. In Smith, L. B. & Thelen, E. (Eds.) *A dynamic systems approach to development applications* (pp. 263–331). Cambridge, MA: MIT Press.

Van Geert, P. (1998). Dynamic modelling of cognitive and language development: From growth processes to sudden jump and multimodality. In Newell, K. M. & Molenaar, P. C. M. (Eds.) *Applications of nonlinear dynamics to developmental process modeling*, (pp. 129–160). Mahwah, NJ: Lawrence Erlbaum.

Voelkle, M. C. & Oud, J. H. (2015). Relating latent change score and continuous time models. *Structural Equation Modeling: A Multidisciplinary Journal, 22*(3), 366–381.

Whittaker, T. A. (2012). Using the modification index and standardized expected parameter change for model modification. *The Journal of Experimental Education, 80*(1), 26–44.

Williams, R. H. & Zimmerman, D. W. (1996). Are simple gain scores obsolete? *Applied Psychological Measurement, 20*, 59–69.

Appendix

Sample *dynr* Code for Fitting the Stochastic BDCS Models in the Illustrative Example.

Freely estimated IC or diffuse fix IC can be specified with the *prep.initial* function. For details, please see script below.

```
data <- dynr.data(yall, id="ID", time="Time",
                  observed=c("read","math"))


meas <- prep.measurement(
  values.load=matrix(c(1,0,0,0,
                       0,0,1,0),ncol=4,byrow=T),
  params.load=matrix(rep("fixed",8),ncol=4),
  state.names=c("readLevel","readSlope","mathLevel","mathSlope"),
  obs.names=c("read","math")
)


## Initial condition speicification with freely estimated parameters ##


initial <- prep.initial(
  values.inistate=c(-1,.5,-.9,.5),
  params.inistate=c('mu_readLevel', 'mu_readSlope','mu_mathLevel',
        'mu_mathSlope'),
  values.inicov=matrix(c(.2,.01,.01,.01,
                         .01,.1,.01,.01,
                         .01,.01,.1,.02,
                         .01,.01,.02,.1),byrow=T,ncol=4),
  params.inicov=matrix(c("v_11","c_12","c_13","c_14",
                         "c_12","v_22","c_23","c_24",
                         "c_13","c_23","v_33","c_34",
                         "c_14","c_24","c_34","v_44"),byrow=T,ncol=4))
```

```
## Diffuse initial condtiion specification ##
#initial covariance is fixed to a diagonal matrix of 10s.
initial <- prep.initial(
  values.inistate=c(-1,.5,-.9,.5),
  params.inistate=c('mu_readLevel', 'mu_readSlope','mu_mathLevel',
        'mu_mathSlope'),
  values.inicov=diag(rep(10,4)),
  params.inicov=diag(rep('fixed',4)))


## Include process noises into the model ##
mdcov <- prep.noise(
  values.latent=matrix(c(.2,0,.01,0,
                         0,0,0,0,
                         .01,0,.2,0,
                         0,0,0,0),byrow=T,ncol=4),
  params.latent=matrix(c("v_readLevel","fixed","c_levels","fixed",
                         "fixed","fixed","fixed","fixed",
                         "c_levels","fixed","v_mathLevel","fixed",
                         "fixed","fixed","fixed","fixed"),byrow=T,ncol=4),
  values.observed=diag(c(.03,.03)),
  params.observed=diag(c('readErrorV','mathErrorV'),2))


formula =list(
  list(readLevel~ (1+beta.read)*readLevel + readSlope
      + gamma.read*mathLevel,
       readSlope~ readSlope,
       mathLevel~ (1+beta.math)*mathLevel + mathSlope
      + gamma.math*readLevel,
       mathSlope~ mathSlope
  ))


dynm   <- prep.formulaDynamics(formula=formula,
                               startval=c(beta.read = -.5, beta.math = -.5,
                                          gamma.read = .3, gamma.math = .03
                               ), isContinuousTime=FALSE)


model.stoch <- dynr.model(dynamics=dynm, measurement=meas,
                          noise=mdcov, initial=initial, data=data,
                          outfile="BDCS.c")
BDCS.stoch <- dynr.cook(model.stoch)
summary(BDCS.stoch)
```

2

DISCRETE- AND SEMI-CONTINUOUS TIME LATENT CHANGE SCORE MODELS OF FLUID REASONING DEVELOPMENT FROM CHILDHOOD TO ADOLESCENCE[1]

Emilio Ferrer

Fluid reasoning (FR) is the capacity to think logically and solve problems in novel situations, independent of acquired knowledge (Cattell, 1957; Horn & Cattell, 1966). This capacity is an essential component of cognitive development (Goswami, 1992), as it serves as a scaffold for acquiring other abilities (Blair, 2006; Cattell, 1971, 1987). FR in childhood accurately predicts performance in school, at university (Green et al., 2017), and in cognitively demanding occupations (Gottfredson, 1997). Indeed, FR is the strongest and most consistent predictor of mathematics achievement between ages 5 and 19 (Taub, Floyd, Keith, & McGrew, 2008).

Although there is evidence linking FR to other cognitive abilities and academic achievement, there is a lack of knowledge about the precise developmental trajectories of FR across the life-span, specifically during the transition from childhood to adolescence. Understanding the time course of these trajectories is important to describe important developmental sequences and to identify potential mechanisms that underlie such pathways. The general objective of this chapter is to investigate the age-related trajectories of FR using a cohort-sequential sample spanning childhood and adolescence. In particular, the goal was to characterize the changes in fluid reasoning from childhood to adolescence, as well as identify potential developmental mechanisms underlying such changes.

Development of Fluid Reasoning

Fluid reasoning is thought to emerge in the first two or three years of life (Cattell, 1971, 1987), after the development of general perceptual, attentional, and motoric capabilities (Horn, 1991; Horn & Noll, 1997). Notably, fluid reasoning follows a different developmental trajectory than crystallized abilities, lending support to the idea that these are separable cognitive functions (Horn, 1991; Horn & Noll, 1997; Schaie, 1996). The psychometric literature indicates that fluid reasoning capacity increases very rapidly in early and middle childhood, continues to increase at a slower rate in late childhood and early adolescence, and reaches asymptotic values in late adolescence and early adulthood, peaking at around age 22 and declining subsequently (McArdle, Ferrer, Hamagami, & Woodcock, 2002). This pattern of growth and decline has been characterized by a double exponential function (McArdle et al., 2002), with features similar to the patterns followed by other cognitive abilities such as processing speed up to adolescence (Kail, 1991; Kail & Ferrer, 2007). This description, however, has not been replicated across other longitudinal data sets, especially with an array of measures of fluid reasoning and an age span ranging from early childhood to late adolescence.

Identifying the precise form that characterizes the changes in fluid reasoning is important to obtain a formal description of its development. Moreover, the parameters of the mathematical model can yield insights regarding possible mechanisms underlying such development. For this goal, longitudinal data are necessary that provide repeated assessments from individuals. Such repeated measures are needed to identify within-person changes over time, as well as individual differences in such changes.

Models to Examine Changes in Fluid Reasoning across Measurement Occasions

Two approaches are implemented to examine the development of fluid reasoning. The first approach utilizes models for identifying changes across measurement occasions (e.g., McArdle & Woodcock, 1997). This approach is based on latent change score models (Ferrer & McArdle, 2010; McArdle, 2001; McArdle & Hamagami, 2001), in particular, a second-order model (2LCS), which is a multivariate extension of latent change score models that incorporates the measurement structure (Ferrer, Balluerka, & Widaman, 2008)[2]. This specification of the model allows for a test of factorial invariance, evaluating whether the FR construct is equivalent across measurement occasions. Given a system of four observed variables, X, Y, W, and Z, measured at t time points for n individuals, this model can be written as:

$$X_{(t)n} = \tau_x + \lambda_x f_{(t)n} + e_{x(t)n},$$

$$Y_{(t)n} = \tau_y + \lambda_y f_{(t)n} + e_{y(t)n},$$

$$W_{(t)n} = \tau_w + \lambda_w f_{(t)n} + e_{w(t)n}, \quad \text{and}$$

$$Z_{(t)n} = \tau_z + \lambda_z f_{(t)n} + e_{z(t)n}, \quad \text{with}$$

$$\Delta f_{(t)n} = \alpha \cdot f_{sn} + \beta \cdot f_{(t-1)n} + v_{\Delta(t)n}, \tag{2.1}$$

where Δf represents change in the factor f at time t, α is a parameter that expresses the influence of an additive component f_s on the change, β is a coefficient representing the effect of the factor at the previous state on the change, and $\nu_{\Delta(t)n}$ is the residual of the latent change. Thus, the trajectory of the latent factor f at any given time t can be written as a function of its initial state plus all the changes accumulated up to time t, as:

$$f_{(t)n} = f_{0n} + \left(\sum_{i=2}^{t} \Delta f(i)n \right). \tag{2.2}$$

Figure 2.1 represents a path diagram for the 2LCS model. This figure depicts four manifest variables that assess fluid reasoning measured over three occasions. At each occasion, the four indicators comprise a fluid reasoning latent factor. Moreover, for each repeated assessment, a new latent variable Δ_{f_t} is created that represents a latent change between the two occasions. To examine associations between the fluid reasoning factor and covariates of interest X (e.g., age), paths can be specified that indicate regression coefficients from those covariates to the initial level of fluid reasoning $(\beta_x \rightarrow f_{0})$, as well as to the changes $(\beta_x \rightarrow \Delta_{[fr]})$.

This 2LCS specification is useful to: (a) evaluate whether or not the same construct of fluid reasoning is being measured across occasions; (b), model within-person changes in the fluid reasoning factor, with attenuated measurement error; (c) identify potential variability in such changes across individuals; and (d) examine possible associations between covariates of interest and the fluid reasoning factor, its initial level and its changes. This is novel in the developmental methodology literature.

Models to Examine Dynamics of Fluid Reasoning and Underlying Developmental Mechanisms

The second approach extends the described LCS model into a specification for capturing age-related changes. For this, age is now used as the underlying time signature. Participants in the empirical dataset ranged in age from 6 to 19 and were measured up to three times, with different test-retest intervals. Specifying an LCS with age as the underlying metric in standard SEM requires creating age bins that accommodate the FR scores for each possible age (Ferrer & McArdle, 2004). This specification will yield a data matrix in which each person has information at two or three of the possible age points and missing data elsewhere. This data matrix matched the data collection design, which was based on a cohort sequential design and replacement attrition strategy, with the goal of obtaining approximately the same amount of data points across all ages in the sample (see Figure 2.2).

Using this approach, one can model the changes in FR across the entire age span. Similarly, this approach allows investigating the potential contribution of covariates of interest to the latent changes. Figure 2.3 is a path diagram of this LCS specification. Here, FR reasoning is modeled as a latent variable at each year (fr_{yr}). Furthermore, for each repeated occasion, a latent variable $\Delta_{y[t]}$ represents the changes in the construct. Such changes are the key components of an LCS

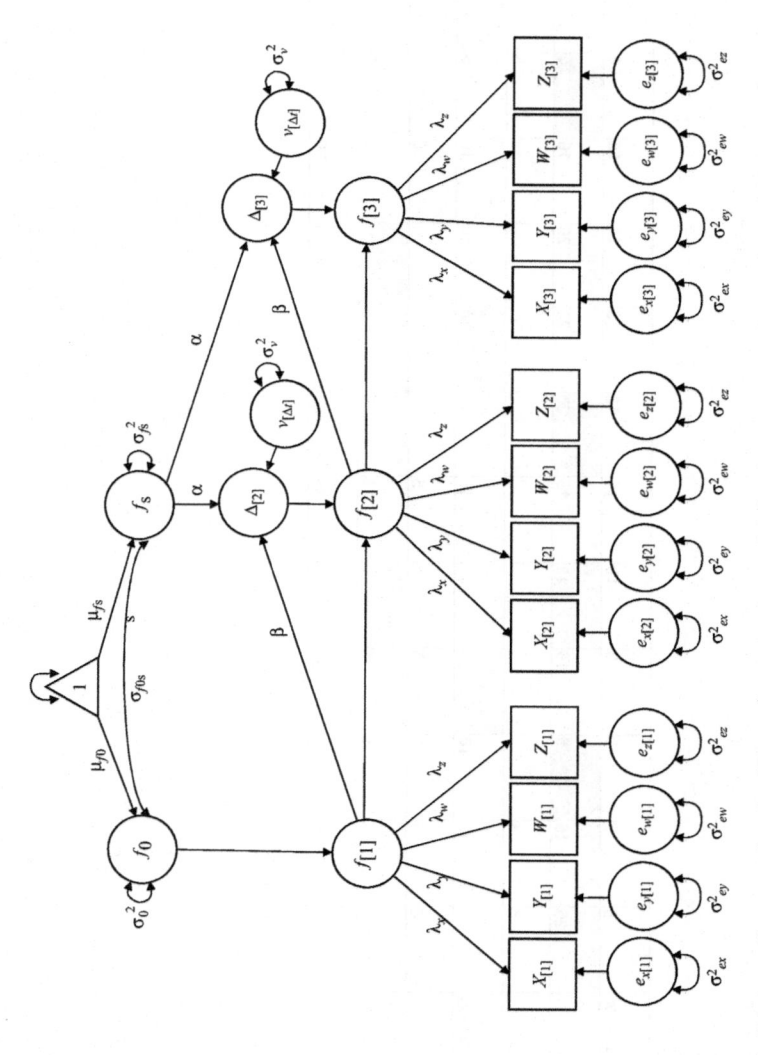

FIGURE 2.1 Path diagram of a second-order latent change score model for three-occasion data. Manifest variables are represented by squares. Latent variables are represented by circles. The triangle represents a constant to estimate the means and intercepts. Although not depicted in this figure, the intercepts of the manifest variables are estimated. Also not depicted in this figure are the covariances among same manifest variables at adjacent time points. Factor loadings are represented as invariant over time.

Time	Subjects	6	7	8	9	10	11	12	13	14	15	16	17	18
T1	new	25	15	15	15	15	15	20	20	20	10	10	10	10
	new	5	5	.	.	.	.	.	.	.		5	5	5
T2	returning	.	10	10	10	10	10	10	10	10	10	5	5	5
	new	5	5	5	5	5	5	.	.	.	5	5	5	5
T3	returning	.	5	5	5	5	5	5	5	5	5	5	5	5
Total		35	35	35	35	35	35	35	35	35	30	30	30	30

FIGURE 2.2 Data collection matrix based on a cohort–sequential design.

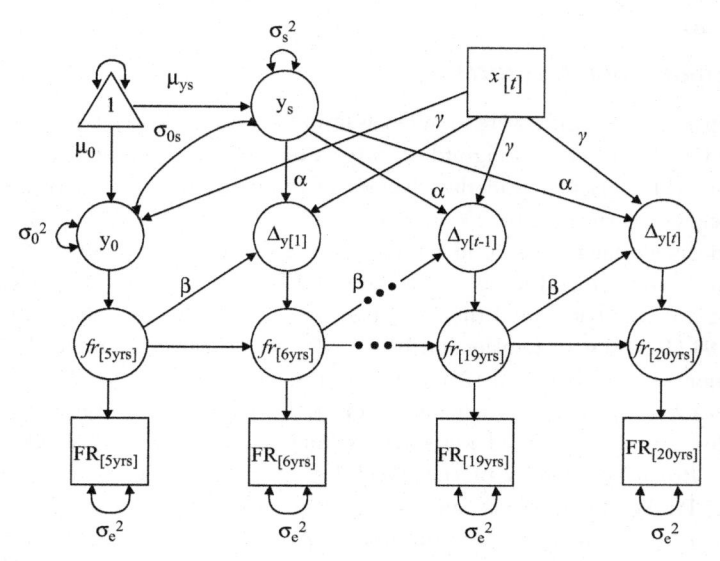

FIGURE 2.3 Path diagram of a latent change score model for multiple-occasion data with age bins as the underlying metric.

model and are a function of: (a) the construct itself as the previous year, quantified by the coefficient β; (b) an additive component y_s, quantified by the coefficient α; and (c) covariates of interest x, quantified by the coefficient γ.

These covariates of interest can be time-invariant or time-varying. Moreover, they can represent levels at any given time as well as changes across occasions, depending on the hypothesis being tested. If, in addition to the influence of the covariate on the main process variable, the investigator is also interested in modeling the covariate over time, such ongoing interrelation can be examined via a bivariate LCS specification (see Ferrer & McArdle, 2010; McArdle, 2009).

One important aspect of the specification depicted in Figure 2.3 is the time metric underlying the process. Because age is a continuous variable, one needs to decide an adequate binning metric. This depiction of yearly bins is a reasonable starting point that, as described previously, matches the data collection. If more precision in the process is desired, smaller bins, such as a half-year, can be created (e.g., McArdle & Bell, 2000). Such specification might also be influenced by the density of data, as finer grain of precision will result in fewer data points, or by features of the study design (Miller & Ferrer, 2017). Alternatively, a model can be specified in which age, the underlying time metric, is truly continuous (Boker, 2001; Boker et al., 2004; Ji & Chow, 2017; Oud & Jansen, 2000; van Montfort, Oud, Voelkle, in press; Voelkle & Oud, 2013, 2015; Voelkle et al., 2012). In these analyses, age bins are used as a semi-continuous metric to investigate the yearly developmental changes in fluid reasoning across childhood and adolescence.

Method

Participants and Measures

Participants in this study were individuals from the *Neural Development of Reasoning Ability* (NORA) study, a longitudinal project designed to examine the behavioral and neural factors that underlie changes in fluid reasoning from childhood to adolescence (Ferrer et al., 2009). Data were available from 201, 121, and 71 individuals at the first, second, and third assessments, respectively. At time 1, the participants ranged in age from 5.00 to 19.1; at time 2, the age range was 6.46 to 20.5; and at time 3 the age range was 7.75 to 21.0. Of the 201 participants, 94 (46.8%) were females and 107 (53.2%) were males. The interval between assessments ranged between 12 and 24 months.

At each assessment, participants completed a battery of cognitive measures, including four standardized measures of fluid reasoning: the *Block Design* and *Matrix Reasoning* subtests of the Wechsler Abbreviated Scale of Intelligence (WISC-R; Wechsler, 1981), and the *Analysis Synthesis* and *Concept Formation* subtests of the Woodcock-Johnson Tests of Achievement (WJ-R; Woodcock & Johnson, 1990). *Block Design* measures the ability to arrange a set of red-and-white blocks in such a way as to reproduce a 2-dimensional visual pattern shown on a set of cards. *Matrix Reasoning* measures the ability to select the geometric visual stimulus that accurately completes a series of stimuli that change along a particular dimension. *Analysis Synthesis* measures the ability to analyze the components of an incomplete logic puzzle and to determine and name the missing components. Participants are given instructions on how to perform an increasingly complex procedure and feedback on the correctness of their responses. *Concept Formation* measures the ability to identify and state the rules for concepts when shown illustrations of both instances and noninstances of the concept. Participants are presented with a complete stimulus set from which to derive the rule for each item and are given feedback regarding the correctness of each response. All the tests are reported to have very high internal consistency and test-retest reliability, ranging from .94 to .95 (McArdle et al., 2002; McGrew et al., 1991).

Data Description

Table 2.1 shows descriptive statistics of each of the four observed variables across the three measurement occasions. This information shows increases in each of the variables from the first to the second occasion, as well as moderate to strong correlations among the four variables at each occasion. From these means and correlations, it is reasonable to expect to extract a robust factor that is common among the four variables and that shows quantitative changes across the two occasions.

Figure 2.4 includes plots for the four tests used in the analyses. In these plots, each line represents an individual's scores across the measurement occasions. Thus, the graphs depict individual trajectories as well as the general pattern of growth for

TABLE 2.1 Descriptive statistics (means, standard deviations, and correlations) for the observed variables of fluid reasoning across the three waves.

	Matrix Reasoning	Block Design	Concept Formation	Analysis Synthesis
Means $t1$	21.794	31.974	23.497	24.748
SD $t1$	7.714	19.119	9.008	5.742
matrix reasoning $t1$	1.000			
block design $t1$	.743	1.000		
concept formation $t1$	.696	.697	1.000	
analysis synthesis $t1$	.691	.574	.690	1.000
Means $t2$	26.256	40.504	27.933	27.042
SD $t2$	6.468	19.94	7.543	4.594
matrix reasoning $t2$	1.000			
block design $t2$	.601	1.000		
concept formation $t2$	.640	.728	1.000	
analysis synthesis $t2$	.652	.685	.774	1.000
Means $t3$	28.750	48.986	31.875	29.426
SD $t3$	4.075	16.854	4.472	3.197
matrix reasoning $t3$	1.000			
block design $t3$	.694	1.000		
concept formation $t3$	.609	.835	1.000	
analysis synthesis $t3$	.645	.647	.773	1.000

Note: $N_{t1} = 201$, $N_{t2} = 121$, $N_{t2} = 71$.

the entire sample. These plots display some general similarities in the shape among the various tests, with curves that rise rapidly during childhood and less rapidly during late adolescence, along with individual differences in the trajectories.

Results

Change in Fluid Reasoning Across Measurement Occasions

The first set of analyses investigated changes in fluid reasoning across the three measurement occasions. For this, a common factor representing fluid reasoning was specified using the four tests. Equivalence of this factor across the three measurement occasions was then examined using longitudinal measurement invariance (Meredith, 1993) to ensure an equal definition of the latent construct over time (Ferrer et al., 2008; Hancock et al., 2001; Sayer & Cumsille, 2001).

These analyses involved a number of increasingly restrictive models, including: (a) configural invariance, indicating that the same indicators of the latent construct are specified at each occasion, regardless of the numerical values of the parameter

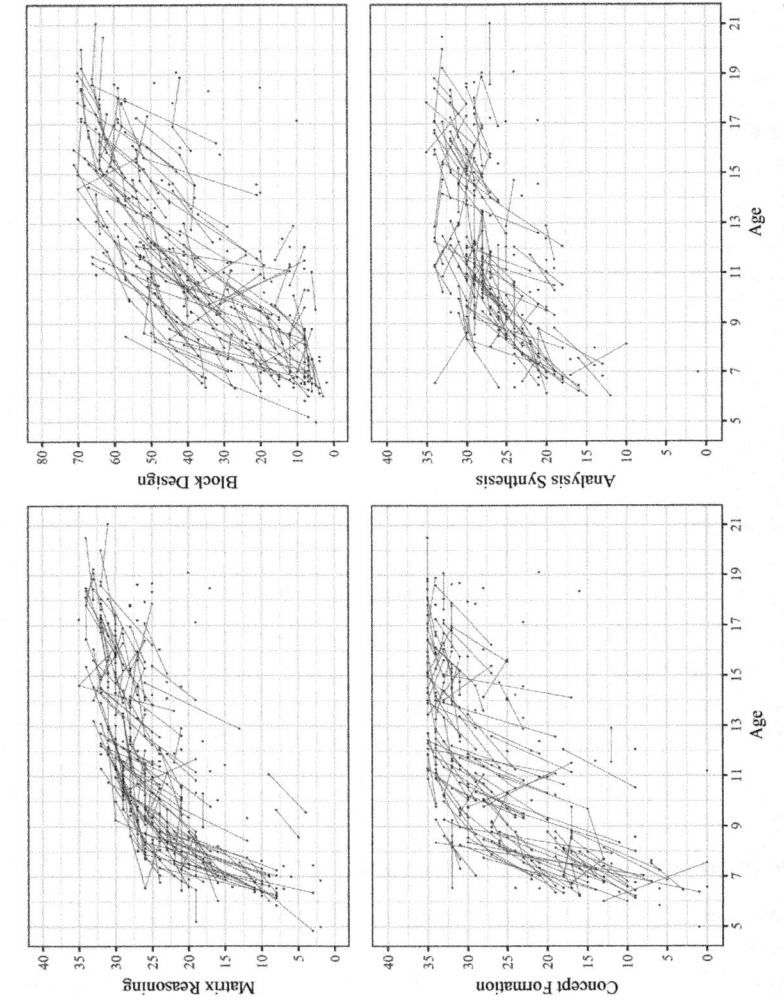

FIGURE 2.4 Individual plots for the four measures of fluid reasoning. Each line represents an individual's scores across the two occasions of measurement. Single dots represent those persons with one score only.

TABLE 2.2 Model fit factorial invariance across measurement occasions.

Invariance Model	χ^2	df	# parameters	$\Delta\chi^2 / \Delta$ df	p	BIC
Configural	140	47	43	–		8856
Weak ($\lambda^=$)	165	53	37	15 / 6	= .025	8849
Strong ($\lambda^= + \tau^=$)*	170	59	31	5 / 6	> .050	8824
Strict ($\lambda^= + \tau^= + \Theta^=$)*	253	67	23	83 / 8	< .001	8864

Note: $N_{t1} = 201$, $N_{t2} = 121$, $N_{t3} = 71$. λ = factor loadings; τ = intercepts; Θ = residual variances. "*" = The factor mean at the second occasion is free to vary.

estimates; (b) weak factorial invariance, where the factor loading of each indicator takes the same numerical value across occasions; (c) strong factorial invariance, where the measurement intercept for each indicator is invariant across time; and (d) strict factorial invariance, requiring that the unique variance for each manifest variable be equal over time (Ferrer et al., 2008).

Model fit results from these analyses are presented in Table 2.2. The model specifying configural invariance represents a baseline against which to evaluate subsequent models. The second model (weak), constrained the factor loadings to be equal across all occasions. This led to a more restricted model, and such restrictions worsened the fit slightly ($\Delta\chi^2 / \Delta df = 15/6$, p = .025). Although statistically significant, the decrease in model fit was not very large and other indices showed better fit (i.e., BIC). The next model (strong) constrained the intercepts to invariance over time. In this case, the resulting model fit did not worsen ($\Delta\chi^2 / \Delta df = 5/6$, p > .05), and the BIC showed the best fit. The final model (strict) specified the unique variances to be invariant over time, and this led to a large decrease in model fit ($\Delta\chi^2 / \Delta df = 83/8$, p < .001). The results from these analyses revealed that both weak and strong factorial invariance are not unreasonable in these data, indicating that the same fluid reasoning construct is being measured at both occasions. Moreover, any observed changes in the means can be modeled as quantitative changes at the factor level.

The next analyses examined changes in the fluid reasoning factor across the three occasions. These analyses involved the second–order latent difference score model with strong invariance specifications described in Equations 2.1 and 2.2, and Figure 2.1.[3] Results from these analyses are presented in Table 2.3. The first block of estimates represents the standardized factor loadings, which were constrained to be equal across occasions. These estimates range from .81 to .86, indicating that all four measures contributed strongly to the latent factor. The second block of estimates represents the factor means. The first parameter (ly_0) is the initial latent level. It was set to zero to identify the model and set the metric of the factor. Given that the four tests had different metric s, a zero mean was deemed reasonable for the fluid reasoning factor. The second mean (ly_s) represents an additive slope that is added to the changes at each occasion. This value was

TABLE 2.3 Estimates of 2LCS model of fluid reasoning across measurement occasions.

	Estimate	S.E.	Est./S.E.
Factor Loadings [ab]			
λ_1 matrix reasoning	.856	.024	36.13
λ_2 block design	.806	.031	26.05
λ_3 concept formation	.863	.025	34.53
λ_4 analysis synthesis	.810	.036	22.50
Factor Means			
μ_0 level ly_0^c	0.00[c]	–	–
μ_s additive slope ly_s	7.092	.673	10.54
Regressions			
β fr$_{t-1} \rightarrow \Delta_t$	−.029	.123	−.239
γ age $\rightarrow ly_0$	1.322	.095	13.88
γ sex $\rightarrow ly_0$	−.189	.629	−.300
γ age $\rightarrow \Delta_2$	−.274	.133	−2.070
γ age $\rightarrow \Delta_3$	−.383	.163	−2.348
γ sex $\rightarrow \Delta_2$	−.320	.481	−.666
γ sex $\rightarrow \Delta_3$	.432	.490	.881
Factor Variances			
σ_0^2 level[d]	8.961	2.666	3.361
σ_s^2 additive slope	3.105	.798	3.889
σ_Δ^2 changes[d]	5.862	1.686	3.476
Model Fit			
χ^2 chi square	198.76		
degrees of freedom	79		
number parameters	35		
CFI	.917		
RMSEA	.088		
(90% CI)	(.073 − .104)		

Note: λ = factor loadings. "a" = parameters were invariant across occasions. "b" = mean of standardized estimates. "c" = parameter fixed. "d" = residual variances. Unique variances are not shown.

statistically different from zero ($\mu_s = 7.09$; $p < .01$), indicating a contribution of 7.09 units to the change across each occasion.

The next block in Table 2.3 includes regression estimates. The first of such regressions is the autoproportion, representing the influence of fluid reasoning at a given occasion on its own changes at the next occasion. This parameter estimate, however, was not reliably different from zero ($\beta = -.029$; $p > .05$), indicating that all the changes are due to the additive slope. The next set of regression coefficients denotes influences from the covariates age and sex on either the initial level or the latent changes. Of these, the only estimates that were reliably different from zero were the path coefficients from age to the initial fluid reasoning level ($\gamma = 1.32$; $p < .01$) and to its changes ($\gamma = -.274$ and $-.383$; $ps < .05$). These estimates indicate that older individuals scored higher in the initial assessment than younger individuals (1.32 units higher per year of age), but they improved less across occasions (.274 and.383 units less per year of age, across the three occasions). The effect of gender and the age by gender interaction (not shown in tables) were not perceptible.

The final block of estimates contains factor variances. Of these, the first and third entries denote residual variances, as the model contains covariates. The first value is the variance in the level ($\sigma_0^2 = 8.96$; $p < .01$). The second estimate represents variability in the additive slope across individuals ($\sigma_s^2 = 3.10$; $p < .05$). The third value is the variance in the latent changes ($\sigma_{fr}^2 = 5.83$; $p < .01$).

Based on these analyses, the expected changes in fluid reasoning were estimated for each individual. The predicted change scores are depicted in Figure 2.5. In line with the results just described, this plot shows a pattern of decline in the expected changes over age, as well as an apparent decrease in variability in such changes across ages.

FIGURE 2.5 Predicted changes in fluid reasoning across the three measurement occasions as a function of age.

Developmental Changes in Fluid Reasoning

The next analyses sought to examine developmental changes in fluid reasoning. This required shifting the underlying time metric from measurement occasion to age, and using the extension of the LCS with age bins. This model contained 15 age bins (from 6 to 20 years of age) as discrete intervals and was aimed to characterize the age-related changes across childhood and adolescence. These analyses were carried out using Mplus (Muthén & Muthén, 2007) and SAS PROC NLMIXED.[4]

Table 2.4 presents results from analyses using a second order LCS model (i.e., LCS with invariant measurement structure). The interpretation of these results is similar to those in the previous analyses, yet some of the parameters are different due to the age specification. For example, as was the case before, each of the observed variables shows a strong and equal contribution to the fluid reasoning

TABLE 2.4 Estimates of 2LCS model of fluid reasoning across age.

	Estimate	S.E.	Est./S.E.
Factor Loadings [a][b]			
λ_1 matrix reasoning	.696	.058	12.02
λ_2 block design	.735	.047	15.75
λ_3 concept formation	.714	.056	12.67
λ_4 analysis synthesis	.703	.061	11.45
Factor Means			
μ_0 level ly_0^c	0.00^c	–	–
μ_s additive slope ly_s	3.692	.391	9.43
Regressions			
β fr$_{t-1} \rightarrow \Delta_t$	−.183	.021	−8.680
γ sex $\rightarrow ly_0$	−.283	1.120	−.253
γ sex $\rightarrow \Delta_t$	−.055	.157	−.350
Factor Variances			
σ_0^2 level^d	14.14	4.44	3.187
σ_s^2 additive slope	.323	.185	1.744
σ_Δ^2 changes^d	.638	.688	.928
Model Fit			
χ^2 chi square	2661		
degrees of freedom	950		
number parameters	19		
CFI	.214		
RMSEA	.096		
(90% CI)	(.092 − .100)		

Note: λ = factor loadings. "a" = parameters were invariant across occasions. "b" = mean of standardized estimates. "c" = parameter fixed. "d" = residual variance. Unique variances are not shown.

factor across all ages. Also similar to the previous analyses, the mean ly_0 represents the initial latent level, but it now corresponds to the youngest age (6 years). The mean ly_s denotes an additive slope ($\mu_s = 3.69$; $p < .01$) that is added to the changes every year. The autoproportion is now different from zero ($\beta = -.183$; $p < .05$), denoting a force that slows down the developmental improvements in fluid reasoning across age, with a larger force for higher levels in fluid reasoning. The coefficients relating gender to the initial level and latent changes are both far from significant, indicating that males and females in this sample can be represented as following a similar developmental path regarding fluid reasoning.

The next goal was to examine the role of brain structure maturation in the described developmental changes of fluid reasoning. For this, a univariate LCS model was specified using fluid reasoning factor scores extracted from the invariance analyses described previously. This model was estimated using maximum likelihood with dual quasi-Newton optimization, as implemented in SAS PROC NLMixed (SAS, 2014), a flexible program that allows constraints such as ensuring predicted values remain in bounds. As covariates, two indicators of brain structure were used: (a) white matter volume (in mm^3) and (b) white matter structural integrity, as measured using fractional anisotropy (i.e., the extent to which water diffuses in one main direction, representing fiber density and myelination).

TABLE 2.5 Estimates of LCS model of fluid reasoning across age with brain covariates.

	Estimate	S.E.	Est./S.E.
Factor Means			
μ_0 level ly_0	−1.66	.121	−13.74
μ_s additive slope ly_s	.185	.019	9.45
Regressions			
β $fr_{t-1} \rightarrow \Delta_t$	−.287	.037	−7.72
γ wm_vol $\rightarrow \Delta_t$	.048	.019	2.51
γ wm_fa $\rightarrow \Delta_t$	.040	020	2.01
Factor Variances			
σ_0^2 level	.366	.120	3.04
σ_s^2 additive slope	.016	007	2.36
$\sigma_{0,s}$ level, slope	.024	.043	.560
σ_{fr}^2 fluid reasoning[d]	.072	.018	4.00
Model Fit			
-2LL	227.7		
number parameters	9		
BIC	271.2		

Note: "d" = residual variance. "wm_vol" = white matter volume. "wm_fa" = white matter fractional anisotropy.

Results from these analyses are reported in Table 2.5. As before, the interpretation of all parameters is the standard in LCS models. A noteworthy difference from previous analyses is that the current model is a univariate specification and the mean of the latent level is not fixed to zero but has a value ($\mu_0 = -1.66$; $p < .01$) representing the initial fluid reasoning scores at the earliest age (6 years). As before, the additive slope ($\mu_s = .185$; $p < .01$) denotes a component that is added linearly to the yearly changes in fluid reasoning. Contributing to such changes are also the parameters listed under "regressions". The first of these is the autoproportion ($\beta = -.287$; $p < .01$), indicating a slowing effect that becomes stronger as fluid reasoning increases over age. The next two parameters represent influences from brain structure to the changes in fluid reasoning. Both estimates are different from zero ($\gamma = .048$ and $.040$; $ps < .05$), indicating that higher levels of white matter volume and structural integrity across the whole brain at any given year are related to developmental improvements in fluid reasoning the following year, across childhood and adolescence.

Discussion

The aims of this chapter were two-fold. The first goal was to examine changes in measures of fluid reasoning observed using a cohort-sequential sample of children and adolescents assessed on a limited number of occasions. The second goal was to investigate age-related changes in fluid reasoning from childhood to late adolescence and to identify potential mechanisms underlying such developmental changes.

Summary of Findings

The first set of results showed that a fluid reasoning factor could be reliably identified from the four psychometric tests used in the analyses. This factor had a robust measurement structure that was deemed invariant over time; that is, the construct had an equal definition across the three measurement occasions (Ferrer et al., 2008; Hancock et al., 2001). This desirable property allowed us to examine changes in the factor scores of fluid reasoning.

Next, within-person changes in fluid reasoning across the three time points were examined using a LCS model with measurement structure. The results here indicated reliable improvements across the three occasions and across the entire longitudinal sample. These improvements were consistent with a maturational account, as compared with a practice-related account: the longer the interval between assessments, the larger the improvement in fluid reasoning. Indeed, practice-related effects would be expected to dominate at shorter delays between assessments. Further, the magnitude of improvement between occasions decreased with age, supporting the idea that the most rapid improvements in fluid reasoning take place during childhood. No differences in such improvements were perceptible between males and females.

To examine changes in fluid reasoning across age, a LCS model was specified using age bins spanning from childhood through adolescence. This model used a very sparse data matrix containing one, two, or three time points per person, but was able to capture the developmental changes across the age span, showing rapid improvements during childhood and early adolescence, and slower changes later on. Results using this model showed that brain structure was predictive of subsequent changes in fluid reasoning. In particular, measures of white matter volume and structural integrity from the entire brain at any given year were associated with improvements in fluid reasoning the following year, across the entire age span, throughout childhood and adolescence.

Methodological and Substantive Implications

Several points seem worth mentioning given these findings. First, a cohort-sequential design is a very useful design to capture developmental changes across a wide age period (Bell, 1954; McArdle et al., 2002). Although these designs typically yield a data matrix with missing information at the individual level, the resulting matrix is sufficient to specify longitudinal models that span the age period. A potential issue derived from this approach is parameter estimation using such sparse data matrix. Hamagami and McArdle (2001) examined this question in a Monte Carlo study where parameters were defined for a population extending 20 years. Results from that study showed that an LCS model could recover the population parameters, even when the initial 20 data points per person were degraded to two data points only. This result was true as long as the two or three data points were randomly drawn across all possible ages and covered the ages where the aimed dynamics were manifest, and all individuals conformed to the simulated model.

In the multi-level framework, fitting models to a sparse data matrix, such as the one in this chapter, using age as a continuous variable is straightforward (McArdle et al., 2002). In structural equation modeling, however, this is not as simple. Only recent developments in this area allow such an implementation where age, as the underlying time metric, is truly continuous (Boker, 2001; Boker et al., 2004; Ji & Chow, 2017; Oud & Jansen, 2000; van Montfort, et al. in press; Voelkle & Oud, 2013, 2015; Voelkle et al., 2012). One benefit of using continuous time modeling is that potential effects do not depend on the specific size of the bin or, more generally, the chosen observation interval. This feature is particularly advantageous when the time interval does not have a particular meaning (e.g., change across grades in school). In this chapter, age bins were used as a way to capture the age-related changes in fluid reasoning (Ferrer & McArdle, 2004; McArdle & Bell, 2000). This specification using age as a semi-continuous metric should approximate the results from a continuous LCS model of lag one (one year of age). One benefit of this approach is that it is easy to implement in standard SEM software, even for multivariate models that include a measurement structure.

From a substantive perspective, more variables and constructs might be needed to understand the constellation of factors that give rise to fluid reasoning and that unfold together during development (Ferrer & McArdle, 2004). Similarly, it appears almost necessary to combine data relative to brain structure and function with behavioral data if we want to move from describing developmental trajectories to understanding mechanisms of development (Crone & Ridderinkhof, 2011). Although expensive, slow, and difficult, the benefits of this approach will likely outweigh the costs.

Notes

1 This work was supported by the National Institute on Neurological Disorders and Stroke (R01 NS057146). I am indebted to Jack McArdle for his advice and many ideas related to this research over the years, starting in graduate school. I am also grateful to my colleague Silvia A. Bunge, with whom I did this research. I thank Kirstie K.J. Whitaker and the research assistants in the Building Blocks of Cognition Laboratory at UC Berkeley for data collection and assistance with the project. I also thank Joel Steele and Joseph Gonzales for their useful input during various phases of these analyses.
2 Not to be confused with second-order in auto-regressive models, where "order" refers to lag, or in continuous time models, where "second-order" refers to acceleration (i.e., change in change).
3 These analyses were carried out in Mplus (Muthén & Muthén, 2007). Code is available upon request.
4 I thank Fumiaki Hamagami, who first programmed LCS models in SAS PROC NLMIXED. Code is available upon request.

References

Bell, R. Q. (1954). An experimental test of the accelerated. *Child Development, 25,* 281–286.

Blair, C. (2006). How similar are fluid cognition and general intelligence? A developmental neuroscience perspective on fluid cognition as an aspect of human cognitive ability. *Behavioral and Brain Sciences, 26,* 109–160.

Boker, S. M. (2001). Differential structural equation modeling of intraindividual variability. In L. Collins & A. Sayer (Eds.), New methods for the analysis of change (pp. 3–28). Washington, DC: American Psychological Association.

Boker, S. M., Neale, M. & Rausch, J. R. (2004). Latent differential equation modeling with multivariate multi-occasion indicators. In K. van Montfort, H. Oud, & A. Satorra (Eds.), Recent developments on structural equation models: Theory and applications (pp. 151–174).Amsterdam, The Netherlands: Kluwer.

Cattell, R. B. (1957). *Personality and motivation structure and measurement.* New York: World.

Cattell, R. B. (1971). Abilities: Their structure, growth and action. Houghton-Mifflin: Boston.

Cattell, R. B. (1987). Intelligence: Its structure, growth and action. Amsterdam: North-Holland.

Crone, E. A. & Ridderinkhof, K. R. (2011). The developing brain: From theory to neuroimaging and back. *Developmental Cognitive Neuroscience, 1,* 101–109.

Ferrer, E., Balluerka, N. & Widaman, K. F. (2008). Factorial Invariance and the specification of second-order latent growth models. *Methodology, 4,* 22–36.

Ferrer, E. & McArdle, J. J. (2004). An experimental analysis of dynamic hypotheses about cognitive abilities and achievement from childhood to early adulthood. *Developmental Psychology, 40*, 935–952.

Ferrer, E. & McArdle, J. J. (2010). Longitudinal modeling of developmental changes in psychological research. *Current Directions in Psychological Science, 19*, 149–154.

Ferrer, E., O'Hare, E. & Bunge, S. A. (2009). Fluid reasoning and the developing brain. *Frontiers in Neuroscience, 3*, 46–51.

Goswami, U. (1992). *Analogical reasoning in children.* Hillsdale, NJ: Lawrence Erlbaum.

Gottfredson, L. S. (1997). Why g matters: The complexity of everyday life. *Intelligence 24*, 79–132.

Green, C. T., Bunge, S. A., Briones, V., Barrow, M. & Ferrer, E. (2017). Fluid reasoning predicts future mathematical performance among children and adolescents. *Journal of Experimental Child Psychology, 157*, 125–143.

Hamagami, F. & McArdle, J. J. (2001). Advanced studies of individual differences linear dynamic models for longitudinal data analysis. In G. Marcoulides & R. Schumacker (Eds.), *Advanced structural equation modeling: New developments and techniques* (pp. 203–246). Mahwah, NJ: Lawrence Erlbaum.

Hancock, G. R., Kuo, W. & Lawrence, F. R. (2001). An illustration of second-order latent growth models. *Structural Equation Modeling, 8*, 470–489.

Horn, J. L. (1991). Measurement of intellectual capabilities: A review of theory. In: McGrew, K. S., Werder, J.K., & Woodcock, R. W. (Eds.), *Woodcock-Johnson technical manual* (pp. 197–246). Allen, TX: DLM Teaching Resources, TX.

Horn, J. L. & Cattell, R. B. (1966). Refinement and test of the theory of fluid and crystallized intelligence. *Journal of Educational Psychology, 57*, 253–270.

Horn, J. L. & Noll, J. (1997). Human cognitive capabilities: Gf-Gc theory. In D. P. Flanagan, J. L. Genshaft, & P. L. Harrison (Eds.), *Contemporary intellectual assessment: Theories, tests, and issues* (pp. 53–91). New York: Guilford Press.

Ji, L. & Chow, S-M. (2017). Methodological issues and extensions to the latent difference score framework. In E. Ferrer & S. M. Boker (Eds.), *Advances in longitudinal models for multivariate psychology.* New York: Taylor & Francis.

Kail, R. (1991). Developmental change in speed of processing during childhood and adolescence. *Psychological Bulletin, 109*, 490–501.

Kail, R. V. & Ferrer, E. (2007). Processing speed in childhood and adolescence: Longitudinal models for examining developmental change. *Child Development, 78*, 1760–1770.

McArdle, J. J. (2001). A latent difference score approach to longitudinal dynamic structural analysis. In R. Cudeck, S. du Toit, & D. Sörbom (Eds.), *Structural equation modeling: Present and future. A Festschrift in honor of Karl Jöreskog* (pp. 341–380). Lincolnwood, IL: Scientific Software International.

McArdle, J. J. (2009). Latent variable modeling of differences in changes with longitudinal data. *Annual Review of Psychology, 60*, 577–605.

McArdle, J. J. & Bell, R. Q. (2000). Recent trends in modeling longitudinal data by latent growth curve methods. In T. D. Little, K. U. Schnabel, & J. Baumert (Eds.), *Modeling longitudinal and multilevel data: Practical issues, applied approaches, and scientific examples* (pp. 69–108). Mahwah, NJ: Lawrence Erlbaum.

McArdle, J. J., Ferrer-Caja, E., Hamagami, F. & Woodcock, R. W. (2002). Comparative longitudinal structural analyses of the growth and decline of multiple intellectual abilities over the life-span. *Developmental Psychology, 38*, 115–142.

McArdle, J. J. & Hamagami, F. (2001). Linear dynamic analyses of incomplete longitudinal data. In L. Collins & A. Sayer (Eds.), New methods for the analysis of change (pp. 137–176). Washington, DC: APA Press.

McArdle, J. J. & Woodcock, J. R. (1997). Expanding test-rest designs to include developmental time-lag components. *Psychological Methods, 2*, 403–435.

McGrew, K. S., Werder, J. K. & Woodcock, R. W. (1991). *Woodcock–Johnson technical manual.* Allen, TX: DLM Teaching Resources.

Meredith, W. M. (1993). Measurement invariance, factor analysis, and factorial invariance. *Psychometrika, 58*, 525–543.

Miller, M. L. & Ferrer, E. (2017). The Effect of sampling-time variation on latent growth curve model fit. *Structural Equation Modeling, 24*, 831–854. https://doi.org/10.1080/10705511.2017.1346476

Muthén, L. K. & Muthén, B. O. (2007). *Mplus user's guide.* 5th edition. Los Angeles, CA: Muthén & Muthén.

Oud, J. H. L. and Jansen, R. A. R. G. (2000). Continuous time state space modeling of panel data by means of SEM. *Psychometrika, 65*, 199–215.

SAS Institute Inc. (2014). SAS/STAT® 13.2 User's Guide. Cary, NC: SAS Institute Inc.

Sayer, A. G. & Cumsille, P. E. (2001). Second-order latent growth models. In L. M. Collins & A. G. Sayer (Eds.), *New methods for the analysis of change* (pp. 179–200). Washington, DC: American Psychological Association.

Schaie, K. W. (1996). *Intellectual development in adulthood.* Cambridge, UK: Cambridge University Press.

Sowell, E. R., Thompson, P. M., et al. (2004). Longitudinal mapping of cortical thickness and brain growth in normal children. *Journal of Neuroscience, 24*(38), 8223–8231.

Taub, G. E., Floyd, R. G., Keith, T. Z. & McGrew, K. S. (2008). Effects of general and broad cognitive abilities on mathematics achievement. *School Psychology Quarterly 23*, 11.

van Montfort, J. Oud, J. H. L. & M. Voelkle (2018). *Continuous time modeling in the behavioral and related sciences.* New York: Springer Verlag.

Voelkle, M. C. & Oud, J. H. L. (2013). Continuous time modelling with individually varying time intervals for oscillating and non-oscillating processes. *British Journal of Mathematical and Statistical Psychology, 66*, 103–126.

Voelkle, M. C. & Oud, J. H. L. (2015). Relating latent change score and continuous time models. *Structural Equation Modeling, 22*, 366–381.

Voelkle, M. C., Oud, J. H., Davidov, E. & Schmidt, P. (2012). An SEM approach to continuous time modeling of panel data: relating authoritarianism and anomia. *Psychological methods, 17*, 176–192.

Wechsler, D. (1981). *Wechsler Intelligence Scale for Children – Revised.* New York: Psychological Corp.

Woodcock, R. W. & Johnson, M. B. (1990). *Woodcock-Johnson Psycho-Educational Battery-Revised.* Allen, TX: DLM.

Appendix

Sample Code for Analyses

Mplus code for 2LCS Model of Fluid Reasoning across Measurement Occasions (Table 2.3)

```
TITLE: Analysis of NORA Behavioral Data;
DATA: FILE = C:\Projects1\NORA_Behavioral\nora_T3.dat;
VARIABLE: NAMES = id ... ;
MISSING = .;
USEVARIABLES = mr1-mr3 bd1-bd3 cf1-cf3 as1-as3 female
               age;
MODEL:
    !Fluid Reasoning Factor at Time 1
    fr1 BY  mr1 (l1_1)
            bd1 (l2_1)
            cf1 (l3_1)
            as1 (l4_1);

    !Fluid Reasoning Factor at Time 2
    fr2 BY  mr2 (l1_1)
            bd2 (l2_1)
            cf2 (l3_1)
            as2 (l4_1);

    !Fluid Reasoning Factor at Time 3
    fr3 BY  mr3 (l1_1)
            bd3 (l2_1)
            cf3 (l3_1)
            as3 (l4_1);

    !LCS Specification
    fr2 ON fr1@1 ; fr3 ON fr2@1 ;
    ld2 BY fr2@1 ; ld3 BY fr3@1 ;
    ly0 BY fr1@1 ;
    lys BY ld2@1 ld3@1 ;

    !LCS Autoproportions
    ld2 ON fr1 (b_1);
    ld3 ON fr2 (b_1);

    !Latent Variable Means
    [fr1@0 fr2@0 fr3@0];
    [ly0@0 lys];
    [ld2@0 ld3@0];

    !Latent Variable Variances/Disturbances
    fr1-fr3@0 (v_f);
    ld2 ld3 (v_ld) ;
```

```
ly0 lys ;
ly0 WITH lys;

!Observed Variables Means
[mr1 mr2 mr3] (t1_1) ;
[bd1 bd2 bd3] (t2_1) ;
[cf1 cf2 cf3] (t3_1) ;
[as1 as2 as3] (t4_1) ;

!Observed Variables Variances
mr1 mr2 mr3; ! (e1_1) ;
bd1 bd2 bd3; ! (e2_1) ;
cf1 cf2 cf3; ! (e3_1) ;
as1 as2 as3; ! (e4_1) ;

!Correlated Uniquenesses (Lag1)
mr1 WITH mr2 (c1_1) ; mr2 WITH mr3 (c1_1) ;
bd1 WITH bd2 (c2_1) ; bd2 WITH bd3 (c2_1) ;
cf1 WITH cf2 (c3_1) ; cf2 WITH cf3 (c3_1) ;
as1 WITH as2 (c4_1) ; as2 WITH as3 (c4_1) ;

!Regressions from Covariates
ly0 ON female age;
ld2 ON female (g_sex1);
ld3 ON female (g_sex2);
ld2 ON age    (g_age1);
ld3 ON age    (g_age2);

OUTPUT: SAMPSTAT STANDARDIZED TECH1 TECH4;
```

Mplus code for 2LCS Model of Fluid Reasoning across Age (Table 2.4)

```
TITLE: Analysis of NORA Behavioral Data;
DATA: FILE = C:\Projects1\NORA_Behavioral\nora_bins.dat;
VARIABLE: NAMES = id ... ;
MISSING = .;
USEVARIABLES = mr1-mr3 bd1-bd3 cf1-cf3 as1-as3 female;
MODEL:
!Fluid Reasoning Latent Variables
ly1  BY mtx6   (11) blk6   (12) cnf6   (13) ans6   (14);
ly2  BY mtx7   (11) blk7   (12) cnf7   (13) ans7   (14);
...
ly15 BY mtx20  (11) blk20  (12) cnf20  (14) ans20  (14) ;
```

```
!LCS Specification
ly2  ON ly1@1;
ly3  ON ly2@1;
...
ly15 ON ly14@1;

dy2  BY ly2@1;
dy3  BY ly3@1;
...
dy15 BY ly15@1;

!Autoproportions
dy2  ON ly1*.001  (b_y);
dy3  ON ly2*.001  (b_y);
...
dy15 ON ly14*.001 (b_y);

!Latent mean and additive slope
lys BY dy2-dy15@1;
ly0 BY ly1@1;

!Latent Variable Means
[ly1-ly15@0] ;
[ly0@0 lys]  ;
[dy2-dy15@0] ;

!Latent Variable Variances/Disturbances
ly1-ly15@0 (v_ly) ;
dy2-dy15 (v_dy);
ly0 lys ;
ly0 WITH lys ;

!Observed Variables Means
[mtx6-mtx20] (t1) ;
[blk6-blk20] (t2) ;
[cnf6-cnf19] (t3) ;
[ans6-ans20] (t4) ;

!Observed Variables Variances
mtx6-mtx20 (e1) ;
blk6-blk20 (e2) ;
cnf6-cnf19 (e3) ;
ans6-ans20 (e4) ;
```

```
!Regressions x->y
dy2  ON female*.0001 (g_y);
dy3  ON female*.0001 (g_y);
...
dy15 ON female*.0001 (g_y);
ly0 ON female;

OUTPUT: STANDARDIZED TECH1 TECH4;
```

SAS code for Estimates of LCS Model of Fluid Reasoning across Age with Brain
Covariates (Table 2.5)

```
TITLE 'LCS Model With Covariates: Total White Matter
 + FA White Matter';

PROC NLMIXED DATA = temp2 METHOD=FIRO;
PARMS m_ly0=-1.52  m_lys=.22 beta=.01 gamma1=.01
      gamma 2=.01
      v_ly0=.50  v_lys=.005  c_0s=.001  v_e=.15 ;

temp1=0-temp15=0;
dy1-dy15=0;

ARRAY Latent[15] temp1-temp15;
ARRAY Dy[15] dy1-dy15;

ly0 = m_ly0 + d_ly0;
lys = m_lys + d_lys;
Latent[1]=ly0;
Dy[1]=0;

DO I=2 to time;
Dy[I]=lys + beta*Latent[I-1] + gamma1*wvc
     + gamma2*faWMc;
Latent[I]=Dy[I] + Latent[I-1];
END;

traject = Latent[time];
MODEL fr ~ NORMAL(traject, v_e);
RANDOM    d_ly0 d_lys ~ NORMAL([0,0],
           [v_ly0,
            c_ls,  v_lys]) SUBJECT=id;
RUN;
```

3

INDIVIDUALLY VARYING TIME METRICS IN LATENT CHANGE SCORE MODELS[1]

Kevin J. Grimm & Ross Jacobucci

Longitudinal data are necessary to study how individuals change over time. When analyzing longitudinal data, a time metric must be chosen to organize the data. Different time metrics can affect the measurement of the within-person change process as well as how the change trajectories from different participants are arranged with respect to one another. This is particularly important when working with data from an accelerated or time unstructured longitudinal study. Data from the National Longitudinal Survey of Youth – Children and Young Adults (NLSY-CYA; Center for Human Resource Research, 2004) is an example of such data. The NLSY-CYA began in 1986 with children of female participants from the National Longitudinal Survey of Youth 1979 (NLSY79) and assessments were scheduled every two years. Participants varied in age at the beginning of the study (i.e., in 1986), and as more children were born to the NLSY79 female participants they were subsequently enrolled into the NLSY-CYA.

Longitudinal data from the NLSY-CYA can be organized with respect to multiple time metrics depending on the particular research question (see also Grimm & Ram, 2011; Grimm, Ram, & Estabrook, 2017). Some example time metrics include *grade in school* for examining school-related processes, *age* (i.e., time since birth) for examining age-related processes, *pubertal age* (i.e., time to/from menarche for females) for examining maturational-related processes, *measurement occasion* for examining processes related to being repeatedly assessed (e.g., retest effects), and *months (or days) since first measurement occasion* for examining processes related to the exposure to the study protocol. In general, the choice of time metric should be based on the research question, but sometimes researchers opt for an alternative time metric because of data constraints, often due to data sparseness (i.e., data incompleteness), and/or model complexity.

When discussing time metrics, there are some time metrics whose values are *discrete*, where the time metric takes on a relatively small number of distinct values.

Examples include *measurement occasion* and *grade in school*. Other time metrics have values that are more or less *continuous*. With a continuous time metric, for example *age*, participants are unlikely to be measured at exactly the same age. We note, however, that almost any time metric can be specified in a discrete or continuous form. For example, if age was measured in days or months since birth, then age may be considered to be a more or less continuous time metric, but if age was rounded to the nearest year, then this age time metric would be more or less discrete. Overall, greater precision in the time-metric is beneficial when modeling change (Aydin, Leite, & Algina, 2014) with less bias in the parameter estimates (Biesanz, Deeb-Sossa, Papadakis, Bollen, & Curran, 2004). However, using a more precise time metric may cause greater convergence issues due to increased data sparseness (O'Rourke, Grimm, & MacKinnon, 2017; Sterba, 2014), particularly when using the structural equation modeling (SEM) framework to estimate parameters of (complex) growth models.

The nature of the time metric is important when studying within-person change with growth models (McArdle, 1986; McArdle & Epstein, 1987; Meredith & Tisak, 1990) because it has an effect on the statistical framework that can be used to estimate the model's parameters (see Ghisletta & Lindenberger, 2003; Willett & Sayer, 1994). With discrete time metrics, the SEM framework and the multilevel modeling (MLM) framework are both viable frameworks for estimating parameters of growth models. Researchers may prefer the SEM framework when modeling change with discrete time metrics because of the availability of absolute and incremental fit indices (e.g., RMSEA, CFI, TLI), which aid in model evaluation and selection, the ease with which different residual structures can be imposed (see Grimm & Widaman, 2010), and the ability to include latent variables (as the outcome of the growth model or as predictors of growth). When the time metric is continuous (often referred to as individually varying), the MLM framework is often preferred because of the ease with which continuous time metrics can be specified in the statistical programs. The SEM framework can handle continuous time metrics (see Sterba, 2014) by treating the timing variables as *definition* variables (Mehta & Neale, 2005); however, some SEM programs do not allow for definition variables making it more challenging or impossible to handle continuous time metrics.

Another class of longitudinal models, known as latent change score models (McArdle, 2001; McArdle & Hamagami, 2001), combine aspects of growth models and the autoregressive model (Jöreskog, 1970) for panel data. Given the inclusion of lagged effects, latent change score models must use a discrete time metric. Due to the necessity of having a discrete time metric, latent change score models have almost always been specified using standard SEM software. The only exception is in Hamagami, Zhang, & McArdle (2009), where WinBUGS (Spiegelhalter, Thomas, Best, & Lunn, 2003), a general statistical program that uses Markov Chain Monte Carlo methods for estimation, was used to estimate model parameters. As noted above, latent change score models have only been specified using a discrete time metric with relatively few unique values – less than 30 (or so) unique values (including Hamagami et al. 2009). Although it is true that latent change score models require a discrete time metric because of the inclusion of lagged effects, researchers typically use a time metric with only a few unique values. Thus, when researchers want to use a continuous time metric, they have discretized the time metric to limit the number of possible values (e.g., McArdle & Grimm, 2010) or opted for a simpler discrete time metric (e.g., measurement occasion) instead of a more continuous time metric (e.g., Small, Dixon, McArdle, & Grimm, 2012). In this chapter, we review the latent change score framework, describe its specification in the SEM framework, and then discuss how to specify latent change score models in the nonlinear MLM framework using `NLMIXED`, and in the Bayesian hierarchical framework using `JAGS` (Plummer, 2003). Both of these frameworks enable the specification of latent change score models with near continuous time metrics. An illustrative example is provided and we highlight the importance of having and using precise time metrics in latent change score models.

Latent Change Score Models

Latent change score models are a collection of longitudinal models used to study within-person change and dynamics. These models combine aspects of latent growth models (Grimm et al., 2017; McArdle & Epstein, 1987; Meredith & Tisak, 1990) to study individual change and autoregressive cross-lag models (Jöreskog, 1974) for studying lagged effects with longitudinal data. To begin our specification of latent change score models, the observed score measured at time t for person i, y_{ti}, is composed of a true score, which we refer to as ly_{ti} (for *latent y*), and a unique score, u_{ti}. This specification follows the ideas of classical test theory, and can be written as

$$y_{ti} = ly_{ti} + u_{ti} \qquad (3.1)$$

The distinction between the latent true score and the unique score is that the latent true scores are allowed to covary over time and the unique scores do not. Building on Equation 3.1, the latent true score at time t for individual i is the sum of the latent true score at time $t-1$, the previous time point, and the true amount of change from time $t-1$ to time t. This can be written as

$$ly_{ti} = ly_{t-1i} + dy_{ti} \qquad (3.2)$$

where ly_{t-1i} is the latent true score at the time $t-1$ and dy_{ti} is the true change score from time $t-1$ to time t (see Grimm, Zhang, Hamagami, & Mazzocco, 2013). In latent change score modeling, we often define an intercept, which represents the latent true score at the first measurement occasion. That is

$$b_{0i} = ly_{1i} \qquad (3.3)$$

where b_{0i} is the intercept and ly_{1i} is the latent true score at the first time point based on the chosen time metric. Thus, the intercept is equivalent to the first latent true score, and has a mean (β_0) and a variance (ϕ_0^2). Now that we defined the basic set-up, we can write the equation for the observed score at time t as

$$y_{ti} = b_{0i} + \sum_{r=2}^{t} dy_{ri} + u_{ti} \qquad (3.4)$$

where b_{0i} is the intercept, $\sum_{r=2}^{t} dy_{ri}$ is the accumulation of change scores with r as an index of t (r^{th} time point) beginning at 2 and going to t, and u_{ti} is the time-dependent residual. Thus, the observed score at each time point is equal to the sum of the initial true score for person i, the summation of latent change scores from the second to the tth time point for person i, and the unique score at time t for individual i.

With this set-up in place, we can now write a model for the latent change scores, which controls the within-person trajectory. Thus, different change equations lead to different shaped trajectories. There are four commonly specified models for the latent change scores, which include the (A) *no change* model, (B) *constant change* model, (C) *proportional change* model, and (D) *dual change* model. The dual change model is the most general of these models and the change equation for this model can be written as

$$dy_t = b_{1i} + \pi \cdot ly_{t-1i} \qquad (3.5)$$

where b_{1i} is the *constant change component* for individual i, which is a between-person factor that adds a constant amount to the changes for person i between consecutive time points, and π is the proportional change parameter that multplies the prior instance of the true score, which leads to expected changes between consecutive time points that are proportional to the prior level of performance. The constant change component is assumed to be normally distributed with a mean (β_1), variance (ϕ_1^2), and the constant change component is allowed to covary with the intercept (ϕ_{10} is the covariance). In the proportional change model, b_{1i} is removed from Equation 3.5, so that expected changes are only proportional to the previous state. In the constant change model, $\pi \cdot ly_{t-1i}$ is removed from Equation 3.5, so that expected changes are constant, which leads to linear changes in the latent true scores, and in the no change model, b_{1i} and $\pi \cdot ly_{t-1i}$ are removed from Equation 3.5, so that no changes over time are expected.

Estimation of Latent Change Score Models

Structural Equation Modeling Framework

Latent change score models are typically specified and estimated in the SEM framework. As such, the longitudinal data are organized in the *wide* or *person-level*

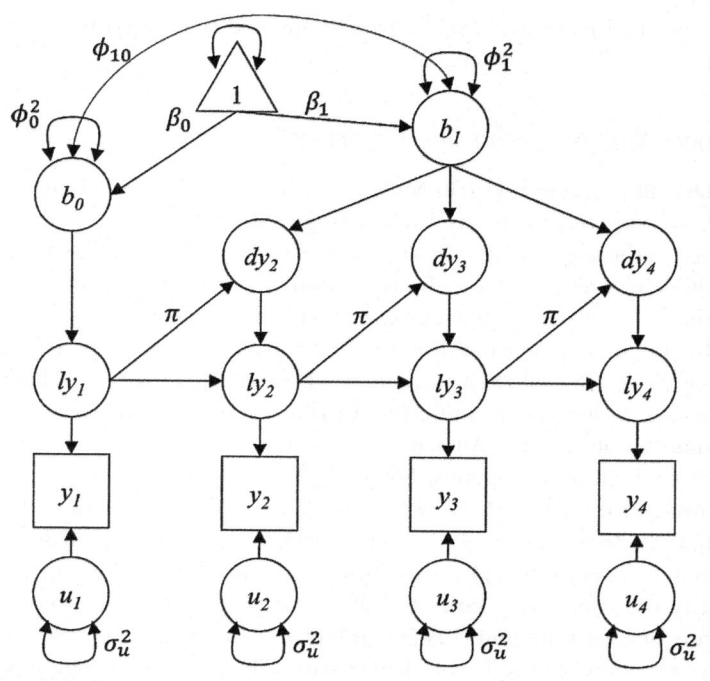

Figure 3.1 Path diagram of the dual change model with four measurement occasions.

format (Singer & Willett, 2003) according to the chosen time metric. As an illustration of the data structure and model, a path diagram of the dual change score model is contained in Figure 3.1 with four measurement occasions. The model in Figure 3.1 can be specified and estimated in any SEM program. As discussed, when the data are organized in the wide or person-level file, the time metric is *discrete*. The data can be complete or incomplete, participants can vary in the number of repeated assessments, and participants can vary in which assessments are observed and which are incomplete. This data structure falls under the first two types of longitudinal data discussed by Sterba (2014), and these data structures are easily handled with the traditional SEM framework.

When longitudinal data have individually varying time points, certain SEM programs may be viable, but the specification would be extensive because latent true scores and latent change scores would need to be specified for every unique time point and additional latent true and change scores may be necessary to maintain a constant time lag (amount of time lapsed) between consecutive true scores (see McArdle, 2001). Thus, while it may be possible to use the SEM framework, it is not efficient. With growth models, researchers often turn to the MLM framework because it easily accommodates such data (see Ghisletta & Lindenberger, 2003). Our focus is on answering whether latent change score models can be specified using available MLM software and we discuss this in the next section.

Nonlinear Multilevel Modeling Framework

The NLMIXED procedure (Littell, Milliken, Stroup, & Wolfinger, 1996), available in SAS, can be used to specify latent change score models. Here, the data are organized in the *long* or *person-period* format (Singer & Willett, 2003), where there are multiple records (one for each observation) per participant (typical set-up for estimating growth models with mixed-effects modeling software). An NLMIXED script for the model depicted in Figure 3.1 is contained in Script 1. The script begins by calling the NLMIXED procedure and the example2 dataset. The variables in the dataset include the identification variable, id, the outcome variable, y, and the timing variable, time. An array is then written to create latent true scores for each of the four time points. Following Equation 3.1, the latent true scores are named ly1 through ly4. Next, the first latent true score is set equal to b_0i, the intercept. In a similar vein, traject, which represents the predicted mean over time, is set equal to ly1 for the first time point. Next, a DO loop is written to specify the latent true scores for all of the time points after the first. The true score at each time point, ly[t], is equal to the prior true score, ly[t-1], plus the equation for the latent change scores. In the dual change model, the latent change scores are equal to the constant change component, b_1i, plus the proportional change parameter, pi, multiplied by the previous latent true score, ly[t-1], following Equation 3.5. In the second line of the DO loop, we need to attach the time metric in the dataset (time) to the time metric of the model (t). Since the variable time goes from 1 to 4, it maps directly onto t, the index of time for the model. Thus, when the variable time is equal to t, the predicted mean over time, traject, is equal to the latent true score at time t.

The MODEL and RANDOM statements follow typical specification for NLMIXED. The MODEL statement identifies the outcome variable, y, which is assumed to be normally distributed with a mean equal to traject, which was previously defined, and a level-1 residual variance equal to sigma2_u. The RANDOM statement defines the random coefficients of the model, which include the intercept, b_0i, and the constant change component, b_1i. These random coefficients are assumed to follow a normal distribution with means, beta_0 and beta_1, and a covariance matrix with elements phi2_0, phi_10, and phi2_1 for the variance of the intercept, the covariance between the intercept and constant change component, and the variance of the constant change component, respectively. The last part of the RANDOM statement is SUBJECT = id, which identifies id as the cluster variable. The final part of the script is the PARMS statement, where starting values for the estimated parameters are provided.

Some important considerations when using NLMIXED for latent change score models are now described. First, participants do not have to be assessed at each

Script 1 **NLMIXED** script for a *Dual Change Score* model with four time points

```
PROC NLMIXED DATA = example2;
    ARRAY ly[4] ly1-ly4;

    ly1 = b_0i;
    traject = ly1;

    DO t = 2 to 4;
        ly[t] = ly[t-1] + (b_1i + pi * ly[t-1]);
        IF time = t THEN traject = ly[t];
    END;

    MODEL y ~ NORMAL(traject, sigma2_u);
    RANDOM b_0i b_1i ~ NORMAL([beta_0, beta_1],
                             [phi2_0,
                              phi_10, phi2_1])
           SUBJECT = id;

    PARMS
        beta_0 = 10     beta_1 = 12     pi = -.5
        phi2_0 = 4      phi_10 = 0      phi2_1 = 1
        sigma2_u = .5;
RUN;
```

measurement occasion. That is, incomplete data can be handled with each observation contributing to the likelihood function. This mimics how full information maximum likelihood functions within the SEM framework. Second, the time-lag must be constant because of the proportional change parameter. However, the need for a constant time-lag is solely at the *latent variable* level and not at the *observed variable* level. Thus, there can be more latent variable scores (`ly[t]`) than observed variable scores in order for the time-lag to remain constant at the latent variable level. Given this, the maximum t, which is 4 in this script, represents the maximum number of latent variable scores needed to keep a constant time lag. For example, in McArdle (2001) participants were assessed in grades 1, 2, 4 and 6. To keep a constant time lag, McArdle (2001) created two phantom variables representing participants' latent true scores in third and fifth grade. Thus, the spacing between consecutive latent true scores was 1 year. To mimic this in **NLMIXED**, six latent true scores would be created, `ly[1]` to `ly[6]`, and the observed scores would only map on to the latent true scores for grades 1, 2, 4 and 6. Third, providing good starting values aid model convergence. Typically, good starting values for the fixed-effects parameters are most important and good starting values for these parameters can be obtained by removing the **RANDOM** statement.

The **NLMIXED** script in Script 1 provides almost identical parameter estimates as those obtained from *Mplus* (Muthén & Muthén, 1998–2015), which was used to estimate the model in the SEM framework (e.g., as represented in Figure 3.1). The benefit of **NLMIXED** is that Script 1 can be easily modified to account for many time points. To do this, there are two main changes. First, the **ARRAY** statement is edited to account for the additional time points. That is, we need to define latent true scores for all points in time between the minimum and maximum values based on the chosen time metric. Second, the upper bound of the **DO** loop is increased to account for all possible time points. We note that the **t** index in the **DO** loop moves in steps of 1 so the smallest step of the timing variable needs to be 1 as well. Thus, if the timing variable is *age* and *age* is measured to two decimal places, then the age variable can be multiplied by 100, so that the timing metric moves in steps of 1.

JAGS

In comparison to the amount of research on Bayesian estimation methods for latent growth models (Zhang, Hamagami, Wang, Grimm, & Nesselroade, 2007), much less work has focused on using Bayesian estimation methods for latent change models. Despite this, Hamagami et al. (2009) demonstrated how this can be accomplished with both univariate and bivariate latent change score models. When using noninformative priors, both Bayesian and maximum likelihood estimation yield similar estimates, even in the presence of missing data. Therefore, we examined Bayesian estimation methods to determine whether similar parameter estimates to the SEM framework (with maximum likelihood estimation) and **NLMIXED** (nonlinear mixed–effects framework with maximum likelihood estimation) could be obtained, and with what level of computational effort. We used the open source Markov Chain Monte Carlo sampler, **JAGS** (Plummer, 2003), interfaced through the **rjags** package (Plummer, Stukalov, & Denwood, 2016) in the R statistical environment (R Core Team, 2016), for model estimation. In contrast to **NLMIXED**, the wide format is used for the data in **JAGS**.

The **model** statement from **JAGS** is contained in Script 2. The script begins with two **for** loops – the first is for persons and the second is for time points (embedded within the **for** loop for persons). In the persons **for** loop, the intercept and constant change latent variables are defined in **b**, which are normally distributed with means in **beta** and the inverse of the covariance matrix in **i_phi**. Additionally, we define the distribution of the outcome at the first time point, contained in **y[i,1]**, which is normal with a mean equal to the latent true score at the first time point, **ly[i,1]**, and an inverse residual variance (precision) equal to **i_sigma2_u**. As in the **NLMIXED** script, the first latent true score is then set equal to the latent variable intercept, **b[i,1]**.

The **for** loop for the repeated measures is then specified from time 2, the second time point, to time **T**, the final time point. Here, the distribution of the

Script 2 **JAGS** script for a *Dual Change Score* model with four time points

```
model {
    for (i in 1:N){
        b[i,1:2]~dmnorm(beta[1:2], i_phi[1:2,1:2])

        y[i,1]~dnorm(ly[i,1], i_sigma2_u)
        ly[i,1]<-b[i,1]

        for (t in 2:T){
            y[i,t]~dnorm(ly[i,t], i_sigma2_u)
            ly[i,t]<-ly[i,t-1]+(pi*ly[i,t-1]+b[i,2])
            }
    }

    i_sigma2_u~dgamma(.001,.001)
    pi~dnorm(0,.00001)
    beta[1]~dnorm(0,.00001)
    beta[2]~dnorm(0,.00001)
    i_phi[1:2,1:2]~dwish(i_phi_e[1:2,1:2],2)

    i_phi_e[1,1]<-1
    i_phi_e[2,2]<-1
    i_phi_e[1,2]<-i_phi_e[2,1]
    i_phi_e[2,1]<-0

    sigma2_u<-1/i_sigma2_u
    phi[1:2,1:2]<-inverse(i_phi[1:2,1:2])
}
```

repeatedly measured outcome is specified and as with the first time point, the outcome at time t, y[i,t], is normally distributed with mean at time t equal to the latent true score at time t, ly[i,t], and the inverse residual variance is i_sigma2_u. Next, the latent true score at each time point, ly[i,t], is set equal to the prior latent true score, ly[i,t-1], plus the equation for the latent change score. In the case of the dual change score model, the latent change score equation is pi, the proportional change parameter, multiplied by the previous latent true score, ly[i,t-1], plus the constant change component, b[i,2]. The two **for** loops are then closed.

In the next section of the script, prior distributions are specified for all esti-mated parameters. The inverse residual variance, i_sigma2_u, is given a gamma distribution prior; the proportional change parameter, pi, and the means of the intercept, beta[1], and constant change component, beta[2], are given normal priors; and the inverse of the latent variable covariance matrix, i_phi, is given a

Wishart distribution for its prior. The elements of `i_phi` are specified as `i_phi_e`, which allows us to give them initial values, which are specified in the next section. In the final two lines of the model statement, the residual variance, `sigma2_u`, and the latent variable covariance matrix, `phi`, are specified as the inverse of the appropriate elements. Noninformative, also known as diffuse, priors were used (see Hamagami et al. [2009] for more detail on prior specification), which leads to the prior having little to no effect on the estimated parameters. In such cases, estimates close to maximum likelihood estimates are often obtained. As with the `NLMIXED` script, an arbitrary number of time points (`T`) can be specified within the script, thus producing more concise code for any number of time points.

Illustrative Example

Data

Longitudinal data from the NLSY-CYA (Center for Human Resource Research, 2004), where children were repeatedly administered the Peabody Individual Achievement Test (PIAT; Dunn & Markwardt, 1970) mathematics assessment, were analyzed for illustrative purposes. These data have been previously analyzed in Grimm et al. (2017) using *grade*, a discrete time metric with seven unique values, as the time metric. A longitudinal plot of the mathematics test scores against *age at testing* is contained in Figure 3.2. There are a total of $2,221$ data points from 932 participants. Participants were measured between one ($n = 45$) and four

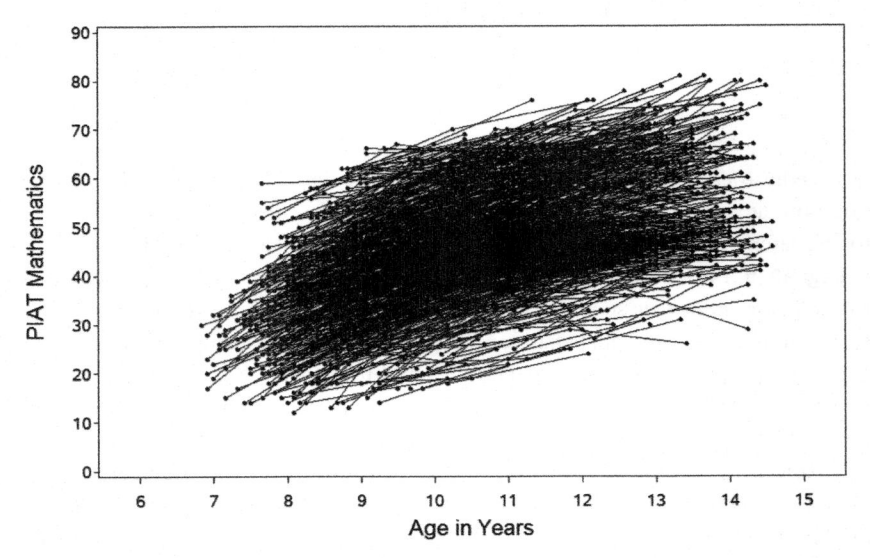

Figure 3.2 Longitudinal plot of the PIAT Mathematics assessment scores against age (measured in months).

($n = 38$) times, with the majority of participants being measured two ($n = 523$) or three ($n = 326$) times. The age variable in the NLSY-CYA is measured to a precision of months and this level of precision is maintained for our analysis.

SAS *Programming*

We programmed the dual change score model using NLMIXED, with the code contained in Script 3. After calling the NLMIXED procedure and nlsy_math_long2 dataset, the latent true scores are defined using an ARRAY statement. The age variable in the NLSY-CYA had a minimum of 82 months and a maximum of 175 months, which leads to 94 potential values. Thus, 94 latent true scores, ly1 through ly94, were created. The first latent true score was set equal to the intercept, b_0i, and traject was also set equal to the intercept, b_0i, following Script 1.

The DO loop follows with the index t going from 2 to 94. The latent true score at each time point, ly[t], is set equal to the prior latent true score, ly[t-1], plus the equation for the latent change scores, which is contained within parentheses. Following the dual change score model, the equation for the latent change scores is equal to the constant change component, b_1i, plus the proportional change

---

Script 3 NLMIXED script for the *Dual Change Score* model fit to the NLSY-CYA data

```
PROC NLMIXED DATA = nlsy_math_long2;
    ARRAY ly[94] ly1-ly94;

    ly1 = b_0i;
    traject = b_0i;

    DO t = 2 to 94;
        ly[t] = ly[t-1] + (b_1i + pi * ly[t-1]);
        IF age = t + 81 THEN traject = ly[t];
    END;

    MODEL math ~ NORMAL(traject, sigma2_u);
    RANDOM b_0i b_1i ~ NORMAL([beta_0, beta_1],
                             [phi2_0,
                              phi_10, phi2_1])
        SUBJECT = id;
    PARMS
        beta_0 = 30    beta_1 = 15    pi = -.02
        phi2_0 = 75    phi_10 = 0    phi2_1 = 6
        sigma2_u = 35;
RUN;
```

---

parameter, `pi`, multiplied by the prior latent true score, `ly[t-1]`. The second line of the `DO` loop mapped the time metric of the data to the time metric of the model. Since the *age* variable goes from 82 to 175, we want to map `age` = 83 (second potential age value) to `t` = 2, `age` = 84 to `t` = 3, and so on. Thus, we write `IF age = t + 81 THEN traject = ly[t]`. This statement also maps `traject`, the predicted mean over time, to the latent true score at time `t`. The remainder of the script follows directly from Script 1 with changes to the starting values provided in the `PARMS` statement.

NLMIXED *Output*

Parameter estimates from `NLMIXED` are labeled according to how they were labeled in the script and are presented in Output 1. The mean of the intercept, `beta_0`, was 21.54 and represents the predicted mean PIAT mathematics score at 82 months. The mean of the constant change component, `beta_1`, was 1.40 and this value in conjunction with the proportional change parameter, `pi`, which was -0.02, control how the mean function changed over time. This combination leads to a decelerating exponential curve that approaches an upper asymptotic level. There was significant between-child differences in true mathematics ability at 82 months, represented by the variance of the intercept, `phi2_0`, and significant between-child differences in the constant change component, represented

---

Output 1 **NLMIXED** output for the *Dual Change Score* model

```
                      Fit Statistics

          -2 Log Likelihood                15641
          AIC (smaller is better)          15655
          AICC (smaller is better)         15655
          BIC (smaller is better)          15689


                    Parameter Estimates

                          Standard
Parameter    Estimate       Error      DF   t Value   Pr > |t|

beta_0        21.5383       0.8472     930    25.42     <.0001
beta_1         1.4043       0.07397    930    18.99     <.0001
pi            -0.02237      0.001573   930   -14.23     <.0001
phi2_0        75.0326      11.8886     930     6.31     <.0001
phi_10         1.2993       0.1793     930     7.25     <.0001
phi2_1         0.05319      0.007356   930     7.23     <.0001
sigma2_u      26.9069       1.4806     930    18.17     <.0001
```

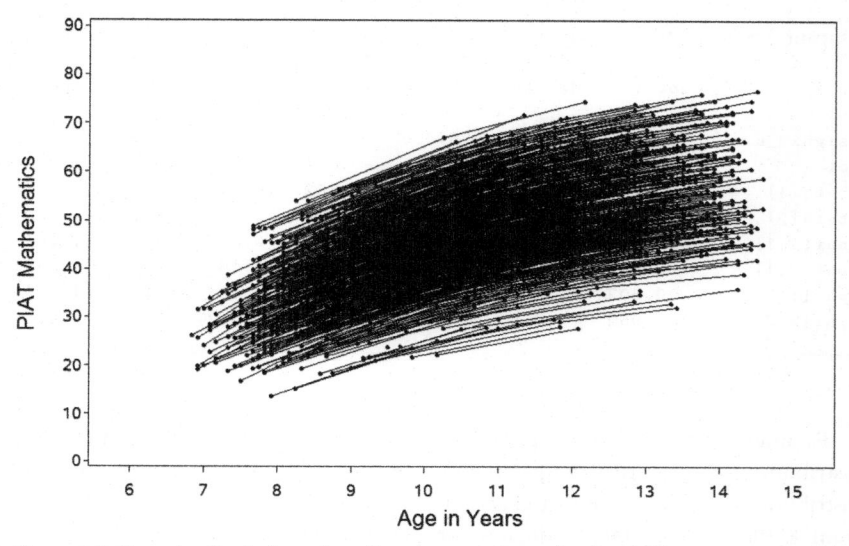

Figure 3.3 Longitudinal plot of predicted scores from the *Dual Change Score* Model.

by `phi2_1`. Children who had higher intercept scores tended to have higher constant change component scores, indicating that these children tended show more change over time. This association was represented by `phi_10`. Last, the residual variance, `sigma2_u`, was 26.91 and represents individual variability that was not accounted for by the dual change score model.

Empirical Bayes estimates of the intercept and constant change component were output, and predicted scores were calculated for each child. These estimates are plotted in Figure 3.3. From these estimates, the exponential nature of the predicted trajectories is evident, as well as the association between the intercept and the constant change component as children higher scores tended to show greater overall rates of change.

JAGS

Script 2 was extended to handle the empirical data (full script can be found at the authors' websites). The data were organized in the wide format with a separate variable for each of the 94 time points. To handle the large amount of missing data, `JAGS` uses *data augmentation*, a process similar to imputation (Merkle, 2011). Given this process, model estimation was expected to take longer than `NLMIXED`. To judge chain convergence, we used the potential scale reduction factor (psrf; Gelman & Rubin, 1992), with the cutoff of 1.1 for all parameters (< 1.1 indicates good chain mixing, thus convergence). The model converged for all parameters after 50,000 samples, taking approximately 2 hours and 10 minutes.

Output 2 Select **JAGS** output for the *Dual Change Score* model

	Lower95	Median	Upper95	Mean	SD	Mode	psrf
sigma2_u	23.482	25.997	28.630	26.019	1.310	25.937	1.000
pi	-0.027	-0.024	-0.021	-0.024	0.001	-0.024	1.012
beta[1]	20.233	21.767	23.245	21.752	0.777	21.775	1.007
beta[2]	1.355	1.482	1.613	1.484	0.068	1.480	1.012
phi[1,1]	59.598	80.356	101.810	80.802	10.887	79.096	1.001
phi[2,1]	0.902	1.217	1.550	1.219	0.167	1.205	1.005
phi[1,2]	0.902	1.217	1.550	1.219	0.167	1.205	1.005
phi[2,2]	0.052	0.066	0.081	0.066	0.007	0.066	1.008

Parameter estimates are displayed in Output 2. In examining the posterior distributions, we see that the parameter estimates (mean or median of posterior distribution) are close, but not exactly the same as the estimated values obtained from **NLMIXED**. The **JAGS** estimates for the fixed–effects parameters (**beta[1]**, **beta[2]**, and **pi**) appear closer to the **NLMIXED** estimates compared to the estimates of the random effects parameters, which tended to be smaller when using **JAGS**. However, using credible intervals to determine the significance of a model parameter, the same conclusions are reached using **JAGS** and **NLMIXED** in that all parameters were significantly different from 0 (0 was not contained within credible interval).

Structural Equation Modeling Software

Two structural equation modeling programs, **Mplus** (Muthén & Muthén, 1998–2015) and **OpenMx** (Boker, Neale, Maes, Wilde, Spiegel, Brick, & Mehta 2011), were used to estimate the dual change score model to the mathematics data contained in Figure 3.2 with *month* as the timing variable. With succinct programming containing multiple statements per line, the **Mplus** script was three pages long and the **OpenMx** script encompassed four pages. **Mplus** was unable to estimate the full model because there was only one observation at 82 months and **Mplus** requires there to be at least two different values for each observed variable. The first variable was removed from the data and the model was re-estimated. **Mplus** converged quickly (18 seconds) and yielded results that were highly similar to those obtained from **NLMIXED**. **OpenMx** was slower to converge (20 minutes), but the model did converge with the full sample. However, **OpenMx** produced a warning message with **Mx Status RED** indicating the results should be interpreted cautiously. The **OpenMx** output is contained in Output 3. The model fit reported by **OpenMx** was identical to the model fit produced by **NLMIXED** and the estimates were highly similar. Both of these scripts are contained on the authors' websites.

Output 3 `OpenMx` output for the *Dual Change Score* Model

```
free parameters:
        name matrix   row   col     Estimate    Std.Error A
1        pi      A  dy83  1y82  -0.02234271    0.00157171
2 sigma2_u      S   y82   y82  27.09930510    1.49059264
3   psi2_0      S   b0i   b0i  72.12637973   11.57374398
4  psi_10       S   b0i   b1i   1.30717950    0.17705272
5   psi2_1      S   b1i   b1i   0.05298880    0.00734041
6  beta_0       M     1   b0i  21.55868778    0.84249813
7  beta_1       M     1   b1i   1.40289165    0.07390640

observed statistics:   2221
estimated parameters:   7
degrees of freedom:   2214
fit value ( -2lnL units ):   15641.3
number of observations:   932
Information Criteria:
          |  df Penalty  |  Parameters Penalty  |  Sample-Size Adjusted
AIC:       11213.2964            15655.30                            NA
BIC:         503.4416            15689.16                      15666.93
```

Discussion

LCS models represent an important framework for modeling and understanding intraindividual change and its determinants. These models are primarily used to study time-dependent change – the effect of prior scores on subsequent changes. Given the incorporation of lagged effects, the time metric must be discrete in nature as opposed to continuous. Because of this and the complexity of model specification, researchers often round the values of a time metric that is more continuous, or researchers opt to use simpler time scales (e.g., *measurement occasion* vs. *age*) when fitting latent change score models. One issue with rounding is that researchers assume the time-lag is constant (within and across participants) when, in fact, it varies between and within participants over time, and the degree of rounding is associated with the ability to accurately estimate model parameters (O'Rourke et al. 2017). For example, using *age in years* with the NLSY-CYA data leads to different conclusions when fitting bivariate latent difference score models compared to when using *age in months*, which highlights the importance of using a fine-grained time metric (O'Rourke et al. 2017). If researchers use a more fine-grained time metric, the programming of latent change score models can become burdensome and the data matrix can become extremely sparse, which can hamper model convergence. Balancing the precision in the time metric with the viability of the model given data sparseness and the model specification is challenging within the SEM framework.

In light of this challenge, we proposed using NLMIXED in SAS as well as JAGS to estimate LCS models. The benefit of these programs is that programming of latent change score models with 10, 100, or 1,000 potential time points is nearly identical. Thus, researchers can use more fine-grained time metrics to increase precision of model estimates, without the programming burden common to using SEM programs to estimate latent change score models. Furthermore, SEM programs can have trouble estimating latent change score models when multiple participants do not share values of the time metric, with NLMIXED demonstrating the ability to adequately estimate such models with these types of data. To illustrate the potential for NLMIXED, we simulated data based on the dual change score model for $N = 200$ participants over $T = 1,000$ time points. Data were then randomly deleted. First, 99.5% of the observations were deleted leaving data from $N = 198$ simulated participants measured between 1 and 13 times over $T = 1,000$ potential time points. NLMIXED converged within one minute and provided estimates close to the population values. Second, 99.7% of the observations were deleted leaving data from $N = 183$ simulated participants measured between 1 and 9 times over $T = 1,000$ potential time points. As before, NLMIXED converged within one minute. Parameter estimates were close to their population values with the exception of the intercept variance, which was underestimated. Specifying and estimating the dual change score model in the SEM framework with $T = 1,000$ variables measured on $N = 183$ or $N = 198$ participants would be challenging to say the least. As a comparison, in the NLSY-CYA there were 94 potential time points for $N = 932$ leading to $87,608$ potential datapoints. There were $2,221$ observations, which is 2.5% of the potential time points and yielding a missing data rate of 97.5%.

Although NLMIXED is a viable alternative to estimating latent change score models and is more flexible than shown here (e.g. a changes to changes model; Grimm, An, McArdle, Zonderman, & Resnick, 2012), the procedure does have limitations for estimating latent change score models. First, although bivariate models can be specified in NLMIXED (Grimm et al. 2017), the residual covariance cannot, which can lead to model misspecification and biased model parameters. Second, latent change score models are sometimes estimated with dynamic noise, where a residual term is added to the latent change score equation (see McArdle, 2001; Equation 3.5). As far as we are aware, this type of residual term cannot be estimated using NLMIXED. If researchers are interested in bivariate and/or dynamic noise models with a finely measured more or less continuous time metric, then WinBUGS or JAGS may be a good alternative (see Hamagami et al. 2009); however, computation is burdensome.

One of the main advantages of the latent change score model framework is the flexibility of which it can be adapted to the idiosyncracies of both research questions and datasets. Furthermore, pairing the latent change score model with Bayesian estimation enhances the flexiblity and the incorporation of theoretical information into the model specification/estimation. For instance, informative priors could have been specified in the JAGS code above, either to reduce the influence of parameters that are of less theoretical interest, or to use previous research to inform the resulting model parameters. Although very little pairing has occurred between the latent change score model and Bayesian estimation, we expect this to change in the future given the rise of Bayesian applications (van de Schoot, Winter, Zondervan-Zwijnenburg, Ryan, & Depaoli, 2017). Particularly given problems with nonconvergence and the latent change score model (O'Rourke et al., 2017), Bayesian estimation is one potential solution to overcoming difficulties with the highly constrained nature of the latent change score model.

Modeling within-person change processes with lagged effects is challenging. When using latent change score models, researchers often make compromises with the nature of the time metric. Using NLMIXED or JAGS for latent change score models enables researchers to be more precise about the time metric, which allows for the idiosyncracies of each longitudinal dataset. That is, there is no longitudinal dataset where all participants are assessed at a consistent interval. It is important to account for this variability in the timing of the assessments, particularly for quickly changing processes. The approaches outlined in this chapter allow researchers to model the data, instead of molding the data to fit the model.

Note

1 Kevin J. Grimm was supported by National Science Foundation Grant REAL-1252463 awarded to the University of Virginia, David Grissmer (Principal Investigator), and Christopher Hulleman (Co-Principal Investigator). Ross Jacobucci was supported by funding through the National Institute on Aging Grant Number T32AG0037.

References

Aydin, B., Leite, W. L., & Algina, J. (2014). The consequences of ignoring variability in measurement occasions within data collection waves in latent growth models. *Multivariate Behavioral Research, 49*, 149–160.

Biesanz, J. C., Deeb-Sossa, N., Papadakis, A. A., Bollen, K. A., & Curran, P. J. (2004). The role of coding time in estimating and interpreting growth curve models. *Psychological Methods, 9*, 30–52.

Boker, S., Neale, M., Maes, H., Wilde, M., Spiegel, M., Brick, T., ... & Mehta, P. (2011). OpenMx: an open source extended structural equation modeling framework. *Psychometrika, 76*, 306–317.

Center for Human Resource Research (2004). *A guide to the 1979–2002 National Longitudinal Survey of Youth.* Washington, DC: US Department of Labor, Bureau of Labor Statistics.

Dunn, L. & Markwardt, F. (1970). *Peabody Individual Achievement Test.* Circle Pines, MN: American Guidance Service.

Gelman, A. & Rubin, D. B. (1992). Inference from iterative simulation using multiple sequences. *Statistical Science, 7*, 457–472.

Ghisletta, P. & Lindenberger, U. (2003). Static and dynamic longitudinal structural analyses of cognitive changes in old age. *Gerontology, 50*, 12–16.

Grimm, K. J., An, Y., McArdle, J. J., Zonderman, A. B. & Resnick, S. M. (2012). Recent changes leading to subsequent changes: Extensions of multivariate latent difference score models. *Structural Equation Modeling: A Multidisciplinary Journal, 19*, 268–292.

Grimm, K. J. & Ram, N. (2011). Growth curve modeling from an SEM perspective. In B. Laursen, T. Little, & N. Card (Eds.), *Handbook of developmental research methods* (pp. 411–431). New York: Guilford Publications.

Grimm, K. J., Ram, N., & Estabrook, R. (2017). *Growth modeling: Structural equation and multilevel modeling approaches.* New York Guilford Publications.

Grimm, K. J. & Widaman, K. F. (2010). Residual structures in latent growth curve analysis. *Structural Equation Modeling: A Multidisciplinary Journal, 17*, 424–442.

Grimm, K. J., Zhang, Z., Hamagami, F., & Mazzocco, M. M. (2013). Modeling nonlinear change via latent change and latent acceleration frameworks: Examining velocity and acceleration of growth trajectories. *Multivariate Behavioral Research, 48*, 117–143.

Hamagami, F., Zhang, Z., & McArdle, J. J. (2009). Modeling latent difference score models using Bayesian algorithms. In S. M. Chow, E. Ferrer, & F. Hsieh (Eds.), *Statistical methods for modeling human dynamics: An interdisciplinary dialogue* (pp. 319–348). New Jersey: Lawrence Erlbaum Associates.

Jöreskog, K. G. (1970). Estimation and testing of simplex models. *British Journal of Mathematical and Statistical Psychology, 23*, 121–145.

Jöreskog, K. G. (1974). Analyzing psychological data by structural analysis of covariance matrices. In D. H Krantz, R. C. Atkinson, R. D. Luce, & P. Suppes (Eds.), *Contemporary developments in mathematical psychology* (vol. 2, pp. 1–56). San Francisco, CA: W. H. Freeman. Francisco.

Littell, R. C., Milliken, G. A., Stroup, W. W., & Wolfinger, R. D. (1996). *SAS system for mixed models*, Cary, NC: SAS Institute Inc.

McArdle, J. J. (1986). Latent variable growth within behavior genetic models. *Behavior Genetics, 16*, 163–200.

McArdle, J. J. (2001). A latent difference score approach to longitudinal dynamic structure analysis. In R. Cudeck, S. du Toit & D. Sörbom (Eds.), *Structural equation modeling: Present and future. A festschrift in honor of Karl Jöreskog* (pp. 1–40). Lincolnwood, IL: Scientific Software International, Inc.

McArdle, J. J. & Epstein, D. (1987). Latent growth curves within developmental structural equation models. *Child Development, 58*, 110–133.

McArdle, J. J. & Hamagami, F. (2001). Latent difference score structural models for linear dynamic analyses with incomplete longitudinal data. In L. M. Collins & A. G. Sayer (Eds.), *New methods for the analysis of change* (pp. 139–175). Washington, DC: American Psychological Association.

McArdle, J. J. & Grimm, K. J. (2010). Five steps in latent curve and latent change score modeling with longitudinal date. In K. van Montford, J. Oud., & A. Satorra (Eds.), *Longitudinal research with latent varibles* (pp. 245–274). Heidlberg, Germany: Springer Verlag.

Mehta, P. D. & Neale, M. C. (2005). People are variables too: multilevel structural equations modeling. *Psychological Methods, 10*, 259–284.

Meredith, W. & Tisak, J. (1990). Latent curve analysis. *Psychometrika, 55*, 107–122.

Merkle, E. C. (2011). A comparison of imputation methods for Bayesian factor analysis models. *Journal of Educational and Behavioral Statistics, 36*, 257–276.

Muthén, L. K. and Muthén, B. O. (1998–2015). *Mplus user's guide* (7th Ed.). Los Angeles, CA: Muthén & Muthén.

O'Rourke, H., Grimm, K. J., & MacKinnon, D. P. (2017). Time metrics and their effects in latent change score models. Manuscript under review.

Plummer, M. (2003). JAGS: A program for analysis of Bayesian graphical models using Gibbs sampling. In K. Hornik, F. Leisch, & A. Zeileis (Eds.), *Proceedings of the 3rd international workshop on distributed statistical computing.*

Plummer, M., Stukalov, A., & Denwood, M. (2016). `rjags` (R package version 4–6, pp. 1–19). Vienna, Austria: The Comprehensive R Archive Network.

R Core Team (2016). R: A language and environment for statistical computing. R Foundation for Statistical Computing, Vienna, Austria. URL www.R-project.org/.

Singer, J. D. & Willett, J. B. (2003). *Applied longitudinal data analysis: Modeling change and event occurrence.* New York Oxford University Press.

Small, B. J., Dixon, R. A., McArdle, J. J., & Grimm, K. J. (2012). Do changes in lifestyle engagement moderate cognitive decline in normal aging? Evidence from the Victoria Longitudinal Study. *Neuropsychology, 26,* 144–155.

Spiegelhalter, D. J., Thomas, A., Best, N., & Lunn, D. (2003). `WinBUGS` manual version 1.4. (MRC Biostatistics Unit, Institute of Public Health, Robinson Way, Cambridge CB2 2SR, UK) www.mrc-bsu.cam.ac.uk/bugs

Sterba, S. K. (2014). Fitting nonlinear latent growth models with individually-varying time points. *Structural Equation Modeling: A Multidisciplinary Journal, 21,* 630–647.

van de Schoot, R., Winter, S., Zondervan-Zwijnenburg, M., Ryan, O., & Depaoli, S. A. (2017). A systematic review of Bayesian papers in psychology: The last 25 years. *Psychological Methods, 22,* 217–239.

Willett, J. B. & Sayer, A. G. (1994). Using covariance structure analysis to detect correlates and predictors of individual change over time. *Psychological Bulletin, 116,* 363.

Zhang, Z., Hamagami, F., Wang, L., Grimm, K. J., & Nesselroade, J. R. (2007). Bayesian analysis of longitudinal data using growth curve models. *International Journal of Behavioral Development, 31,* 374–383.

4

LATENT CHANGE SCORE MODELS WITH CURVILINEAR CONSTANT BASES

Fumiaki Hamagami & John J. McArdle

Introduction

In mathematics, the difference equation is a rule that regulates sequential states of a variable of interest in a longitudinal process in discrete time steps. McArdle and Hamagami (2001) realized that a latent curve model was merely a methodological means to delineate a certain shape of growth trajectories. The latent curve approach does not account for what induces change, which in turn determines a growth trajectory. The latent slope or rate of change in the latent curve model is static for each individual, meaning that the latent rate of change is a time invariant unobserved score and its quantity does not change over time. Until the publication of an innovative methodological paper (McArdle, 2001), we have not formally seen the structural equation model in which a difference equation is integrated into a structural equation and difference scores are used as a regulatory means to determine sequential temporal states of a variable in a longitudinal process. In this model, an unobserved latent change score is time variant, meaning that its quantity changes over time for each individual. Most importantly, latent change is a focal point of analyses.

With the advent of this methodological idea, we witnessed a plethora of research papers in which the latent change score model was applied to analyze repeated measures data, examining what accounted for change in variables. For example, Ferrer and McArdle (2004) extensively examined the dynamic relationship between cognitive ability and academic achievement during the pre-adult period and tested Cattell's investment theory of crystallized ability and fluid reasoning (see also, Ferrer, McArdle, Shaywits, Holahan, Marchinone, & Shaywits, 2007; McArdle, Hamagami, Meredith & Bradway, 2000) . In Grimm (2008), application of the bivarate latent change score model led to the conclusion that early reading comprehension was an important determinant for a conceptual understanding of algebraic knowledge and practical use of mathematical concepts. Grimm (2007) investigated whether or not the affective mental state of children influenced academic progress over time through the bivariate latent change score model. Hishinuma et al. (2012) similarly showed that depressive state of adolescents negatively influenced change in GPA through the bivariate latent change score model for the ordinal variables. The discrete dynamical system analyses in McArdle, Hamagami, Jones, Jolesz, Kikinis, Spiro, and Albert (2004) implied that a structural state in the lateral ventricle size in the brain had an untoward effect on change in memory in elderly adults.

The purpose of this study is to introduce a variant of the latent change score model that can be used as a possible alternative discrete dynamical model for analyses of longitudinal data. In McArdle's dual change score model, latent change is determined by two components: (1) an individualized time invariant latent constant score and (2) a feedback effect of the time dependent preceding latent score. As a consequence, these two determinants generate a growth curve derived from combinatorial effects of linear and autoregressive exponential functions. The shape of growth curves is dictated by the quantitative size of an individualized initial state, the quantitative size of an individualized additive constant, strength of self-feedback coefficient, and the quantitative state of an individualized preceding latent score. Theoretically, an individualized initial state and additive constant can range from $-\infty$ to ∞, a self-feedback coefficient can range from $-\infty$ to ∞, and an individualized preceding latent score can range from $-\infty$ to ∞. In spite of these theoretical wide ranges of unknown latent component scores and self-feedback parameters, a fundamental shape of the resultant growth curve is a shape formed by a combinatorial effect of linear and exponential functions. Figure 4.1 illustrates fundamental growth patterns that are derived from the univariate dual change score model. As a whole, we can expect four types of expected trajectories based on the univariate dual change score model: (1) accelerated explosive growth, (2) accelerated explosive decline or terminal drop, (3) a positive partial adjustment growth curve, or gradual increase towards an asymptotic plateau, and (4) a negative partial adjustment curve, or gradual decline towards an asymptotic nadir.

A simple question arises. Is the dual change score model good for repeated measures data that seemingly show quadratic curves? The answer is probably not in the long run. If an observation period captures an incremental phase of the quadratic form, the dual change score model could suffice. However, once an observation period encounters a maximum and enters into the decline phase of the growth curve, the univariate dual change score model is no longer sufficient to delineate such a nonlinear curve. This chapter proposes an alternative latent change model to deal with repeated measures with such nonlinear characteristics.

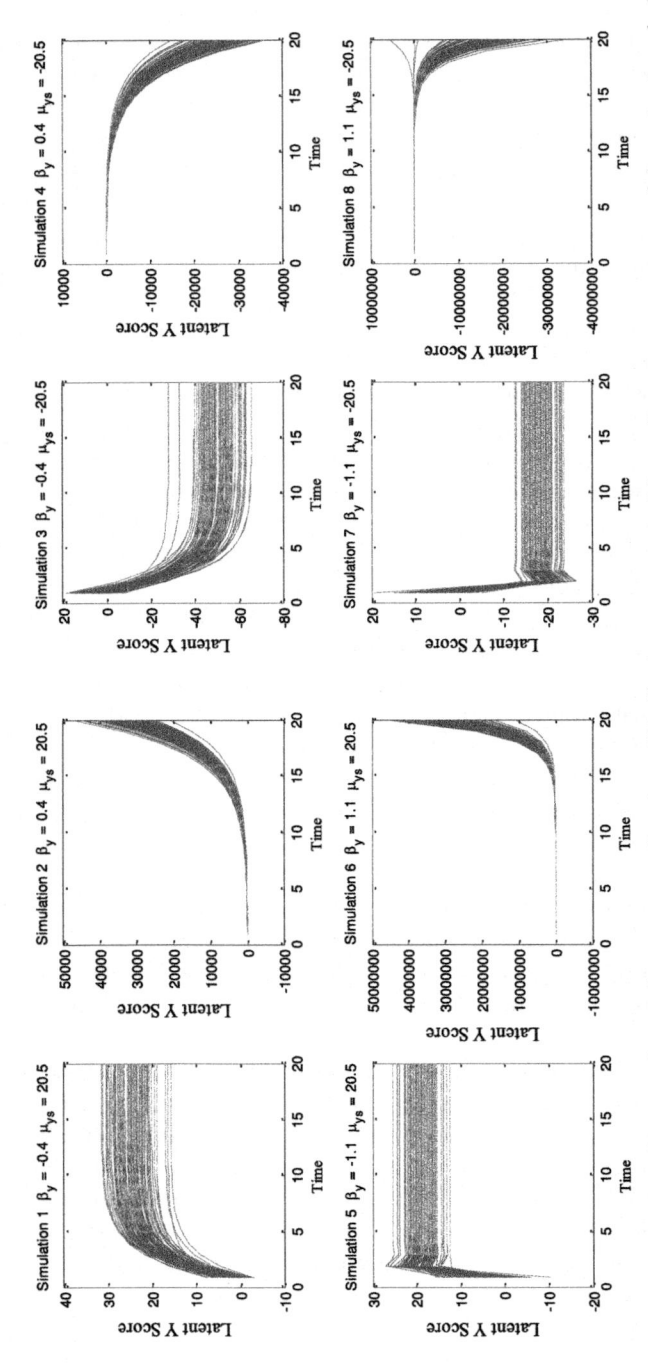

FIGURE 4.1 A series of expected growth curves as a function of feedback parameters and latent linear constant scores of the univariate dual change score model.

Methods

The dynamical system is about an evolutionary process of some measurable events over time. When we are interested in how something changes, concept of the dynamical system allows us to discover a underlying systematic regularity in that evolutionary process that underlies data. When we investigate something over time, we are keen to understand critical essence of the longitudinal process. We ponder why the process behaves in a particular manner over time. We contemplate what causes these changes in a systematic way. We need to take a snapshot of essence that is a critically important part of the dynamical process. We hope that a picture of the momentary state will impart something very critical that eventually lets us find an underlying rule of the dynamical system.

We record event history of something at a sequence of time. Recording of the variables are invariably taken at a discrete time sequence, because we cannot keep recording snapshots of something in an infinitesimally small interval like an interval of every second. We hope that the measurements we take in an intermittent manner would inform us of something very essential for the system process.

When we collect measurements of selected variables for our investigation, we presume that these measurements represent the "state" of the dynamical system of the variables of interest. However, this representation of the state is one slice of the "state space" that encompasses all possible states of the system process. Our aim is to discover a rule of the system that accounts for the sequential snapshots of the events, hopefully approximating to a unique slice within the state space of the hidden dynamical system.

The latent change score model is used to analyze sequential measurements of multiple individuals collected over periods of times and to identify an undiscovered rule that determines a discrete dynamical system. Once we deduce the critical rule of the discrete dynamical system through careful analyses, we are able to forecast a unique state within the state space governed by the rule of dynamical system.

A rule that determines the dynamical system is a latent change score (McArdle, 2001; McArdle & Hamagami, 2001). Our task is to deduce what accounts for latent change. A latent change score is a difference between two consecutive latent scores. Algebraically, a difference score is defined as

$$\Delta y[t]_i = y[t]_i - y[t-1]_i. \tag{4.1}$$

where $\Delta y[t]_i$ is a latent difference score for an individual at time t, $y[t]_i$ is an individualized latent score at t, and $y[t-1]_i$ is an individualized latent score at the preceding time.

When we rearrange the latent change score equation, the current latent score is the sum of the preceding latent score and the latent change score, i.e.,

$$y[t]_i = \Delta y[t]_i + y[t-1]_i. \tag{4.2}$$

TABLE 4.1 Algebraic expression of consecutive latent scores with an initial score and cumulative latent change scores.

	A current latent score	A current latent score expressed with an initial score and cumulative latent change scores
t	$y[t]_i$	$y[t]_i = y[1]_i + \sum_{k=2}^{t} \Delta y[k]_i$
1	$y[1]_i$	$y[1]_i = L_i$
2	$y[2]_i = y[1]_i + \Delta y[2]_i$	$y[2]_i = L_i + \Delta y[2]_i$
3	$y[3]_i = y[2]_i + \Delta y[3]_i$	$y[3]_i = L_i + \left\{ \Delta y[2]_i + \Delta y[3]_i \right\}$
4	$y[4]_i = y[3]_i + \Delta y[4]_i$	$y[4]_i = L_i + \left\{ \Delta y[2]_i + \Delta y[3]_i + \Delta y[4]_i \right\}$
5	$y[5]_i = y[4]_i + \Delta y[5]_i$	$y[5]_i = L_i + \left\{ \Delta y[2]_i + \Delta y[3]_i + \Delta y[4]_i + \Delta y[5]_i \right\}$
6	$y[6]_i = y[5]_i + \Delta y[6]_i$	$y[6]_i = L_i + \left\{ \Delta y[2]_i + \Delta y[3]_i + \Delta y[4]_i + \Delta y[5]_i + \Delta y[6]_i \right\}$
t	$y[t]_i = y[t-1]_i + \Delta y[t]_i$	$y[t]_i = L_i + \left\{ \Delta y[2]_i + \Delta y[3]_i + \cdots + \Delta y[t-1]_i + \Delta y[t]_i \right\}$

Latent change scores represent a critical rule of the discrete dynamical system. An equation of the relationship between the current latent score and the past latent score forms a "recurrence" equation that informs us of an individualized future state within the state space of the dynamical system. Obviously, each individual stays at a specific unique state within the state space and his/her future state is uniquely determined.

Once an initial score is determined, a temporal sequence of individualized latent scores is calculated given the rule of the dynamical system. Table 4.1 shows that a sequence of individualized latent scores is determined by an initial latent score and summation of the consecutive latent change scores up to the specific time period. For example, the latent score at time 2 is the sum of an initial score and a latent change score at time 2. At the third time period, the latent score is now the sum of an initial score and two latent change scores, the previous and current change scores. In this way, a new change score is added to a cumulative collection of the previous change scores in order to calculate the current latent score.

Latent Constant Change Score Model

The constant change score model is equivalent to the linear latent growth model. For the latent constant change score, we define an individualized latent change score as

$$\Delta y[t]_i = S_i, \tag{4.3}$$

where $\Delta y[t]_i$ is an individualized latent change score at t time period and S_i is an individualized constant. An individualized latent change score is simply a latent

TABLE 4.2 A relationship among t, and latent change scores at t, and cumulative sums of change scores at t for the constant change score model.

t	$\Delta y[t]_i = S_i$	$\sum_{k=2}^{t} \Delta y[k]_i = (t-1)S_i.$
1	0	0
2	S_i	S_i
3	S_i	$S_i + S_i = 2S_i$
4	S_i	$2S_i + S_i = 3S_i$
5	S_i	$3S_i + S_i = 4S_i$
6	S_i	$4S_i + S_i = 5S_i$
t	S_i	$(t-2)S_i + S_i = (t-1)S_i$

constant specific to an individual. The latent change score does not change across time periods for a specific individual. In other words, each individual has a specific change score that does not change. Thus, a solution of the latent change score is simply a latent linear growth model as shown below,

$$y[t]_i = L_i + \sum_{k=2}^{t} \Delta y[k]_i = L_i + \sum_{k=2}^{t} S_i = L_i + (t-1)\, S_i. \tag{4.4}$$

Table 4.2 shows the relationship among t, latent change scores at t, and cumulative sums of change scores at t for the constant change score model. It clearly shows that at each time point, a linear constant is added to the cumulative sum at the previous time point.

By adding a time variant individualized error term e[t]$_i$, a manifest score Y[t]$_i$ is

$$Y[t]_i = y[t]_i + e[t]_i = L_i + \sum_{k=2}^{t} \Delta y[k]_i + e[t]_i = L_i + \sum_{k=2}^{t} S_i + e[t]_i. \tag{4.5}$$

Latent Quadratic Constant Change Score Model

A quadratic latent growth curve can be fitted through the latent change score model approach. In the quadratic form, a latent change score is

$$\Delta y[t]_i = \{2(t-2)+1\} Q_i,\ but\ \Delta y[1]_i = 0 \tag{4.6}$$

where Q$_i$ is a latent quadratic constant score for an individual. This latent change equation reduces to

$$y[t]_i = L_i + \sum_{k=2}^{t} \Delta y[k]_i = L_i + \sum_{k=2}^{t} \{2(k-2)+1\} Q_i = L_i + (t-1)^2 Q_i. \tag{4.7}$$

Table 4.3 shows that loadings of the quadratic factor on latent change scores lead to quadratic coefficients for the quadratic factor of the latent quadratic curve.

TABLE 4.3 A relationship among t, and latent change scores at t, and cumulative sums of change scores at t.

t	$\Delta y[t]_i = \{2(t-2)+1\}Q_i$	$\sum_{k=2}^{t} \Delta y[k]_i = (t-1)^2 Q_i.$
1	0	0
2	$1Q_i$	$1Q_i$
3	$3Q_i$	$1Q_i+3Q_i=4Q_i$
4	$5Q_i$	$4Q_i+5Q_i=9Q_i$
5	$7Q_i$	$9Q_i+7Q_i=16Q_i$
6	$9Q_i$	$16Q_i+9Q_i=25Q_i$
t	$\{2(t-2)+1\}Q_i$	$(t-2)^2 Q_i + \{2(t-2)+1\}Q_i = (t-1)^2 Q_i$

A manifest score for the latent quadratic change score model is expressed as

$$Y[t]_i = L_i + \sum_{k=2}^{t} \Delta y[k]_i + e[t]_i = L_i + \sum_{k=2}^{t} \{2(k-2)+1\}Q_i + e[t]_i$$

$$= L_i + (t-1)^2 Q_i + e[t]_i \qquad (4.8)$$

For the full quadratic form, a latent change score is

$$\Delta y[t]_i = S_i + \{2(t-2)+1\}Q_i, \text{ but } \Delta y[1]_i = 0 \qquad (4.9)$$

and

$$y[t]_i = L_i + \sum_{k=2}^{t} \Delta y[k]_i = L_i + \sum_{k=2}^{t} \{S_i + \{2(k-2)+1\}Q_i\}$$

$$= L_i + (t-1)S_i + (t-1)^2 Q_i. \qquad (4.10)$$

A manifest score is

$$Y[t]_i = L_i + \sum_{k=2}^{t} \Delta y[t]_i + e[t]_i = L_i + \sum_{k=2}^{t} \{S_i + \{2(t-2)+1\}Q_i\} + e[t]_i$$

$$= L_i + (t-1)S_i + (t-1)^2 Q_i + e[t]_i. \qquad (4.11)$$

Using the latent change score approach, we can now add a self-feedback effect of the previous latent score on the current latent change, which becomes a quadratic form of a dual change score model. i.e.,

$$\Delta y[t]_i = \beta y[t-1]_i + S_i + \{2(t-2)+1\}Q_i, but \Delta y[1]_i = 0. \qquad (4.12)$$

Thus, the latent curve of the quadratic dual change score model becomes highly complex,

$$y[t]_i = y[t-1]_i + \Delta y[t]_i = y[t-1]_i + \{\beta y[t-1]_i + S_i + \{2(t-2)+1\}Q_i\}$$

$$= (1+\beta)y[t-1]_i + S_i + \{2(t-2)+1\}Q_i, \qquad (4.13)$$

where

$$y[t-1]_i = (1+\beta)\,y[t-2]_i + S_i + \{2\,(t-3)+1\}\,Q_i. \tag{4.14}$$

The solution for the recurrent equation is

$$y[t]_i = \left\{\frac{-1+(1+\beta)^{t-1}}{\beta}\right\} S_i + \left\{-\frac{2t\beta - \beta + 2 - 2(1+\beta)^{t-1}}{\beta^2}\right\} Q_i + (1+\beta)^{t-1}\,L_i. \tag{4.15}$$

An equation for an observed score is

$$Y[t]_i = \left\{\frac{-1+(1+\beta)^{t-1}}{\beta}\right\} S_i + \left\{-\frac{2t\beta - \beta + 2 - 2(1+\beta)^{t-1}}{\beta^2}\right\} Q_i$$
$$+ (1+\beta)^{t-1}\,L_i + e[t]_i. \tag{4.16}$$

A path diagram for the quadratic dual change score model is shown in Figure 4.2. A difference between the quadratic dual change score model and the linear dual change score model is that in the former, a latent variable representing a quadratic shape is added to the structure of the linear change score model.

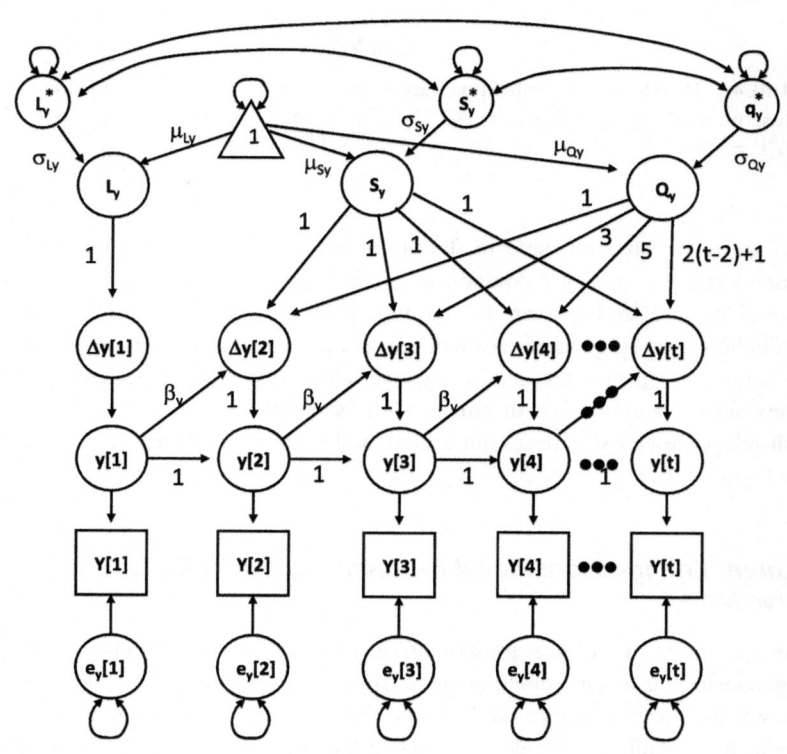

FIGURE 4.2 A path diagram of the full quadratic dual change score model.

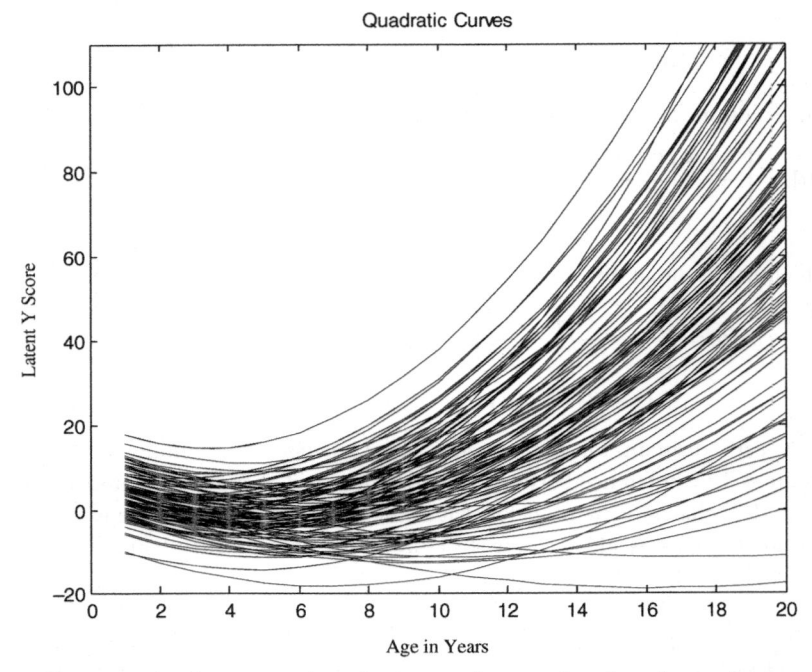

FIGURE 4.3 Randomly generated quadratic growth curves based on the quadratic constant score model ($\mu_{\text{Ly}} = 5$, $\mu_{\text{Sy}} = -2.5$, $\mu_{\text{Qy}} = .3$, $\sigma_{\text{Ly}} = 5$, $\sigma_{\text{Sy}} = .5$, $\sigma_{\text{Qy}} = .1$, N = 100, T = 20).

If we set means and standard deviations for the initial condition, the linear constant and the quadratic constant as $\mu_{\text{Ly}} = 5$, $\mu_{\text{Sy}} = -2.5$, $\mu_{\text{Qy}} = .3$, $\sigma_{\text{Ly}} = 5$, $\sigma_{\text{Sy}} = .5$, $\sigma_{\text{Qy}} = .1$ and generate 100 random quadratic growth curves with T = 20, we obtain expected quadratic growth curves that are shown in Figure 4.3. Using the same set of parameters plus a negative self-feedback $\beta_{\text{y}} = -.2$, we generate a new set of random growth curves with N = 100 and T = 20. A negative feedback parameter suppresses the growth and curbs down trajectories in general (see Figure 4.4).

A Latent Change Score Model Representing Latent Basis Curve Model

Unlike a simple latent linear growth curve, a latent basis curve can be any growth shape, including linear, spline, angular concave, or any other non-linear shape. A latent basis growth curve can be fitted through the latent change score model approach (McArdle, 2009). We showed that the linear latent curve model could be expressed in a latent change score model. By adding a time variant basis coefficient

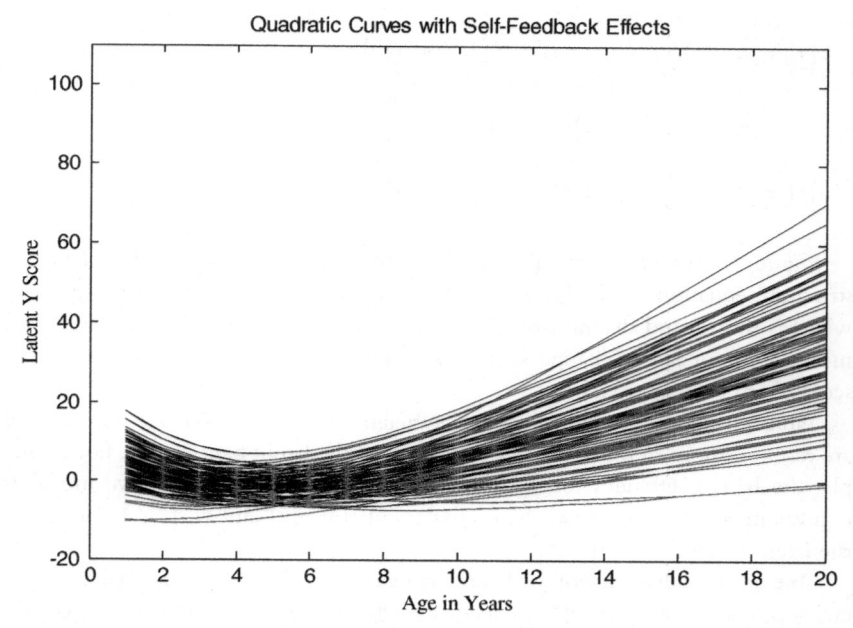

FIGURE 4.4 Randomly generated quadratic growth curves based on the quadratic dual change score model ($\mu_{Ly} = 5$, $\mu_{Sy} = -2.5$, $\mu_{Qy} = .3$, $\sigma_{Ly} = 5$, $\sigma_{Sy} = .5$, $\sigma_{Qy} = .1$, $\beta_y = -.2$, N = 100, T = 20).

for the linear constant factor, a latent change score becomes

$$\Delta y[t]_i = \alpha[t] S_i, \tag{4.17}$$

where $\alpha[t]$ is a time variant basis coefficient for the constant factor S_i. An expected latent score is now expressed as

$$y[t]_i = L_i + \sum_{k=2}^{t} \Delta y[k]_i = L_i + \sum_{k=2}^{t} \alpha[k] S_i. \tag{4.18}$$

However, one constraint needs to be imposed. One of these basis coefficients needs to be fixed at a certain value. Let us say, at the time period t = 2, $\alpha[2] = 1.00$. Assuming there are 5 time periods in data, an expected score at each time period is calculated as

$$y[1]_i = L_i \tag{4.19}$$

$$y[2]_i = L_i + \sum_{k=2}^{2} \Delta y[k]_i = L_i + \alpha[2] S_i = L_i + S_i \tag{4.20}$$

$$y[3]_i = L_i + \sum_{k=2}^{3} \Delta y[k]_i = L_i + \alpha[2] S_i + \alpha[3] S_i = L_i + (\alpha[2] + \alpha[3]) S_i \tag{4.21}$$

$$y[4]_i = L_i + \sum_{k=2}^{4} \Delta y[k]_i = L_i + \alpha[2]S_i + \alpha[3]S_i + \alpha[4]S_i$$

$$= L_i + (\alpha[2] + \alpha[3] + \alpha[4])S_i \tag{4.22}$$

$$y[5]_i = L_i + \sum_{k=2}^{5} \Delta y[k]_i = L_i + (\alpha[2] + \alpha[3] + \alpha[4] + \alpha[5])S_i. \tag{4.23}$$

Figure 4.5 shows two path diagrams. The first diagram on the left depicts a structural equation model for a latent basis curve based on a latent change score, whereas the second diagram on the right depicts an ordinary latent basis curve model without latent change scores. We obtain the equivalent expected latent scores from both approaches.

Table 4.4 shows how time variant coefficients of the latent change score model are re-expressions of time variant coefficients of the latent basis curves. For example, the basis coefficient for y[3] labeled $\beta1$ in the latent basis curve model is equivalent to the sum of two basis coefficients for y[2] and y[3] or 1 and $\alpha1$ in the latent change score model

One unique advantage of the latent change score with time variant basis coefficients is that we can now add self-feedback effects of the preceding latent score on the current latent change scores. For the ordinary approach, it is impossible to test such a hypothesis. The model is called the latent triple change score model due to three determinants that make up the latent change score. They are: (1) time variant basis coefficients, (2) an individualized constant, and (3) self-feedback coefficients.

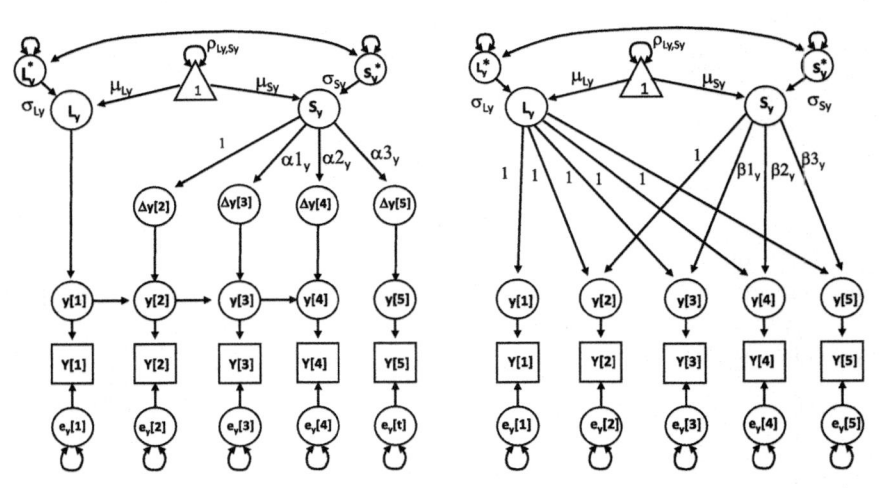

FIGURE 4.5 Path diagrams representing latent basis models. *Note*: the diagram on the left represents a structural equation model of latent basis curves by a latent difference score approach, whilst that on the right represents a structural equation model of an ordinary latent growth curve modeling approach.

TABLE 4.4 Equivalence of time variant basis coefficients between the ordinary latent curve model and the latent time variant change score model.

Time Period (t)	Time Variant Basis coefficients used for the ordinary latent curve model $\beta[t]$	Latent Time Variant Basis Change Score Model $\sum_{k=2}^{t} \alpha[t] S_i$
1	$0 =$	$0 =$
2	$1 =$	$1 =$
3	$\beta 1$	$1 + \alpha 1$
4	$\beta 2$	$1 + \alpha 1 + \alpha 2$
5	$\beta 3$	$1 + \alpha 1 + \alpha 2 + \alpha 3$

The equation of the latent change score becomes

$$\Delta y[t]_i = \alpha[t] S_i + \beta_y y[t-1]_i. \tag{4.24}$$

Expected latent scores are

$$y[t]_i = L_i + \sum_{k=2}^{t} \Delta y[k]_i = L_i + \sum_{k=2}^{t} \left\{ \alpha[k] S_i + \beta_y y[k-1]_i \right\}. \tag{4.25}$$

Expected scores of the first 5 latent scores are computed as

$$y[1]_i = L_i \tag{4.26}$$

$$y[2]_i = y[1]_i + \Delta y[2]_i = L_i + \alpha[2] S_i + \beta_y y[1]_i$$
$$= L_i (1 + \beta_y) + S_i \tag{4.27}$$

$$y[3]_i = y[2]_i + \Delta y[3]_i = \alpha[3] S_i + (1 + \beta_y) y[2]_i$$
$$= \alpha[3] S_i + (1 + \beta_y) \left\{ L_i (1 + \beta_y) + S_i \right\}$$
$$= \alpha[3] S_i + (1 + \beta_y) S_i + L_i (1 + \beta_y)^2 \tag{4.28}$$

$$y[4]_i = y[3]_i + \Delta y[4]_i = \alpha[4] S_i + (1 + \beta_y) y[3]_i$$
$$= \alpha[4] S_i + (1 + \beta_y) \left\{ \alpha[3] S_i + (1 + \beta_y) S_i + L_i (1 + \beta_y)^2 \right\}$$
$$= \alpha[4] S_i + (1 + \beta_y) \alpha[3] S_i + S_i (1 + \beta_y)^2 + L_i (1 + \beta_y)^3 \tag{4.29}$$

$$y[5]_i = y[4]_i + \Delta y[5]_i = \alpha[5] S_i + (1 + \beta_y) y[4]_i$$
$$= \alpha[5] S_i + (1 + \beta_y) \left\{ \alpha[4] S_i + (1 + \beta_y) \alpha[3] S_i + S_i (1 + \beta_y)^2 + L_i (1 + \beta_y)^3 \right\}$$
$$= \alpha[5] S_i + (1 + \beta_y) \alpha[4] S_i + (1 + \beta_y)^2 \alpha[3] S_i + S_i (1 + \beta_y)^3 + L_i (1 + \beta_y)^4. \tag{4.30}$$

Clearly, the model generates non–linear trajectories with combinatorial effects of various elements including the level factor score, the slope factor score, sizes and magnitude of basis coefficients, and size and magnitude of the self-feedback effect.

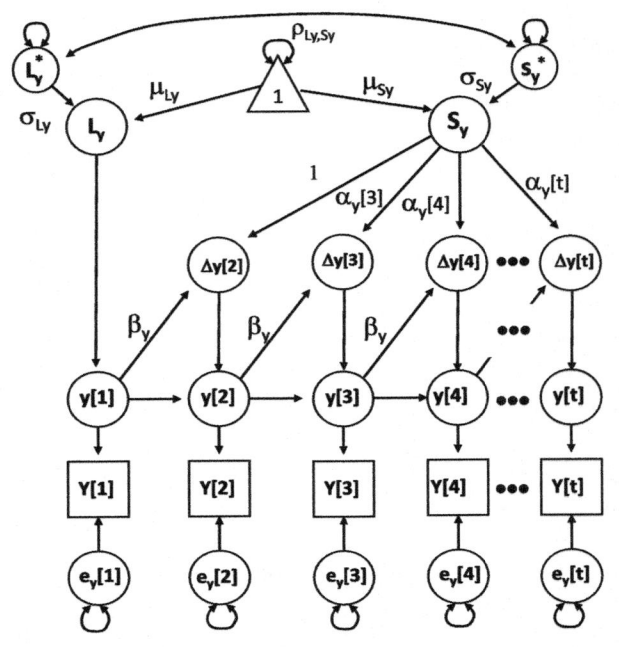

FIGURE 4.6 A path diagram representing a triple change score model.

A path diagram of the triple change score model is presented in Figure 4.6.

We simulated latent curves based on two models: (1) the constant change score model with time variant basis coefficients, and (2) the triple change score model. Parameters used for simulation are as follows: Mean of the level factor $\mu_{Ly} = 5$; mean of the slope factor $\mu_{Sy} = 20$; standard deviation of the level factor $\sigma_{Ly} = 5$; standard deviation of the slope factor $\sigma_{Sy} = 5$; basis coefficients $\alpha[t] = [0 \; 1 \; .5 \; .5 \; -1]$; self-feedback $\beta_y = .3$; a number of time period $T = 5$; and the sample size $N = 100$. Latent trajectories generated by two different models show apparently different trajectories. With time variant basis coefficients applied, trajectories start off low, then hit an apex, then abate. By applying a positive feedback effect of the preceding latent score on the current change score, trajectories hold off a downturn trend at the end.

Bivariate Latent Quadratic Curve Model Based on Latent Change Score Approach

Bivariate latent quadratic curves are constructed simply by a system of two latent change scores which are determined by two components: (1) an individualized linear constant, and (2) an individualized quadratic constant with a time variant

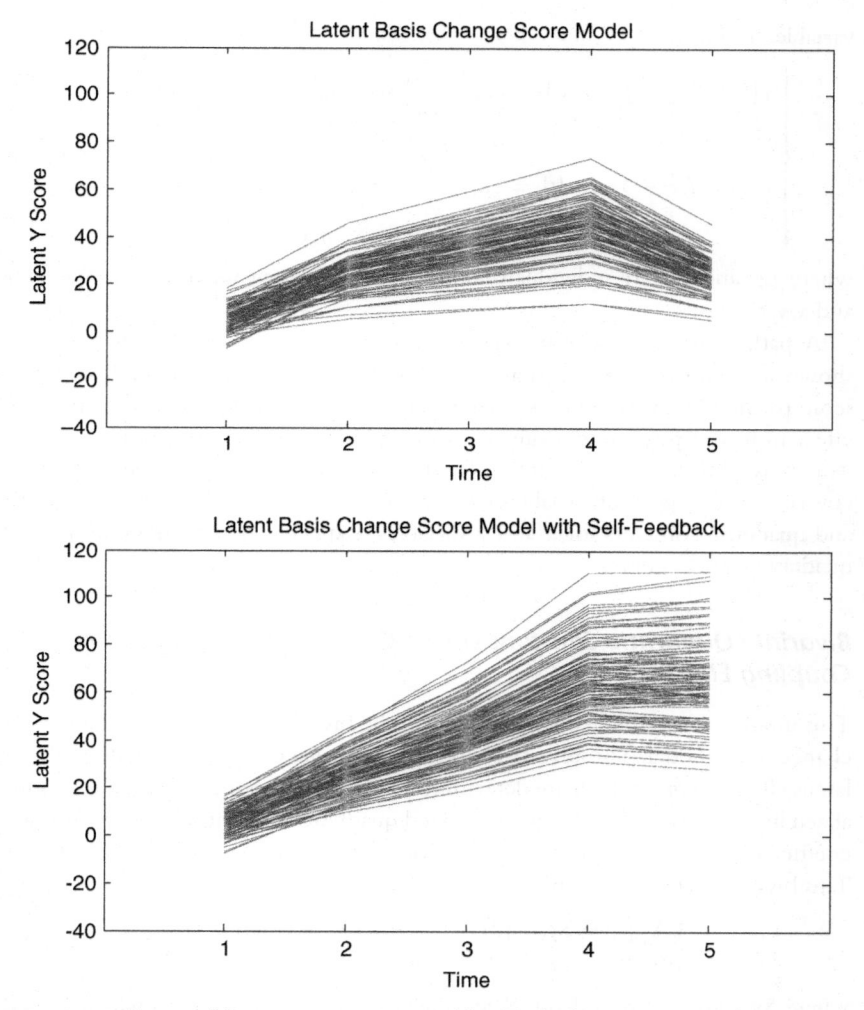

FIGURE 4.7 Expected latent curves contrasted by (1) the latent constant change score model with time variant basis coefficients, and (2) the triple change score model.

coefficient. The bivariate latent quadratic constant model is expressed as

$$\begin{cases} \Delta y[t]_i = Sy_i + \{2(t-2)+1\} Qy_i \\ \Delta x[t]_i = Sx_i + \{2(t-2)+1\} Qx_i \end{cases}, \tag{4.31}$$

where Sy_i and Sx_i are individualized linear constants for $\Delta y[t]_i$ and $\Delta x[t]_i$, and Qy_i and Qx_i are individualized quadratic constants for $\Delta y[t]_i$ and $\Delta x[t]_i$, respectively. These latent change scores are used to calculate expected scores of y and x variables as follows,

$$\begin{cases} y[t]_i = Ly_i + \sum_{k=2}^{t} \Delta y[t]_i = Ly_i + \sum_{k=2}^{t} \{Sy_i + \{2(t-2)+1\} Qy_i\} \\ \qquad = Ly_i + (t-1) Sy_i + (t-1)^2 Qy_i \\ x[t]_i = Lx_i + \sum_{k=2}^{t} \Delta x[t]_i = Lx_i + \sum_{k=2}^{t} \{Sx_i + \{2(t-2)+1\} Qx_i\} \\ \qquad = Lx_i + (t-1) Sx_i + (t-1)^2 Qx_i \end{cases}, \quad (4.32)$$

where Ly_i and Lx_i are individualized scores for the latent initial conditions for y and x variables.

A path diagram for the bivariate quadratic constant change score model is shown in Figure 4.8. In the figure, the self-feedback effect from the past latent score to the present latent change score does not appear, nor does the coupling effect from the past latent score of one variable to the present change score of its counterpart. Covariance among latent scores of x and y are accounted for by covariance among latent variables representing initial conditions, linear constants, and quadratic constants for x and y variables. Expected latent curves are merely quadratic growth curves.

Bivariate Quadratic Constant Latent Change Score Model with Coupling Effect

This model adds mutual coupling effects to the bivariate quadratic constant latent change score model. This bivariate model is constructed simply by a system of two latent change scores which are determined by three components: (1) an individualized linear constant, (2) an individualized quadratic constant with a time variant coefficient, and (3) a coupling effect from the preceding counterpart variable. This bivariate latent quadratic constant model is expressed as

$$\begin{cases} \Delta y[t]_i = Sy_i + \{2(t-2)+1\} Qy_i + \gamma_{yx} x[t-1]_i \\ \Delta x[t]_i = Sx_i + \{2(t-2)+1\} Qx_i + \gamma_{xy} y[t-1]_i \end{cases}, \quad (4.33)$$

where Sy_i and Sx_i are individualized linear constants for $\Delta y[t]_i$ and $\Delta x[t]_i$, Qy_i and Qx_i are individualized quadratic constants for $\Delta y[t]_i$ and $\Delta x[t]_i$, respectively, and γ_{yx} and γ_{xy} are coupling parameters that are regression effects of the previous score of one variable to the current latent change score of the counterpart (i.e., $x[t-1]_i \rightarrow \Delta y[t]_i$ or $y[t-1]_i \rightarrow \Delta x[t]_i$). These latent change scores are used to calculate the general latent score of y and x variables as follows:

$$\begin{cases} y[t]_i = y[t-1]_i + \Delta y[t]_i = y[t-1]_i + Sy_i + \{2(t-2)+1\} Qy_i + \gamma_{yx} x[t-1]_i \\ x[t]_i = x[t-1]_i + \Delta x[t]_i = x[t-1]_i + Sx_i + \{2(t-2)+1\} Qx_i + \gamma_{xy} y[t-1]_i \end{cases}. \quad (4.34)$$

This model assumes that there is a significant cross–lag effect of one latent variable to the latent change score of the counterpart. The autoregressive effect is deemed trivial in this model. An example of a path diagram is presented in Figure 4.9.

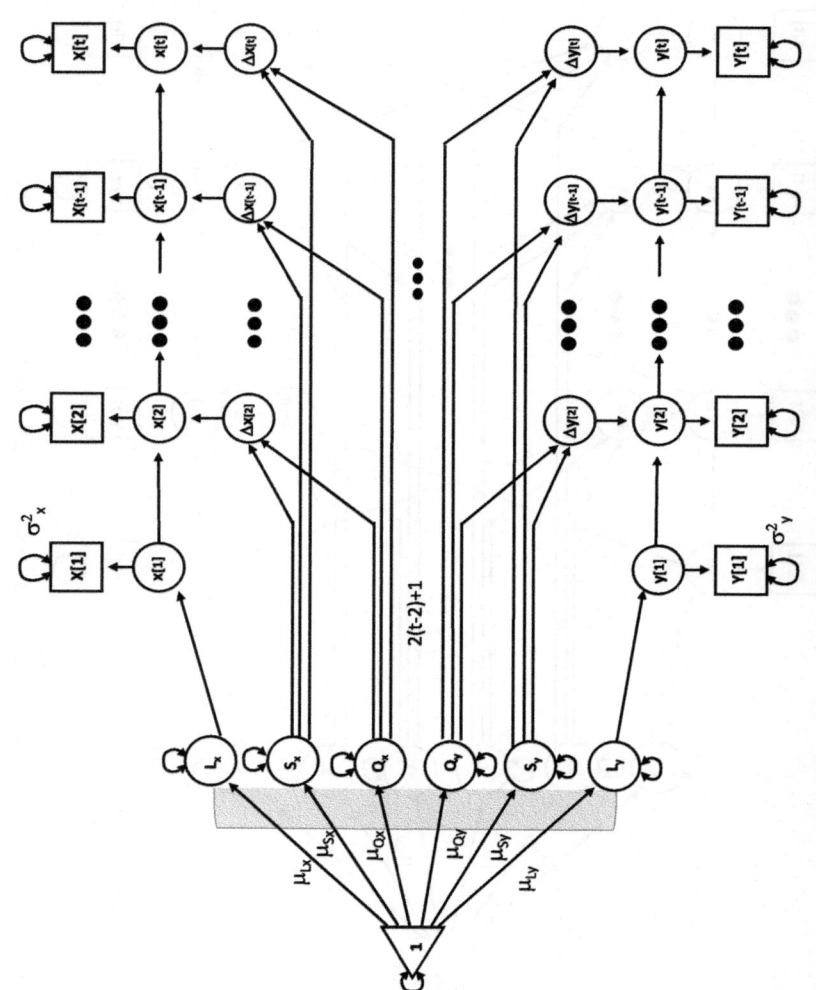

FIGURE 4.8 A path diagram representing a bivariate system of latent quadratic constant change score model. *Note:* a shaded area in light blue indicates that initial conditions, linear constants, and quadratic constants are correlated.

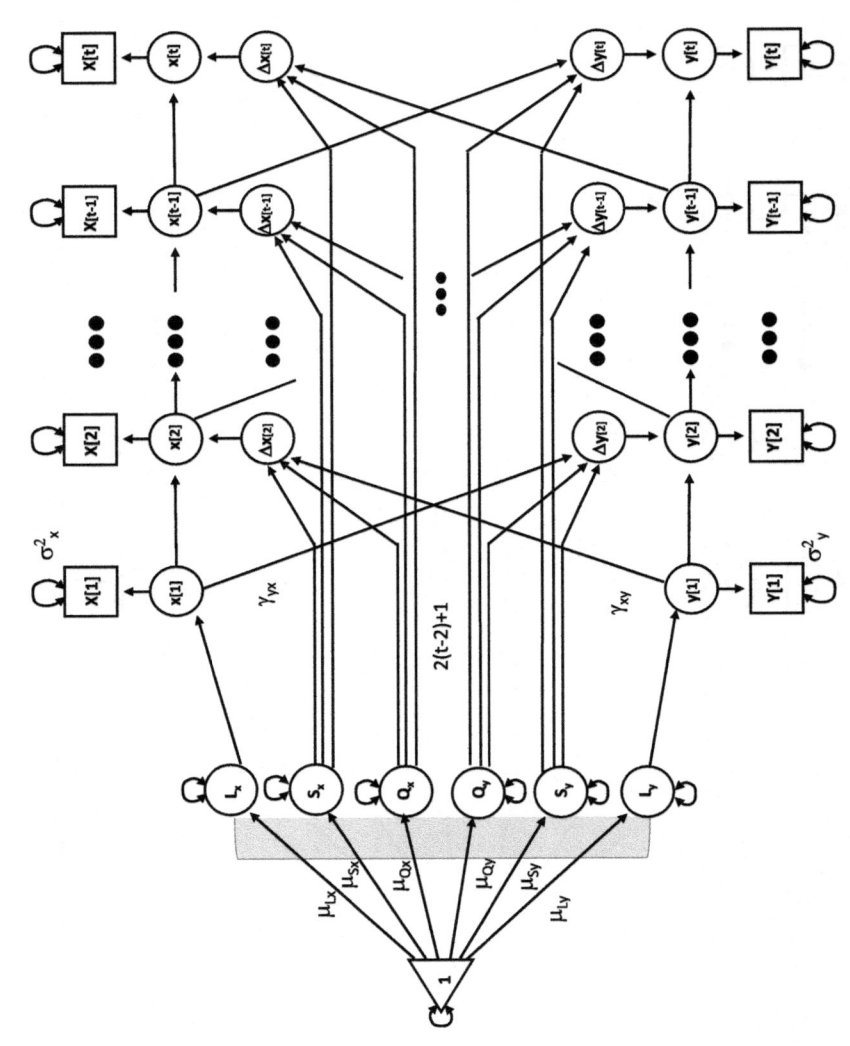

FIGURE 4.9 A path diagram of bivariate quadratic constant change score model with mutual coupling effects.

A set of simulated latent curves for a bivariate quadratic constant model is shown in Figure 4.10. Parameters of the bivariate model are as follows: means of an initial condition, a linear constant, and a quadratic constant for latent scores for y are $\mu_{Ly} = 20$, $\mu_{Sy} = 10.5$, $\mu_{Qy} = .8$; means of an initial condition, a linear constant, and a quadratic constant for latent scores for x are $\mu_{Lx} = 20$, $\mu_{Sx} = 20.5$, $\mu_{Qx} = -.7$; standard deviations of an initial condition, a linear constant, and a quadratic constant for latent scores for y are $\sigma_{Ly} = 10$, $\sigma_{Sy} = 2$, $\sigma_{Qy} = .2$; standard

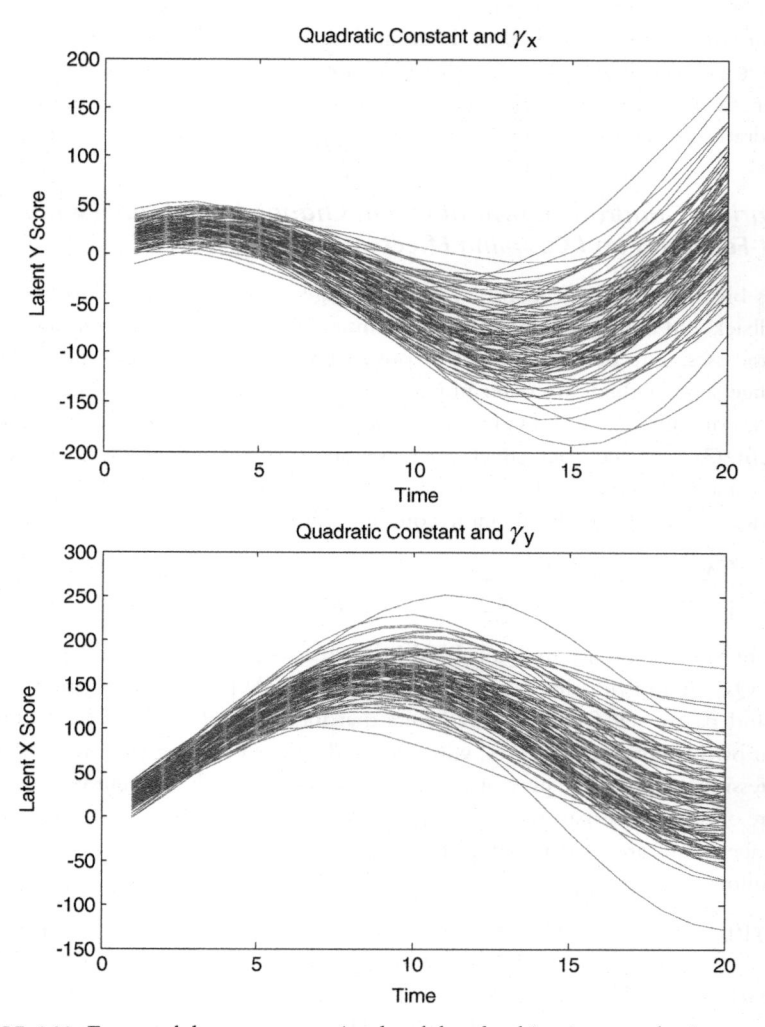

FIGURE 4.10 Expected latent curves simulated by the bivariate quadratic constant change score model with mutual coupling effects.

deviations of an initial condition, a linear constant, and a quadratic constant for latent scores for x are $\sigma_{Lx} = 10$, $\sigma_{Sx} = 2$, $\sigma_{Qx} = .2$. The coupling effect of $x[t{-}1]_i \rightarrow \Delta y[t]_i$ is $\gamma_{yx} = -.25$ and the coupling effect of $y[t-1]_i \rightarrow \Delta x[t]_i$ is $\gamma_{xy} = .25$. The model generated 100 individualized bivariate latent curves for latent variables y and x with 20 time periods. The coupling effects on the latent change scores apparently distort a simple quadratic latent curve of both x and y latent scores. It is no longer straightforward to predict latent scores of latent quadratic curves once the coupling effect is applied on the latent change score.

We also examined how strength of coupling effects would influence an overall shape of growth curves by manipulating sizes of coupling parameters. Expected latent curves of x and y dyad of different simulations do differ in terms of overall trajectories (see Figure 4.11). In these latent curves, we do not observe any characteristics of quadratic growth curves. Without coupling effects in the bivariate quadratic constant score model, all of these trajectories are quadratic curves.

Bivariate Quadratic Constant Latent Change Score Model with Self-Feedback and Coupling Effect

This bivariate quadratic constant latent change score model contains both self-feedback and coupling effects that determine latent change scores for both y and x processes. This bivariate model is constructed simply by a system of two latent change scores which are determined by four components: (1) an individualized linear constant, (2) an individualized quadratic constant with a time variant coefficient, (3) a self-feedback effect of its own process from the previous time period, and (4) a coupling effect from the preceding companion variable to its own latent change . Bivariate latent quadratic constant model is expressed as

$$
\begin{cases}
\Delta y[t]_i = Sy_i + \{2(t-2)+1\}\, Qy_i + \beta_y y[t-1]_i + \gamma_{yx} x[t-1]_i \\
\Delta x[t]_i = Sx_i + \{2(t-2)+1\}\, Qx_i + \beta_x x[t-1]_i + \gamma_{xy} y[t-1]_i
\end{cases}, \quad (4.35)
$$

where Sy_i and Sx_i are individualized linear constants for $\Delta y[t]_i$ and $\Delta x[t]_i$, Qy_i and Qx_i are individualized quadratic constants for $\Delta y[t]_i$ and $\Delta x[t]_i$, respectively. β_y and β_x are self-feedback parameters that indicate influences of past states on their own latent change scores, whilst γ_{yx} and γ_{xy} are coupling parameters that are regression effects of the previous score of one variable to the current latent change score of the counterpart (i.e., $x[t{-}1]_i \rightarrow \Delta y[t]_i$ or $y[t{-}1]_i \rightarrow \Delta x[t]_i$). These latent change scores are used to calculate the general latent score of y and x variables as follows:

$$
\begin{cases}
y[t]_i = y[t-1]_i + \Delta y[t]_i = y[t-1]_i + Sy_i + \{2(t-2)+1\}\, Qy_i + \beta_y y[t-1]_i \\
\qquad\qquad + \gamma_{yx} x[t-1]_i \\
x[t]_i = x[t-1]_i + \Delta x[t]_i = x[t-1]_i + Sx_i + \{2(t-2)+1\}\, Qx_i + \beta_x x[t-1]_i \\
\qquad\qquad + \gamma_{xy} y[t-1]_i
\end{cases}
$$

$$(4.36)$$

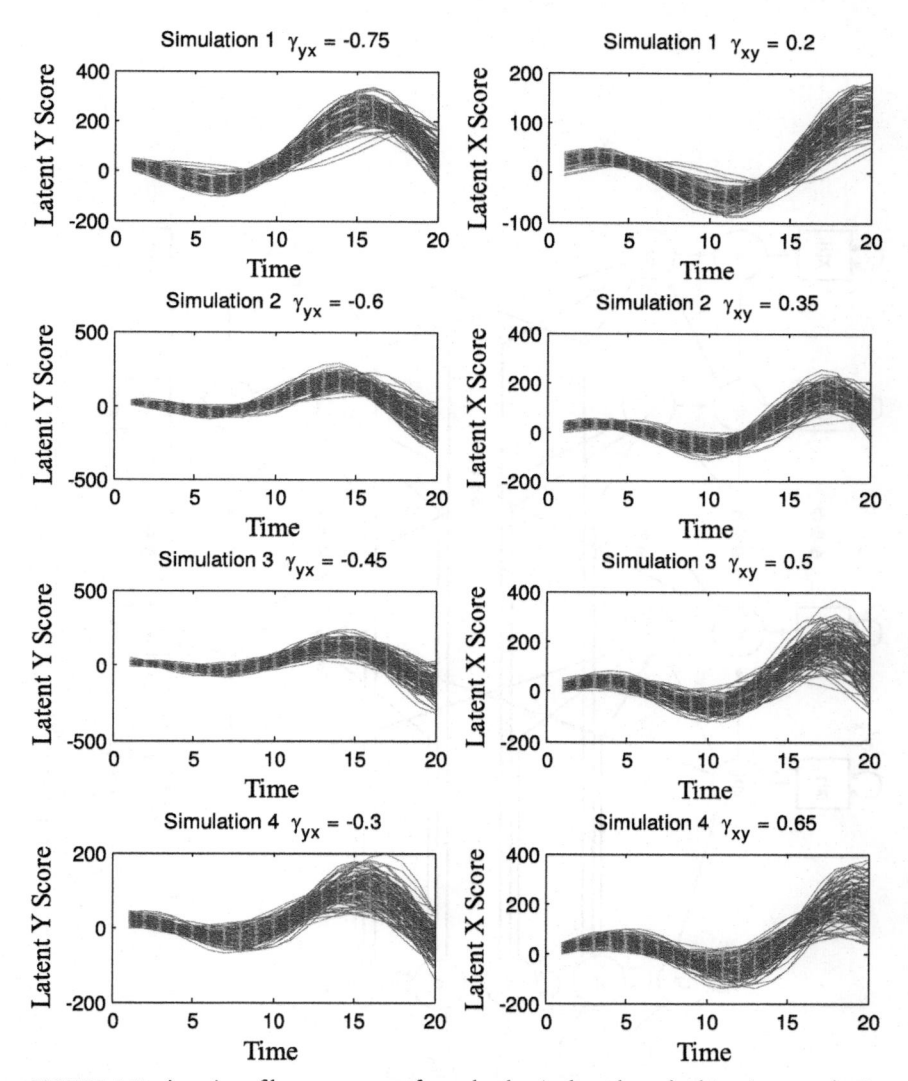

FIGURE 4.11 A series of latent curves of x-y dyad pairs based on the bivariate quadratic constant change score model with mutual coupling parameters. Four simulations differ in terms of coupling parameters.

This model assumes that there is a significant cross-lag effect of one latent variable to the latent change score of the counterpart. In addition, the autoregressive effect is considered a significant contributor in the change process. An example of a path diagram is presented in Figure 4.12.

We generated a series of simulated growth curves based on the full bivariate quadratic basis change score model. Parameters of the bivariate model are as

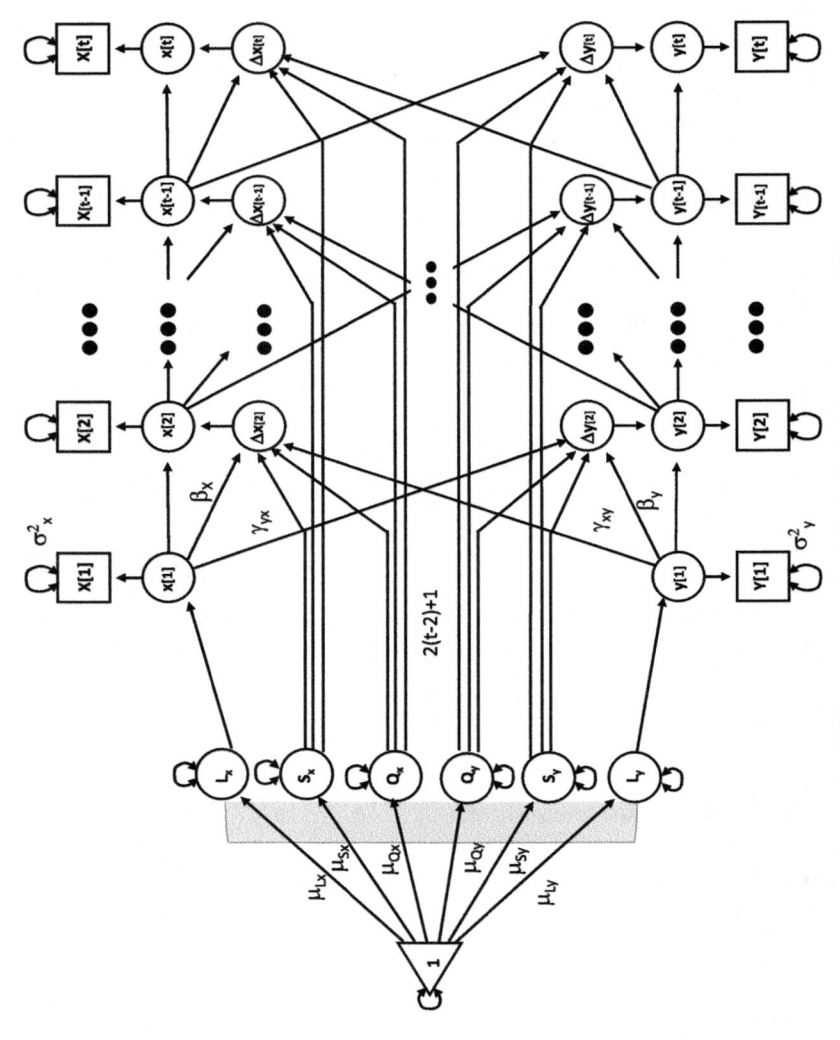

FIGURE 4.12 A path diagram representing the full bivariate quadratic basis dual change score model.

follows: means of an initial condition, a linear constant, and a quadratic constant for latent scores for y are $\mu_{Ly} = 20$, $\mu_{Sy} = 1.5$, $\mu_{Qy} = .4$; means of an initial condition, a linear constant, and a quadratic constant for latent scores for x are $\mu_{Lx} = 20$, $\mu_{Sx} = 2.5$, $\mu_{Qx} = -.6$; standard deviations of an initial condition, a linear constant, and a quadratic constant for latent scores for y are $\sigma_{Ly} = 10$, $\sigma_{Sy} = .5$, $\sigma_{Qy} = .1$; standard deviations of an initial condition, a linear constant, and a quadratic constant for latent scores for x are $\sigma_{Lx} = 10$, $\sigma_{Sx} = .5$, $\sigma_{Qx} = .1$. The coupling effect of $x[t-1]_i \to \Delta y[t]_i$ is $\gamma_{yx} = -.55$ and the coupling effect of $y[t-1]_i \to \Delta x[t]_i$ is $\gamma_{xy} = .25$. The self-feedback effect of $y[t-1]_i \to \Delta y[t]_i$ is $\beta_y = -.5$ and the coupling effect of $x[t-1]_i \to \Delta x[t]_i$ is $\beta_x = -.5$. We simulated 100 bivariate latent curves for latent variables y and x with 20 time points using above-mentioned parameters. For the next three sets of simulation, we gradually increased self-feedback parameters of both y and x by .3 for each simulation model. Thus, for Simulation 2, $\beta_x = -.2$ and $\beta_y = -.2$; for Simulation 3, $\beta_x = .1$ and $\beta_y = .1$; for Simulation 4, $\beta_x = .4$ and $\beta_y = .4$. Figure 4.13 displays these latent growth curves based on these four simulation models. These curves are nonlinear. In general, latent curves of each simulation are distinguishable from those of other simulations. These curves are characterized by irregular undulations. Some curves show multiple local minima or local maxima. These features of expected latent curves are not obtainable by the straightforward bivariate linear constant dual change score model. By just adding the quadratic constant to the bivariate model, it is apparent that the bivariate latent change score model becomes flexible enough to accommodate repeated measures data showing irregular nonlinear growth patterns.

Discussion

In the prevailing and mainstream description of the latent change score model, the additive constant is treated as a time-invariant normally distributed latent variable and each individual is assigned a distinct unique quantity (Ghisletta & McArdle, 2012; Hamagami & McArdle, 2007; McArdle, 2009; McArdle & Grimm, 2010; McArdle & Nesselroad, 2014; McArdle & Prindle, 2008). This quantity remains unchanged across time. In the new model, we proposed that this additive constant can be manipulated so that a contributive constant to a latent change score can be of a nonlinear functional form and the value of the latent constant can be time-dependent. In our delineation of the new model, we mainly used a quadratic functional form. We found that the nonlinear basis of the additive constant could dramatically influence the trajectory shape of the expected growth curve of the latent score. Even with a simple nonlinear additive constant such as a quadratic function basis, an overall growth curve exhibits multiple local minima and maxima, granted that the bivariate change score model is formed with a time dependent constant basis. This finding leads us to believe that repeated measures with overall nonlinear trajectory patterns can be applied to our new model

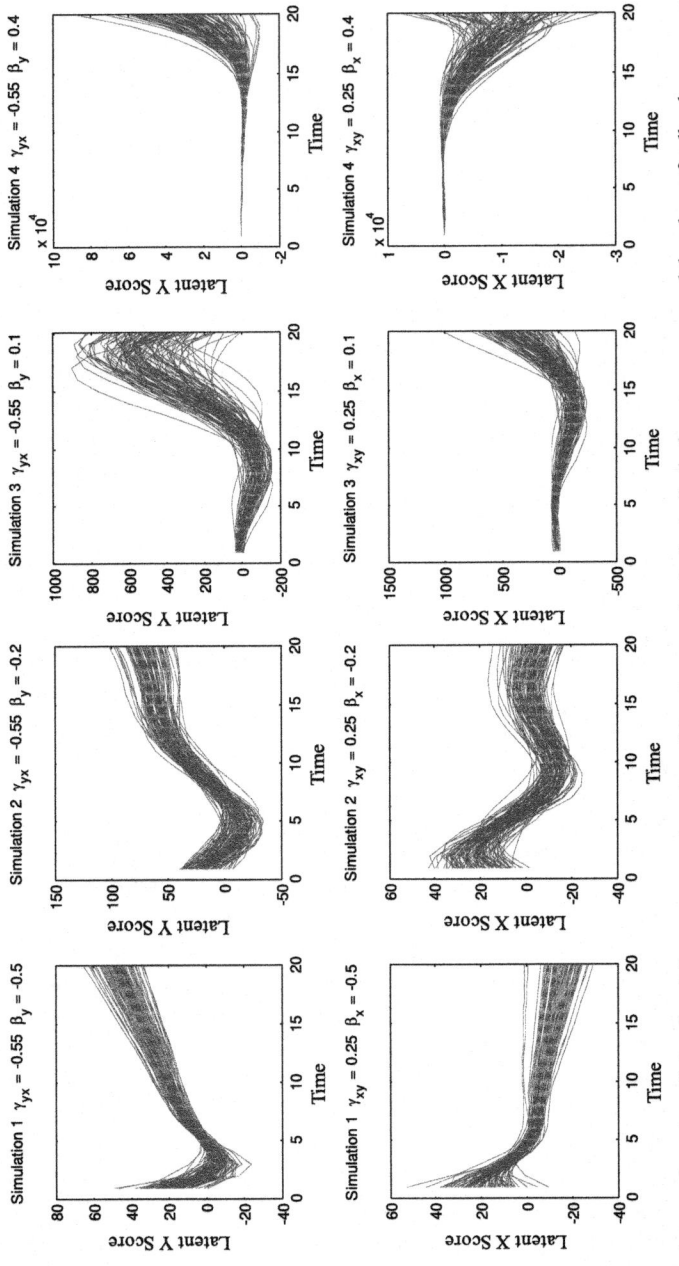

FIGURE 4.13 A series of simulated latent curves based on bivariate quadratic basis dual change score models where feedback parameters are incremented by .3 for both companion variables at each subsequent simulation model.

and test a dynamical hypothesis as to what induces change in something and still obtain a good fit to these nonlinear longitudinal data.

In view of the quadratic constant latent change score model, we can consider 10 possible alternative bivariate models to test dynamical hypotheses. They are:

(1) There is no dynamical relationship between two companion variables x and y. Within each companion variable, change scores are not influenced by their own prior states.

(2) Latent change of y is affected by the prior state of y itself, whereas latent change of x is not. There is no cross-lag impact on latent change.

(3) Latent change of y is not related by the prior state of y itself, whereas latent change of x is influenced by the previous state of x. There is no cross-lag impact on latent change.

(4) There are significant temporal relationships between latent change and the preceding state in both companion variables. However, latent change is not impacted by the opposite variable.

(5) Latent change in y is solely influenced by the prior state of the companion latent variable x, whilst latent change in x is not leveraged by the prior state of y. However, there is no self-feedback effect of either companion variable.

(6) Latent change in y is not impacted by the prior state of the companion latent variable x nor its own prior state, whilst latent change in x is under the influence of the prior state of y but not affected by its own previous state.

(7) Both latent change variables are impacted by the previous state of their counterpart alone. Mutual coupling effects are predominant determinants of change scores.

(8) Both latent change variables are impacted by their own preceding states. In addition, latent change in y is impacted by the previous state of x. Both latent changes receive significant feedback from their own previous states. However, latent change in y is influenced by the counterpart. Thus, x is dominant over y.

(9) Both latent changes receive significant feedback from its own previous state. The companion variable y dominantly affects latent change in x.

(10) The prior states in both x and y exert impact on their own latent change, as well as latent change in the companion variable.

These 10 hypotheses are summarized in Table 4.5.

In view of an additional nonlinear constant basis in latent change, we can pragmatically strategize piecemeal steps in bivariate discrete dynamical analyses. First, it is not required that a constant variable is included in the latent change score equation. Auxiliarily, it is not required that constant variables are inserted in the latent change score equations of both companion variables. It is testable that only

TABLE 4.5 A list of alternative bivariate quadratic constant score latent change score models.

Bivariate Latent Change Score Model	Determinants for latent change scores for y				Determinants for latent change scores for x			
	Lin	Quad	Feedback	Coupling	Lin	Quad	Feedback	Coupling
$\Delta y[t] = S_y + Q_y\{2(t-2)+1\}$ $\Delta x[t] = S_x + Q_x\{2(t-2)+1\}$	S_y	Q_y			S_x	Q_x		
$\Delta y[t] = S_y + Q_y\{2(t-2)+1\}+\beta_y\, y[t-1]$ $\Delta x[t] = S_x + Q_x\{2(t-2)+1\}$	S_y	Q_y	β_y		S_x	Q_x		
$\Delta y[t] = S_y + Q_y\{2(t-2)+1\}$ $\Delta x[t] = S_x + Q_x\{2(t-2)+1\}+\beta_x\, y[t-1]$	S_y	Q_y			S_x	Q_x	β_x	
$\Delta y[t] = S_y + Q_y\{2(t-2)+1\}+\beta_y\, y[t-1]$ $\Delta x[t] = S_x + Q_x\{2(t-2)+1\}+\beta_x\, y[t-1]$	S_y	Q_y	β_y		S_x	Q_x	β_x	
$\Delta y[t] = S_y + Q_y\{2(t-2)+1\}+\gamma_{yx}\, x[t-1]$ $\Delta x[t] = S_x + Q_x\{2(t-2)+1\}$	S_y	Q_y		γ_{yx}	S_x	Q_x		
$\Delta y[t] = S_y + Q_y\{2(t-2)+1\}$ $\Delta x[t] = S_x + Q_x\{2(t-2)+1\}+\gamma_{xy}\, y[t-1]$	S_y	Q_y			S_x	Q_x		γ_{xy}
$\Delta y[t] = S_y + Q_y\{2(t-2)+1\}+\gamma_{yx}\, x[t-1]$ $\Delta x[t] = S_x + Q_x\{2(t-2)+1\}+\gamma_{xy}\, y[t-1]$	S_y	Q_y		γ_{yx}	S_x	Q_x		γ_{xy}
$\Delta y[t] = S_y + Q_y\{2(t-2)+1\}+\beta_y\, y[t-1]+\gamma_{yx}\, x[t-1]$ $\Delta x[t] = S_x + Q_x\{2(t-2)+1\}+\beta_x\, y[t-1]$	S_y	Q_y	β_y	γ_{yx}	S_x	Q_x	β_x	
$\Delta y[t] = S_y + Q_y\{2(t-2)+1\}+\beta_y\, y[t-1]$ $\Delta x[t] = S_x + Q_x\{2(t-2)+1\}+\beta_x\, y[t-1]+\gamma_{xy}\, y[t-1]$	S_y	Q_y	β_y		S_x	Q_x	β_x	γ_{xy}
$\Delta y[t] = S_y + Q_y\{2(t-2)+1\}+\beta_y\, y[t-1]+\gamma_{yx}\, x[t-1]$ $\Delta x[t] = S_x + Q_x\{2(t-2)+1\}+\beta_x\, y[t-1]+\gamma_{xy}\, y[t-1]$	S_y	Q_y	β_y	γ_{yx}	S_x	Q_x	β_x	γ_{xy}

latent change in y is impacted by an additive constant, whilst that in x is not. In this case, the latent variable y has underlying linear change, while the latent variable x is characterized as stable at equilibrium, unless latent change is disturbed by the prior state of its own or the counterpart. Furthermore, it is not required that both linear and quadratic constant variables need to be inserted in the latent change equation for the quadratic latent change model. It is reasonable that only the quadratic constant is included in the change equation, leaving out the linear additive constant. When observation periods are short (e.g., 3 occasions), not only are nonlinear constant variables not necessary, but the model might be unidentifiable due to the fact that there are 21 unknown parameters of variance and covariance terms amongst initial conditions, linear constants and quadratic constants in the bivariate full quadratic model. Table 4.6 itemizes a series of specific conditions of latent change scores for x and y in terms of impact of latent constants on latent change scores. Each condition is differentiated by which and how many latent constants are specified in the bivariate latent change equation. There are 16 particularized conditions for the bivariate latent change model with additional inclusion of the quadratic constant . For each particular condition, 10 alternative models are testable as described before (see Table 4.5 for model specification). Therefore, 160 alternative bivariate quadratic constant change models in total are available in consideration of 16 distinct conditions and 10 alternative testable models for each distinct condition. As a practice, it is not needed to examine all 160 alternative models. Which models need to be tested is up to a researcher's own judgment.

When the number of measurement occasions is limited (e.g., less than 4 repeated measurements), we do not expect to see nonlinear empirical growth curves replete with irregular undulations . In this situation, it is not necessary to add a curvilinear basis to the latent change equation. On the other hand, when the frequency of measurement occasions increases and empirical growth curves are no longer straightforwardly linear, we have an opportunity to test more complex dynamic hypotheses by adding a curvilinear constant to the latent change equation. As a general rule, we might quantitatively test tenability of contending dynamical models by means of the likelihood ratio tests under the maximum likelihood estimation and weighted least square estimation approaches. However, under the robust maximum likelihood estimation when the multivariate normal distribution assumption for observed variables is violated, the Satorra-Bentler scaled Chi-square difference test need to be applied to choose the most viable model among alternative nested models (Satorra & Bentler, 2001, 2009). For example, to test dominance of the past influence of the latent score of x on the change score in y, we run two models. The null model includes two coupling parameters in the bivariate change score model. The alternative model includes only the coupling parameter from the past x latent score to the y latent change score. These two models are nested. Therefore, we can use a Chi-square difference test to see if removing one coupling parameter from the model significantly

TABLE 4.6 Alternative conditions of linear and quadratic constant bases impacting on latent change in x and y companion variables.

Conditions of latent change scores (Δy and Δx) in terms of types of additive constants	Condition Number	Impact on Δy		Impact on Δx	
		Linear Constant	Quadratic Constant	Linear Constant	Quadratic Constant
No Constant	1				
Unbalanced Linear Constant – Only Δy includes the linear constant	2	S_y			
Unbalanced Linear Constant – Only Δx includes the linear constant	3			S_x	
Balanced Linear Constant Only – both Δy and Δx include only linear constants	4	S_y		S_x	
Unbalanced Quad Constant Only – Only Δy includes the quadratic constant	5		Q_y		
Unbalanced Quad Constant Only – Only Δx includes the quadratic constant	6				Q_x
Balanced Quad Constant Only – both Δy and Δx include quadratic constants	7		Q_y		Q_x
Unbalanced Linear Quad Constant – Only Δy includes both linear and quadratic constant	8	S_y	Q_y		
Unbalanced Linear Quad Constant – Δy includes only linear constant and Δx includes only quadratic constant	9	S_y			Q_x
Unbalanced Linear Quad Constant – Δy includes only quadratic constant and Δx includes only linear constant	10		Q_y	S_x	
Unbalanced Linear Quad Constant – Only Δx includes both linear and quadratic constants	11			S_x	Q_x
Unbalanced Linear Quad Constant – Δy includes only linear constant and Δx includes both constants	12	S_y		S_x	Q_x
Unbalanced Linear Quad Constant – Δy includes both constants and Δx includes only linear constant	13	S_y	Q_y	S_x	
Unbalanced Linear Quad Constant – Δy includes only quadratic constant and Δx includes both constants	14		Q_y	S_x	Q_x
Unbalanced Linear Quad Constant – Δy includes both constants and Δx includes only quadratic constant	15	S_y	Q_y		Q_x
Balanced Full Linear Quadratic Constant	16	S_y	Q_y	S_x	Q_x

changes a numerical value of χ^2. If a model fit significantly deteriorates by setting a null constraint on one coupling parameter, then we might conclude that a coupling parameter from y to x is also needed, thus we can conclude that impacts on latent change scores are bi-lateral.

In summary, we suggested a new way to formulate latent change scores distinct from the traditional latent change score. A functional difference is made by adding nonlinear additive constant bases which are time-dependent. By doing so, we observed that overall expected growth trajectories were replete with irregular undulations, local maxima, and local minima. Thus, this new latent change model seems better suited to be tested when observed trajectories of longitudinal data follow irregular nonlinear patterns.

References

Ferrer, E., & McArdle, J. J. (2004). An experimental analysis of dynamic hypotheses about cognitive abilities and achievement from childhood to early adulthood. *Developmental Psychology, 40*, 935–952.

Ferrer, E., McArdle, J. J., Shaywitz, B. A., Holahan, J. N., Marchione, K., & Shaywitz, S. E. (2007). Longitudinal models of developmental dynamics between reading and cognition from childhood to adolescence. *Developmental Psychology, 43*, 1460–1473.

Ghisletta, P. & McArdle, J. J. (2012). Teacher's corner: Latent curve models and latent change score models estimated in R. *Structural Equation Modeling, 19*, 651–682.

Grimm, K. J. (2007). Multivariate longitudinal methods for studying developmental relationships between depression and academic achievement. *International Journal of Behavioral Development, 31*, 328–339.

Grimm, K. J. (2008). Longitudinal associations between reading and mathematics. *Developmental Neuropsychology, 33*, 410–426.

Hamagami, F. & McArdle, J. J. (2007). Dynamic extensions of latent difference score models. In S. M. Boker & M. L. Wegner (Eds.), *Quantitative methods in contemporary psychology* (pp. 47–85). Mahwah, NJ: Erlbaum.

Hishinuma, E. S., Chang, J. Y., McArdle, J. J., & Hamagami, F. (2012). Potential causal relationship between depressive symptoms and academic achievement in the Hawaiian high schools health survey using contemporary longitudinal latent variable change models. *Developmental Psychology, 48*, 1327–1342.

McArdle, J. J. (2001). A latent difference score approach to longitudinal dynamic structural analysis. In R. Cudeck, S. du Toit, and D. Sörbom (Eds.), *Structural equation modeling: Present and future. A Festschrift in honor of Karl Jöreskog* (pp. 341–380). Lincolnwood, IL: Scientific Software International.

McArdle J. J. (2009). Latent variable modeling of differences and changes with longitudinal data. *Annual Review of Psychology, 60*, 577–605

McArdle, J. J. & Grimm, K. J. (2010). Five steps in latent curve and latent change score modeling with longitudinal data. In K. van Montfor, J. H. L. Oud, & A. Satorra (Eds.), *Longitudinal research with latent variables* (pp. 245–274). New York: Springer.

McArdle, J. J. & Hamagami, F. (2001). Linear dynamic analyses of incomplete longitudinal data. In L. Collins & A. Sayer (Eds.), *New methods for the analysis of change* (pp. 137–176). Washington, DC: APA Press.

McArdle, J. J., Hamagami, F., Jones, K., Jolesz, F., Kikinis, R., Spiro, A., III, & Albert, M. S. (2004). Structural modeling of dynamic changes in memory and brain structure using longitudinal data from the normative aging study. *Journal of Gerontology: Psychological Sciences, 59B*, 294–304.

McArdle, J. J., Hamagami, F., Meredith, W., & Bradway, K. P. (2000). Modeling the dynamic hypotheses of Gf-Gc theory using longitudinal life-span data. *Learning and Individual Differences, 12*, 53–79.

McArdle, J. J. & Nesselroade, J. R. (2014). *Longitudinal data analysis using structural equation models.* Washington, DC: American Psychological Associations.

McArdle, J. J., & Prindle, J. J. (2008). A latent change score analysis of a randomized clinical trial in reasoning training. *Psychology and Aging, 23*, 702–719.

Satorra, A., & Benter, P. M. (2001). A scaled difference chi-square test statistic for moment structure analysis. *Psychometrika, 66*, 507–514.

Satorra, A., & Benter, P. M. (2009). Ensuring positiveness of the scaled difference chi-square test statistic. *Psychometrika, 75*, 243–248.

5

REGULARIZED ESTIMATION OF MULTIVARIATE LATENT CHANGE SCORE MODELS

Ross Jacobucci & Kevin J. Grimm

Regularized Estimation of Multivariate Latent Change Score Models

With longitudinal data, although a number of statistical frameworks are available for analysis, the use of structural equation modeling has become increasing popular. Hypotheses about change trajectories, determinants of change, along with other components can be formulated as a sequence of models, each representing a specific theoretical formulation. For instance, it is common to first start with a *No Change* model, typically formulated as a model with only an intercept term. Next, a *Linear Change* model can be tested, generally resulting in a better fit to the data if respondents do in fact exhibit change across the time span. Finally, various nonlinear formulations can be tested, each representing a quantitative and qualitative difference with previously tested models. Each model in the sequence tests a specific hypothesis about the functional form of change.

Although testing a sequence of models, varying in their degree of complexity, is most commonly done using the latent growth curve modeling framework (McArdle & Epstein, 1987; Meredith & Tisak, 1990), the latent change score (LCS) framework (McArdle, 2001; McArdle & Hamagami, 2001) has been used in an increasing amount of research over the last decade. The LCS model can be used to test a rich array of linear and nonlinear models, allowing researchers to examine different influences of change across time. Additionally, the LCS framework can be extended to the bivariate space (and beyond) to assess the reciprocal relationship between changes in constructs over time. It is because of these rich extensions beyond the latent growth curve modeling framework that we focus this chapter on exploring and examining additional extensions of the LCS framework. Before our discussion of various extensions that incorporate regularization, we provide a brief overview of both univariate and bivariate latent change score models.

Latent Change Score Framework

The LCS framework for studying longitudinal change shares similarities with both the autoregressive cross-lagged model (Jöreskog, 1970, 1974; Usami, Hayes, & McArdle, 2016) and the latent curve model (McArdle & Epstein, 1987; Meredith & Tisak, 1990). The LCS framework allows for the examination of both linear and nonlinear change across time (age) in the univariate case, with extensions to examining change both within and between constructs in the case of multivariate LCS models (McArdle, 2001).

Traditional testing with the LCS framework includes examining models that include *No Change*, *Constant Change*, *Proportional Change*, and finally, a combination of both proportional and constant effects in the *Dual Change Model* (McArdle & Hamagami, 2001). Beyond these four univariate models, few extensions have been proposed. Proposed extensions include the *Changes to Changes* models (Grimm, An, McArdle, Zonderman, & Resnick, 2012), *Latent Acceleration* models (Hamagami & McArdle, 2007), and Bayesian estimation for both the univariate and bivariate LCS models (Hamagami, Zhang, & McArdle, 2009).

To describe the model, we begin with true score theory where an observed score at age $t(Y[age]_n)$ for respondent n is composed of a theoretical true score $(y[age]_n)$ and a unique score $(u[age]_n)$. This can be written as

$$Y[age]_n = y[age]_n + u[age]_n. \tag{5.1}$$

In this model, change over age (time) can be seen as a difference between the true score at the current age minus true score at the age in the prior year $(age - 1)$, such that

$$\Delta y[age]_n = y[age]_n - y[age - 1]_n. \tag{5.2}$$

Across the entirety of the age span, total change manifests itself as the initial true level plus the summation of all previous true changes, such that

$$y[age]_n = y[0]_n + \sum_{r=1}^{r=age} (\Delta y[r]_n) \tag{5.3}$$

where $y[0]_n$ is the initial true level and $\sum_{r=1}^{r=age} (\Delta y[r]_n)$ is the summation of changes until the current *age*.

Univariate Latent Change Score Model. Although we omit detail regarding all of the possible specification of the univariate LCS model, we follow the specification guidelines from Grimm et al. (2012). This involves specifying four different models: (a) the proportional change model where $\Delta y[age]_n = \pi \cdot y[age - 1]_n$, where π is an estimated autoproportion parameter; (b) constant change where $\Delta y[age]_n = \alpha_{2n}$ where α_{2n} is the constant change component; (c) the dual change model which is a combination of both (a) and (b) where $\Delta y[age]_n = \alpha_{2n} + \pi \cdot y[age - 1]_n$; and (d) the changes to changes model where prior changes influence subsequent changes is added to model (c) $\Delta y[age]_n = \alpha_{2n} + \pi \cdot \gamma[age-1]_n + \phi \cdot \Delta y[age-1]_n$. Each of the four models allows for different influences of change and different degrees of nonlinearity.

Bivariate Latent Change Score Model. A fully specified bivariate model, for variables X and Y, can be written as

$$\Delta y[t]_n = \alpha_y \cdot s_{yn} + \pi_y \cdot \gamma[t-1]_n + \phi_y \cdot \Delta y[t-1]_n + \gamma_{yx} \cdot x[t-1]_n + \xi_{yx}$$
$$\cdot \Delta x[t-1]_n \tag{5.4}$$
$$\Delta x[t]_n = \alpha_x \cdot s_{xn} + \pi_x \cdot x[t-1]_n + \phi_x \cdot \Delta x[t-1]_n + \gamma_{xy} \cdot \gamma[t-1]_n + \xi_{xy}$$
$$\cdot \Delta y[t-1]_n$$

where the univariate changes to changes model is specified in addition to coupling parameters, γ and ξ, where effects from the other variable are included. The two coupling parameters add influence from the previous time and the prior latent change of the other variable, respectively. This results in fitting seven models: (a) no coupling; (b) only γ_{yx}; (c) only γ_{xy}; (d) both γ_{yx} and γ_{xy}; (e) model d $+\xi_{yx}$; (f) model d $+\xi_{xy}$; (g) model d $+\xi_{yx}$ and ξ_{xy}. A path diagram of the bivariate changes to changes model is depicted in Figure 5.1. Parameter labels in Figure 5.1 correspond to the specification in Equation 5.4, with latent variables depicted as circles and observed variables as squares. Following Grimm and colleagues (2012), the best fitting univariate model from each scale is then used in the bivariate LCS models, which tests the coupling between constructs X and Y.

Choosing a final model is typically done using one of multiple information criteria, such as the Akaike Information Criteria (AIC; Akaike, 1973), the Bayesian Information Criteria (BIC; Schwarz, 1978), and the sample size-adjusted Bayesian information criterion (aBIC; Sclove, 1987). There are deficiencies in using information criteria to choose amongst LCS models (Usami et al., 2016); however, using absolute fit indices can be difficult because in many cases the covariance coverage is low, preventing the calculation of such fit indices based on a saturated model.

The choice of a final bivariate (and univariate) model tells a very distinct story regarding the dynamic relationship between the variables of interest. For example, if model *b* fits best, this leads us to believe that the previous level of X exerts a significant influence on subsequent change in Y, whereas not including the same relationship from Y to changes in X does not significantly impact model fit, leading us to believe this relationship may not hold in the population. Additionally, the same interpretation holds if either models *e* or *f* fit best, but instead pointing to the significant influence that previous change in one variable has on subsequent change on the other variable. Despite the complexity of each bivariate model, each subsequent model only examines the influence of one additional parameter, allowing us to examine nuanced relationships between both X and Y.

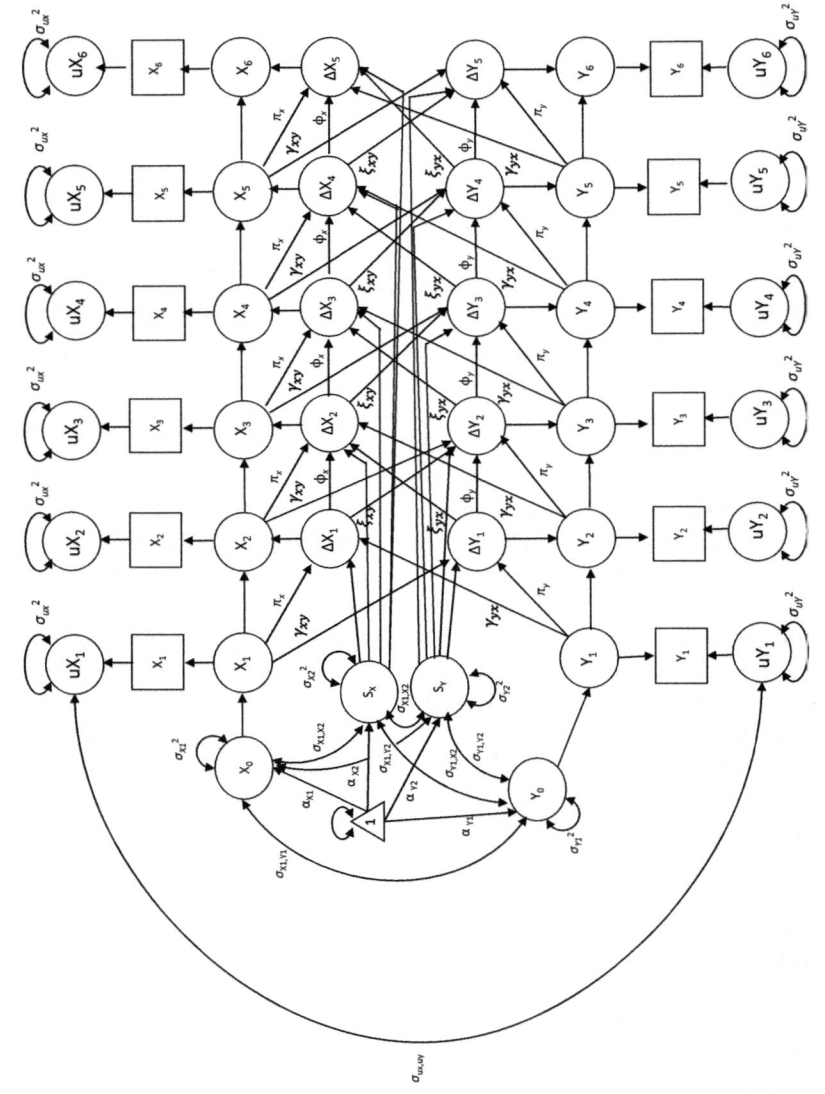

FIGURE 5.1 Diagram of the Bivariate Latent Change Score Model.

Exploratory Model Specification and Testing

With longitudinal SEM, most work has been focused on confirmatory modeling – the sequence of models is specified *a priori*, each corresponding to a competing theoretical formulation of change. Less work has focused on exploratory modeling. The work on exploratory modeling has focused in the context of latent growth curve models (McArdle & Epstein, 1987; Meredith & Tisak, 1990). In this, models can be tested with anywhere from a linear model with fixed factor loadings from the slope, to the latent basis growth model, which can be seen as an exploratory approach to determining the optimal shape of development (Grimm, Steele, Ram, & Nesselroade, 2013).

Despite work on exploratory modeling of change, increasing the flexibility *across* models, not just *within*, has received far less research. For example, testing the no change, linear change, and nonlinear change models represents a *discrete* form of model testing, with no flexibility in testing models that lie in between each of these formulations. This form of testing can be altered to introduce flexibility into the model testing sequence by constraining individual parameters in each model. For instance, maximum likelihood estimation (MLE) of the linear growth curve model adds freely estimated mean and variance parameters to the latent variable slope factor. The addition of constraints on the mean and variance of the slope factor results in a model that exists somewhere in the continuum between a *no change* and *linear change* models. Where in this continuum depends on the level of constraint, a smaller constraint results in parameter estimates closer to *linear change* model, whereas a greater constraint is closer to the *no change* model.

One particular scenario that proves problematic when using discrete model selection is when one of the models fails to converge. For instance, when the amount of incompleteness is high, the LCS model has increasing amounts of nonconvergence (O'Rourke, Grimm, & MacKinnon, 2017). The question that remains is how to interpret a model that has not converged. Particularly in the case when the most complex model (nonlinear change) does not converge, does this mean that linear change is the best fitting model? This dilemma is purely a product of discrete model fitting, where there is a large jump in complexity from one model to the next in the sequence. By increasing the flexibility in model testing, allowing for a continuum of models to be tested, it provides the opportunity to glean the maximum amount of information from a dataset.

Rationale

To overcome a number of these limitations in LCS model testing, we propose the incorporation of regularization (described below) for constraining parameters within the LCS model to allow for simpler, more flexible model testing. Particularly using the dual change score model, this allows us to test models ranging from highly nonlinear, to linear, to the intercept only models. Ultimately, this simplifies the model testing procedure. Furthermore, this approach is particularly useful in models where parameters are typically constrained to be equal over time, which is often the case in LCS models. For example, the autoproportion parameter is often constrained to be equal over time (in the dual change model) and it is difficult to detect efficiently where invariance may or may not hold. The same is true for bivariate LCS models as the autoproportion and coupling parameters are often constrained to be equal over time.

In this chapter, we introduce multiple ways for regularization to be used with the LCS model. One of these is a proposal of a penalized difference approach, where penalties are applied to the difference between the constrained estimates (parameters estimates are the same across time) and freely estimated effects. We also demonstrate the use of penalizing parameters in the bivariate LCS models. In this, we use a hierarchical approach to test the range of models, ranging from *no* to *full* coupling, with one, instead of four models (or seven if including changes to changes coupling). To understand this form of model testing, we first present an overview of regularization and how this can be incorporated into both frequentist and Bayesian SEM estimation.

Regularization

The question that remains in testing models that lie on the continuum between traditionally specified models is how to systematically estimate models with constraints on specific parameter estimates. In the past, users of LISREL were able to place interval restrictions on parameter estimates (Rindskopf, 2012). However, this did not represent a systematic method that relied on a fit criterion to choose amongst many possible restrictions that could be placed on a parameter. In contrast, the method of regularization tests a sequence of models, each placing a varying degree of constraint on individual parameter estimates, while typically choosing among the sequence of constraints by examining performance on a holdout sample. The two most common forms of regularization are *Ridge Regression* (Hoerl & Kennard, 1970) and the *Least Absolute Shrinkage and Selection Operator* (Lasso; Tibshirani, 1996). In the case of using ordinary least squares regression, Lasso estimates can be found by optimizing the expression

$$\sum_{i=1}^{n} \left(Y_i - \beta_0 - \sum_{p=1}^{P} \beta_p X_{ip} \right)^2 + \lambda \sum_{p=1}^{P} |\beta_p| \qquad (5.5)$$

In Equation 5.5, the left side of the expression is the traditional residual sum of squares from OLS regression. λ is a constant, such that $\lambda \geq 0$. In Lasso regression, the l_1-norm (absolute value) is used, instead of l_2-norm (squared) as in Ridge. In Lasso, the β parameters shrink and, in many cases, β parameters are shrunken all the way to zero; thus performing a form of subset selection (for more detail, see Hastie, Tibshirani, & Friedman, 2009; Tibshirani, 1996). Although there are a number of sparser penalties available (see Jacobucci, 2017), one worth detailing is the adaptive lasso (Zou, 2006). In this, each penalized parameter is scaled by its maximum likelihood estimate, which overcomes the propensity for the lasso to over-constrain large parameters (Fan & Li, 2001).

In the context of frequentist regularization, both Lasso and Ridge regression has been extended for use with SEMs, termed regularized structural equation modeling (RegSEM; Jacobucci, Grimm, & McArdle, 2016). RegSEM builds upon the traditional maximum likelihood (ML) fit function for SEM models,

$$F_{ML} = \log(|\Sigma|) + tr\left(C * \Sigma^{-1}\right) - \log(|C|), \tag{5.6}$$

and adds an element to the cost function

$$F_{regsem} = F_{ML} + \lambda P(\cdot). \tag{5.7}$$

where λ is the regularization parameter, taking on a value between zero and infinity, and $P(\cdot)$ is a general function for summing parameters. When λ is zero, ML estimation is performed.

Particularly in more complex SEM models, due to the highly constrained nature of regularization, RegSEM convergence can be problematic. It is in this domain that Bayesian forms of regularization may be most useful. In the same way that frequentist regularization has been extended to SEM from regression, Bayesian regularization has been detailed in the context of regression (e.g. Kyung, Gill, Ghosh, & Casella, 2010; Park & Casella, 2008) as well as in SEM (Guo, Zhu, Chow, & Ibrahim, 2012; Feng, Wu, & Song, 2017; Jacobucci & Grimm, 2017; Lu, Chow, & Loken, 2016; Muthén & Asparouhov, 2012).

For Bayesian estimation, specific to our purpose is the recent implementation of M*plus*' (Muthén & Muthén, 1998–2015) Bayesian SEM (Muthén & Asparouhov, 2012) small variance priors. Similar in a sense to using previous research to inform the choice of the prior distribution, the use of small variance priors that are centered around zero restricts the influence of non-target (e.g. cross-loadings) parameters. Small variance priors can lead to less biased estimates compared to when small parameter estimates, not of empirical interest, are inappropriately constrained to zero. This allows for more flexibility in model creation, where, through the use of restrictive priors, unimportant or uninformative parameters can be pared away.

The use of small variance priors in Bayesian estimation has been formulated equivalently with regularization in frequentist regression (Kyung et al., 2010; Park & Casella, 2008, Tibshirani, 1996). That is, decreasing the prior variance in Bayesian estimation is equivalent to increasing the level of penalization in frequentist regularization. In the case of Ridge regression, a small variance prior with a normal distribution is used to constrain estimates and the Ridge estimate is the mean of the posterior distribution (Park & Casella, 2008; Tibshirani, 1996). In the case of Lasso regression, a small variance prior with a Laplace distribution is used to constrain estimates and the Lasso estimate is the mode of the posterior distribution (Park & Casella, 2008; Tibshirani, 1996).

Although there are a number of different formulations of Bayesian regularization, for the purposes of the applications in this chapter, we will focus on the hierarchical adaptive Lasso prior, in line with Feng et al. (2017), of which we will term the Bayesian adaptive Lasso (BaLasso). A hierarchical model is one in which a prior on a specific parameter is further given a probabilistic specification, known as a hyperparameter (see Chapter 5 in Gelman, Carlin, Stern, & Rubin, 2014). In contrast to testing multiple different prior variances (e.g. 30 models) to find a best-fitting final model, the use of a hierarchical prior allows for testing only one model, using the data to explicitly estimate the optimal prior on the parameters of interest.

Purpose

Our goal in pairing the LCS model with regularization is to demonstrate a more flexible approach to model testing. This will be demonstrated through the use of three examples, each demonstrating different types of penalties. The first adds penalties to the proportional change parameter in the dual change model, testing varying degrees of nonlinearity to the expected trajectory. The second example proposes a two-step procedure to capture the difference between allowing the proportional change parameter to be freely estimated across time and constraining the proportional change parameter to be invariant across time. This procedure allows us to test whether the assumption of constraining this parameter over time holds. In the third example, we add penalties to the coupling parameters in the bivariate LCS model, necessitating the testing of only one, instead of multiple models. Programming scripts for each example are available from both author's websites.

Univariate LCS Regularization

To provide a more concrete example of the use of both types of regularization, we examine both BaLasso and RegSEM methods with the dual change model and longitudinal data from the Wechsler Intelligence Scale for Children dataset ($N = 204$; Osborne & Suddick, 1972), which contains four measurement occasions (ages 6, 7, 9, and 11 years). For this analysis, we used the verbal scale. This examination can be conceptualized as testing whether the addition of the proportional change parameter, which increases the nonlinearity in the individual trajectory, is necessary and allows us to test models ranging from the constant change model to the dual change model. All parameters in the dual change model are either freely estimated or given diffuse priors[1] (see Hamagami et al., 2009), outside of the penalties (RegSEM) and small variance priors (BaLasso) added to the proportional change. In RegSEM, the fit function becomes

$$F_{regsem} = F_{ML} + \lambda|\pi|. \tag{5.8}$$

Starting with an unpenalized model ($\lambda = 0$), we tested 40 penalty values, ranging from $\lambda = 0$ to $\lambda = 3.9$ in increments of .1. For the BaLasso, the prior on π was

$$\pi \sim N(0, \psi_j \tau_j^2)$$

$$\tau_j^2 \sim Gamma(1, \frac{\gamma_j^2}{2}) \tag{5.9}$$

$$\psi_j^{-1} \sim Gamma(\alpha, \beta)$$

$$\gamma_j^2 \sim Gamma(\alpha, \beta)$$

with α set to 1 and β as .05 following the recommendations by Feng et al. (2017). This prior on a prior, resulting in a gamma mixture of normals, capitalizes on the fact that the Laplace distribution can be expressed as a scale mixture of normal distributions with independent exponentially distribution variances (i.e. Gamma with $\alpha = 1$; Andrews & Mallows, 1974). In comparison to the M*plus* small variance priors, which put a normal distribution prior on each parameter, the formulation in Equation 5.9 results in mean posterior distribution estimates that are closer to zero, while also allowing some estimates to be closer to what they would be with diffuse priors. One can think of this as a diffuse prior for significant parameters that influence the fit of the model, and highly constrained priors for those parameters that are not influential. Models were estimated in the R statistical environment (R Core Team, 2017) using the `regsem` package (Jacobucci, 2017) for the RegSEM Lasso model, and the `rjags` package (Plummer, 2016) to interface JAGS (Plummer, 2003) for the BaLasso model.

The maximum likelihood and the Bayesian estimation with diffuse prior results are displayed in Table 5.1. For the RegSEM results, the BIC only got worse (higher) as the value of the penalty increased and the model failed to converge when the penalty reached 2.2. Thus, using RegSEM, we concluded that the unpenalized dual change model was the best fitting model. For BaLasso, the model converged after 100,000 samples with thinning equal to 3. The mean estimates from the posterior distributions are displayed in Table 5.1.

The interesting thing to note is how the mean of the constant change component (α_2) was shrunken towards the estimate from the constant change model, 4.67 (other parameters not displayed). This occurs due to the dependence between the proportional change parameter and the mean of the slope. As the proportional change parameter was shrunken towards zero, the mean of the slope correspondingly moved towards the parameter estimate in the constant change model. As a result, the BaLasso model only resulted in a small amount of shrinkage towards the constant change model. Given the results from both RegSEM and BaLasso, we concluded that the dual change model was appropriate for this data,

TABLE 5.1 Parameter estimates for the dual change score model.

Parameters	MLE	Diffuse Bayes	BaLasso
α_1	19.17	19.17	19.22
α_2	−1.84	−1.88	−1.34
π	0.43	0.43	0.40
σ_1^2	18.35	18.23	18.40
σ_2^2	1.14	1.16	1.06
σ_{12}	−2.91	−2.84	−2.37
σ^2	11.19	11.41	11.46
Fit	BIC = 5028	DIC = 4586	DIC = 4587

Note: BIC = the Bayesian Information Criterion; DIC = the Deviance Information Criterion; α is the mean of the intercept (α_1) and the slope (α_2); σ is the variance of the intercept (σ_1^2), the slope (σ_2^2), and the covariance between slope and intercept (σ_{12}); σ^2 is the residual variance at each time point, constrained to be equal across time.

as the BaLasso model led to a small amount of shrinkage and RegSEM chose a model equivalent to the unpenalized maximum likelihood estimation. Given this, there is an important proportional effect from the previous time point leading to the subsequent change, in addition to the additive effect on change from the constant change component. This results in a nonlinear model, comprising both linear and proportional change.

In a second step, we tested whether the nonlinear change was influenced from the previous time point (proportional change), the previous change (changes to changes), or both (model *d* in the univariate formulation). This involves testing a fully specified univariate model, and penalizing both the autoproportion and changes to changes parameters. However, similar to penalizing the autoproportion parameter, the best fitting model, across regularization methods, kept both parameters as non–zero. As a result, we do not present these results further.

Time-Varying Effects Regularization

The problems with non–convergence in the LCS model creates problems not only in model selection, but also in parameter estimation. Furthermore, the proportional change parameters are often held invariant across time, but this assumption is rarely challenged or tested. This constraint is imposed for theoretical interpretation, but also to limit the number of freely estimated parameters as a way to prevent problems with estimation. To overcome these limitations when fitting LCS models, we propose a two-step procedure that we term the *penalized difference* approach. In this, we can use either Bayesian or frequentist forms of regularization.

This two-step process can be accomplished in the following manner. In the first step, the autoproportion parameters are constrained to be equal across time, resulting in a single estimate. In the second step, a deviation parameter is created, capturing the difference between the time-varying parameter estimate and the time-constrained estimate at each time point. Thus, any parameter estimate that differs meaningfully from the invariant estimate should have a deviation parameter that is non-zero. This can be used as a final, more flexible model, or to inform subsequent analyses that incorporate adjustments to the initial model to take into account the time-varying effects discovered in the second step. Note that one alternative procedure is to use the estimate from step one as the prior mean for each parameter in the second step. We prefer to use the penalized difference approach, as it captures the amount that each autoproportion parameter *deviates* from the invariance assumption.

To examine this two-step procedure, we conducted a small-scale simulation study. We simulated data adhering to the dual change model with six time points and a sample of 500. The proportional change parameter was simulated to have an estimate of 0 for the first two change factors, and 0.2 for the last three change factors. Using 100 replications, we compared two models using both frequentist and Bayesian regularization. In the first step, the invariance model constrained the autoproportion parameter to be equal over time. In the second model, the parameter estimate for the autoproportion parameter in the first model was used to create a deviation parameter. In this, each proportional change parameter was

$$\pi_j = \pi_1 + dev_j.$$
$$dev_j \sim N(0, .01) \tag{5.10}$$

where π_j is the autoproportion parameter at time j, π_1 is the autoproportion parameter from model 1, and dev_j is the deviation parameter at time j. For the prior on dev_j we chose a small variance normal distribution (Ridge) with a variance of .01. Our main concern was not deriving posterior mean estimates at zero, but instead to capture an interpretable deviation parameter, while also removing bias from other model parameters.

For frequentist regularization, estimation was formulated as

$$F_{diffLasso} = F_{ML} + \lambda |dev_j| \tag{5.11}$$

where dev_j is the vector of deviations for each freely estimated π_j from the estimate of π in step 1 using ML. Although we could have used one of multiple types of penalty, we chose the Lasso for its ability to set the deviations to 0. In this, although the unconstrained estimates start at points away from π and their simulated estimates, as the penalty increases, these parameters become closer and closer to π. Because of difficulties in deriving the effective degrees of freedom in this approach, we used five-fold cross-validation and the Chi-square fit statistic to choose a final model.

TABLE 5.2 Percent bias for each method.

	Simulated	Inv.	Free	Bayes	diffLasso
Parameters					
α_1	1.00	−0.56	−0.39	−0.73	−0.03
α_2	1.00	−32.24	9.19	3.99	−5.10
π_1	0	26.07	−9.17	3.15	5.77
π_2	0	26.07	−4.62	4.42	2.82
π_3	0.20	6.07	−2.93	0.19	1.67
π_4	0.20	6.07	−2.10	0.61	0.98
π_5	0.20	6.07	−1.08	1.02	1.07
σ_1^2	0.50	−7.87	0.32	−0.98	−1.72
σ_2^2	0.50	−17.41	12.14	6.47	−0.46
σ_{12}	0.10	−5.54	2.40	0.74	−1.35
σ^2	1.00	0.75	0.32	−0.29	0.01

Note: α is the mean of the intercept (α_1) and the slope (α_2); σ is the variance of the intercept (σ_1^2), the slope (σ_2^2), and the covariance between slope and intercept (σ_{12}); σ^2 is the residual variance at each time point, constrained to be equal across time. Inv. refers to the model with invariant autoproportion parameters, Free to the model with freely estimated autoproportion parameters, Bayes and diffLasso refer to both Bayesian and RegSEM estimation, respectively, of the peanlized difference method.

The percent bias for each method is displayed in Table 5.2. For the autoproportion parameters, both the invariant model and the model that freely estimated each parameter had the largest amounts of bias. Difficulties in the estimation of these parameters resulted in biased estimates for the slope mean for each of the four models. For the entire model, both the Bayesian and diffLasso models has lower amounts of bias in comparison to both ML models. In comparing both of these models that used deviation parameters, Bayesian estimation resulted in higher bias for the slope variance, while the diffLasso model had high bias for the slope mean and for the first autoproportion parameter. However, differences in performance were almost negligible. Therefore, preference for one form of difference estimation can be given to software familiarity, as each require completely dissimilar frameworks for testing.

Bivariate LCS Regularization

To demonstrate the utility of conducting regularized estimation with the bivariate LCS model, we used both the verbal and performance scales from the WISC dataset. Traditionally, in the bivariate LCS model, the following sequence of models are tested: no coupling, X to Y coupling, Y to X coupling, and dual coupling. Omitting the ξ parameters, the dual coupling model is depicted in Figure 5.1. Once these four models are tested, one or multiple of various fit indices are used to choose a best fitting model. However, as mentioned before, this model testing procedure can be hampered by non-convergence of specific solutions, leaving researchers with uncertainty regarding what model is best, and what this says about the underlying relationship between processes.

The model testing procedure that we propose for bivariate LCS models is similar to what was used with the dual change model. Instead of penalizing the proportional change parameter, we add BaLasso[2] priors to both coupling parameters. This can be seen as a hierarchical form of testing, one that encompasses the four models traditionally used in the model testing sequence. If either or both of the coupling parameters are estimated as non-significant, with mean posterior estimates near zero, this leads us to believe that this directional parameter is unnecessary to understand the dynamic relationship between the two constructs. More so, this one step procedure simplifies the model testing process for researchers, whilst allowing a greater degree of flexibility in constraining the model to adhere to previous knowledge in the subject area. Additionally, we included the RegSEM adaptive lasso. The sequence of penalties was added to both coupling parameters, using the BIC to choose among this sequence of models.

The same prior specification as depicted in Equation 5.9 was used for both coupling parameters, while all other parameters were estimated using diffuse priors as specified in Hamagami, Zhang, and McArdle (2009). The results are displayed in Table 5.3.

In examining the coupling parameters in Table 5.3, it is clear that the path from verbal to performance is much stronger than the reciprocal path. The coupling parameter from performance to verbal was estimated as near zero with the BaLasso, and was zero with RegSEM ALasso, whereas the other coupling parameter had a much larger estimate, which was *significant* according to the credible intervals. Therefore, according to this model, we concluded that prior levels of verbal ability influenced future changes in performance ability. More specifically, those that were higher in prior verbal ability had greater subsequent increases in performance ability.

Discussion

The purpose of this chapter was to introduce a number of novel methods that increase the flexibility in assessing longitudinal change with the LCS framework. We proposed three different strategies: penalizing the proportional change parameter; assessing invariance of the autoproportion parameter by using a penalized difference approach; and finally a single hierarchical model to test the presence of coupling in the bivariate LCS model. Our focus is less on the three specific examples, and more on the introduction of a new way of thinking about model evaluation. The use of both frequentist and Bayesian regularization methods opens the door to many more types of application than just the three detailed here.

TABLE 5.3 Parameter estimates for the bivariate LCS model.

Parameters	BaLasso		RegSEM ALasso
	Mean	95% Int	Est.
α_{V1}	19.29	18.59, 20.00	19.25
α_{V2}	−2.27	−4.48, −.02	−2.23
α_{P1}	18.37	17.15, 19.61	18.30
α_{P2}	1.27	−1.19, 3.51	1.03
π_V	.42	.22, .62	.45
π_P	−.37	−.54, −.19	−.41
σ_{V1}^2	17.43	13.02, 22.06	18.22
σ_{V2}^2	.99	.33, 1.75	1.04
$\sigma_{V1,V2}$	−2.75	−5.01, −.56	−3.03
σ_{P1}^2	56.51	42.47, 70.82	58.76
σ_{P2}^2	4.93	2.52, 7.37	5.53
$\sigma_{P1,P2}$	2.76	−2.07, 7.90	2.92
$\sigma_{V1,P1}$	26.36	19.99, 33.35	26.31
$\sigma_{V2,P2}$	.83	.07, 1.63	1.00
$\sigma_{V1,P2}$	−3.39	−6.17, −.79	−4.04
$\sigma_{V2,P1}$	−3.51	−7.24, −.24	−3.48
σ_V^2	12.18	10.47, 13.87	11.68
σ_P^2	22.13	19.33, 24.95	21.50
$\gamma_{V,P}$	.74	.51, .97	0.80
$\gamma_{P,V}$	.03	−.01, .18	0

Note: α is the mean of the intercept (α_1) and the slope (α_2); $\gamma_{V,P}$ is the coupling parameter from Verbal to Performance; σ is the variance of the intercept (σ_1^2), the slope (σ_2^2), and the covariance between slope and intercept (σ_{12}); σ^2 is the residual variance at each time point, constrained to be equal across time. For RegSEM ALasso, the BIC was used to choose a final model.

Regularization allows for more flexibility, in both simplifying the model testing process, while promoting the incorporation of more complex specifications.

With the three proposed methods that alter the way of testing LCS models, additional simulation work is required to understand the settings in which the methods work or do not work. Particularly with the bivariate coupling, simulation studies are warranted to test whether using sparse hierarchical priors captures the true model better than discrete model testing. Specifically, given that the influence of a prior is determined by the sample size, this hierarchical approach is expected to demonstrate variability in performance across both small and large sample sizes.

Across the three examples, one limitation to RegSEM was problems with convergence, derived from pairing constrained estimation with a model that was highly constrained to begin with. As the RegSEM optimization methods (see Jacobucci, 2017) improve, we expect increased pairing of RegSEM with the various LCS models. In the second example, with penalizing the difference with the time–constrained parameter estimate, a frequentist penalization method has been worked out with RegSEM. This entails directly adding the difference between the time-constrained estimate and current parameter estimate to Equation 5.11. However, a number of difficulties remain in implementing this approach. In the future, particularly with large sample sizes, we expected RegSEM to hold an advantage in this form of testing given the ability of RegSEM Lasso to push parameter estimates all the way to zero, thus simplifying the process of variable/parameter selection.

The use of the hierarchical BaLasso is just one implementation of hierarchical Bayesian regularization methods. In comparison to the BaLasso, two specific methods that accomplish setting parameter estimates to zero are the spike-and-slab (Ishwaran & Rao, 2005; Lu et al. 2016; O'Hara & Sillanpää, 2009) and Horseshoe (Carvalho, Polson, & Scott, 2009) priors (see Jacobucci & Grimm, 2017 for a comparison in SEM). Particularly with large models, setting parameters directly to zero could be advantageous, due to simplifying inference. We expect an increased incorporation of Bayesian regularization into structural equation models in the future.

In conclusion, this chapter introduced a framework for incorporating regularization into the LCS framework. Across both univariate and bivariate LCS models, using both frequentist and Bayesian regularization allowed for a simplified process in choosing a *best* model, while also increasing the plasticity of the LCS model to incorporate additional parameterizations. We expect that researchers are able tailor their specific research questions to incorporate aspects of the three examples presented. The three novel ways of pairing regularization and the LCS model represent a small subset of possible applications and modifications. We look forward to seeing additional proposals in this arena going forward.

Notes

1 Note that in this specification, outside the context of regularization, both the frequentist and Bayesian specifications are expected to give similar results (Hamagami et al., 2009).
2 We solely use the BaLasso with the Bivariate model given problems with RegSEM and model convergence. The complex, highly constrained nature of the Bivariate LCS model make frequentist estimation particularly problematic.

References

Akaike, H. (1973). Information theory and an extension of the maximum likelihood principle. In B. N. Petrov & F. Csaki (Eds.), *Second International Symposium on Information Theory.* (pp. 267–281). Budapest: Akademiai Kiado.

Andrews, D. F. and Mallows, C. L. (1974). Scale mixtures of normal distributions. *Journal of the Royal Statistical Society. Series B, 36*, 99–102.

Carvalho, C. M., Polson, N. G., & Scott, J. G. (2009). Handling sparsity via the horseshoe. Journal of Machine Learning Research W&CP, *5*(73–80), 2009.

Gelman, A., Carlin, J. B., Stern, H. S., & Rubin, D. B. (2014). Bayesian data analysis (Vol. 2). Boca Raton, FL Chapman & Hall/CRC.

Grimm, K. J., An, Y., McArdle, J. J., Zonderman, A. B., & Resnick, S. M. (2012). Recent changes leading to subsequent changes: Extensions of multivariate latent difference score models. *Structural Equation Modeling: A Multidisciplinary Journal, 19*, 268–292.

Grimm, K. J., Steele, J. S., Ram, N., & Nesselroade, J. R. (2013). Exploratory latent growth models in the structural equation modeling framework. *Structural Equation Modeling: A Multidisciplinary Journal, 20*, 568–591.

Guo, R., Zhu, H., Chow, S.-M., & Ibrahim, J. G. (2012). Bayesian lasso for semiparametric structural equation models. *Biometrics, 68*, 567–577.

Fan, J., & Li, R. (2001). Variable selection via nonconcave penalized likelihood and its oracle properties. *Journal of the American Statistical Association, 96*(456), 1348–1360.

Feng, X.-N., Wu, H.-T., & Song, X.-Y. (2017). Bayesian regularized multivariate generalized latent variable models. *Structural Equation Modeling: A Multidisciplinary Journal, 24*(3), 341–358.

Hamagami, F., & McArdle, J. J. (2007). Dynamic extensions of latent difference score models. In S. M. Boker, & M. J. Wenger (Eds.), *Data analytic techniques for dynamical systems*. Mahwah, NJ: Lawrence Erlbaum Associates.

Hamagami, F., Zhang, Z., & McArdle, J. J. (2009). Modeling latent difference score models using Bayesian algorithms. In S. M. Chow, E. Ferrer, & F. Hsieh (Eds), *Statistical methods for modeling human dynamics: An interdisciplinary dialogue* (pp. 319–348). New Jersey: Lawrence Erlbaum Associates.

Hastie, T., Tibshirani, R., & Friedman, J. (2009). *The elements of statistical learning*. New York Springer.

Hoerl, A. E. & Kennard, R. W. (1970). Ridge regression: Biased estimation for nonorthogonal problems. *Technometrics, 12*(1), 55–67.

Ishwaran, H. & Rao, J. S. (2005). Spike and slab variable selection: frequentist and Bayesian strategies. *Annals of Statistics, 33*, 730–773.

Jacobucci, R., Grimm, K. J., & McArdle, J. J. (2016). Regularized structural equation modeling. *Structural Equation Modeling: A Multidisciplinary Journal, 23* (4), 555–566.

Jacobucci, R. (2017). regsem: Performs regularization on structural equation models. R package version 0.6.3. https://cran.r-project.org/package=regsem

Jacobucci, R. (2017). regsem: Regularized Structural Equation Modeling. arXiv preprint arXiv:1703.08489.

Jacobucci, R. & Grimm, K. J. (2018). Comparison of frequentist and Bayesian regularization in structural equation modeling. *25*(4), 639–649.

Jöreskog, K. G. (1970). Estimation and testing of simplex models. *British Journal of Mathematical and Statistical Psychology, 23*, 121–145.

Jöreskog, K. G. (1974). Analyzing psychological data by structural analysis of covariance matrices. In: Atkinson, R. C., Krantz, D. H., Luce, R. D., Suppas, P. (Eds.) Contemporary developments in mathematical psychology. San Francisco: Freeman; pp. 1–56.

Kyung, M., Gill, J., Ghosh, M., & Casella, G. (2010). Penalized regression, standard errors, and Bayesian lassos. *Bayesian Analysis, 5*(2), 369–411.

Lu, Z. H., Chow, S. M., & Loken, E. (2016). Bayesian factor analysis as a variable-selection problem: Alternative priors and consequences. *Multivariate Behavioral Research, 51*(4), 519–539.

McArdle, J. J. (2001). A latent difference score approach to longitudinal dynamic structure analysis. In R. Cudeck, S. du Toit & D. Sörbom (Eds.), *Structural equation modeling: present and future. A festschrift in honor of Karl Jöreskog* (pp. 1–40). Lincolnwood, IL: Scientific Software International, Inc.

McArdle, J. J. & Epstein, D. (1987). Latent growth curves within developmental structural equation models. *Child Development, 58*, 110–133.

McArdle, J. J. & Hamagami, F. (2001). Latent difference score structural models for linear dynamic analyses with incomplete longitudinal data. In L. M. Collins, & A. G. Sayer (Eds.), *New methods for the analysis of change* (pp. 139–175). Washington, DC: American Psychological Association.

Meredith, W. & Tisak, J. (1990). Latent curve analysis. *Psychometrika, 55*, 107–122.

Muthén, B., & Asparouhov, T. (2012). Bayesian structural equation modeling: A more flexible representation of substantive theory. *Psychological Methods, 17*, 313–335.

Muthén, L. K. & Muthén, B. O. (1998–2015). M*plus user's guide*. 7th Edition. Los Angeles, CA: Muthén & Muthén

O'Hara, R. B. & Sillanpää, M. J. (2009). A review of Bayesian variable selection methods: What, how and which. *Bayesian Analysis, 4*, 85–11

O'Rourke, H., Grimm, K. J., & MacKinnon, D. P. (2017). Time metrics and their effects in latent change score models. Manuscript under review.

Osborne, R. T. & Suddick, D. E. (1972). A longitudinal investigation of the intellectual differentiation hypothesis. *Journal of Generic Psychology, 121*, 83–89.

Park, T. & Casella, G. (2008). The Bayesian lasso. *Journal of the American Statistical Association, 103*(482), 681–686.

Plummer, M. (2003). Jags: A program for analysis of Bayesian graphical models using gibbs sampling. *In Proceedings of the 3rd international workshop on distributed statistical computing* (Vol. 124, p. 125).

Plummer, M. (2016). rjags: Bayesian Graphical Models using MCMC. R package version 4–6. https://CRAN.R-project.org/package=rjags

R Core Team. (2017). R: A language and environment for statistical computing [Computer software manual]. Vienna, Austria.

Rindskopf, D. (2012). Next steps in Bayesian structural equation models: Comments on, variations of, and extensions to Muthén and Asparouhov (2012). *Psychological Methods, 17*, 336–339.

Schwarz, G. (1978). Estimating the dimension of a model. *The Annals of Statistics, 6*, 461–464.

Sclove, S. L. (1987). Application of model-selection criteria to some problems in multivariate analysis. *Psychometrika, 52*, 333–343.

Tibshirani, R. (1996). Regression shrinkage and selection via the lasso. *Journal of the Royal Statistical Society. Series B (Methodological), 58* (1), 267–288.

Usami, S., Hayes, T., & McArdle, J. J. (2016). Inferring longitudinal relationships between variables: Model selection between the latent change score and autoregressive cross-lagged factor models. *Structural Equation Modeling: A Multidisciplinary Journal, 23*, 331–342.

Zou, H. (2006). The adaptive lasso and its oracle properties. *Journal of the American Statistical Association, 101*(476), 1418–1429.

6

THE RETICULAR ACTION MODEL[1]

A Remarkably Lasting Achievement

Steven M. Boker

For readers whose first experience of Structural Equation Modeling (SEM) occurred within the past 40 years, the Reticular Action Model (RAM) approach to SEM may seem obvious. However, prior to McArdle (1978) first presenting his formulation, this way of approaching data analysis differed from contemporary approaches in fundamental ways. I will approach this chapter with a more personal perspective than is the norm. The reason for this is that I was living in Denver at the time of RAM's development and had the good fortune to be friends with Jack McArdle while he was a postdoc with John Horn. Jack and I met most Thursdays for lunch at a Mexican restaurant or in his basement office where he used me as a sounding board for the arguments, algebra, and diagrams that underlie the RAM model. These discussions were of equal parts matrix algebra and graph theory; defining characteristics of the RAM way of specifying models. The current chapter will begin with some historical context, give an exposition of why the RAM model was a breakthrough, and then trace some of the developments that RAM has enabled.

Setting the Stage

Tukey wrote, "The important question about methods is not 'How' but 'Why.' ... In explaining why, we must remember that every method is to some extent the child of the time of its development." (Tukey, 1954, p. 33). With this in mind, I will begin with a short history of data analysis from a path analytic perspective, to provide historical context for the shift in thinking that led to the development of the RAM model and the surprising capabilities that it made available to modelers (see Li et al., 1975; Wolfle, 1999, 2003, for further historical accounts of path analysis).

Karl Pearson (1896) developed the *correlation coefficient* which is, at its heart, an average cross product between two mean centered variables then rescaled to be in units of the product of the root mean squares of the same variables. Keep in mind that the cross products and sums of squares (or covariance and variance) are essentially the same operation on either two variables or one variable respectively.

From this idea of averaging sums of squares as a measure of the relatedness of variables, Spearman (1904) built his method of *factor analysis*. The method can be framed such that an unobserved variable would be the common cause for a number of observed variables and could be estimated as a system of simultaneous equations with unobserved common factor(s) on the right-hand side of each equation and one equation for each observed variable.

Sewall Wright (1918) derived *path coefficients* that decomposed a single observed correlation into multiple parts and thereby demonstrated a general size factor as well as leg and skull size factors in rabbits. Two years later, he wrote, "The correlation between two variables can be shown to equal the sum of the products of the chains of path coefficients along all of the paths by which they are connected." (Wright, 1920, p 330) and used this property to demonstrate heritable traits in piebald guinea pigs. Wright also worked out what we now call the *components of correlation*.

It can be shown that the squares of the path coefficients measure the degree of determination by each cause. If the causes are independent of each other, the sum of the squared path coefficients is unity. If the causes are correlated, terms representing joint determination must be recognized. The complete determination of X [...] by factor A and the correlated factors B and C, can be expressed by the equation: $a^2 + b^2 + c^2 + 2bcr_{BC} = 1$ (Wright, 1920, p 329)

Wright's seminal articles not only established the basis of structural equation modeling, but also provided the first examples of path diagrams (see Figure 6.1). Wright used his path diagrams to explain the implications of his equations, thus demonstrating that these path diagrams were more than just a convenience, but had a fundamental relationship to the equations (see McArdle & Aber, 1990, for an SEM analysis of Wright's data). In an article published the next year, Wright (1921) again combined the use of the path diagrams and simultaneous equations to illustrate a variety of structural models. He makes the important point that one should not interpret these equations as being statements of causality, but only as being structures of correlations. It is beguiling to think that the left-hand side of the simultaneous equations of SEM are outcomes of the right-hand side. But the equals sign is not the same as a "stores into" operator; equality only expresses a network of balances of the left- and right-hand sides. This balancing of accounts is at the heart of SEM, but some model formulations encourage causal interpretation more than others (Pearl, 2003).

Wright's path analysis method did not immediately become popular. Parameters of systems of simultaneous equations with constraints were difficult to estimate from data when "Computer" was not a noun applied to a machine, but rather was

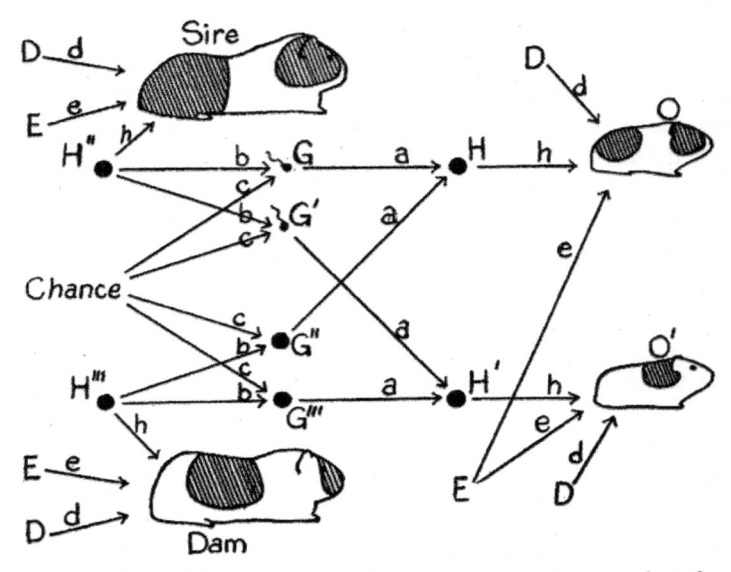

FIGURE 6.1 The first published example of a path diagram. Note modern features of SEM including the exogenous variable labeled "Chance", common environment (E), unique environment (D) and additive genetic paths (a) constrained to equality across generations (Wright, 1920).

a job title for people who calculated arithmetic operations as a profession and used paper and pencil as tools. Wright took an approach that would now be called an *instrumental variables* approach, isolating parts of the model and estimating them independently (see, e.g., Bollen, 1996; Kirby & Bollen, 2009, for a modern use of this technique). In 1934, Wright proposed that the method of path coefficients could be converted into Pearson's partial regression coefficients, but it was another 20 years before the method began to attract attention.

Tukey gave an idea of how far path analysis had faded into the background when he wrote

> ... I had heard of path coefficients repeatedly. The surprise came when I found that I did not know anything about path analysis, although after some study it seemed to be natural and useful. After coming to the point where I thought I understood it moderately well, it occurred to me to wonder why I had not known about it before.
>
> *Source*: (Tukey, 1954, p.35)

Tukey (1954) and later Turner and Stevens (1959) proposed that unstandardized (what Turner and Stevens called "concrete") coefficients be used for path analysis and that reciprocal relations be allowed in path analytic models.

Wright's responses (1960a, 1960b) to Tukey brought the discussion of path analysis back into the literature. Wright mentions that overdetermined systems may be estimated if one can "...obtain a compromise solution by the method of least squares..." (Wright, 1960a, p. 198). At the time, the method used for obtaining solutions to overdetermined models was not simultaneous equations optimization, but instead isolating instrumental variables and then solving one equation at a time.

Cattell, steeped in the traditions of factor analysis, argued that the notion of factors arranging themselves in a pyramid with fewer factors at higher levels was an inevitable mathematical artifact and not a proof of hierarchical structure of psychological constructs (see Figure 6.2).

> One mathematical rule, when communalities are used, is that one cannot take out as many factors as there are variables. Consequently, a hundred variables may define, say, only twenty primaries (*n.b.*, first order factors), and twenty primaries must yield fewer second order factors, and so on. But the fact that a number of higher order factors as great as the number of variables or lower order factors cannot be mathematically defined for lack of a sufficiency of variables is no proof that they do not exist.
>
> *Source*: R. B. Cattell (1965)

In that chapter, Cattell argued for a *reticular* (i.e., network or directed graph) structure for latent variables, as shown in Figure 6.3 adapted from his chapter. This model includes all possible reciprocal regression relations between variables and first-order factors. Cattell states that he did not draw all the possible reciprocal relations from the second-order factors in order "to avoid overcrowding".

After mainframe computers started to become commonplace in the 1950s and 1960s, improved techniques for optimization became available, and interest was revived. Duncan (1966) reviewed Wright's articles in detail and brought path

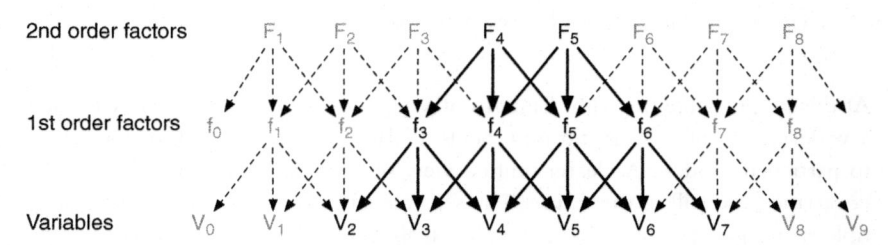

FIGURE 6.2 Alternative explanation for a pyramidal organization of higher order factors. If only variables V2 through V7 are measured, a hierarchical structure is inevitable. Figure adapted from Cattell (1965, p. 234) who captioned his figure, "False hierarchy in an essentially reticular structure."

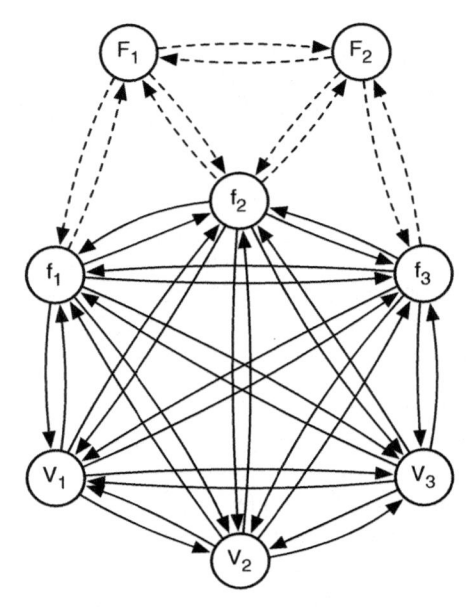

FIGURE 6.3 Cattell's reticular structure presages modern *network* or *graph* models. Figure is adapted from Cattell (1965, p. 236) who captioned his figure, "Possible interactions of a set of eight distinct influences."

coefficients and path analysis to wider attention in the social sciences. Duncan recognized the value in path diagrams being an exact representation of the underlying algebra and complained:

> Causal diagrams are appearing with increasing frequency in sociological publications. Most often, these have some kind of pictorial or mnemonic function without being isomorphic with the algebraic and statistical properties of the postulated system of variables—or, indeed without having a counterpart in any clearly specified system of variables at all.
>
> (Duncan, 1966, p. 3)

At this point, while the path diagrams of Wright provided a unified way to view a wide variety of models, fitting models to data involved algorithms specialized to particular models. A clearer unified view of linear structure of correlation or covariance was still in the future. The separate languages used in ANOVA, multiple regression, factor analysis, and path analyses also inhibited unification of the field.

Jöreskog (1970) first presented a unified matrix-oriented model for the relations between variables. Goldberger noted the relationship between Jöreskog's formulation and Wright's path coefficients models and published a review in order to "redress economists' neglect of the work of Sewall Wright." (Goldberger,

1972, p. 979). Goldberger organized a series of meetings between members of the psychometric (including Jöreskog), econometric, and sociological (including Duncan) communities. At the first of these, Jöreskog (1973) presented his Linear Structural Relations (LISREL) model. LISREL allowed the specification of a wide variety of statistical models within the framework of its matrices.

Each matrix in the LISREL system of specification corresponded to part of an SEM model. Once the matrices were specified, the same optimization procedure could be used to obtain parameter estimates from the model, no matter which model was input into the matrices. This was an incredible improvement over the previously idiosyncratic methods for estimation and accelerated the adoption of SEM in the social and behavioral sciences. One property of the LISREL system is that it provides definitions of how the matrices should be used and thus structures the thinking of modelers. This has the benefit of providing instructional support for someone first learning how to create statistical models. It also has the disadvantage of reducing the probability that someone will innovate new structural relations that are not easily described within the LISREL framework. It was not uncommon for researchers in the 1970s and 1980s to speak of "tricking LISREL" into fitting the model they had in mind.

Starting in the late 1960s (e.g., Cohen, 1968) and accelerating in the late 1970s, people in the variety of fields of data analysis began to realize that there were many commonalities between what had been considered to be separate types of statistical models. For instance, Cohen (1978) derived a proof that interactions and partialed products were the same thing. Bentler and Weeks (1976) used the LISREL formulation to illuminate similarities and differences between principal components analysis and factor analysis as he presented a model for what he called structural factor analysis. Bentler and Weeks (1979) expanded on the theme to show how several kinds of models were all special cases of the LISREL formulation. McDonald proposed a set of principals that could be "... applied to give a unified treatment of a wide range of models for multivariate data, including models that have not yet been proposed." (McDonald, 1979, p. 22). Fraser and McDonald (1988) developed this idea as the COSAN software, which was later incorporated into SAS.

The Breakthrough: RAM Algebra and RAM Path Analysis

Here our history has come to the time where McArdle introduced the RAM specification. Consider the milieu of the late 1970s. While room-sized mainframe computers are the way that LISREL models are fit, there is a new microcomputer that has just been released and that seems to be promising: the Apple II. Maybe some day people will be able to fit SEM models right on their own desks rather than waiting overnight for green-bar printouts from the data center. An easy, general way of specifying structural models might revolutionize how we go about converting our theories into testable hypotheses.

In 1978, as a postdoc at the University of Denver, McArdle first presented his ideas about how one might go about organizing theories drawn with path diagrams into a set of matrices that could then be optimized with respect to observed data (McArdle, 1978). This was followed a few months later by a presentation at the American Psychological Association's annual meeting, where he called his method the Reticular Analysis Model (McArdle, 1979). The basic idea is that Wright's path diagrams provided a representation of the structure of a covariance matrix. The diagrams had four kinds of elements: manifest variables, latent variables, single headed arrows, and double headed arrows. LISREL matrices make a distinction between manifest variables and latent variables that result in a particular structure of relations. For instance, in which matrix a regression coefficient is placed depends on whether it is predicting a manifest variable or a latent variable.

McArdle worked out that if one were to put regression coefficients for both manifest and latent variables into a single matrix, $\mathbf{A}$, one could radically reduce the total number of required matrices from LISREL's 8 or 10 matrices down to just 3. Similar logic applied to the covariance coefficients: A single matrix, $\mathbf{S}$, for covariances of all the variables could suffice. The well-known formula for the covariance of linear combinations could then be used to calculate the total model-implied covariance, $\mathbf{R}_{total}$, of the all the variables (manifest and latent):

$$\mathbf{R}_{total} = (\mathbf{I}+\mathbf{A})\mathbf{S}(\mathbf{I}+\mathbf{A})' \qquad (6.1)$$

However, his formula does not always work. Suppose we have three standardized variables, x_1, x_2, and x_3. Suppose further that

$$x_3 = b_2 x_2 + e_3 \qquad (6.2)$$

$$x_2 = b_1 x_1 + e_2 . \qquad (6.3)$$

There are five total variables in this system of equations: x_1, x_2, and x_3 are manifest, while e_2, and e_3 are model-implied, i.e., latent. If we set the rows and columns to be in the order $\{x_1, x_2, x_3, e_2, e_3\}$, then we can set $\mathbf{A}$ to

$$\mathbf{A} = \begin{bmatrix} 0 & 0 & 0 & 0 & 0 \\ b_1 & 0 & 0 & 1 & 0 \\ 0 & b_2 & 0 & 0 & 1 \\ 0 & 0 & 0 & 0 & 0 \\ 0 & 0 & 0 & 0 & 0 \end{bmatrix} \qquad (6.4)$$

Note that the position of b_1 in $\mathbf{A}[2,1]$ represents that the regression coefficient b_1 is predicting x_2 from x_1. Similarly, the position of b_2 in $\mathbf{A}[3,2]$ represents that the regression coefficient b_2 is predicting x_3 from x_2. Also note that the latent variables e_2 and e_3 have an implied coefficient of 1.0 in Equations 6.2 and 6.3, so 1.0 is placed into the appropriate cells of $\mathbf{A}$.

In the same way, we can set up the variances and covariances that are to be estimated in the matrix **S**, where

$$\mathbf{S} = \begin{bmatrix} 1.0 & 0 & 0 & 0 & 0 \\ 0 & 0 & 0 & 0 & 0 \\ 0 & 0 & 0 & 0 & 0 \\ 0 & 0 & 0 & var(e_2) & 0 \\ 0 & 0 & 0 & 0 & var(e_2) \end{bmatrix} \tag{6.5}$$

Note that the variances of x_1, e_2, and e_3 are along the diagonal ($var(x_1) = 1.0$, since it is standardized. The variances of x_2, and x_3 are set to zero, since their variances are completely accounted for by Equations 6.2 and 6.3.

However, now we find that Equation 6.1 does not follow Wright's path analysis rule that "The correlation between two variables can be shown to equal the sum of the products of the chains of path coefficients along all of the paths by which they are connected." (Wright, 1920, p 330). This can be easily seen by substituting Equation 6.3 into Equation 6.2. In order to calculate the products of the regression chain ($b_2 b_3$), we can calculate $\mathbf{A}^2$ and so now the sum of the products of the regression chain becomes

$$\mathbf{A} + \mathbf{A}^2 \tag{6.6}$$

and so

$$\mathbf{R}_{total} = (\mathbf{I} + \mathbf{A} + \mathbf{A}^2)\mathbf{S}(\mathbf{I} + \mathbf{A} + \mathbf{A}^2)' \tag{6.7}$$

Given that $\mathbf{I} = \mathbf{A}^0$, for each chain of regression coefficients of length n, we need to find

$$\mathbf{A}^0 + \mathbf{A}^1 + \mathbf{A}^2 + \ldots + \mathbf{A}^n, \tag{6.8}$$

a sum of a continued product (McDonald, 1978).

But now suppose that our model has a cyclic relation by adding one more path:

$$x_3 = b_2 x_2 + e_3 \tag{6.9}$$

$$x_2 = b_1 x_1 + e_2 \tag{6.10}$$

$$x_1 = b_3 x_3 + e_1. \tag{6.11}$$

By the same logic as above, the sum of the products of the regression chain now becomes an infinite sum of a continued product,

$$\mathbf{R}_{total} = (\mathbf{A}^0 + \mathbf{A}^1 + \mathbf{A}^2 + \mathbf{A}^3 + \ldots + \mathbf{A}^\infty)\mathbf{S}(\mathbf{A}^0 + \mathbf{A}^1 + \mathbf{A}^2 + \mathbf{A}^3 + \ldots + \mathbf{A}^\infty)' \tag{6.12}$$

which would seem to be much harder to calculate. However, as McArdle (1980) and McArdle and McDonald (1984) noted,

$$(\mathbf{I} - \mathbf{A})(\mathbf{A}^0 + \mathbf{A}^1 + \mathbf{A}^2 + \mathbf{A}^3 + \ldots + \mathbf{A}^\infty) = \mathbf{I} + (\mathbf{A} - \mathbf{A}) + (\mathbf{A}^2 - \mathbf{A}^2) + (\mathbf{A}^3 - \mathbf{A}^3) \ldots$$

$$= \mathbf{I}$$

So therefore

$$(\mathbf{A}^0 + \mathbf{A}^1 + \mathbf{A}^2 + \mathbf{A}^3 + \ldots + \mathbf{A}^\infty) = (\mathbf{I} - \mathbf{A})^{-1}$$

which means that

$$\mathbf{R}_{total} = (\mathbf{I} - \mathbf{A})^{-1}\mathbf{S}((\mathbf{I} - \mathbf{A})^{-1})' \tag{6.13}$$

applies to sums of products of coefficient chains of any length. This simple formula for the model implied covariance for all the variables can be filtered to just the measured variables, by constructing an appropriate *measured variables × total variables* matrix, $\mathbf{F}$, with a single 1.0 in each row corresponding to that measured variable's position in the $\mathbf{A}$ and $\mathbf{S}$ matrices. This, finally, is the RAM model which calculates $\mathbf{R}_{exp}$, the model-expected covariance matrix

$$\mathbf{R}_{exp} = \mathbf{F}(\mathbf{I} - \mathbf{A})^{-1}\mathbf{S}((\mathbf{I} - \mathbf{A})^{-1})'\mathbf{F}' . \tag{6.14}$$

McDonald was the first to propose the notion of a general, two-matrix solution to the expected covariances of an SEM model (McDonald, 1978, p. 61). His model was not isomorphic to Wright's tracing rules, but it was influential in McArdle's proposal later that year (McArdle, 1978). Equation 6.14 appears in the discussion at the end of Bentler and Weeks (1979). However, while they recognize that

> It appears more general than [6] (*n.b.* the foundational equation in their article), and because it allows essentially all possible measurement levels and multivariate regressions, it also includes Weeks' (1978) seemingly more complex model [19]. Such a conclusion ignores some complexities of the problem.
>
> (Bentler & Weeks, 1979, p. 181)

At the time, Bentler and Weeks did not appear to completely understand the generality of the model, nor the implications for path analysis. However, in subsequent years, Equation 6.14 became the foundation of Bentler's EQS software.

One of McArdle's main contributions were how he realized that the calculations performed in Equation 6.14 mapped isomorphically to the set of path analysis rules originally defined by Wright (1920, 1934). Thus, each covariance in the model-expected covariance matrix, $\mathbf{R}_{exp}$ could be decomposed into additive *components of covariance*. Each component of covariance is the outcome of one traced path or, alternatively, one additive part of the matrix equation calculating $\mathbf{R}_{exp}$. This one-to-one correspondence, i.e., isomorphism, allows a path diagram to be a specification for one and only one matrix equation and similarly the matrix equation specifies one and only one path diagram. For this isomorphism to exist, McArdle (1980) realized that there was a missing diagrammatic element in previous path diagrams: there was not a diagrammatic element for variance terms in the $\mathbf{S}$ matrix. In standardized models – where the variance is fixed at 1.0 for all latent and observer predictors – the omitted variance terms had been assumed.

But many path diagrams drawn without variance terms are ambiguous, and this impedes replication of analyses. The development of the double-headed arrow from a variable to itself as representing a non-zero element in the **S** matrix allowed for an isomorphic (one to one) relationship between diagrams and equations and led to the development of automatic graphic user interfaces for SEM.

Some Personal History

The first RAM-style path diagrams appeared in print (Horn & McArdle, 1980; McArdle, 1979, 1980) around the time when I first met Jack McArdle. At the time I had just published *Graphtrix*, a software package for text and graphics printing on the Apple II (Boker, 1980).Jack called me up for technical support on how to use it to include path diagrams into his manuscripts. We were both located in Denver, and so we met for lunch. Thus began a set of wide ranging discussions on the elements of path diagrams, graph theory, and why the double-headed arrow variance term was so important to tracing rules. In these early diagrams (1979, 1980), McArdle's innovative representation of variance terms was already present; however, variances and covariances did not yet include arrows at the ends of the arcs. A second graphical innovation in RAM diagrams is the use of a triangle to represent a column of ones in the data, so that models for means can be specified in the path diagram (McArdle, 1986; McArdle & Epstein, 1987).

As McArdle presented his ideas it became evident that he was driven to implement the most general network of relations, the reticular relations proposed by Cattell (1965). I argued that "reticular" was an unnecessarily obscure term – why did he not just call it Network Analysis Modeling. In his usual light-hearted manner, McArdle replied that the acronym NAM had obvious negative associations for many Americans. But primarily, he wanted to honor Cattell's contribution in helping generalize latent structure away from the strict input-output causal implications that had previously dominated statistical modeling.

There is a subtle point here. Input-output designs such as factor analysis, multiple regression, and mediation models all encourage the modeler to think in causal terms. On the other hand, a network model with feedback (reciprocal relations) is better framed in terms of bidirectional coupling or resonance. Strict causality becomes irrelevant in a highly connected feedback network. The answer to the causality question is always "yes", no matter which two variables and no matter in which order one picks. Modern network and dynamical systems models have recently begun to be analyzed in terms of impulse response resonance, sidestepping the causality question entirely. In this way, McArdle was 30 years ahead of his time.

The **A** and **S** matrices have unique placement for each possible regression coefficient and each variance/covariance relation. McArdle said that one could think of the matrices as starting with a zero in every cell and add each regression coefficient or variance/covariance from a theory into the matrices. However, he said, one could also consider the matrices as starting as entirely filled and then zero out the regression coefficients and variance/covariances that *should not* appear in the diagram. The point here is a result from cognitive psychology: we tend to see what *is* present rather than what *is not* present. Structural equation modeling involves the balance between what is and what is not present in a path diagram. By focusing on what is not in the diagram, one focuses on the constraints that provide an opportunity for misfit. McArdle said this was akin to Sir Arthur Conan Doyle's Sherlock Holmes short story, *Silver Blaze*:

> Gregory (Scotland Yard detective): "Is there any other point to which you would wish to draw my attention?"
> Holmes: "To the curious incident of the dog in the night-time."
> Gregory: "The dog did nothing in the night-time."
> Holmes: "That was the curious incident."
>
> (Doyle, A.C., 1894, p. 22)

McArdle's point is well taken. The single- and double-headed arrows that are missing from a path diagram are exactly what makes a theory testable using goodness of fit statistics. The fact that many published path diagrams are artifactually missing critical elements that in fact existed in the calculation of a model's expectation has been a source of great consternation to McArdle, and he has crusaded to persuade SEM users to publish *complete* diagrams (e.g., Figure 6.4). The RAM-style path diagram is now a well-established and often recommended standard (e.g., McDonald & Ho, 2002)

Out of these discussions, in 1982 I developed the RAMpath algorithm that allowed automatic computer-generated path diagrams from matrices (Boker, McArdle, & Neale, 2002). This algorithm was first implemented in order to automatically determine the longest regression chain, so that the expected covariance matrix for a RAM-style model could be calculated without taking an inverse; thus enabling model-expected covariance matrices to be estimated on an early 48 kilobyte Apple II. Later, McArdle and I developed software that would automatically highlight each component of covariance one at a time on a path diagram (McArdle & Boker, 1990). This algorithm has since been used in software including Mx (Neale, Boker, Xie, & Maes, 1999), RAMONA (Browne & Mels, 1998), COSAN (Fraser & McDonald, 1988), OpenMx (Boker, Neale, Maes, Wilde, Spiegle, Brick, et al., 2009; Neale, Hunter, Pritikin, Zahery, Brick, Kirkpatrick, et al., 2016), Ωnyx (Oertzen, Brandmaier, & Tsang, 2015), and the R packages SEM (Fox, 2009) and RAMpath (Zhang, McArdle, Hamagami, & Grimm, 2012).

One early argument against the RAM formulation for use in model estimation is that its matrices are large and sparse. McArdle's argument was the Moore's law – the exponential increase in transistor density on CPUs – would make this efficiency penalty irrelevant. In his view, the bottleneck was not CPU time, but rather the time of the creative scientist. By making model specification as easy

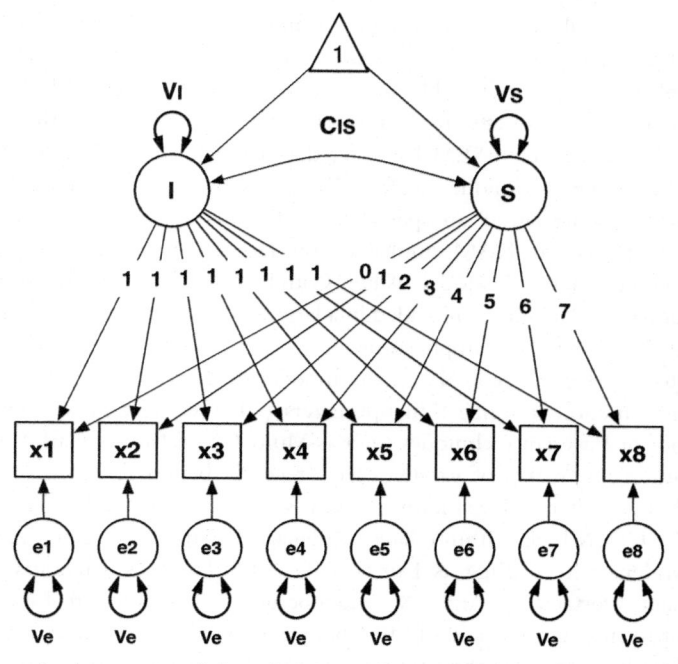

FIGURE 6.4 An intercept and slope latent growth curve model. Note the use of fixed basis functions to calculate the slope and intercept.

as possible, more creative data science would be accomplished. If one scientist spent more time attempting to shoehorn his theory into a cumbersome modeling framework, whereas another scientist was able to translate her theory into a model more quickly and with fewer errors, then she would likely be the first to publish.

In the meantime, another advantage has become apparent. Due to the close link between graph theory and the model specification, techniques such as power equivalent models (Oertzen, 2010), RAMpart (Pritikin, Hunter, Oertzen, Brick, & Boker, 2017) and the RAMpath algorithm have allowed many common RAM-style models to automatically be more computationally efficient than the equivalent LISREL or MPlus specifications.

How Our Thinking About Modeling Has Changed

One important aspect of RAM is that it refocuses attention from the specifics of a particular modeling framework and brings to the foreground the psychological theory that is to be tested without few constraints on how that theory is instantiated in a model. This can be frustrating for those new to SEM, since there is a great deal of cognitive support provided by statistical techniques such as ANOVA and its regression alter-ego, the general linear model (GLM). New psychologists are trained to think in terms of predictors and outcomes. This is a useful technique for generalizing average effects to a population when combined with data from controlled experiments. However, the logic of ANOVA and GLM break down when conclusions are drawn from observational or quasiexperimental data. This can be illustrated in SEM by using the fact that ANOVA and GLM (and many other earlier techniques such as Factor Analysis, Principal Components, and Canonical Correlation) are special cases of RAM.

The "Reticular" in RAM emphasizes the fact that SEM needs to be understood as being a network model. When Cattell (1965) proposed the idea of any observational model being embedded in a larger network of unobserved relations, few understood the wider implications. One of McArdle's main advances was to instantiate this idea of a general network model in a way that it could be estimated using cost function minimization optimizers (whether least squares, maximum likelihood, or Bayesian techniques such as Multi-Chain Monte Carlo). Methods for examining networks of variables have recently begun to evolve past RAM into techniques such as Exploratory Graph Analysis (EGA) (Golino & Epskamp, 2017), the GIMME algorithm (Gates, Molenaar, Hillary, Ram, & Rovine, 2010; Gates, Molenaar, Iyer, Nigg, & Fair, 2014), and SEM Trees (Brandmaier, 2011; Brandmaier, Oertzen, McArdle, & Lindenberger, 2013). These techniques are a testament to how far the field of SEM has progressed since the days when it was yet unclear how each separate type of statistical model related to one another. Even more impressive, our theories are beginning to break free of the trap of

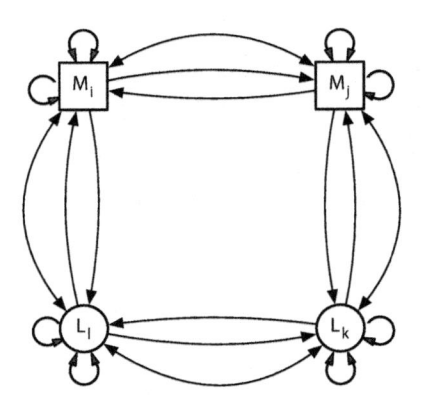

FIGURE 6.5 A reticule of variables (after Horn & McArdle, 1980, p. 194). Note that this diagram differs from Horn and McArdle in that arrows have been added to the covariance arcs and variances have been added to comply with McArdle's later full statement of RAM path diagrams. Single-headed arrows from variables to themselves represent stability coefficients in an autoregressive sense. In the reticule it is useful to interpret single-headed arrows as being effects occurring across time and double-headed arrows as being contemporaneous. In this way, it the reticule can be seen as the basic building block of modern network algorithms.

directed-effects causal thinking that has kept us from understanding the implications of resonant recurrent networks of relations – from appreciating Cattell's *reticule* as illustrated by Horn & McArdle (1980) in Figure 6.5.

Another important consequence of the RAM model and its isomorphic correspondence to path diagrams is that the way we discuss statistical models and teach SEM has been transformed. When students come into my office to ask questions about their theories and models, they overwhelmingly choose to bring a path diagram with them. In this way we can quickly communicate about the implications of models. After learning the tracing rules, students begin to actively explore the consequences of adding or subtracting regression relations in their models. This was made very clear to me when a second-year graduate student came to see me after an SEM class period. She was excited and said she had just won her first argument with her advisor. She said she proved her point to her advisor using tracing rules and he was forced to agree. The didactic power of complete and isomorphic path diagrams is not to be underestimated.

The Future of RAM

The RAM model is not a static concept. It has been extended in several ways, for instance to account for multi-group and mixture distribution models. It has been used to fit state space and dynamical systems models such as Latent Differential Equations (LDE) (Boker, Neale, & Rausch, 2004).Recently, the OpenMx team has been exploring new extensions that have enabled multilevel models. The power of the RAM philosophy here can be seen in the efficiency of the RAMpart (Pritikin et al., 2017) model, an efficiency that derives from a graph theoretic transformation developed by von Oertzen (2010), where the portions of the RAM model that need to be inverted can be automatically isolated from the remainder of the multilevel model. Current work has been focusing on efficient and compact methods for estimating variances and covariances of products of variables. This will require an extension of the RAM matrices and new tracing rules. The RAM philosophy of *reticular action* of a network has been central to this work.

In short, the RAM model has been unreasonably influential in the development of the field of SEM over the past 40 years. I hope you will join me in thanking Jack McArdle for his incredibly helpful insights into the reticular structure of the network of relations between variables.

Notes

1 Funding for this work was provided in part by NIH Grant 1R21DA024304 and the Max Planck Institute for Human Development. Any opinions, findings, and conclusions or recommendations expressed in this material are those of the authors and do not necessarily react the views of the National Institutes of Health.

References

Bentler, P. M. (1976). Multistructure statistical model applied to factor analysis. *Multivariate Behavioral Research*, *11*(1), 3–25.

Bentler, P. M. & Weeks, D. G. (1979). Interrelations among models for the analysis of moment structures. *Multivariate Behavioral Research*, *14*(2), 169–186.

Boker, S., Neale, M., Maes, H., Wilde, M., Spiegel, M., Brick, T., ... (2009). *OpenMx: Multipurpose software for statistical modeling*. University of Virginia, Department of Psychology, Box 400400, Charlottesville, VA 22904. http://openmx.psyc.virginia.edu

Boker, S. M. (1980). *Graphtrix*. Denver, CO: Data Transforms, Inc.

Boker, S. M., McArdle, J. J., & Neale, M. C. (2002). An algorithm for the hierarchical organization of path diagrams and calculation of components of covariance between variables. *Structural Equation Modeling*, *9*(2), 174–194.

Boker, S. M., Neale, M. C., & Rausch, J. (2004). Latent differential equation modeling with multivariate multi-occasion indicators. In K. van Montfort, H. Oud, & A. Satorra (Eds.), *Recent developments on structural equation models: Theory and applications* (pp. 151–174). Dordrecht, Netherlands: Kluwer Academic Publishers.

Bollen, K. A. (1996). An alternative two stage least squares (2SLS) estimator for latent variable equations. *Psychometrika*, *61*(1), 109–121.

Brandmaier, A. M. (2011). *Permutation distribution clustering and structural equation model trees*. Unpublished doctoral dissertation, Universität des Saarlandes. (Unpublished doctoral dissertation)

Brandmaier, A. M., Oertzen, T. von, McArdle, J. J., & Lindenberger, U. (2013). Structural equation model trees. *Psychological methods*, *18*(1), 71.

Browne, M. W. & Mels, G. (1998). *RAMONA: SYSTAT for Windows: Advanced Applications (Ver. 8)*. SYSTAT.

Cattell, R. B. (1965). Higher order factor structures and reticular-vs-hierarchical formulae for their interpretation. In C. Banks & P. L. Broadhurst (Eds.), *Studies in psychology* (pp. 223–266). London: University of London Press.

Cohen, J. (1968). Multiple regression as a general data-analytic system. *Psychological Bulletin*, *70*(6), 426.

Cohen, J. (1978). Partialed products are interactions; partialed powers are curve components. *Psychological Bulletin*, *85*(4), 858–866.

Doyle, A. C. (1894). *The memoirs of Sherlock Holmes*. New York: Harper & Brothers.

Duncan, O. D. (1966). Path analysis: Sociological examples. *The American Journal of Sociology*, *72*(1), 1–16.

Fox, J. (2009). *sem: Structural Equation Models*. (R package version 0.9–19)

Fraser, C., & McDonald, R. P. (1988). Cosan: Convariance structure analysis. *Multivariate Behavioral Research*, *23*(2), 263–265.

Gates, K. M., Molenaar, P. C., Hillary, F. G., Ram, N., & Rovine, M. J. (2010). Automatic search for fmri connectivity mapping: an alternative to granger causality testing using formal equivalences among sem path modeling, var, and unified sem. *Neuroimage*, *50*(3), 1118–1125.

Gates, K. M., Molenaar, P. C., Iyer, S. P., Nigg, J. T., & Fair, D. A. (2014). Organizing heterogeneous samples using community detection of gimme-derived resting state functional networks. *PloS one*, *9*(3), e91322.

Goldberger, A. S. (1972). Structureal equation methods in the social sciences. *Econometrica*, *40*(6), 979–1001.

Golino, H. F. & Epskamp, S. (2017). Exploratory graph analysis: A new approach for estimating the number of dimensions in psychological research. *PloS one, 12*(6), e0174035.

Horn, J. L. & McArdle, J. J. (1980). Perspectives on mathematical and statistical model building (masmob) in aging research. In L. W. Poon (Ed.), *Aging in the 1980s: Contemporary perspectives.* Washington, DC: American Psychological Association.

Jöreskog, K. G. (1970). A general method for analysis of covariance structures. *Biometrika,* 239–251.

Jöreskog, K. G. (1973). A general method for estimating a linear structural equation system. In A. S. Goldberger & O. D. Duncan (Eds.), *Structural equation models in the social sciences* (pp. 85–112). New York: Seminar.

Kirby, J. B. & Bollen, K. A. (2009). Using instrumental variable tests to evaluate model specification in latent variable structural equation models. *Sociological Methodology, 39*(1), 327–355.

Li, C. C., et al. (1975). *Path analysis-a primer.* Pacific Grove, CA: The Boxwood Press.

McArdle, J. J. (1978). *A structural view of structural models.* (Paper presented at the Winter Workshop on Latent Structural Models Applied to Developmental Data, University of Denver)

McArdle, J. J. (1979). The development of general multivariate software. In J. Hirschbuhl (Ed.), *Proceedings of the association for the development of computer-based instruction.* Akron, OH: University of Akron Press.

McArdle, J. J. (1980). Causal modeling applied to psychonomic systems simulation. *Behavior Research Methods & Instrumentation, 12*(2), 193–209.

McArdle, J. J. (1986). Latent growth within behavior genetic models. *Behavior Genetics, 16,* 163–200.

McArdle, J. J. & Aber, M. S. (1990). Patterns of change within latent variable structural equation modeling. In A. von Eye (Ed.), *New statistical methods in developmental research* (pp. 151–224). New York: Academic Press.

McArdle, J. J. & Boker, S. M. (1990). *Rampath.* Hillsdale, NJ: Lawrence Erlbaum.

McArdle, J. J. & Epstein, D. (1987). Latent growth within developmental structural equation models. *Child Development, 58*(1), 110–133.

McArdle, J. J. & McDonald, R. P. (1984). Some algebraic properties of the Reticular Action Model for moment structures. *British Journal of Mathematical and Statistical Psychology, 37,* 234–251.

McDonald, R. P. (1978). A simple comprehensive model for the analysis of covariance structures. *British Journal of Mathematical and Statistical Psychology, 31*(1), 59–72.

McDonald, R. P. (1979). The structural analysis of multivariate data: A sketch of a general theory. *Multivariate Behavioral Research, 14*(1), 21–38.

McDonald, R. P. & Ho, M.-H. R. (2002). Principles and practice in reporting structural equation analyses. *Psychological Methods, 7,* 64–82.

Neale, M., Hunter, M., Pritikin, J., Zahery, M., Brick, T., Kirkpatrick, R., et al. (2016). Openmx 2.0: Extended structural equation and statistical modeling. *Psychometrika, 81*(2), 535–549. (PMCID: 25622929)

Neale, M. C., Boker, S. M., Xie, G., & Maes, H. H. (1999). *Mx: Statistical modeling.* (Box 126 MCV, Richmond, VA 23298: Department of Psychiatry, 5th Edition)

Oertzen, T. von.(2010). Power equivalence in structural equation modeling. *British Journal of Mathematical and Statistical Psychology, 63*(2), 257–272.

Oertzen, T. von, Brandmaier, A., & Tsang, S. (2015). Structural equation modeling with Ωnyx. *Structural Equation Modeling: A Multidisciplinary Journal*, *22*(1), 148–161.

Pearl, J. (2003). Causality: models, reasoning and inference. *Econometric Theory*, *19*(675–685), 46.

Pearson, K. (1896). Mathematical contributions to the theory of evolution. iii. regression, heredity, and panmixia. *Philosophical Transactions of the Royal Society of London. Series A*, *187*, 253–318.

Pritikin, J. N., Hunter, M. D., Oertzen, T. von, Brick, T. R., & Boker, S. M.(2017). Many-level multilevel structural equation modeling: An efficient evaluation strategy. *Structural Equation Modeling: A Multidisciplinary Journal*, 1–15.

Spearman, C. (1904). General intelligence objectively determined and measured. *American Journal of Psychology*, *15*, 201–293.

Tukey, J. W. (1954). Causation, regression, and path analysis. In O. Kempthorne, T. A. Bancroft, J. W. Gowen, & J. L. Lush (Eds.), *Statistics and mathematics in biology* (pp. 35–66). Ames, IA: Iowa State College Press.

Turner, M. E., & Stevens, C. D. (1959). The regression analysis of causal paths. *Biometrics*, *15*(2), 236–258.

Weeks, D. G. (1978). *Structural equation systems on latent variables within a second order measurement model*. University of California, Los Angeles. (Unpublished doctoral dissertation)

Wolfle, L. M. (1999). Sewall Wright on the method of path coefficients: An annotated bibliography. *Structural Equation Modeling*, *6*(3), 280–291.

Wolfle, L. M. (2003). The introduction of path analysis to the social sciences, and some emergent themes: An annotated bibliography. *Structural Equation Modeling*, *10*(1), 1–34.

Wright, S. (1918). On the nature of size factors. *The Annals of Mathematical Statistics*, *3*, 367–374.

Wright, S. (1920). The relative importance of heredity and environment in determining the piebald pattern of guinea-pigs. *Proceedings of the National Academy of Sciences*, *6*, 320–332.

Wright, S. (1921). Correlation and causation. *Journal of Agricultural Research*, *20*(7), 557–585.

Wright, S. (1934). The method of path coefficients. *The Annals of Mathematical Statistics*, *5*, 161–215.

Wright, S. (1960a). Path coefficients and path regressions: alternative or complementary concepts? *Biometrics*, *16*(2), 189–202.

Wright, S. (1960b). The treatment of reciprocal interaction, with or without lag, in path analysis. *Biometrics*, *16*(3), 423–445.

Zhang, Z., McArdle, J. J., Hamagami, A., & Grimm, K. (2012). *Rampath: Structural Equation Models*. (R package version 0.4)

Measurement and Testing Issues in Longitudinal Modeling

7

SMALL SAMPLE CORRECTIONS TO MODEL FIT CRITERIA FOR LATENT CHANGE SCORE MODELS[1]

Sarfaraz Serang

Small Sample Corrections to Model Fit Criteria for Latent Change Score Models

Structural equation modeling (SEM) is a flexible modeling framework that encompasses a broad set of statistical models. One common misconception about SEM is that it should only be used in large samples. Although it is unclear where specifically this notion originated, it has been proliferated to students of SEM by introductory texts. For example, Loehlin recommends that "structural equation modeling should not be considered a small-sample technique" (Loehlin, 2004, p. 59). Kline concurs, claiming "it is generally true that SEM is a large-sample technique" (Kline, 2011, p. 11).

General rules of thumb have been proposed regarding minimum sample sizes required to use SEM. Some have recommended sample sizes must be merely greater than $N = 100$ (Gorsuch, 1983), whereas others suggest samples of size $N = 500$ or more (Comrey & Lee, 1992). Others tie their sample size recommendations to features of the model being estimated. For example, Nunnally (1967) advises 10 observations per variable, while Bentler and Chou (1987) suggest 5 to 10 observations per estimated parameter. However, such rules of thumb have severe limitations, as the minimum sample size required is influenced by a variety of factors, including number of variables, model specification, parameter values, and amount of missing data (MacCallum, Widaman, Zhang, & Hong, 1999; Wolf, Harrington, Clark, & Miller, 2013).

Thus, researchers with smaller samples ($N \leq 100$) have turned to alternative modeling frameworks. One popular choice is the mixed-effects modeling framework, due in part to literature demonstrating this framework's capabilities in handling smaller samples (e.g. Bell, Morgan, Schoenberger, Kromrey, & Ferron, 2014; Maas & Hox, 2005). Longitudinal models can be specified as mixed-effects models, and as such enjoy these properties as well. In fact, these models can be fit to samples of as few as $N = 12$ individuals (Brammer, 2003; Muth et al., 2016). On the other hand, the longitudinal SEM literature has little research demonstrating its effectiveness in small samples (Bollen & Curran, 2006; McNeish & Harring, 2017).

Due to its generality, the SEM framework subsumes many statistical techniques as special cases. Although the notion that SEM is a large sample technique may hold true for certain latent variable models such as factor analysis models, it need not be the case for simpler models. For example, even a simple linear regression model can be fit as a structural equation model, yielding identical parameter estimates as traditional methods such as regression with least squares. If a model of interest does not require a large sample when fit in an alternative framework, and this model can be equivalently specified as a structural equation model, it stands to reason that the SEM framework would not require a large sample either.

Indeed, the simple linear regression model is not the only model that can be shown to be a special case of SEM; equivalencies across frameworks have also been demonstrated for longitudinal models. Meredith and Tisak (1990) demonstrated that repeated measures ANOVA was a special case of their more general latent curve analysis. Soon after, Willett and Sayer (1994) showed that longitudinal mixed-effects models could easily be specified as structural equation models in LISREL notation, clarifying the links between the two frameworks. Curran (2003) expanded on this work to demonstrate that a broad range of mixed-effects models could be estimated as structural equation models. As such, it is clear that models for how individuals change over time can be fit in the SEM framework, even for small samples.

One major advantage of using the SEM framework to fit longitudinal models is its access to global model fit criteria (Chou, Bentler, & Pentz, 1998; McNeish & Harring, 2017). Unavailable in the mixed-effects framework, these model fit criteria allow for the evaluation of how well a model fits the data. Consider the maximum likelihood fit function with mean structure included:

$$F_{ML} = ln|\boldsymbol{\Sigma}| - ln|\mathbf{S}| + tr\left[(\mathbf{S} - \boldsymbol{\Sigma})\,\boldsymbol{\Sigma}^{-1}\right] + (\mathbf{M} - \boldsymbol{\mu})'\boldsymbol{\Sigma}^{-1}(\mathbf{M} - \boldsymbol{\mu}) \qquad (7.1)$$

where $\mathbf{S}$ is the covariance matrix of the observed variables, $\boldsymbol{\Sigma}$ is the model-implied or expected covariance matrix, $\mathbf{M}$ is the mean vector of the observed variables, and $\boldsymbol{\mu}$ is the model-implied mean vector. The log-likelihood function is maximized when F_{ML} is minimized. The most basic global model fit criterion (and the one upon which the others discussed are based) is the model Chi-square test statistic, defined as

$$T_{ML} = (N - 1)F_{ML} \qquad (7.2)$$

where N is the sample size. Under the null hypothesis that the specified mean and covariance structures are correct, in large samples, T_{ML} follows a central Chi-square distribution with degrees of freedom equal to the degrees of freedom of the model, denoted df. As such, T_{ML} is a measure of misfit, quantifying the extent to which the model fails to reproduce the observed data.

As sample size grows, so too does the power of T_{ML} to detect even minor discrepancies between the model and the data. Thus, approximate fit indices have been developed in order to better evaluate model fit. In this study, we focus on the root mean square error of approximation (RMSEA; Steiger, 2016; Steiger & Lind, 1980). The RMSEA is defined as

$$\text{RMSEA} = \sqrt{\max\left(\frac{T_{ML} - df}{df(N-1)}, 0\right)} \qquad (7.3)$$

Although the sampling distribution of T_{ML} follows a Chi-square distribution in large samples (e.g. $N \geq 200$), it does not follow this distribution in small samples ($N < 200$; Curran, Bollen, Paxton, Kirby, & Chen, 2002; Hu & Bentler, 1999). This trickles down to the approximate fit indices, given that they are based on T_{ML} (Herzog & Boomsma, 2009). For example, the sample RMSEA overestimates its population counterpart in samples of sizes of less than $N = 200$, leading to positive bias (Curran, Bollen, Chen, Paxton, & Kirby, 2003). Furthermore, these shortcomings are exhibited under ideal conditions in which models are correctly specified and data follow a multivariate normal distribution. Needless to say, performance does not improve when these assumptions are not met (Fouladi, 2000; Nevitt & Hancock, 2004).

To address these concerns, a correction can be applied which transforms T_{ML} so that it follows a Chi-square distribution even in small samples. Unfortunately, an exact mathematical transformation to achieve this does not exist (Fujikoshi, 2000; Yuan, Tian, & Yanagihara, 2015). As a result, all such corrections are heuristic in nature (Herzog, Boomsma, & Reinecke, 2007; McNeish & Harring, 2017). Several small sample corrections (SSCs) for T_{ML} have been proposed. This study focuses on two in particular, due to their favorable performances in the methodological literature: those by Bartlett (1950) and Yuan (2005). In small samples, the sampling distribution of T_{ML} tends to have a heavier tail, exhibiting values of T_{ML} that are larger than those expected under the Chi-square distribution it intends to follow. In these situations, T_{ML} must be scaled down in order for its sampling distribution to better approximate its corresponding Chi-square distribution. Both of the aforementioned SSCs aim to achieve this in similar ways.

Bartlett (1950) suggested an SSC defined as

$$T_{BA} = \left(1 - \frac{2t + 4f + 5}{6(N-1)}\right) T_{ML} \qquad (7.4)$$

where t is the number of observed variables and f is the number of latent variables. Originally developed for exploratory factor analysis, T_{BA} adjusts T_{ML} by a function of the number of variables, both observed and latent, as well as the sample size. One attractive feature is that it can easily be calculated post hoc. Another is that its sampling distribution is asymptotically identical to that of T_{ML}. For small samples, however, T_{BA} more closely approximates a Chi-square distribution than T_{ML} (Fouladi, 2000; Herzog & Boomsma, 2009; Herzog et al., 2007; Nevitt & Hancock, 2004).

One drawback of Bartlett's correction is that it was originally intended for exploratory factor analysis, and as such is not ideal for more general models of covariance structure analysis such as those employed in SEM. This is in part due to the extent of the penalty placed on latent variables, which can be too high in confirmatory settings. To address this, Yuan (2005) proposed a slight modification of T_{BA}, defined as

$$T_{YU} = \left(1 - \frac{2t + 2f + 7}{6(N-1)}\right) T_{ML} \tag{7.5}$$

Yuan (2005) noted that the exploratory factor model and the confirmatory factor model are identical for $f = 1$, and as such his correction is identical to that of Bartlett's in this case. However, when $f > 1$, exploratory factor models estimate far more parameters than their confirmatory counterparts. Because the number of parameters estimated in the model does not enter into the correction directly, T_{YU} attempts to reduce the penalty indirectly imposed by T_{BA} through the coefficient of f. In T_{BA}, each additional latent variable decreases the correction factor by $\frac{\partial T}{\partial f} = \frac{-2}{3(N-1)}$, whereas in T_{YU}, the correction is only reduced by $\frac{\partial T}{\partial f} = \frac{-1}{3(N-1)}$ (Herzog & Boomsma, 2009). As such, T_{YU} does not penalize the number of latent factors as heavily as T_{BA}, since the addition of latent factors in a confirmatory factor analysis (CFA) model leads to fewer additional parameters estimated than the addition of latent factors in exploratory factor models. Because of this, for confirmatory models typically seen in SEM, generally $T_{BA} < T_{YU}$ for $f > 1$.

Several studies have examined the properties of T_{BA} and T_{YU} in the context of CFA models (Fouladi, 2000; Herzog & Boomsma, 2009; Herzog et al., 2007; Nevitt & Hancock, 2004). However, CFA models have different attributes than the longitudinal models of interest here. Longitudinal data are typically more expensive to collect given that they require repeated observations on the same individuals over time. As such, longitudinal models usually involve fewer observed variables than CFA models. Incomplete data are also more of a concern for longitudinal studies, since subjects often drop out of the study as time passes. Both of these impact on how SSCs correct T_{ML}: the former results in a reduction of t. while the latter implies that N overestimates the amount of information available in the data.

At this time, the only study examining SSCs in the context of longitudinal models is that of McNeish and Harring (2017). Specifically, they use the latent growth curve model (LGM; McArdle & Epstein, 1987; Meredith & Tisak, 1990), amongst the most popular longitudinal models specified in the SEM framework. The LGM proposes that the trajectory of an individual's scores over time is the result of some unobserved underlying process with some added random error. While the shape of this trajectory is assumed to be the same for all individuals, each person is permitted to have their own parameter values, which are assumed to take on a prespecified distributional form.

For the case in which all individuals are measured at the same time points (though this can easily be extended to allow for individual measurement schedules without loss of generality), the LGM can be written in the SEM framework as

$$Y_i = \Lambda \eta_i + e_i \tag{7.6}$$

where Y_i is a $t \times 1$ vector of observed scores, Λ is a $t \times f$ matrix of factor loadings, η_i is a $f \times 1$ vector of latent factor scores, and e_i is a $t \times 1$ vector of residuals. The factor scores can be decomposed into fixed effects, α, and random effects, ζ_i, such that

$$\eta_i = \alpha + \zeta_i \tag{7.7}$$

The random effects and residuals each follow a multivariate normal distribution such that $\zeta_i \sim N(0, \Psi)$ and $e_i \sim N(0, \Theta)$, where Ψ is the $f \times f$ covariance matrix for the random effects and Θ is the $t \times t$ covariance matrix for the residuals. Inserting Equation (7.7) into Equation (7.6) yields

$$Y_i = \Lambda \alpha + \Lambda \zeta_i + e_i \tag{7.8}$$

with expected mean vector (μ) and covariance matrix (Σ)

$$\mu = \Lambda \alpha$$
$$\Sigma = \Lambda \Psi \Lambda' + \Theta \tag{7.9}$$

McNeish and Harring (2017) compare the performances of T_{ML}, T_{BA}, and T_{YU} in the context of this model. As mentioned above, they point out that most structural equation models are fit using full information maximum likelihood (FIML) estimation, which does not impute values for missing data. Instead, FIML allows each individual to contribute to the likelihood function based on only their observed scores. As such, a dataset containing N individuals with missing data does not contain N individuals' worth of information for the purposes of the SSCs. Since N overestimates the amount of information available, SSCs do not correct T_{ML} as much as they should.

To address this, McNeish and Harring (2017) suggest a missing data correction (MDC) involving replacing N in T_{BA} and T_{YU} with an effective sample size, $C^2 N$. Here, C is the proportion of observed elements in the data matrix, conceptualized as a measure of data quality. For example, consider a sample in which $N = 100$ individuals were measured at 10 time points each. The resulting data matrix would contain $100 \times 10 = 1,000$ cells. If 90% of these cells were complete, than $C = 0.9$, and $C^2 N = 81$. The substitution of $C^2 N$ for N into the equations for T_{BA} and T_{YU} thus creates analogous corrections to be used in the presence of missing data. One useful property of this MDC is that, if the data are complete, $C^2 = 1$ so that the effective sample size will be N and the corrected value of the test statistic will be identical to its complete data counterpart.

McNeish and Harring (2017) studied the performance of the test statistics under different sample sizes, numbers of time points, and percentages of missing data. Similar to the findings of previous studies, T_{ML} performed extremely poorly. Even with complete data, at $N = 20$ it exhibited a type I error rate near 35% with 8 time points. On the other hand, T_{BA} and T_{YU} were all able to control type I error rates well when data were complete. When data were incomplete, the SSCs on their own were inadequate, requiring the MDC to be applied before being able to maintain control over type I error rates. The authors also found that the MDC was required in the calculation of the RMSEA. Overall, they recommend T_{YU} in small samples when data are complete, and T_{BA} when data are incomplete.

Though McNeish and Harring (2017) discuss the application of SSCs in LGMs, no attention has yet been given to other longitudinal structural equation models. For example, consider the latent change score model (LCSM; Hamagami & McArdle, 2001; McArdle, 2001; McArdle & Hamagami, 2001), another popular approach to model change in the SEM framework. The LCSM describes growth by explicitly modeling change scores from one time point to the next. The LCSM can be written as follows. According to classical test theory (McDonald, 1999), the observed scores from an individual i at time *time* can be written as a combination of true scores and errors, such that

$$Y_{i,time} = y_{i,time} + e_{i,time} \tag{7.10}$$

where the true scores are allowed to covary over time and the errors follow a multivariate normal distribution with uncorrelated errors. Then, the change score between a given time point and the one immediately preceding it can be written as

$$\Delta y_{i,time} = y_{i,time} - y_{i,time-1} \tag{7.11}$$

It is upon these change scores that hypotheses are made. For example, in a *no change* model, Equation (7.11) reduces to

$$\Delta y_{i,time} = 0 \tag{7.12}$$

indicating that no change occurs over time. A *constant change* model can also be formulated in which individuals are proposed to change by the same amount from time point to time point. This model can be written as

$$\Delta y_{i,time} = s_i \tag{7.13}$$

where s_i is an individual specific constant change component with mean μ_s and variance σ_s^2. Combining this with Equation (7.10), we can write the model for the original observed variables as

$$Y_{i,time} = y_{i,1} + (time - 1) s_i + e_{i,time} \tag{7.14}$$

Figure 7.1 displays path diagrams for both the LGM and the constant change score model. It can easily be seen that these models are equivalent (Ghisletta &

McArdle, 2012), yielding identical model expectations and fit statistics. However, the number and role of latent variables in each model differs, leading to differences in the calculation of SSCs.

Though the LGM has been studied in small samples with missing data, the LCSM has received no such attention in this context. The consensus in the literature is that the sampling distribution of T_{ML} relies heavily on asymptotic behavior and is therefore resoundingly inadequate when used in small samples. However, it remains unclear whether T_{BA} and T_{YU} can remedy this situation. Both have been recommended under various circumstances, but whether these recommendations hold for the LCSM in small samples with missing data is unknown. Additionally, both have severe limitations. This stems in part from the notion that all were intended to be used for models with a significant measurement component. That is, they were derived for models in which latent variables are conceptualized as unobserved constructs inferred from the relationships between observed variables. However, in longitudinal SEM, latent variables represent something entirely different: parameters associated with growth and dynamic processes.

This distinction manifests itself in the correction factors of the SSCs. Both T_{BA} and T_{YU} shrink T_{ML} by an amount proportional to the number of latent variables, f. Consider a CFA model with k indicators per factor (k is therefore a positive integer). As a function of observed variables, t, the number of latent variables can be represented as $f = \frac{t}{k}$. For the LGM however, f is not a function of t, but rather the functional form of the growth. For the linear growth model for

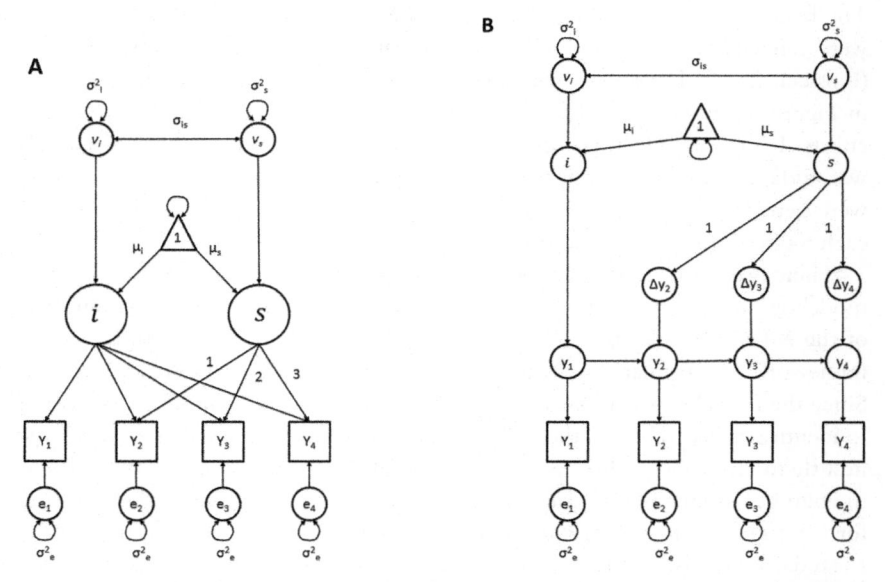

FIGURE 7.1 Path diagrams for equivalent models for change in the (A) LGM framework and (B) LCSM framework.

example, one would obtain $f = 2$ for all t. Finally, the LCSM contains the highest number of latent variables, given that the true scores are explicitly modeled in the matrix algebra. For the constant change model, $f = 2t + 1$. This is troubling for two reasons. First, f varies drastically depending on the model, which in turn can proportionally distort the correction factor. Second, T_{BA} and T_{YU} are not invariant under model respecification. If a model for linear growth were to be fit in the LGM and LCSM frameworks (using the constant change score model), they would obtain identical values of T_{ML} because both models are equivalent and will yield the same model fit, but different values of T_{BA} and T_{YU} because each model contains a different number of latent variables. The performance of the RMSEA also requires further evaluation. Even if an SSC is able to approximate its reference Chi-square distribution well, its RMSEA may not perform well, or vice versa.

The purpose of this chapter is to examine the performance of measures of model fit for the LCSM in small samples with missing data. Of particular interest is the performance of SSCs in this endeavor. The next section consists of a simulation study to investigate this. The following section provides an empirical example using data on cognitive change in which this subject plays a key role. The chapter concludes with a discussion of the results accompanied by some thoughts on how future research should proceed.

Methods

The behavior of the SSCs was studied via a Monte Carlo simulation study. Data were generated and analyzed in R (R core team, 2014), using the *lavaan* package (Rosseel, 2012). Data were generated according to the growth model provided in Figure 7.1, varying levels of the factors of interest to better understand their effects. Following a factorial design, every possible combination of factor levels was studied. For each condition (each combination of factor levels), 1,000 datasets were generated to serve as replications. T_{ML}, T_{BA}, and T_{YU} were calculated for each replication in each condition.

There were five main factors whose influence was of interest: sample size, modeling framework, number of time points, amount of missing data, and use of the MDC. Sample size had four levels: $N = 20$, 30, 50, and 100. Modeling framework, the primary focus of this study, had two levels: LGM and LCSM. Since the model expectations for each of these models are identical (thus leading to identical values of T_{ML}), the differences across levels for this factor would manifest themselves only in how SSCs treat each of the formulations. With regard to the number of time points, datasets had either $t = 4$ or $t = 8$ time points. The data for $t = 4$ conditions simply consisted of the odd numbered time points from the $t = 8$ data. The use of the same (albeit masked) data was intended to remove the influence of sampling fluctuations inherent in randomly generated data in order to make these two levels as comparable as possible.

The amount of missing data was also varied, either 0% (representing complete data) or 20% missing data. The 20% missing data conditions were created by subjecting each data point in the corresponding complete data condition to a 20% chance of being obscured, resulting in data missing completely at random, or MCAR. Thus, the value of C varied across datasets, but on average, it was approximately 20%. As with the number of time points, this was done to remove the influence of sampling fluctuations to make complete data conditions as comparable as possible to missing data conditions. Finally, the effectiveness of the MDC, as proposed by McNeish and Harring (2017), was evaluated. SSCs were calculated with and without MDCs, to determine if they improved the performance of the SSCs.

Two outcomes were of interest. The first was the type I error rate, which was calculated for each test statistic in each condition. An alpha level of 0.05 was used as the nominal rate, as is common in the social sciences. Conditions for which the type I error rate exceeded this were undesirable given that this too often leads to the rejection of, in our case, the population model. However, type I error rates too far below the nominal level are also undesirable, given that they reflect low power, a concern already present in small samples. Type I error rates between 2.5% and 7.5% were considered acceptable, not deviating too far from the nominal rate of 5% (Bradley, 1978). The second outcome of interest was the RMSEA. Following McNeish and Harring (2017), the median RMSEA among all replications in each condition was calculated in order to serve as a representative estimate of approximate model fit. This provides a sense of the typical RMSEA one would expect in each condition. Values of the RMSEA below 0.06 are typically judged to have acceptable approximate model fit (Hu & Bentler, 1999).

Results

Type I error rates are displayed in Table 7.1. As expected, these rates were inflated for T_{ML}: in no condition did they drop below 6%. T_{ML} exhibited its best performance when $t = 4$ and data were complete. In this condition, only the $N = 20$ case had rates beyond the acceptable bounds of 8.8%. However, rates grew substantially with additional time points. For example, when considering the condition just mentioned, rates grew from 8.8% to 25.9%, simply by increasing the number of time points from $t = 4$ to $t = 8$. The impact of missing data is also worth noting. When $t = 8$, type I error rates skyrocketed from 25.9% to 96.3% for $N = 20$, only managing to fall below 10% for samples of $N = 100$. Clearly, T_{ML} on its own cannot control type I error well in small samples.

Modeling Framework

SSCs did a much better job, though their ability to control type I error rates was more sensitive to the influence of some factors rather than others. The most

TABLE 7.1 Simulation study results – type I error rates. Values outside the acceptable range of .025 and .075 are given in bold.

t	Miss.	MDC	T	LGM				LCSM			
				$N=20$	$N=30$	$N=50$	$N=100$	$N=20$	$N=30$	$N=50$	$N=100$
4	0%		T_{ML}	**.088**	.065	.065	.062	**.088**	.065	.065	.062
			T_{BA}	.032	.034	.045	.052	**.003**	**.010**	.029	.039
			T_{YU}	.038	.037	.045	.053	**.015**	**.023**	.039	.046
	20%	Yes	T_{ML}	**.153**	**.106**	.071	**.077**	**.153**	**.106**	.071	**.077**
		Yes	T_{BA}	.044	.031	.038	.053	**.000**	**.002**	**.011**	.035
		Yes	T_{YU}	.050	.041	.039	.055	**.015**	**.013**	.028	.048
		No	T_{BA}	**.079**	.062	.048	.061	.025	**.014**	.028	.049
		No	T_{YU}	**.085**	.064	.051	.062	.051	.032	.038	.053
8	0%		T_{ML}	**.259**	**.147**	**.109**	**.076**	**.259**	**.147**	**.109**	**.076**
			T_{BA}	**.018**	**.020**	.048	.045	**.000**	**.000**	**.000**	**.013**
			T_{YU}	.028	.030	.050	.046	**.000**	**.002**	**.015**	.028
	20%	Yes	T_{ML}	**.963**	**.613**	**.179**	**.095**	**.963**	**.613**	**.179**	**.095**
		Yes	T_{BA}	**.701**	**.392**	.051	.047	**.000**	**.000**	**.000**	**.005**
		Yes	T_{YU}	**.749**	**.405**	.058	.049	**.001**	.071	**.007**	**.016**
		No	T_{BA}	**.895**	**.477**	**.084**	.053	**.000**	**.097**	**.008**	**.016**
		No	T_{YU}	**.903**	**.485**	**.086**	.055	**.430**	**.358**	.033	.038

influential factor in determining type I error rates was the framework within which the model was fit. Models fit using the LCSM framework (thus contributing a higher f to the calculation of the SSCs) exhibited unilaterally lower type I error rates compared to when models were fit in the LGM framework. The problem with this is that, similar to the findings of McNeish and Harring (2017), the SSCs seemed to control type I error rates relatively well when using the LGM framework. As a result, type I error rates for the LCSM condition were often too small.

Consider, for example, the conditions with complete data and $t = 4$. When fit in the LGM framework, type I error rates for the SSCs fell within the acceptable range for all sample sizes. However, when fit in the LCSM framework, SSCs overcorrected and the rates did not rise to acceptable levels until sample size reached $N = 50$ or more. A similar phenomenon was observed when data were missing (and the MDC was used). Keeping with $t = 4$, for the LGM condition, all type I error rates were very near their nominal levels. Yet in the LCSM condition, a sample of $N = 50$ or more was required. In fact, for T_{BA} in particular, even $N = 50$ was not enough; a sample of $N = 100$ was necessary.

Graphically, the role of the modeling framework can be seen in Figure 7.2. Figure 7.2 displays the distributions of each of the test statistics fit in both frameworks for $N = 20$, $t = 4$, and missing data with the MDC employed. The reference distribution they aimed to approximate, the Chi-square distribution with 8 degrees of freedom, is shown as a solid line. Compared to the Chi-square distribution, the distribution of T_{ML} is clearly too heavy-tailed. However, both

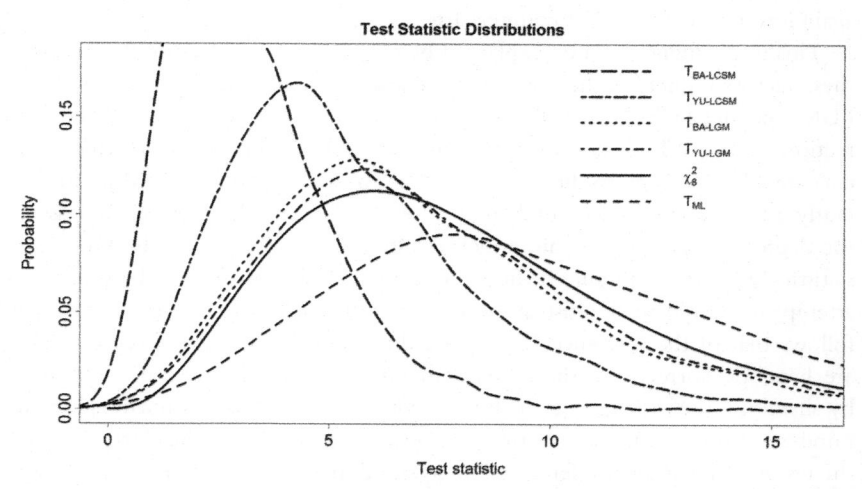

FIGURE 7.2 Distributions of test statistics fit in both frameworks for $N = 20$, $t = 4$, and 20% missing data with the MDC employed.

SSCs fit using the LGM framework were able to shrink T_{ML} adequately. As such, when using the LGM framework, both SSCs approximated the Chi-square distribution relatively well, leading to acceptable type I error rates. However, when using the LCSM framework, both SSCs overcorrected (T_{BA} more so than T_{YU}), resulting in test statistics and consequently type I error rates that were far too small.

Number of Time Points

The number of time points also appeared to play an important role in type I error rates of SSCs. This came as no surprise, given that it entered directly into their calculation. However, its pattern of effects was not as consistent as that of the modeling framework. For example, consider the LGM condition with complete data. As mentioned earlier, type I error rates fell within the acceptable range for $t = 4$. However, when $t = 8$, the SSCs overcorrected leading to type I error rates that were lower, especially when T_{BA} was applied to smaller sample sizes such as $N = 20$ and $N = 30$.

One interesting feature to note is that, unlike the effect of modeling framework, the effect of the number of time points was not unilateral. That is, whereas fitting the model in the LCSM framework led to reduction in type I error rates for all conditions when compared to the LGM framework, the same was not true when increasing the number of time points. This can be seen in the example just mentioned. Whereas raising the number of time points lowered type I error rates for both SSCs for $N = 20$ and $N = 30$, increasing time points *raised* type I error rates slightly for $N = 50$. Finally, for $N = 100$, these rates for $t = 8$ were once again lower than their $t = 4$ counterparts.

This phenomenon can be explained by examining the nature of how each of these factors influences the SSC. In comparing modeling frameworks, both the LGM and the LCSM have identical values of T_{ML} and differ only in the correction factor. When increasing the number of time points in the data, more data are added leading to different values of T_{ML} across conditions. More importantly, the increase in the number of observed variables leads to an increase in the degrees of freedom of the model, resulting in a different distribution of test statistics which also require a different reference Chi-square distribution. SSCs attempt to transform the distribution of the test statistics so that it more closely follows that of the reference Chi-square distribution. However, since the SSCs are heuristic corrections, the increase in time points is compensated for solely by shrinking the distribution of the test statistics by a factor proportional to the number of time points. Since the true relationship between the distribution of the test statistics and the reference Chi-square distribution is certainly much more complex, this mapping is inherently flawed, with the imperfections manifesting themselves in the fluctuations of type I error rates across conditions. As such, when increasing the number of time points, it is not unreasonable to observe departures from the monotonic decrease in type I error rates seen for modeling framework comparisons.

This point regarding the impact of adding additional time points is further exemplified by the inconsistencies in the direction of type I error rate changes with respect to other factors. For example, when fitting LCSMs, overcorrections to the SSCs were amplified. Since LCSMs overcorrected too much as is, the combination of this as well as the overcorrection due to the increase in the number of time points led to type I error rates near 0. However, in other cases, SSCs did not correct enough when the number of time points was increased. For the LGM condition with missing data (and the MDC used), type I error rates shifted from being acceptable for all sample sizes at $t = 4$ to exceeding 70% when $t = 8$ for $N = 20$. Even for $N = 30$, rates were far too large at 40%, before stabilizing at acceptable levels at $N = 50$ and above.

Missing Data Corrections

The effects of missing data vary based on the other conditions. When MDCs were not used, the presence of missing data led to increases in type I error rates. This is unsurprising, given that in the presence of missing data, MDCs reduced the denominator of the SSCs, thus increasing the amount by which SSCs shrank T_{ML}. Without MDCs, N overrepresented the amount of information available in the data, thereby reducing the amount by which SSCs shrank T_{ML}. As a result, corrected test statistics remained too large, leading to higher type I error rates.

The effectiveness of the MDCs, however, depended on the modeling framework. When fitting LGMs with missing data, MDCs allowed SSCs to reach acceptable type I error rates using smaller samples. For example, for $t = 4$, SSCs with MDCs exhibited acceptable type I error rates even at $N = 20$, whereas without MDCs, samples of size $N = 30$ were required. Similarly, for $t = 8$, SSCs with MDCs required samples of size $N = 50$ for acceptable type I error rates, whereas those without MDCs needed $N = 100$. However, when fitting LCSMs, this same advantage did not hold. As discussed earlier, the type I error rates for SSCs applied to LCSMs were too small, and the MDCs only made them even smaller. As such, their use was counterproductive for LCSMs.

One combination of conditions resulted in excessively high type I error rates: conditions with both 20% missing data and $t = 8$. In particular, these high rates occurred for the smaller sample size conditions, that of $N = 20$ and $N = 30$. The LGM conditions appeared more problematic. When no MDC was used, type I error rates were about 90% for $N = 20$ and about 48% for $N = 30$. Rates were slightly better (though still far too high) when the MDC is used, with rates of about 70% for $N = 20$ and about 40% for $N = 30$. With regard to the use of

LCSMs, the overcorrection of the SSCs seemed to hold these rates in check. The only exception was when no MDC was used, where T_{YU} had 43% type I error rates for $N = 20$ and 36% for $N = 30$. Curiously, corresponding rates for T_{BA} were under 10% for both sample sizes, though it should be noted that both were outside the acceptable range. Overall, it appears that the combination of 20% missing data and $t = 8$ was too much to control for the SSCs for sample sizes of $N = 20$ and $N = 30$, though these extremely high rates were reined in for samples of size $N = 50$ or more.

RMSEA

Results were much more favorable for the RMSEA. Considering conditions for which the median RMSEA was below 0.06 (Hu & Bentler, 1999) to have acceptable approximate fit, all conditions for which samples were of size $N = 50$ or more would be judged as having acceptable model fit. Results for T_{ML} are given in Table 7.2. As we can see, the median RMSEA was a bit too large in all conditions for $N = 20$. It was also too high for the smaller sample size conditions when $t = 8$, likely due to the issues resulting from the increase in degrees of freedom already discussed.

When calculated using SSCs, median RMSEAs were excellent. In fact, outside of those conditions that exhibited excessively high type I error rates, median RMSEAs for SSCs were zero in all conditions. When LGMs were fit with 20% missing data, $t = 8$, and no MDC was used, median RMSEA was 0.23 for $N = 20$, 0.11 for $N = 30$, and 0.02 for $N = 50$. When the MDC was employed, the RMSEA was 0.18 for $N = 20$, and 0.09 for $N = 30$. When LCSMs were fit to data with 20% missingness (without the MDC) and $t = 8$, T_{YU} exhibited a median RMSEA of 0.14 for $N = 20$ and 0.06 for $N = 30$. As mentioned, median RMSEA was zero for all other conditions. The exceptional performance of the RMSEA, particularly for the LCSM conditions, is likely due to the SSCs tendency to shrink the test statistic too much. Since we desire RMSEAs to be as close to zero as possible, the index benefits a great deal from the overcorrection of the SSCs.

TABLE 7.2 Simulation study results – median RMSEA for T_{ML}. Values above the acceptable range of 0.060 are given in bold.

t	Miss. %	$N = 20$	$N = 30$	$N = 50$	$N = 100$
4	0%	**0.062**	0.000	0.000	0.000
	20%	**0.096**	0.050	0.000	0.000
8	0%	**0.107**	**0.064**	0.036	0.015
	20%	**0.300**	**0.147**	0.053	0.022

Empirical Example

Also relevant is the extent to which the results found in the previous section hold when comparing models. For example, it can be of interest to determine whether a model hypothesizing change over time (e.g. the LGM or LCSM) fits the data better than a model presuming no change (the *intercept-only* or *no change* model). This comparison is typically done using the likelihood ratio test, which takes the difference in model fit to determine whether the gains achieved by fitting the more complex model are worthwhile. However, if the test statistics used in this test are inflated in small samples, as observed in the previous section, they may not retain their properties and therefore produce discordant results. Here, this is examined in an empirical dataset.

The data come from the Cognition and Aging in the USA (CogUSA) study, a national longitudinal study of age-related changes in cognition in adults. Though the full sample is much larger, only a small subset of $N = 43$ individuals is examined here, with 28% missing data. These individuals were chosen such that each individual contributed up to four measurements, the first of which was taken between the ages of 53 and 54 years and the last of which was taken before the age of 61 years. All data were collected via telephone interviews. The outcome of interest is the Number Series score, a test from the Woodcock Johnson Psychoeducational Test Battery (WJ-III; Woodcock, McGrew, & Mather, 2001; Woodcock & Mather, 2001), adapted for administration over the telephone. The Number Series test is a measure of quantitative reasoning in which participants are given a series of numbers from which they must derive the numerical pattern and provide the missing number in the sequence. The trajectories of the scores are given in Figure 7.3.

The no change model as well as the constant change model were fit to the data in both the LGM and LCSM frameworks. Constant change models were similar to those in Figure 7.1, with the no change models simply omitting the components associated with changes. For T_{ML}, both the no change model ($T_{ML}(11) = 16.225$, $p = .133$) and the constant change model ($T_{ML}(8) = 7.051$, $p = .531$) showed acceptable fit. That said, the SSCs also demonstrated acceptable fit, given that their fit only improves upon that of T_{ML}. When fit in the LGM framework, Bartlett's correction yielded $T_{BA}(11) = 14.072$, $p = .258$, for the no change model and $T_{BA}(11) = 5.895$, $p = .659$, for the constant change model. Yuan's correction led to $T_{YU}(11) = 13.818$, $p = .243$, for the no change model and $T_{YU}(8) = 6.005$, $p = .647$. Of course, the corresponding LCSM SSCs were smaller. Bartlett's correction resulted in $T_{BA}(11) = 10.525$, $p = .484$, for the no change model and $T_{BA}(11) = 4.354$, $p = .824$, for the constant change model. Yuan's correction yielded $T_{YU}(11) = 12.298$, $p = .342$ for the no change model and $T_{YU}(8) = 5.243$, $p = .732$ for the constant change model.

The interesting finding lies in the likelihood ratio test statistics. Beginning with T_{ML}, the resulting value is $T_{ML}(3) = 9.174$, $p = .027$, indicating that the constant

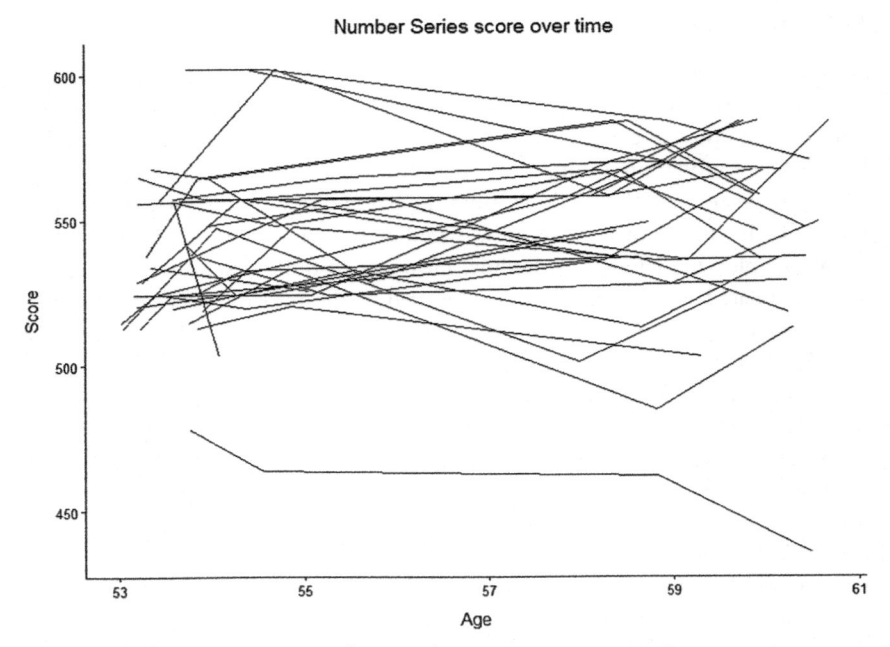

FIGURE 7.3 Change trajectories for Number Series score across time.

change model fits better than the no change model. When fitting the models as LGMs, results concurred for both Bartlett's ($T_{BA}(3) = 8.177$, $p = .042$) and Yuan's ($T_{YU}(3) = 7.813$, $p = .045$) corrections. However fitting the models as LCSMs led to the opposite conclusion, as both Bartlett's ($T_{BA}(3) = 6.171$, $p = .104$) and Yuan's ($T_{YU}(3) = 7.064$, $p = .070$) corrections preferred the no change model over the constant change model.

This finding is in line with the results of the simulation, indicating that SSCs overcorrect when applied to LCSMs, leading to test statistics that are smaller and thus p-values that are larger, manifesting itself in type I error probabilities below the nominal level. One can imagine that, since the likelihood ratio test statistic is calculated by taking the difference between two test statistics, even if both were reduced too much, the difference between them might not be affected. However, since the correction factors are multiplicative, they reduce the larger test statistic, in this case that of the no change model, by more than they do the smaller, that of the constant change model. This brings the two closer together, leading to an even smaller difference between them.

Discussion

The primary focus of this study was to better understand the performance of SSCs in LCSMs with missing data. The simulation study found that when applied to LCSMs, SSCs generally overcorrected T_{ML}, resulting in values that were too small and thus type I error rates below the nominal level, as well as zero or near zero values for the RMSEA. This also led to a substantial reduction in power. Adding more time points did not alleviate this problem, though its effects varied depending on the other conditions. A similar conclusion can be drawn for the presence of incomplete data in that their influence depended on other conditions. MDCs served to lower type I error rates, which had both desirable and undesirable consequences. For LGMs, whose type I error rates in smaller samples were too high, use of the MDC was beneficial since it reduced these rates to more closely align with nominal levels. However for LCSMs, whose type I error rates were too low, MDCs lowered them even further, thereby compounding the problem.

In their study of LGMs, McNeish and Harring (2017) recommend T_{YU} for complete data and T_{BA} for incomplete data. With regard to LCSMs, the current study found that although both SSCs performed similarly, T_{YU} exhibited a slight edge over T_{BA} across the board. This is due to the amount by which both correct T_{ML}. Since for LCSMs both overcorrect T_{ML}, T_{YU} outperforms T_{BA} since it shrinks T_{ML} by a proportionately lesser amount. Thus, the distribution of T_{YU} more closely approximates that of T_{ML} than the distribution of T_{BA}.

Results showed that the RMSEAs were better able to judge model fit. When SSCs were used, median RMSEA was zero in all but the most extreme conditions studied. This is likely due to the fact that SSCs shrink T_{ML}, which in turn shrinks the RMSEA. Since smaller values of the RMSEA are preferable, the shrinking improves its ability to identify a model that fits well. However, this is also likely to diminish its ability to accurately identify a model that fits poorly as a poorly fitting model. Since only data–generating models were fit to the data, the extent to which the RMSEA would fail to identify a poorly fitting model as such is unknown. Yet, it would not be surprising if it were to have difficulty doing so, revealing its performance in this study to be only one side of a double-edged sword.

The empirical example demonstrated that the framework within which a model is fit can lead to opposing results even when comparing models using the likelihood ratio test. When LGMs were fit, SSCs concluded that the constant change model was preferred over the no change model. However, when LCSMs were fit, SSCs selected the no change model, indicating that no changes occurred in Number Series scores over time. Of course, since the data are real empirical data, it is unknown which (if either) conclusion is correct. Yet, the notion that two opposing conclusions can be reached by fitting two equivalent models is concerning.

One potential solution for this problem is to use an SSC that is invariant under model specification. That is, if two equivalent models are fit to the data, the SSC should correct T_{ML} in the same way, regardless of the framework within which the model is specified. The best performing SSC in the literature to adhere to this condition was developed by Swain (1975). Swain's correction is defined as

$$T_{SW} = \left(1 - \frac{t\left(2t^2+3t-1\right)-q\left(2q^2+3q-1\right)}{12df\left(N-1\right)}\right) T_{ML} \qquad (7.15)$$

where

$$q = \frac{\sqrt{1+4t(t+1)-8df}-1}{2} \qquad (7.16)$$

By using df in the calculation instead of f, T_{SW} becomes invariant to model respecification. However, it has two major weaknesses. First, in the context of longitudinal models, T_{SW} has been shown to be inferior to both T_{BA} and T_{YU} with regard to its ability to control type I error rates (McNeish & Harring, 2017). Second, the radical in Equation 7.16 imposes a constraint on the data, since the quantity underneath must be non-negative. It can easily be shown that this constraint amounts to an inequality such that the number of time points, t, must be less than or equal to the number of parameters estimated in the model.

Although this constraint is not typically problematic in factor analytic contexts which estimate a large number of parameters, it can be for longitudinal models which estimate relatively few. For example, given the way in which the models here have been specified thus far, the no change model estimates only 3 parameters, while the constant change model estimates 6. Thus, if one wished to compare the fit of these models, one would be limited to at most 3 time points of data to do so, since the value of the correction factor would not be calculable beyond this. Aside from failing to reward those who measure the process of interest more often, the difficulties in finding reliable change patterns using only 3 time points of data should not be underestimated, especially if these trajectories are nonlinear.

That said, additional work is needed on this topic. Specifically, the results of this study suggest that a new SSC is needed: one that is more appropriate for longitudinal models in general. Though the form of this new SSC has a great deal of flexibility, it should possess the following four properties. First, the new SSC should be asymptotically equivalent to T_{ML}. That is, the influence of the correction should decrease as sample size increases, becoming absent entirely for a sample of infinite size. Second, the new SSC should be invariant to model specification. If two models are identical with regard to model expectations, then the value of the new SSC should be the same for both models. This represents a shift away from using the number of latent variables as part of the correction factor. Third, the new SSC should never penalize the researcher for collecting more variables. In the longitudinal case, this translates to the idea that the SSC should not perform worse if the researcher were to continue the study and obtain data at more time points, ideally rewarding the researcher for doing so. Finally, the new SSC should be able to account for missing data and perform well in its presence. The MDC used should be of the form such that it, in effect, deactivates itself when data are complete. Otherwise, it should adequately characterize the quality of the observed information in the data. Such an SSC would be of great use to researchers with small samples wishing to evaluate how well longitudinal models fit their data.

Note

1 This work was supported in part by funding from the National Institute on Aging grant number 3R37AG007137. The author would like to thank Jack McArdle for the perspective and inspiration leading to this work.

References

Bartlett, M. S. (1950). Tests of significance in factor analysis. *British Journal of Psychology (Statistical Section)*, *3*, 77–85.

Bell, B. A., Morgan, G. B., Schoeneberger, J. A., Kromrey, J. D., & Ferron, J. M. (2014). How low can you go? *Methodology*, *10*, 1–11.

Bentler, P. M. & Chou, C. H. (1987). Practical issues in structural modeling. *Sociological Methods & Research*, *16*, 78–117.

Bollen, K. A. & Curran, P. J. (2006). *Latent curve models: A structural equation perspective.* Hoboken, NJ: Wiley.

Bradley, J. V. (1978). Robustness? *British Journal of Mathematical and Statistical Psychology*, *31*, 144–152.

Brammer, R. J. (2003). Modelling covariance structure in ascending dose studies of isolated tissues and organs. *Pharmaceutical Statistics*, *2*, 103–112.

Chou, C. P., Bentler, P. M., & Pentz, M. A. (1998). Comparisons of two statistical approaches to study growth curves: The multilevel model and the latent curve analysis. *Structural Equation Modeling*, *5*, 247–266.

Comrey, A. L., & Lee, H. B. (1992). *A first course in factor analysis.* Hillsdale, NJ: Erlbaum.

Curran, P. J. (2003). Have multilevel models been structural equation models all along? *Multivariate Behavioral Research*, *38*, 529–569.

Curran, P. J., Bollen, K. A., Chen, F., Paxton, P., & Kirby, J. B. (2003). Finite sampling properties of the point estimates and confidence intervals of the RMSEA. *Sociological Methods & Research*, *32*, 208–252.

Curran, P. J., Bollen, K. A., Paxton, P., Kirby, J., & Chen, F. (2002). The noncentral Chi-square distribution in misspecified structural equation models: Finite sample results from a Monte Carlo simulation. *Multivariate Behavioral Research*, *37*, 1–36.

Fouladi, R. T. (2000). Performance of modified test statistics in covariance and correlation structure analysis under conditions of multivariate nonnormality. *Structural Equation Modeling*, *7*, 356–410.

Fujikoshi, Y. (2000). Transformations with improved chi-squared approximations. *Journal of Multivariate Analysis*, *72*, 249–263.

Ghisletta, P. & Mcardle, J. J. (2012). Latent curve models and latent change score models estimated in R. *Structural Equation Modeling*, *19*, 651–682.

Gorsuch, R. L. (1983). *Factor analysis*, 2nd edition. Hillsdale, NJ: Erlbaum.

Hamagami, F. & McArdle, J. J. (2001). Advanced studies of individual differences linear dynamic models for longitudinal data analysis. In G. Marcoulides & R. Schumacker

(Eds.), *New developments and techniques in structural equations modeling* (pp. 203–246). Mahwah, NJ: Lawrence Erlbaum Associates, Inc.

Herzog, W. & Boomsma, A. (2009). Small-sample robust estimators of noncentrality-based and incremental model fit. *Structural Equation Modeling, 16,* 1–27.

Herzog, W., Boomsma, A., & Reinecke, S. (2007). The model-size effect on traditional and modified tests of covariance structures. *Structural Equation Modeling, 14,* 361–390.

Hu, L. T. & Bentler, P. M. (1999). Cutoff criteria for fit indexes in covariance structure analysis: Conventional criteria versus new alternatives. *Structural Equation Modeling, 6,* 1–55.

Kline, R. B. (2011). *Principles and practice of structural equation modeling*. New York: Guilford Press.

Loehlin, J. C. (2004). *Latent variable models: An introduction to factor, path, and structural equation analysis*. Mahwah, NJ: L. Erlbaum Associates.

Maas, C. J. & Hox, J. J. (2005). Sufficient sample sizes for multilevel modeling. *Methodology, 1,* 86–92.

MacCallum, R. C., Widaman, K. F., Zhang, S., & Hong, S. (1999). Sample size in factor analysis. *Psychological Methods, 4,* 84–99.

McArdle, J. J. (2001). A latent difference score approach to longitudinal dynamic structural analyses. In R. Cudeck, S. duToit, & D. Sorbom (Eds.), *Structural equation modeling: Present and future* (pp. 342–380). Lincolnwood, IL: Scientific Software International.

McArdle, J. J. & Epstein, D. (1987). Latent growth curves within developmental structural equation models. *Child Development, 58,* 110–133.

McArdle, J. J. & Hamagami, F. (2001). Latent difference score structural models for linear dynamic analyses with incomplete longitudinal data. In L. M. Collins & M. Sayer (Eds.), *New methods for the analysis of change* (pp. 139–175). Washington, DC: American Psychological Association.

McNeish, D. & Harring, J. R. (2017). Correcting model fit criteria for small sample latent growth models with incomplete data. *Educational and Psychological Measurement, 77,* 990–1018.

Meredith, W. & Tisak, J. (1990). Latent curve analysis. *Psychometrika, 55,* 107–122.

Muth, C., Bales, K. L., Hinde, K., Maninger, N., Mendoza, S. P., & Ferrer, E. (2015). Alternative models for small samples in psychological research: Applying linear mixed effects models and generalized estimating equations to repeated measures data. *Educational and Psychological Measurement, 76,* 64–87.

Nevitt, J., & Hancock, G. R. (2004). Evaluating small sample approaches for model test statistics in structural equation modeling. *Multivariate Behavioral Research, 39,* 439–478.

Nunnally, J. C. (1967). *Psychometric theory*. New York: McGraw-Hill.

R Core Team. (2014). *R: A language and environment for statistical computing*. Vienna, Austria: R Foundation for Statistical Computing.

McDonald, R. P. (1999). *Test theory: A unified treatment*. London: Lawrence Erlbaum.

Rosseel, Y. (2012). Lavaan: An R package for structural equation modeling. *Journal of Statistical Software, 48*(2), 1–36.

Steiger, J. H. (2016). Notes on the Steiger–Lind (1980) handout. *Structural Equation Modeling, 23,* 777–781.

Steiger, J. H. & Lind, J. C. (1980, May). *Statistically-based tests for the number of common factors*. Paper presented at the annual meeting of the Psychometric Society, Iowa City, IA.

Swain, A. J. (1975). *Analysis of parametric structures for variance matrices* (Unpublished doctoral dissertation). Department of Statistics, University of Adelaide, Adelaide, Australia.

Willett, J. B. & Sayer, A. G. (1994). Using covariance structure analysis to detect correlates and predictors of individual change over time. *Psychological Bulletin, 116*, 363–381.

Wolf, E. J., Harrington, K. M., Clark, S. L., & Miller, M. W. (2013). Sample size requirements for structural equation models: An evaluation of power, bias, and solution propriety. *Educational and Psychological Measurement, 73*, 913–934.

Woodcock, R. W. & Mather, N. (2001). *Woodcock-Johnson Tests of Achievement-Examiner's Manual, Standard and Extended Manual.* Riverside, IL: The Riverside Publishing Company.

Woodcock, R. W., McGrew, K. S., & Mather, N. (2001). *Woodcock-Johnson III cognitive battery and achievement battery.* Riverside, IL: The Riverside Publishing Company.

Yuan, K.-H. (2005). Fit indices versus test statistics. *Multivariate Behavioral Research, 40*, 115–148.

Yuan, K.-H., Tian, Y., & Yanagihara, H. (2015). Empirical correction to the likelihood ratio statistic for structural equation modeling with many variables. *Psychometrika, 80*, 379–405.

8

ON INTERINDIVIDUAL DIFFERENCES IN INTRAINDIVIDUAL CHANGES

Lijuan Wang & Miao Yang

Introduction

Baltes and Nesselroade's (1979) seminal chapter identifies five rationales for conducting longitudinal research: (1) direct identification of intraindividual changes; (2) direct identification of interindividual differences in intraindividual changes; (3) examining interrelationships in intraindividual changes; (4) analyses of causes (determinants) of intraindividual changes; and (5) analyses of causes (determinants) of interindividual differences in intraindividual changes. McArdle and Nesselroade's (2014) book on longitudinal data analysis using structural equation modeling was nicely organized by the five rationales. In this chapter, we discuss two statistical issues related to the second rationale. Specifically, the first issue is on how to appropriately and powerfully detect interindividual differences in intraindividual changes by variance testing, and the second issue is on the consequences of ignoring interindividual differences in intraindividual changes on statistical inferences about latent factor means or fixed effects. For both issues, we use linear growth curve modeling as a tool to facilitate the discussion.

In the following sections, we first review the development of latent curve modeling and describe a generic latent linear growth curve model. Next, we review and discuss four different statistical tests coupled with either constrained or unconstrained estimation for detecting interindividual differences in intraindividual changes. The boundary issue is considered during the discussion and the performance (Type I error rate and power) of the various variance testing approaches is compared and discussed. Then, we discuss the consequences of ignoring interindividual differences in intraindividual changes on point estimation and standard error estimation of latent factor means in linear growth curve modeling. Analyses of real longitudinal data are conducted to demonstrate the main points of each issue. We end this chapter with recommendations and future research directions.

Latent Curve Modeling

Historically, repeated measures ANOVA and MANOVA have been introduced and applied to study intraindividual changes and individual differences in changes over time. However, these traditional methods can be of limited use because of the restrictive assumptions these methods make about missing data and/or the covariance structure of repeated measures (e.g., Hedeker & Gibbons, 2003; Maxwell & Delaney, 2004). To solve some of the problems, latent curve modeling (LCM) was developed, in which structural equation modeling (SEM) techniques are used for studies of growth processes (e.g., McArdle, 1986; McArdle & Epstein, 1987; Meredith & Tisak, 1990). Jack McArdle is among the first researchers, if not the first researcher, who cleverly used SEM for growth curve analysis. Nowadays, growth curve models are widely used for longitudinal data analysis. In these models, random effects of change (e.g., Bryk & Raudenbush, 1987; Laird & Ware, 1982; Singer & Willett, 2003) or latent change factors (e.g., McArdle, 1986; McArdle & Epstein, 1987; Meredith & Tisak, 1990) are included to capture the correlated data structure of longitudinal data, which allow direct modeling of both intraindividual changes and individual differences in changes.

Following McArdle & Nesselroade (2014), a linear latent curve model can be algebraically expressed as

$$y_{it} = b_{1i} + b_{2i} Time_t + e_{it}, \tag{8.1}$$

$$b_{1i} = \beta_1 + u_{1i}, \tag{8.2}$$

$$b_{2i} = \beta_2 + u_{2i}. \tag{8.3}$$

The interpretations of the model parameters depend on how the time variable is centered. For example, when the time variable is centered at the first time point (e.g., $Time = 0, 1, \ldots, T - 1$), b_{1i} is the latent initial level score of individual i and b_{2i} is individual i's latent linear rate of change. e_{it} describes the deviations between the observed scores of the response variable Y and the fitted scores for individual i at time point t.

The variances of e_{it} are usually assumed to be homogeneous across different individuals and time points in the multilevel modeling framework. In the latent growth curve modeling (or SEM) framework, the variances of e_{it} are usually assumed to be the same across individuals, but can be allowed to differ across time. McArdle and Nesselroade (2014) discussed whether these unique variances should be constrained to be the same over time. Their suggestions were that typically "all changes over time should be part of the common latent variables" (page 104) and thus the unique variances should be constrained to be the same value. However, if researchers have an prior reason for relaxing this constraint, varying unique variances over time can be informative. Thus, McArdle and Nesselroade (2014) suggested that one should not uncritically allow the unique variances to differ across time just to achieve better model fits. Because we do not have a prior belief about the unique variances, we follow the suggestion made in McArdle and Nesselroade (2014) to constrain the residual variances to be the same across individuals and time. In this case, the variance of e_{it}, σ_e^2, describes the average intraindividual variability around the individual change trajectories.

Equation (8.1) models the intraindividual change trajectory of individual i. By contrast, β_1 and β_2 in Equations (8.2) and (8.3), the means of the latent factors b_1 and b_2, describe the change trajectory of the "average" person in the population. Specifically, β_1 is the average initial level and β_2 is the average linear rate of change. u_{1i} and u_{2i} are usually assumed to follow a multivariate normal distribution with means of zero and covariance matrix $\mathbf{G} = \begin{pmatrix} \sigma_I^2 & \sigma_{IS} \\ \sigma_{IS} & \sigma_S^2 \end{pmatrix}$. The variance component σ_I^2 quantifies individual differences in latent initial levels and σ_S^2 quantifies individual differences in latent linear rates of change. The covariance term σ_{IS} describes the relation between the latent initial levels and latent linear rates of change. With the inclusion of the two unique factors (u_1 and u_2) for the latent change factors (b_1 and b_2), we can detect individual differences in intraindividual changes by statistically testing whether the intercept and linear slope variances are significantly different from 0.

When the time variable is centered around the middle time point, the interpretations of the terms related to the intercepts are different, whereas those of the terms related to the linear slopes stay the same. Specifically, with the new centering scheme for time, b_{1i} becomes the latent middle-status level of individual i and β_1 becomes the average middle-status level. In addition, σ_I^2 quantifies individual differences in latent middle-status levels and σ_{IS} describes the relation between the latent middle-status levels and latent linear rates of change. However, the interpretations about β_2, σ_S^2, and σ_e^2 do not change. Therefore, statistical inferences about β_2 and σ_S^2 are invariant to the centering scheme of the time variable.

To illustrate our main points on the two issues, we will use a subset of a longitudinal data set containing data from 204 children repeatedly measured at ages 6–11 by the Wechesler Intelligence Scale for Children (WISC). The data are balanced in that all the participants were measured in the spring before they entered the first grade, at the end of the first grade, at the end of third grade, and also upon the completion of the fifth grade. The full data have been used in other research publications (e.g., McArdle & Epstein, 1987; McArdle & Nesselroade, 2014). The sub-sample used in this chapter was obtained by selecting children whose mothers' education levels are 12 years or above ($N = 46$). The response variable is verbal ability. Using ideas of the Reticular Action Model (RAM) specification (e.g., McArdle, 2005; McArdle & Boker, 1990; McArdle & McDonald, 1984) and mimicking the path diagrams in Chapter 7 of McArdle and Nesselroade (2014),

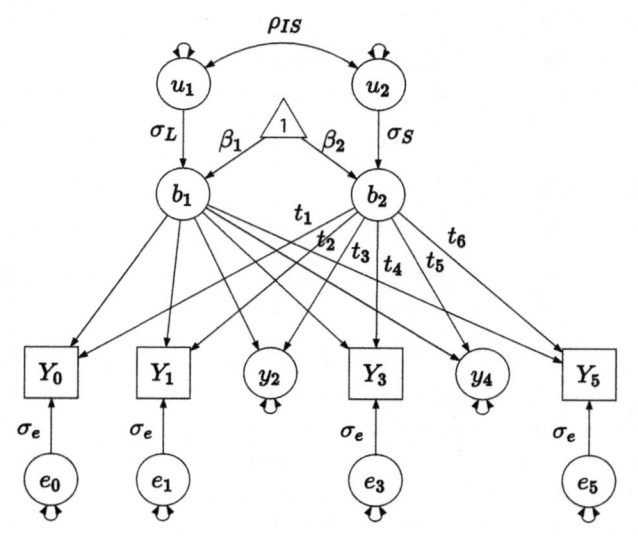

FIGURE 8.1 A path diagram of the latent linear growth curve model for the WISC data.

Figure 8.1 displays a path diagram of the growth curve model in Equations (8.1) to (8.3) for the WISC data.

Variance Testing for Detecting Interindividual Differences in Intraindividual Changes

In this section, we discuss the issue of how to detect interindividual differences in intraindividual changes. We use the detection of individual differences in linear slopes as an example for describing different kinds of variance tests and discussing their features and performance.

Specific vs. Generalized Variance Tests

For testing a variance component in a growth curve model, the Wald test and the likelihood ratio (LR) tests are two widely used statistical tests (e.g., Fitzmaurice, Laird, & Ware, 2011; Singer & Willett, 2003; Verbeke & Molenberghs, 2009). For each variance test, two test forms can be adopted: a specific test vs. a generalized test (e.g., Hertzog, von Oertzen, Ghisletta, & Lindenberger, 2008; Ke & Wang, 2015). A specific variance test examines whether the variance itself is 0, whereas a generalized variance test tests whether both the variance and the related covariance(s) are 0. For example, for testing the linear slope variance in Equation (8.3), a generalized variance test examines the null hypothesis of $H_0 : \sigma_S^2 = 0$ and $\sigma_{IS} = 0$. A specific variance test, however, focuses on only the linear slope variance and the null hypothesis is $H_0 : \sigma_S^2 = 0$. Therefore, we discuss the following four variance tests: the specific Wald test (WS), the generalized Wald test (WG), the specific likelihood ratio test (LRS), and the generalized likelihood ratio test (LRG).

For conducting the specific or generalized Wald tests, only one model needs to be fit, in which the three elements in $\mathbf{G} = \begin{pmatrix} \sigma_I^2 & \sigma_{IS} \\ \sigma_{IS} & \sigma_S^2 \end{pmatrix}$ are freely estimated (Model M_2). The WS test examines the null hypothesis, $H_0 : \sigma_S^2 = 0$, by computing the test statistic, $W_S = \frac{\hat{\sigma}_S^4}{\hat{C}_{\sigma_S^2}}$, where $\hat{C}_{\sigma_S^2}$ is an estimate of the variance of $\hat{\sigma}_S^2$. The WS test statistic is compared to χ_1^2 (chi-squared distribution with $df = 1$)[1]. In contrast, the WG test examines the null hypothesis, $H_0 : \left(\sigma_S^2, \sigma_{IS}\right)' = \mathbf{0}$, by computing the statistic, $W_G = \left(\hat{\sigma}_S^2, \hat{\sigma}_{IS}\right)\left[\hat{C}_{\sigma_S^2, \sigma_{IS}}\right]^{-1}\left(\hat{\sigma}_S^2, \hat{\sigma}_{IS}\right)'$, where $\hat{C}_{\sigma_S^2, \sigma_{IS}}$ is an estimate of the covariance matrix of $\left(\hat{\sigma}_S^2, \hat{\sigma}_{IS}\right)'$. The WG test statistic is compared to the reference distribution, χ_2^2 (chi-squared distribution with $df = 2$).

For conducting the LR tests, however, two nested models need to be fit. σ_I^2 is freely estimated in both models, but there are different constraint specifications for σ_S^2 and σ_{IS} across the two models. Specifically, for the LRS test, both Model M_0 (both σ_S^2 and σ_{IS} are constrained to be 0) and Model M_1 (σ_S^2 is freely estimated but σ_{IS} is constrained to be 0) are fit. The deviance statistic, $T_S = T_0 - T_1$, where T_0 and T_1 denote the -2 log likelihood (-2LL) values of models M_0 and M_1 respectively, is compared to χ_1^2 for testing $H_0 : \sigma_S^2 = 0$. For the LRG test, both Model M_0 and Model M_2 (σ_S^2 and σ_{IS} are freely estimated) are fit. The deviance statistic, $T_G = T_0 - T_2$, where T_0 and T_2 denote the -2LL values of models M_0 and M_2 respectively, is compared to χ_2^2 for testing $H_0 : \left(\sigma_S^2, \sigma_{IS}\right)' = \mathbf{0}$.

McArdle and Nesselroade (2014) had an interesting discussion about the specific vs. generalized variance tests:

> any change in the variance and covariance contribution of the slope is due to the combination of the slope variance and covariance together. Thus, any test of the mean changes from the baseline is based on one df, whereas any changes in the covariance from baseline are based on at least two df. This is not an unusual idea, but it is an idea that is often overlooked
>
> *Source*: McArdle and Nesselroade (2014), page 98

It appears that McArdle and Nesselroade (2014) endorsed the generalized variance tests.

Unconstrained vs. Constrained Estimation and the Boundary Issue

Two estimation procedures can be used to estimate variance components in growth curve modeling: unconstrained vs. constrained estimation. Constrained estimation restricts variance estimates to be nonnegative, whereas unconstrained estimation allows inadmissible estimates (e.g., negative variance estimates). When unconstrained estimation is applied, there is no boundary problem and thus standard inference procedures can be used (e.g., Savalei & Kolenikov, 2008). For example, the aforementioned T and W test statistics follow the χ^2 distributions. When constrained estimation is applied, however, one meets the boundary problem. That is, the regularity condition which requires the true parameter value to be an interior point in the parameter space can be violated. Specifically, the true parameter value under the null hypothesis, 0, is on the boundary of the parameter space (e.g., Stoel, Garre. Dolan, & Van den Wittenboer, 2006) when only admissible (nonnegative) variances are allowed. This violation could cause the aforementioned statistical tests to fail. Specifically, the null distributions of the test statistics are no longer chi-squared distributions.

To deal with the boundary problem under constrained estimation, mixtures of chi-squared distributions (denoted as the mixture distribution approach) have been proposed and used as the reference distributions for the LR tests (e.g., Self & Liang, 1987; Stoel et al., 2006; Stram & Lee, 1994). Here, we briefly review the rationale behind the mixture distribution approach. Under constrained estimation (only nonnegative variance estimates are allowed) and under the null hypothesis of zero variance, there are equal chances of observing positive variance estimates and zero variance estimates. When only positive variance estimates are considered, it is well established that T and W asymptotically follow χ^2 distributions with degrees of freedom equal to 2 for the generalized variance tests and 1 for the specific variance tests. When only zero variance estimates are considered, however, the degrees of freedom reduce to 1 for the generalized tests and 0 for the specific tests, because σ_S^2 can be treated as a fixed/known parameter with its value at 0 in the full models (Models M_2 and M_1 respectively). When all samples are considered, T and W follow equally weighted mixtures of χ^2 distributions, i.e., $.5\chi_1^2 + .5\chi_2^2$ for the generalized tests and $.5\chi_0^2 + .5\chi_1^2$ for the specific tests. Note that when the significance level alpha is set to be .05, the critical values of $.5\chi_1^2 + .5\chi_2^2$ and $.5\chi_0^2 + .5\chi_1^2$ are 5.14 and 2.71 (see a table of critical values in Fitzmaurice et al., 2011, p. 670), which are smaller than the critical values of χ_2^2 and χ_1^2, 5.99 and 3.84, respectively. Therefore, the use of the mixture distribution approach for addressing the boundary issue is asymptotically sound and protects against selection of a model that is too parsimonious in the covariance structure.

For more complex tests of variance components (e.g., testing 2 or more variances simultaneously), the weights for the chi-squared distributions in the mixture distribution approach are often unknown and thus need to be estimated, for example, via Monte Carlo simulations. This could hinder the wide use of the mixture distribution approach. To ease the problem, a simpler but "somewhat ad hoc" method for handling the boundary issue is to use 0.10 instead of 0.05 for the alpha value (denoted as the alpha correction approach). The adjustment in the alpha level also aims at protecting against too conservative test results and thus selection of a model that is too parsimonious (Fitzmaurice et al., 2011, p. 209). The rationale of this correction is that testing whether a variance is greater than zero, whilst knowing that variances are always nonnegative under constrained estimation is similar to conducting a one-sided test instead of a two-sided test. For testing one variance component (e.g., σ_S^2) at a time, the alpha correction approach provides an ad hoc approximate test when coupled with the generalized variance tests, because admissible covariance components can be negative, and an exact variance test when coupled with the specific variance tests. For example, for the generalized tests, the critical value from $.5\chi_1^2 + .5\chi_2^2$ at $\alpha = 0.05$ is 5.14. whereas the critical value from χ_2^2 at $\alpha = 0.10$ is 4.61. Therefore, for the generalized tests, the alpha correction approach would yield more liberal results than the mixture distribution approach. For the specific tests, however, the critical value from $.5\chi_0^2 + .5\chi_1^2$ at $\alpha = 0.05$ is 2.71, the same as the critical value from χ_1^2 at $\alpha = 0.10$. In this case, for the specific tests, the alpha correction approach would yield, by no coincidence, an identical result as the mixture distribution approach.

How Are the Tests Conducted in Practice?

Among the four variance tests (WS, WG, LRS, and LRG), the specific Wald (WS) test probably is the most frequently used one in practice. For example, PROC SAS MIXED and Mplus, two widely used statistical programs for growth curve modeling, by default, produce p values for the WS test (in the Z test form) when Model $M2$ is fit. The default outputs have promoted the use of the WS test. It should be noted that there are a few major differences in how PROC MIXED and Mplus implement the WS test. Specifically, the default estimation procedure of SAS PROC MIXED is constrained estimation. Under constrained estimation, PROC MIXED outputs the p value of a variance test based on a one-sided WS test (can also be viewed as using the alpha correction approach). Because WS is a specific test, the p values from the alpha correction approach and the mixture distribution approach are the same for testing one variance component, as discussed earlier in the chapter. Thus, the boundary issue is theoretically addressed in PROC MIXED when constrained estimation is used. In addition, PROC MIXED has an option of allowing negative variance estimates (using 'NOBOUND') and thus could implement unconstrained estimation. Under unconstrained estimation, there is no boundary problem. The p value of a variance test from PROC MIXED with NOBOUND is based on a two-sided WS test. In contrast, the default estimation procedure of Mplus is unconstrained estimation. The p value of a variance test from Mplus is also appropriately based on a two-sided WS test. One can constrain a variance to be nonnegative in Mplus and the estimation procedure becomes constrained estimation. Under constrained estimation, the p value of a variance test from Mplus is still based on a two-sided WS test, which does not take the boundary issue into account.

For the LRG and LRS tests, two nested models need to be fit. The $-2LL$ and LL values of the two models can be directly obtained from the outputs of SAS PROC MIXED and Mplus respectively. Thus either the LRG or LRS tests can be easily implemented by computing T_G or T_S and their p values with chosen reference distributions.

For the WG test, only Model $M2$ needs to be fit. However, it is less straightforward to conduct the WG test in SAS or Mplus. Because $W_G = \left(\hat{\sigma}_S^2, \hat{\sigma}_{IS}\right)\left[\hat{C}_{\sigma_S^2, \sigma_{IS}}\right]^{-1}\left(\hat{\sigma}_S^2, \hat{\sigma}_{IS}\right)'$, one could first obtain the estimated covariance matrix of $\left(\hat{\sigma}_S^2, \hat{\sigma}_{IS}\right)'$, $\hat{C}_{\sigma_S^2, \sigma_{IS}}$, and then use the test statistic formula to compute the WG test statistic and the p value with a chosen reference distribution. Specifically, for obtaining the estimated covariance matrix of $\left(\hat{\sigma}_S^2, \hat{\sigma}_{IS}\right)'$ in Mplus and SAS PROC MIXED, one can use TECH3 and ASYCOV, respectively.

Performance of the Various Tests Under the Two Estimation Procedures

Previous simulation results indicated that the generalized LR test is often preferable (e.g., better type I error rates and larger empirical power) to the specific Wald test for testing a variance component of change (e.g., Hertzog et al., 2008). Additionally, it has been found that the specific LR test often yielded smaller power than the generalized LR test for detecting individual differences in change (e.g., Hertzog et al., 2008). However, these results could be entangled, because there are two influential factors: factor 1 (LR vs. Wald) and factor 2 (specific vs. generalized). In addition, the performance of the generalized Wald variance test had not been studied. To fill in the research gap, Ke and Wang (2015) extended previous work (e.g., Hertzog et al., 2008) by considering both the specific and generalized forms for both the Wald and LR tests and comparing the performance of these four methods under both constrained and unconstrained estimation for detecting individual differences in change. They conducted Monte Carlo simulations for evaluating the methods for linear growth curve modeling. For the simulation study design, please refer to Ke and Wang (2015). Here we review some findings found in Ke and Wang (2015) with a focus on the performance (Type I error rates and empirical power) of the various tests under the normality assumption. For methods of addressing the nonnormality problem for detecting individual differences in change and simulation results under nonnormality, please read Ke and Wang (2015).

Type I Error Rates

A Type I error rate above .075 is considered as too liberal and below .025 as too conservative (Bradley, 1978). The first and the last column blocks of Table 8.1 summarize the empirical Type I error rates of the four tests under various conditions when the regular χ^2 critical values, $\chi^2_{1,0.05} = 3.86$ or $\chi^2_{2,0.05} = 5.99$, were used for the specific and generalized tests respectively. The results showed that under constrained estimation, all four tests had their type I error rates substantially smaller than the nominal level, 0.05, indicating that the four tests under constrained estimation were too conservative. This is due to the boundary problem.

Therefore, methods addressing the boundary issue are indeed needed under constrained estimation. Under unconstrained estimation, the Type I error rates from the four tests were close to the nominal level. However, the WS and WG tests were too liberal when the number of participants was as small as 50 and the number of time points was as large as 10.

To address the boundary problem under constrained estimation, the mixture distribution approach (Mix. of $\chi^2_{\alpha=0.05}$) and the alpha correction approach ($\chi^2_{\alpha=0.10}$) were applied and the results are listed in the middle two column blocks of Table 8.1. After applying either approach, the Type I error rates became closer to the nominal level, indicating that either approach was somewhat effective. Between the two approaches, as expected, the mixture distribution approach yielded more conservative results than the alpha correction approach for the generalized variance tests (WG and LRG). Also as expected, for the two specific tests (WS and LRS), the Type I error rates were all the same across the two approaches (Constrained with Mix. of $\chi^2_{\alpha=0.05}$ vs. Constrained with $\chi^2_{\alpha=0.10}$ in Table 8.1). Under constrained estimation, the WS tests with either the mixture distribution approach or the alpha correction approach still yielded overly conservative test results under most studied conditions, especially when the sample size was small (e.g., $N \leq 200$). The LRG test with the alpha correction approach yielded more liberal results and the WG test with the mixture distribution approach resulted in a bit conservative results under some conditions. The LRG test coupled with the mixture distribution approach under constrained estimation had well controlled Type I error rates, which were also comparable to the good Type I error rates from LRG under unconstrained estimation.

Statistical Power

In terms of statistical power, generally, Ke and Wang (2015) found that: (1) the generalized tests had higher power than the corresponding specific tests when the correlation between the latent intercept and linear slope factors is not zero, whereas the specific tests had higher power than the corresponding generalized tests when the correlation is zero; (2) the tests under constrained estimation yielded slightly higher power than the corresponding tests under unconstrained estimation; and (3) a Wald test generally had less power than the corresponding likelihood ratio test.

When the covariance between the latent intercept and change factors, σ_{IS}, is not zero, under constrained estimation, the LRG test yielded highest power, followed by the WG test, the LRS test, and the WS test. When $\sigma_{IS} = 0$, however, a different pattern was observed. That is, generally, the LRS test yielded the highest power followed by the LRG test, the WS test, and the WG test. Under unconstrained estimation, they found a similar pattern in terms of the relative power of the tests.

TABLE 8.1 Empirical Type I error rates from different methods for normal data. Constrained: constrained estimation; Unconstrained: unconstrained estimation. WS: specific Wald test, WG: generalized Wald test, LRS: specific LR test, and LRG: generalized LR test. N: the number of participants. The bold and italic entries are larger than .075 or smaller than .025, respectively. $\chi^2_{\alpha=0.05}$ and $\chi^2_{\alpha=0.10}$ used the regular Chi-squared distribution as the reference distribution with an alpha level of 0.05 and 0.10 respectively. Mix. of $\chi^2_{\alpha=0.05}$ used $.5\chi^2_{df-1}+.5\chi^2_{df}$ as the reference distribution with an alpha level of 0.05 (specific variance tests: $df=1$; generalized variance tests: $df=2$).

	5 time points of data															
	Constrained with $\chi^2_{\alpha=0.05}$				Constrained with Mix. of $\chi^2_{\alpha=0.05}$				Constrained with $\chi^2_{\alpha=0.10}$				Unconstrained with $\chi^2_{\alpha=0.05}$			
N	WS	WG	LRS	LRG	WS	WG	LRS	LRG	WS	WG	LRS	LRG	WS	WG	LRS	LRG
50	*.006*	*.022*	*.021*	.031	*.020*	.035	.044	.052	*.020*	.051	.044	.068	.059	.071	.057	.057
100	*.012*	*.020*	*.023*	.031	.032	.034	.046	.048	.033	.049	.046	.064	.057	.060	.052	.054
200	*.014*	*.024*	*.021*	.034	.029	.039	.042	.051	.029	.055	.042	.063	.050	.054	.047	.052
500	*.019*	*.024*	*.024*	.029	.043	.040	.048	.047	.043	.054	.048	.063	.050	.050	.049	.047

	10 time points of data															
	Constrained with $\chi^2_{\alpha=0.05}$				Constrained with Mix. of $\chi^2_{\alpha=0.05}$				Constrained with $\chi^2_{\alpha=0.10}$				Unconstrained with $\chi^2_{\alpha=0.05}$			
N	WS	WG	LRS	LRG	WS	WG	LRS	LRG	WS	WG	LRS	LRG	WS	WG	LRS	LRG
50	*.005*	*.025*	*.021*	.034	*.015*	.037	.038	.050	*.015*	.049	.038	.065	**.076**	**.089**	.057	.059
100	*.008*	*.019*	*.020*	.029	*.023*	.033	.040	.044	*.023*	.046	.040	.058	.062	.071	.054	.051
200	*.010*	*.023*	*.022*	.032	.028	.037	.045	.047	.028	.050	.045	.063	.057	.062	.051	.054
500	*.016*	*.021*	*.021*	.029	.035	.037	.045	.045	.035	.051	.045	.059	.047	.047	.044	.047

In general, the LR tests were more powerful than the corresponding Wald tests. The only exception was found in the conditions with negative intercept-change correlations, i.e., $\rho_{IS} < 0$. Under these conditions, the specific LR test was less powerful than the specific Wald test regardless of estimation procedures. This result is consistent with Hertzog et al. (2008).

Recommendations with Considering Both Type I Error Rates and Power

Among all the studied tests, Ke and Wang (2015) found that the generalized LRG test coupled with the mixture distribution approach under constrained estimation had both well controlled Type I error rates and higher power for testing individual differences in change than the other studied tests when ρ_{IS} is nonzero. When the correlation is 0, the specific likelihood ratio test (LRS) coupled with either the mixture distribution approach or the alpha correction approach under constrained estimation is recommended. Therefore, the endorsement of the generalized variance tests in McArdle and Nesselroade (2014) was supported. Between the mixture distribution approach and the alpha correction approach under constrained estimation, we recommend the mixture distribution approach for better controlled type I error rates for the generalized tests. However, when the model is more complicated and multiple variances are involved in the testing, the weights for the mixture distribution approach may not be easily obtained. In this case, weights can be obtained by simulations (Stoel et al., 2006) or one can use the alpha correction approach for its simplicity.

Under the scenario of zero true latent slope variance, nonconvergence may occur in practice when the model with the unique slope factor u_2 is fit to a data set under constrained estimation. However, nonconvergence can also occur when a truly complex growth curve model (e.g., u_2 is needed in the model) is fit to very sparse data or data with fewer time points (e.g., Singer & Willett, 2003). To deal with convergence, we recommend unconstrained estimation instead of uncritically constraining the variance of a latent change factor to be zero for achieving convergence. The consequences of uncritically constraining a variance component to be zero will be studied in the next section. In addition, we agree with Savalei & Kolenikov (2008) that constrained estimation is less informative about the sources of misfit compared to unconstrained estimation. When multiple models with different mean and covariance structures are evaluated, unconstrained estimation may be more helpful for detecting sources of misfit than constrained estimation.

A Real Data Analysis Example

Here, we use the WISC data to numerically illustrate the performance of the studied variance tests under both constrained and unconstrained estimation. To be consistent with the real data analysis example under the second issue, the time variable was centered around the middle point such that the time values are -2.25, -1.25, 0.75 and 2.75 for the four time points or -2.25, -1.25, 0.25, 0.75, 1.75, and 2.75 for t_1 to t_6 in Figure 8.1. We fit three versions of the model in Equations (8.1) to (8.3) to the data. They are Models M_0 (M_0: both σ_S^2 and σ_{IS} are constrained to be 0), M_1 (M_1 : σ_S^2 is freely estimated, but σ_{IS} is constrained to be 0), and M_2 (M_2: both σ_S^2 and σ_{IS} are freely estimated). The analyses were conducted in SAS PROC MIXED with the restricted ML estimator, a widely used one in practice (e.g., Fitzmaurice et al. 2011). We used the 'NOBOUND' option to implement the unconstrained estimation procedure (i.e., allow negative variance estimates). The point estimates and standard error estimates of all the model parameters (fixed effects and variance components) and the model fit indices were exactly the same from constrained and unconstrained estimation. This is because both the intercept and linear slope variance estimates were not close to 0 in the three models for the current application example.

For conducting the Wald specific and Wald generalized tests, model M_2 was fit. Specifically, for WS, we have $W_S = \frac{\hat{\sigma}_S^4}{\hat{C}_{\sigma_S^2}} = \frac{0.84^2}{0.43^2} = 3.77$. For WG, we used PROC MIXED with ASYCOV to obtain the estimated covariance matrix of σ_S^2 and σ_{IS}, $\hat{C}_{\sigma_S^2,\sigma_{IS}} = \begin{pmatrix} 1.35 & \\ 2.86 & 12.80 \end{pmatrix}$, which was the same under either unconstrained or constrained estimation. Then we have $W_G = (\hat{\sigma}_S^2, \hat{\sigma}_{IS}) \left[\hat{C}_{\sigma_S^2,\sigma_{IS}}\right]^{-1} (\hat{\sigma}_S^2, \hat{\sigma}_{IS})' = (0.84, 3.07) \begin{pmatrix} 1.35 & \\ 2.86 & 12.80 \end{pmatrix}^{-1} (0.84, 3.07)' = 7.94$. For the LR specific test, both Models M_0 and M_1 were fit and the $-2LL$ values were 1143.0 and 1137.6, regardless of whether constrained or unconstrained estimation was used. Thus, $T_S = T_0 - T_1 = 1143.0 - 1137.6 = 5.4$. For the LR generalized test, both Models M_0 and M_2 were fit and the $-2LL$ values were 1143.0 and 1127.2, regardless of the use of constrained vs. unconstrained estimation. Thus, $T_G = T_0 - T_2 = 1143.0 - 1127.2 = 15.8$.

Table 8.2 lists the p values from the four tests coupled with different methods of p-value calculations. First, under either constrained or unconstrained estimation, WS coupled with the regular $\chi^2_{df=1}$ as the reference distribution (theoretically inappropriate under constrained estimation but appropriate under unconstrained estimation) had the highest p value, .052, and thus yielded the most conservative test result. Under constrained estimation, WS coupled with the alpha correction approach or the mixture distribution approach (theoretically appropriate) had the second highest p value, .026. The results showed that the WS test was indeed too conservative for this example. Second, WG was found to be more powerful than LRS, but less powerful than LRG. The estimated correlation between latent intercept and linear slope factors from Model M_2, r_{IS}, is .75, which is statistically significantly different from 0 ($z = 2.77$, $p = .006$). Thus, the real data analysis results were consistent with the simulation results in Ke & Wang (2015)

TABLE 8.2 Test statistics and p values from the various variance testing approaches for the real data example ($N = 46$ with 4 time points). Constrained: constrained estimation; Unconstrained: unconstrained estimation. WS: specific Wald test, WG: generalized Wald test, LRS: specific LR test, and LRG: generalized LR test.

	Constrained						Unconstrained with $\chi^2_{\alpha=0.05}$		
	test statistic	*reference distr.*	*p-value*	*p-value (alpha correction)*	*reference distr.*	*p-value*	*test statistic*	*reference distr.*	*p-value*
WS	3.77	$\chi^2_{df=1}$	0.052	0.026	$.5\chi^2_{df=0} + .5\chi^2_{df=1}$	0.026	3.77	$\chi^2_{df=1}$	0.052
WG	7.94	$\chi^2_{df=2}$	0.019	0.0095	$.5\chi^2_{df=1} + .5\chi^2_{df=2}$	0.012	7.94	$\chi^2_{df=2}$	0.019
LRS	5.4	$\chi^2_{df=1}$	0.020	0.010	$.5\chi^2_{df=0} + .5\chi^2_{df=1}$	0.010	5.4	$\chi^2_{df=1}$	0.020
LRG	15.8	$\chi^2_{df=2}$	0.00037	0.00018	$.5\chi^2_{df=1} + .5\chi^2_{df=2}$	0.00022	15.8	$\chi^2_{df=2}$	0.00037

under the conditions of $\rho_{IS} \neq 0$. Third, the tests that considered the boundary issue (either through the alpha correction approach or the mixture distribution approach) under constrained estimation were more efficient than those under unconstrained estimation. Fourth, in this example, under constrained estimation, the results from the alpha correction approach and the mixtrue distribution approach were the same for the specific tests, whereas the results from the alpha correction approach were a bit liberal for the generalized tests. Overall, our real data analysis results were consistent with the simulation results in Hertzog et al. (2008) and Ke & Wang (2015).

Note that the default output from SAS PROC MIXED is based on the WS test coupled with the alpha correction approach or the mixture distribution approach ($p = .026$), whereas the default output from Mplus is based on the WS test coupled with using the regular chi-squared distribution ($df = 1$) as the reference distribution ($p = .052$). Thus, if one simply uses the default outputs, the variance test results tend to be too conservative.

Consequences of Over-Simplifying Covariance Structures in Linear Growth Curve Modeling

In the real data example described in the previous section, when we used the WS test with the regular chi-squared distribution as the reference distribution, the resulting p value was .052 for testing $H_0 : \sigma_S^2 = 0$. In this case, one fails to reject the null hypothesis that there are individual differences in the linear slopes. Accordingly, researchers may remove the linear slope variance component from the model and use a simplified covariance structure in growth curve modeling, following the parsimony principle (e.g., Fitzmaurice et al., 2011; Singer & Willett, 2003; Verbeke & Molenberghs, 2009). In behavioral research, underpowered studies are not rare but rather prevalent and persistent (e.g., Cohen, 1992; Maxwell, 2004). In practice, a variance test could be under-powered, especially because sample size planning is more often based on detecting group differences in average changes instead of on detecting variance components (e.g., Fan, 2003; Muthén & Curran, 1997; Zhang & Wang, 2009) when designing a longitudinal study. In this case, Type II errors may have occurred and thus as Fitzmaurice et al. (2011) indicated, the model with a simplified covariance structure may be oversimplified and ultimately misspecified in terms of the covariance structure. Another contributing factor of using an oversimplified covariance structure is nonconvergence. When nonconvergence occurs, many analysts simplify a growth curve model through the covariance structure and this could also lead to the use of an over-simplified/mis-specified covariance structure, for example, as criticized in Gurka, Edwards, & Muller (2011).

In this section, we discuss the consequences of over-simplifying covariance structures on inferences about latent factor means or fixed effects in linear growth curve modeling via a real data analysis example. Specifically, we are interested in comparing the results from the real data analysis example to the findings and suggestions in the current literature. We hope our real data analysis example will deepen researchers' understanding of the consequences of over-simplifying covariance structures.

Four Models with Different Covariance Structures

For this real data analysis example, we used the same data from the previous section. We fit four linear growth curve models with the same mean structure but different covariance structures to the data. The mean structure is described in Equations (8.1) to (8.3) or Figure 8.1 with the time variable centered around the middle time point. For the covariance structures, in Model A, interindividual differences in both the latent intercept and linear slope factors b_1 and b_2 are modeled. Thus, Model A is the same as Model $M2$ in the previous section. In Model B, the unique factor u_1 of the latent intercept factor b_1 is omitted from Model A. In Model C, the unique factor u_2 of the latent linear slope factor b_2 is omitted from Model A, and in Model D – the unique factors u_1 and u_2 of latent factors b_1 and b_2 are omitted from Model A. More specifically, when u_1 is omitted, we have $\sigma_I^2 = \sigma_{IS} = 0$ and thus the mid-point levels are not allowed to differ across individuals. When u_2 is omitted, we have $\sigma_S^2 = \sigma_{IS} = 0$ and thus the linear rates of change are not allowed to differ across individuals. The resulting covariance structure is the compound symmetry structure (e.g., Maxwell & Delaney, 2004). Furthermore, when both u_1 and u_2 are omitted, $\sigma_I^2 = \sigma_S^2 = \sigma_{IS} = 0$ and thus the model reduces to a general linear model in which the correlated data structure within an individual is completely ignored. Model D is an example of using unilevel analysis methods on multilevel data or conducting regression analyses for growth curve modeling.

The analyses were conducted in SAS PROC MIXED with the restricted ML estimator. We also used the 'NOBOUND' option to facilitate the unconstrained estimation procedure. In fact, when u_1 (the unique factor of latent intercept) is omitted, Model B did not converge without using the 'NOBOUND' option (i.e., under constrained estimation) and the ML variance estimate of the latent linear slope factor were negative (-0.95) with the 'NOBOUND' option. Therefore, nonconvergence occurred in this real data analysis example and may lead to wrong model selection decisions. Table 8.3 lists the results from the four models fitted to the WISC data.

Point Estimates of the Latent Factor Means or Fixed Effects

From Table 8.3, we can clearly see that the ML point estimates of the latent factor means or fixed effects were identical across the four models. This is not by coincidence and is consistent with the literature. When a model belongs to a family of linear growth curve models with balanced and complete data,

TABLE 8.3 Results of fitting four growth curve models with different covariance structures to the real data ($N = 46$ with 4 time points). Estimate: point estimate; s.e.: ML standard error estimate. na means not applicable.

| | Model A: u_1 and u_2 included | | Model B: u_1 omitted | | Model C: u_2 omitted | | Model D: u_1 and u_2 omitted | | Robust | |
	estimate	s.e.	estimate	s.e.	estimate	s.e.	estimate	s.e.	estimate	s.e.
					Latent factor means					
β_1	34.58	0.72	34.58	0.48	34.58	0.72	34.58	0.46	34.58	0.71
β_2	5.33	0.20	5.33	0.20	5.33	0.17	5.33	0.24	5.33	0.20
					Variance-covariance components					
σ_I^2	20.07	5.10	na	na	19.05	5.10	na	na	na	na
σ_{IS}	3.07	1.11	na	na	na	na	na	na	na	na
σ_S^2	0.84	0.43	−0.95	0.53	na	na	na	na	na	na
σ_e^2	15.77	2.33	42.14	5.09	19.84	2.40	38.68	4.05	na	na

Lange & Laird (1989) have proved that under normality, the ML estimator for the fixed effects is identical to the OLS estimator for any number of random effects. Although Lange & Laird (1989) derived the proofs under the mixed-effects modeling framework, researchers have shown the equivalence of using different modeling frameworks (e.g., mixed-effects modeling vs. structural equation modeling) for growth curve analysis with balanced data (e.g., Curran, 2003; Grimm, Ram, & Hamagami, 2016; MacCallum, Kim, Malarkey, & Kiecolt-Glaser, 1997; Phanalp, Du, Braungart-Ricker, & Wang, 2017). Here, the four models are four linear growth curve models with the same mean structure and the longitudinal data are balanced and complete. Furthermore, the four models differ in only the number of random effects. Thus, the findings from Lange & Laird (1989) can be applied to this example. That is, the ML estimates of the latent factor means from the four models were all equal to one another.

Standard Error Estimates of the Latent Factor Mean Estimates

From Table 8.3, we can see that the standard error estimates of the latent factor mean estimates sometimes differed and sometimes were the same across the models. Specifically, when the latent intercept variance is constrained to be 0 (u_1 is omitted; Model B), the standard error estimate of the latent intercept mean estimate (0.48) was smaller than that from Model A (0.72; the model with both u_1 and u_2 included), whereas the standard error estimate of the latent linear slope mean estimate (0.20) was the same as that from Model A. When the latent linear slope variance is constrained to be 0 (u_2 is omitted; Model C), the standard error estimate of the latent intercept mean estimate (0.72) was the same as that from Model A, whereas the standard error estimate of the latent linear slope mean estimate (0.17) was smaller than that from Model A (0.20). When both the latent factor variances are constrained to be 0 (both u_1 and u_2 are omitted; Model D), the standard error estimate of the latent intercept mean estimate (0.46) was smaller than that from Model A (0.72), whereas the standard error estimate of the latent linear slope mean estimate (0.24) was larger than that from Model A (0.20).

Are the patterns we found from this real data analysis example consistent with the findings or suggestions from the current literature? In the literature, researchers have extensively studied and discussed the performance of using compound symmetry (the model including u_1 but omitting u_2 or the intercept random effect only model; a historically widely assumed/used covariance structure), for real longitudinal data analysis. For example, Box (1954 a, b) and McCall & Appelbaum (1973) have demonstrated inflated Type I error rates of testing fixed effects when falsely assuming compound symmetry in the analysis of variance framework (also see Maxwell & Delaney, 2004). More recently, Gurka et al. (2011) proved that falsely assuming compound symmetry creates biased tests and confidence intervals (inflated Type I error rates) for fixed effect inferences in linear mixed modeling with complete and balanced data and normal errors, in both small and large samples. Therefore, our real data analysis results were consistent with the literature showing that removing the latent linear slope factor variance (omitting u_2 but keeping u_1 in the model) can lead to overly small standard error estimates and thus overly liberal test results concerning the intercept mean.

Furthermore, the current literature tends to suggest inflated Type I error rates in testing fixed effects in multilevel modeling when an over-simplified Level-2 covariance structure is used. For example, Mass and Hox (2004; page 428) noted that "the consequences of using uni-level analysis methods on multilevel data are well known: the parameter estimates are unbiased but inefficient, and the standard errors are negatively biased, which results in spuriously 'significant' effects" (also see Hox, 2010, page 5). More recently, in a highly cited article by Barr, Levy, Scheepers, & Tily (2013), the authors stated that "Based on theoretical analysis and Monte Carlo simulations, we will argue the following...Failure to include maximal random-effects structures in LMEMs (when such random effects are present in the underlying populations) inflates Type I error rates." (page 257). In other words, the current common knowledge is that standard errors of fixed effect estimates are underestimated with over-simplification of the covariance structure of a multilevel model. Our real data analysis example, however, showed that this common knowledge is not always correct. Specifically, when the uni-level analysis was done (the model with omitting both u_1 and u_2, Model D, fit to the data), the standard error estimate of the linear slope factor mean (0.24) was actually larger than that from the model with both u_1 and u_2 included (0.20; Model A).

To figure out why such patterns exist for the differences in the standard error estimates of fixed effect estimates across the four models, Wang, Yang, and Liu (2018) analytically derived the closed-form asymptotic differences in variance and standard error estimates of fixed effect (or latent factor mean) estimates. For one of their derivations, they centered the time variable around the mid-point so that the derivation results could have simple and closed forms. The derivation results showed that: (1) when the random intercept or random slope is omitted, the variance of the fixed-effects intercept or slope estimate is underestimated respectively; and (2) when both the random intercept and random slope are omitted, the variances of the fixed-effects intercept and slope estimates could be underestimated or overestimated. Their derived formulas systematically showed the conditions where Type I error rates are inflated or deflated and quantified the extent of over-estimation or under-estimation in variance or standard error estimates of fixed effect estimates. The derivation results were consistent with the real data analysis results presented earlier in the chapter, confirming that the common knowledge is not always correct.

Robust Standard Error Estimates

A robust ("sandwich" type) standard error estimator (implemented by using the 'EMPIRICAL' option in SAS PROC MIXED) has been suggested for handling covariance structure mis-specifications and/or distribution assumption violations (e.g., Huber, 1967; Liang & Zeger, 1986; White, 1980). Here, we applied it to obtain robust standard error estimates of the latent factor mean estimates and the results are listed in Table 8.3 under the robust column. Note that the robust results are the same for all the four models with different covariance structures because they share the same mean structure. The robust standard error estimates were very close to the ML standard error estimates from the model with both u_1 and u_2 included. There are two implications. First, the model with both u_1 and u_2 included (Model A) is "robust" in terms of the covariance structure for this data set. Second, for the models with the simplified covariance structures (Models B to D), the robust standard error estimates were different from the ML standard error estimates, indicating that it is likely that those simplified models have mis-specified covariance structures.

With regard to the robust standard error estimator, we want to further discuss several points. First, even though robust methods may provide valid inferences about mean structures or fixed effects in models with mis-specified covariance structures, a correctly specified covariance structure can help researchers better understand inter-individual differences in change, which often is a research question of interest (e.g., Baltes & Nesselroade, 1979; McArdle & Nesselroade, 2014; Verbeke & Molenberghs, 2009). Therefore, it is often important and useful to figure out an appropriate covariance structure for growth curve analysis. Second, when missing data exist, robust methods can provide valid inferences for the fixed effects only under strict assumptions (missing completely at random; Liang & Zeger, 1986). Third, the performance of robust methods under small sample size conditions still needs to be studied for complex longitudinal models.

General Discussion

As Baltes and Nesselroade (1979) and McArdle and Nesselroade (2014) emphasized, it is important to identify and study interindividual differences in intraindividual changes. For the covariance structure specification of growth curve modeling, there are various recommendations. For example, Gurka et al. (2011) recommended "backwards selection" with starting with an unstructured pattern. Verbeke & Molenberghs (2009) also suggested that one can start with a "saturated" model and then perform "model deduction" to investigate whether some random effects can be removed. We generally agree with their recommendation, given that there is sufficient accuracy and power in variance testing and model selection. Thus, it is important to use a valid and more powerful variance testing approach. In the discussion of the first issue, we have generally recommended the generalized variance tests coupled with the mixture distribution approach under constrained estimation, because they yielded well controlled Type I error rates and higher statistical power. We do not recommend the Wald specific test, because the results are too conservative, although it may be the easiest for one to obtain the

WS test result. In practice, variance testing can be underpowered (e.g., Hertzog et al., 2008; Ke & Wang, 2015) and model selection criteria such as AIC and BIC may lead to inaccurate decisions, especially when the sample size is small (e.g., Liu, Rovine, & Molenaar, 2012). Thus, the backwards selection approach may lead to over-simplified covariance structures.

For appropriately specifying the covariance structure for a growth curve analysis, in addition to the use of variance tests and model selection criteria, we recommend conducting sensitivity analysis by: (1) fitting various covariance structures with and without using robust standard error estimators to the data; and (2) comparing the inference results on the latent factor means or fixed effects from the various models/methods. If the results from a model with a simplified covariance structure are different from those from a model with a more complex covariance structure, it may indicate that the simplified covariance structure is over-simplified and thus mis-specified. If the inference results from a model with a simplified covariance structure are similar to those from a model with a more complex covariance structure, we are more confident with the inferences.

In this chapter, we used linear growth curve modeling as an example to discuss the two related issues about interindividual differences in intraindividual changes. In psychological and behavioral research, the latent true change trajectories can be nonlinear (e.g., Grimm et al., 2011; McArdle, Ferrer-Caja, Hamagami, & Woodcock, 2002; McArdle, Grimm, Hamagami, Bowles, & Meredith, 2009; McArdle & Wang, 2008; Wang & McArdle, 2008). For nonlinear growth curve modeling, the performance of different variance testing approaches for detecting interindividual differences in nonlinear changes and the consequences of misspecifying covariance structures on inferences about the nonlinear mean structures should be investigated in future research.

In summary, we hope this chapter can help researchers understand the features of various variance testing approaches for detecting interindividual differences in intraindividual changes and thus use an appropriate one under their research context. We also hope that after reading this chapter, researchers can be more aware of the severe consequences of having an oversimplified covariance structure in linear growth curve modeling and thus avoid their use in growth curve analyses.

Note

1 Another form of the WS test is $\frac{\hat{\sigma}_S^2}{S.E.(\hat{\sigma}_S^2)}$ where $S.E.(\hat{\sigma}_S^2)$ is the square root of $\hat{C}_{\sigma_S^2}$, a standard error estimate of $\hat{\sigma}_S^2$. $\frac{\hat{\sigma}_S^2}{S.E.(\hat{\sigma}_S^2)}$ is compared to the standard normal distribution. The two forms of the WS test are statistically equivalent and thus lead to identical results. We use $\frac{\hat{\sigma}_S^4}{\hat{C}_{\sigma_S^2}}$ here only for the purpose of easing the comparison with the other variance tests.

References

Baltes, P. B. & Nesselroade, J. R. (1979). History and rationale of longitudinal research. In J. R. Nesselroade & P. B. Baltes (Eds.), *Longitudinal research in the study of behavior and development* (pp. 1–39). New York: Academic Press, Inc.

Barr, D. J., Levy, R., Scheepers, C., & Tily, H. J. (2013). Random effects structure for confirmatory hypothesis testing: Keep it maximal. *Journal of Memory and Language, 68*(3), 255–278.

Box, G. E. P. (1954a). Some theorems on quadratic forms applied in the study of analysis of variance problems. I: effect of inequality of variance in the one-way classification. *The Annals of Mathematical Statistics, 25*(2), 290–302. Retrieved from www.jstor.org/stable/2236731

Box, G. E. P. (1954b). Some theorems on quadratic forms applied in the study of analysis of variance problems, ii. effects of inequality of variance and of correlation between errors in the two-way classification. *The Annals of Mathematical Statistics, 25*(3), 484–498. Retrieved from www.jstor.org/stable/2236831

Bradley, J. V. (1978). Robustness? *British Journal of Mathematical and Statistical Psychology, 31*, 144–152.

Bryk, A. S. & Raudenbush, S. W. (1987). Application of hierarchical linear models to assessing change. *Psychological Bulletin, 101*(1), 147–158.

Cohen, J. (1992). A power primer. *Psychological Bulletin, 112*(1), 155–159.

Curran, P. J. (2003). Have multilevel models been structural equation models all along? *Multivariate Behavioral Research, 38*(4), 529–569.

Fan, X. (2003). Power of latent growth modeling for detecting group differences in linear growth trajectory parameters. *Structural Equation Modeling, 10*(3), 380–400.

Fitzmaurice, G. M., Laird, N. M., & Ware, J. H. (2011). *Applied longitudinal analysis*, 2nd edition. Wiley series in probability and statistics.

Grimm, K. J., Ram, N., & Estabrook, R. (2016). *Growth modeling: Structual equation and multilevel modeling approaches*. New York Guilford.

Grimm, K. J., Ram, N., & Hamagami, F. (2011). Nonlinear growth curves in developmental research. *Child Development, 82*(5), 1357–1371.

Gurka, M. J., Edwards, L. J., & Muller, K. E. (2011). Avoiding bias in mixed model inference for fixed effects. *Statistics in Medicine, 30*(22), 2696–2707.

Hedeker, D. & Gibbons, R. D. (2003). *Applied longitudinal data analysis*. New York: Wiley-Interscience.

Hertzog, C., von Oertzen, T., Ghisletta, P., & Lindenberger, U. (2008). Evaluating the power of latent growth curve models to detect individual differences in change. *Structural Equation Modeling: A Multidisciplinary Journal, 15* (4), 541–563.

Hox, J. J. (2010). *Multilevel analysis: Techniques and applications* (second ed.). New York: Routledge.

Huber, P. J. (1967). The behavior of maximum likelihood estimates under nonstandard conditions. In *Proceedings of the fifth berkeley symposium on mathematical statistics and probability* (Vol. 1, pp. 221–233).

Ke, Z. & Wang, L. (2015). Detecting individual differences in change: Methods and comparisons. *Structural Equation Modeling, 22*(3), 382–400.

Laird, N. M. & Ware, J. H. (1982). Random-effects models for longitudinal data. *Biometrics, 38*, 963–974.

Lange, N. & Laird, N. M. (1989). The effect of covariance structure on variance estimation in balanced growth-curve models with random parameters. *Journal of the American Statistical Association, 84*(405), 241–247.

Liang, K.-Y. & Zeger, S. L. (1986). Longitudinal data analysis using generalized linear models. *Biometrika, 73*(1), 13–22.

Liu, S., Rovine, M. J., & Molenaar, P. (2012). Selecting a linear mixed model for longitudinal data: repeated measures analysis of variance, covariance pattern model, and growth curve approaches. *Psychological Methods, 17*(1), 15.

Maas, C. J. & Hox, J. J. (2004). The influence of violations of assumptions on multilevel parameter estimates and their standard errors. *Computational Statistics & Data Analyisis, 46*(3), 427–440.

MacCallum, R. C., Kim, C., Malarkey, W. B., & Kiecolt-Glaser, J. K. (1997). Studying multivariate change using multilevel models and latent curve models. *Multivariate Behavioral Research, 32*, 215–253.

Maxwell, S. E. (2004). The persistence of underpowered studies in psychological research: Causes, consequences, and remedies. *Psychological Methods, 9*(2), 147–163.

Maxwell, S. E. & Delaney, H. D. (2004). *Designing experiments and analyzing data: A model comparison perspective,* 2nd edition. New York: Taylor & Francis Group.

McArdle, J. J. (1986). Latent variable growth within behavior genetic models. *Behavior Genetics, 16*, 163–200.

McArdle, J. J. (2005). The development of RAM rules for latent variable structural equation modeling. In A. Madeau & J. J. McArdle (Eds.), *Contemporary advances in psychometrics* (pp. 225–273). Mahwah, NJ: Lawrence Erlbaum Associates, Inc.

McArdle, J. J. & Boker, S. M. (1990). *RAMpath: A computer program for automatic path diagrams*. Hilldale, NJ: Erlbaum.

McArdle, J. J. & Epstein, D. (1987). Latent growth curves within developmental structural equation models. *Child Psychology, 58*, 110–133.

McArdle, J. J., Ferrer-Caja, E., Hamagami, F., & Woodcock, R. W. (2002). Comparative longitudinal structural analyses of the growth and decline of multiple intellectual abilities over the life span. *Developmental psychology, 38*(1), 115–142.

McArdle, J. J., Grimm, K. J., Hamagami, F., Bowles, R. P., & Meredith, W. (2009). Modeling life span growth curves of cognition using longitudinal data with multiple samples and changing scales of measurement. *Psychological Methods, 14*, 126–149.

McArdle, J. J. & McDonald, R. P. (1984). Some algebraic properties of the reticular action model for moment structures. *British Journal of Mathematical and Statistical Psychology, 27*, 234–251.

McArdle, J. J. & Nesselroade, J. R. (2014). *Longitudinal data analysis using structural equation models*. Washington, DC: American Psychological Association.

McArdle, J. J. & Wang, L. (2008). Modeling age-based turning points in longitudinal life-span growth curves of cognition. *Applied Data Analytic Techniques for Turning Points research*, pp. 105–128.

McCall, R. B. & Appelbaum, M. I. (1973). Bias in the analysis of repeated-measures designs; some alternative approaches. *Child Development, 44*, 401–415.

Meredith, W. & Tisak, J. (1990). Latent curve analysis. *Psychometrika, 55*, 107–122.

Muthén, B. O. & Curran, P. J. (1997). General longitudinal modeling of individual differences in experimental designs: A latent variable framework for analysis and power estimation. *Psychological Methods, 2*(4), 371.

Planalp, E. M., Du, H., Braungart-Rieker, J. M., & Wang, L. (2017). Growth curve modeling to studying change: A comparison of approaches using longitudinal dyadic data with distinguishable dyads. *Structural Equation Modeling: A Multidisciplinary Journal, 24*(1), 129–147.

Savalei, V. & Kolenikov, S. (2008). Constrained versus unconstrained estimation in structural equation modeling. *Psychological Methods, 13*, 150–170.

Self, S. G. & Liang, K.-Y. (1987). Asymptotic properties of maximum likelihood estimators and likelihood ratio tests under nonstandard conditions. *Journal of American Statistic Association, 82*, 605–610.

Singer, J. D. & Willett, J. B. (2003). *Applied longitudinal data analysis modeling change and event occurrence.* New York: Oxford University Press.

Stoel, R. D., Garre, F. G., Dolan, C., & van den Wittenboer, G. (2006). On the likelihood ratio test in structural equation modeling when parameter are subject to boundary constraints. *Psychological Methods, 4*, 439–455.

Stram, D. & Lee, J.-W. (1994). Variance components testing in the longitudinal mixed effects model. *Biometrics, 50*, 1171–1177.

Verbeke, G. & Molenberghs, G. (2009). *Linear mixed models for longitudinal data* (3rd ed.). New York: Springer Series in Statistics.

Wang, L. & McArdle, J. J. (2008). A simulation study comparison of bayesian estimation with conventional methods for estimating unknown change points. *Structural Equation Modeling: A Multidisciplinary Journal, 15*, 52–74.

Wang, L., Yang, M., & Liu, X. (2018). The impact of over-simplifying the between-subject covariance structure on inferences of fixed effects in modeling nested data. *Structural Equation Modeling.*

White, H. (1980). A heteroskedasticity-consistent covariance matrix estimator and a direct test for heteroskedasticity. *Econometrica, 48*(4), 817–838.

Zhang, Z. & Wang, L. (2009). Statistical power analysis for longitudinal data using SAS. *Behavioral Research Methods, 41*(4), 1083–1094.

9

SAMPLE SIZE AND MEASUREMENT OCCASION PLANNING FOR LATENT CHANGE SCORE MODELS THROUGH MONTE CARLO SIMULATION[1]

Zhiyong Zhang & Haiyan Liu

Introduction

Longitudinal data collection and data analysis are becoming a norm for psychological research (e.g., Grimm, Ram, & Estabrook, 2016; McArdle & Nesselroade, 2014). A longitudinal design often involves data collection on multiple variables from multiple participants at multiple times. Despite the increased cost and complexity, there are many advantages to collecting longitudinal data. For example, a longitudinal design naturally enables a researcher to study change and related phenomena. In addition, inter-individual differences in change can also be investigated.

Growth curve models are probably the most widely used technique for analyzing longitudinal data, benefiting from the fact that a growth curve model can be fitted from a structural equation modeling (SEM) framework (e.g., McArdle, 1986, 1998; McArdle & Anderson, 1990; McArdle & Bell, 1998; McArdle & Epstein, 1987; McArdle & Hamagami, 1992; McArdle & Nesselroade, 2014). With the increasing use of longitudinal design, it is not surprising that more and more complex models and methods have been developed. For example, in order to deal with missing data, full information maximum likelihood methods, multiple imputation, and Bayesian methods have been developed and used (e.g., Enders, 2011; Lu, Zhang, & Cohen, 2013). To deal with non-normal data, robust methods have been proposed (e.g., Yuan & Zhang, 2012; Zhang, 2013; Zhang, Lai, Lu, & Tong, 2013).

A difficult issue in longitudinal research is to model the nonlinear trajectory of data. With more data collection, a linear growth curve model is often not sufficient. When moving to nonlinear models, issues such as computational difficulty can arise (e.g., Grimm, Ram, & Hamagami, 2011; Wang & McArdle, 2008).

Linearizing a nonlinear model provides an efficient way to deal with such difficulties. Although the method based on Taylor expansion is well known (e.g., Browne, 1993; Neale & McArdle, 2000), it is less well known that the latent change score models (LCSMs) provide a potentially more efficient way to model nonlinear trajectories.

Proposed by McArdle and colleagues, LCSMs combine difference equations with growth curves to study change in longitudinal studies (e.g., McArdle, 2000; McArdle & Hamagami, 2001; Hamagami & McArdle, 2007a; Hamagami, Zhang, & McArdle, 2010). In such models, change is directly modeled, which is often the focus of a longitudinal study. As we will show shortly, the models allow to easily accommodate certain nonlinear growth trajectories. In addition to the univariate LCSMs, bivariate LCSMs have also been proposed to model the inter-relationship between two growth processes (e.g., McArdle & Hamagami, 2001).

Fitting a LCSM in the SEM framework is easy to understand but can be tedious. It can be done with almost any SEM software. Recently, Ghisletta & McArdle (2012) showed how to estimate a univariate LCSM using different R packages, including Lavaan (Rosseel, 2012), OpenMx (Boker, Neale, Maes, Wilde, Spiegel, Brick & pthers, 2011), and sem (Fox, 2006). More recently, Zhang et al. (2015) automated the estimating procedure for the typical univariate and multivariate LCSMs through an R package RAMpath that is developed based on RAM notations (Boker, McArdle, & Neale, 2002; McArdle & Boker, 1990).

The importance of conducting statistical power analysis at the beginning of a study is universally accepted (e.g., Cohen, 1988; Hedges & Rhoads, 2010). Without adequate statistical power, the validity of statistical conclusions from all kinds of research is endangered (e.g., Cohen, 1988; Hedges & Rhoads, 2010; Myors & Wolach, 2014; Shadish, Cook, & Campbell, 2002). For example, without a carefully planned sample size, a study can easily fail to detect an existing effect by chance, which in turn creates problems for replication or cross-validation. Although there are studies on sample size planning and power calculation for growth curve analysis (e.g., Zhang & Wang, 2009), we are not aware of any discussion on such design issues for LCSMs.

To fill the gap, this study proposes a Monte Carlo based method to determine the required sample size and/or the number of measurement occasions for both univariate and bivariate LCSMs. The method can obtain the power for testing each individual parameter of the models such as the change rate and coupling parameters. We also implement the Monte Carlo procedure in a free R package RAMpath (Zhang et al., 2015).

In the rest of the chapter, we first present the univariate and bivariate LCSMs. Then, we introduce the Monte Carlo based method for power analysis. After that, we show how to conduct power analysis for LCSMs through several examples using our developed software. We conclude the chapter with discussion and future directions.

A Univariate Latent Change Score Model

Let $Y[t]_n$ denote the data from the nth $(n = 1, \ldots, N)$ participant at time t $(t = 1, \ldots, T)$ of a sample consisting of N participants measured for T times. The first part of an LCSM is a measurement error model where an observed score $Y[t]_n$ is the sum of the latent true score $y[t]_n$ and the measurement error/uniqueness score $ey[t]_n$:

$$Y[t]_n = y[t]_n + ey[t]_n. \tag{9.1}$$

It is generally assumed that the error follows a normal distribution with mean 0 and variance *varey*. The second part of the model builds the relationship between consecutive latent true scores so that the current score at time t is equal to the sum of the true score at the previous time $t - 1$ and the change score, $dy[t]_n$, from time $t - 1$ to time t:

$$y[t]_n = y[t - 1]_n + dy[t]_n. \tag{9.2}$$

This effectively defines the change score as

$$dy[t]_n = y[t]_n - y[t - 1]_n. \tag{9.3}$$

Note that in the classic LCSM, the relationship between consecutive latent true scores is deterministic, although it is not required to be so. The third part of the model concerns the modeling of the difference scores. One way is to model the difference score at time t as the sum of a linear constant effect ys and the proportional change from time $t - 1$ such that

$$dy[t]_n = ys_n + \beta_y \times y[t - 1]_n, \tag{9.4}$$

where β_y is a compound rate of change.

Given the three part of the model, we can model the observed score as

$$
\begin{aligned}
Y[t]_n &= y[t]_n + ey[t]_n \\
&= y[t - 1]_n + dy[t]_n + ey[t]_n \\
&= (1 + \beta_y)y[t - 1]_n + ys_n + ey[t]_n.
\end{aligned} \tag{9.5}
$$

Successively expressing the above equation will lead to

$$
\begin{aligned}
Y[t]_n &= (1 + \beta_y)y[t - 1]_n + ys_n + ey[t]_n \\
&= (1 + \beta_y)(y[t - 2]_n + dy[t - 1]_n) + ys_n + ey[t]_n \\
&= (1 + \beta_y)^2 y[t - 2]_n + (1 + \beta_y)ys_n + ys_n + ey[t]_n \\
&= (1 + \beta_y)^{t-1}y[1]_n + [1 + (1 + \beta_y) + \ldots + (1 + \beta_y)^{t-2}]ys_n + ey[t]_n \\
&= (1 + \beta_y)^{t-1}y0_n + [1 + (1 + \beta_y) + \ldots + (1 + \beta_y)^{t-2}]ys_n + ey[t]_n
\end{aligned} \tag{9.6}
$$

where $y0_n$ is the initial latent score and note that the latent score at time t follows

$$y[t]_n = (1 + \beta_y)^{t-1} y0_n + [1 + (1 + \beta_y) + \ldots + (1 + \beta_y)^{t-2}] ys_n. \qquad (9.7)$$

Clearly, the observed and latent scores behave as a nonlinear function of time and therefore can capture the nonlinear trajectory, except when $\beta_y = 0$. To visually show this, we plot the latent scores with different values for β_y in Figure 9.1. The basic LCSM can only handle this specific type of nonlinearity with exponential changes. For other types of nonlinearity, more complex LCSMs are needed.

The initial latent score and the linear constant change score can be correlated. In the model, they are assumed to have a bivariate normal distribution

$$\begin{pmatrix} y0_n \\ ys_n \end{pmatrix} \sim MN \left[\begin{pmatrix} my0 \\ mys \end{pmatrix}, \begin{pmatrix} vary0 & vary0ys \\ vary0ys & varys \end{pmatrix} \right] \qquad (9.8)$$

with MN denoting a multivariate, here bivariate, normal distribution. Therefore, the initial latent score follows a normal distribution with mean $my0$ and variance $vary0$ and the constant change score also follows a normal distribution with mean mys and variance $varys$. The covariance between them is $vary0ys$ with the correlation expressed as

$$\rho_{y0ys} = \frac{vary0ys}{\sqrt{vary0 \times varys}}. \qquad (9.9)$$

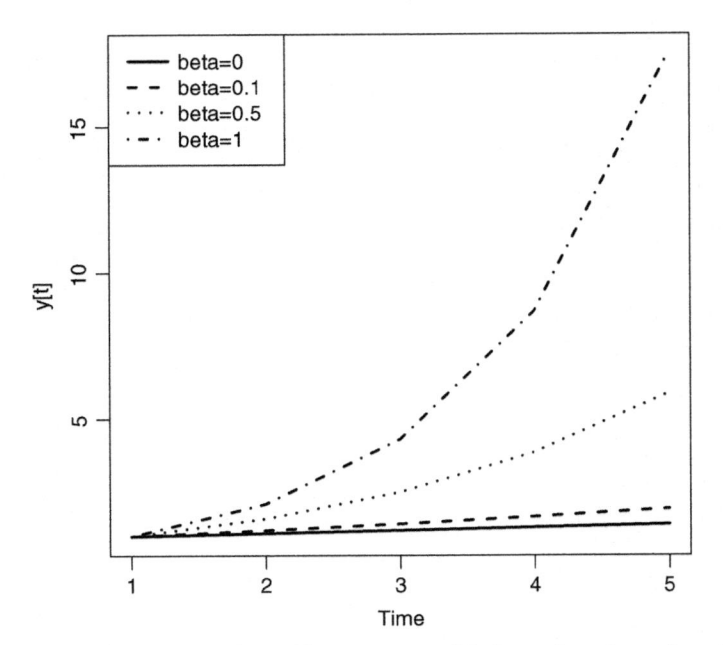

FIGURE 9.1 The trajectory plot of latent scores $y[t]$ from time 1 to time 5 with different β_y values.

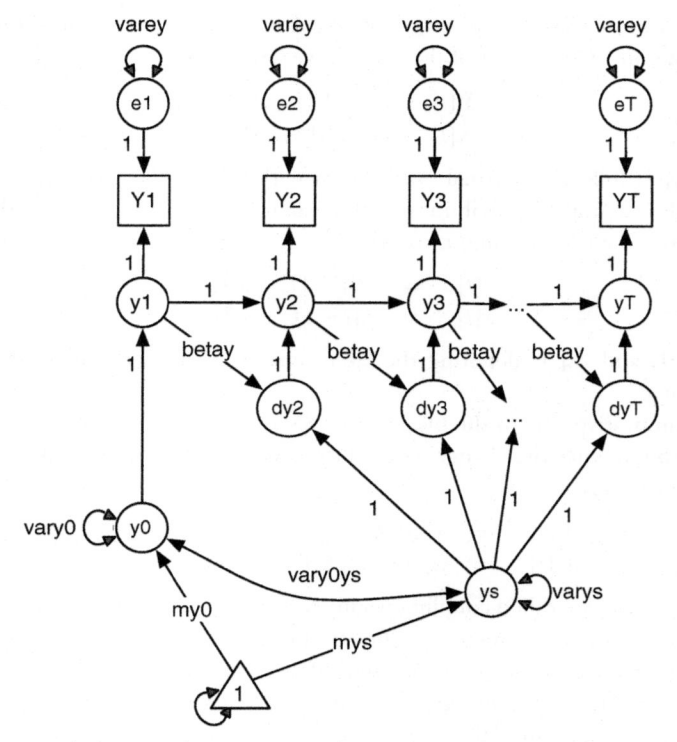

FIGURE 9.2 Path diagram for a univariate latent change score models.

Using a path diagram, this model is portrayed in Figure 9.2. In the path diagram, squares represent observed variables, while circles represent latent variables. A single-headed arrow is for deterministic parameters such as regression coefficients, or factor loadings, while a double-headed arrow represents stochastic parameters such as variance and covariance. A triangle represents a constant. Any arrow originating from the triangle represents an intercept or mean of variables pointed by the arrow. We matched the notations in the formulas and in the path diagram. For simplification, we removed the brackets and the subscripts for the variables in the path diagram.

A Bivariate Latent Change Score Model

A bivariate LCSM is first a combination of two univariate LCSMs. Above and beyond that, it allows the two processes represented by the LCSMs to interact with each other. Let $Y[t]_n$ and $X[t]_n$ denote the observed data on the two variables X and Y, respectively, from the nth ($n = 1, \ldots, N$) participant at time t

$(t = 1, \ldots, T)$ of a sample consisting of N participants measured for T times. For the measurement error part of the model, we have

$$
\begin{aligned}
Y[t]_n &= y[t]_n + ey[t]_n \\
X[t]_n &= x[t]_n + ex[t]_n,
\end{aligned}
\tag{9.10}
$$

where $ey[t]_n$ follows a normal distribution with mean 0 and variance $varey$ and $ex[t]_n$ follows a normal distribution with mean 0 and variance $varex$. For the latent score from time $t - 1$ to time t, we have

$$
\begin{aligned}
y[t]_n &= y[t-1]_n + dy[t]_n \\
x[t]_n &= x[t-1]_n + dx[t]_n,
\end{aligned}
\tag{9.11}
$$

with $dy[t]_n$ and $dx[t]_n$ denoting the latent change scores for the two variables, respectively.

The innovative part of the bivariate LCSM is to allow the latent score of one variable to influence the change score of the other variable. Specifically, we model the change scores as

$$
\begin{aligned}
dy[t]_n &= ys_n + \beta_y \times y[t-1]_n + \gamma_y x[t-1]_n \\
dx[t]_n &= xs_n + \beta_x \times x[t-1]_n + \gamma_x y[t-1]_n
\end{aligned}
\tag{9.12}
$$

where γ_y and γ_x are called coupling parameters. γ_y represents the effect of x on the change score of y and γ_x represents the effect of y on the change score of x. We let $x0$ be the initial latent score and xs be the constant change for x. A multivariate normal distribution is assumed for the initial latent scores and constant changes for the two variables such that

$$
\begin{pmatrix} y0_n \\ ys_n \\ x0_n \\ xs_n \end{pmatrix} \sim MN \left[\begin{pmatrix} my0 \\ mys \\ mx0 \\ mxs \end{pmatrix}, \begin{pmatrix} vary0 & vary0ys & varx0y0 & vary0xs \\ vary0ys & varys & varx0ys & varxsys \\ varx0y0 & varx0ys & varx0 & varx0xs \\ vary0xs & varxsys & varx0xs & varxs \end{pmatrix} \right].
\tag{9.13}
$$

Using a path diagram, a bivariate LCSM is portrayed in Figure 9.3.

Statistical Power Analysis Based on Monte Carlo Simulation

Statistical power analysis concerns the power of a test to detect an effect different from the null. For a model with a set of parameters θ, one can conduct power analysis for one or a subset of parameters, denoted by τ, to investigate whether they are equal to 0 or known values τ_0. Therefore, the null and alternative hypotheses of interest are

$$
H_0 : \tau = \tau_0 \text{ vs. } H_1 : \tau \neq \tau_0.
\tag{9.14}
$$

Existing procedures for power evaluation are mostly based on the Wald test or the likelihood ratio test. The Wald test statistic is defined as

$$
T = (\hat{\tau} - \tau_0)' \hat{\Phi}^{-1} (\hat{\tau} - \tau_0)
\tag{9.15}
$$

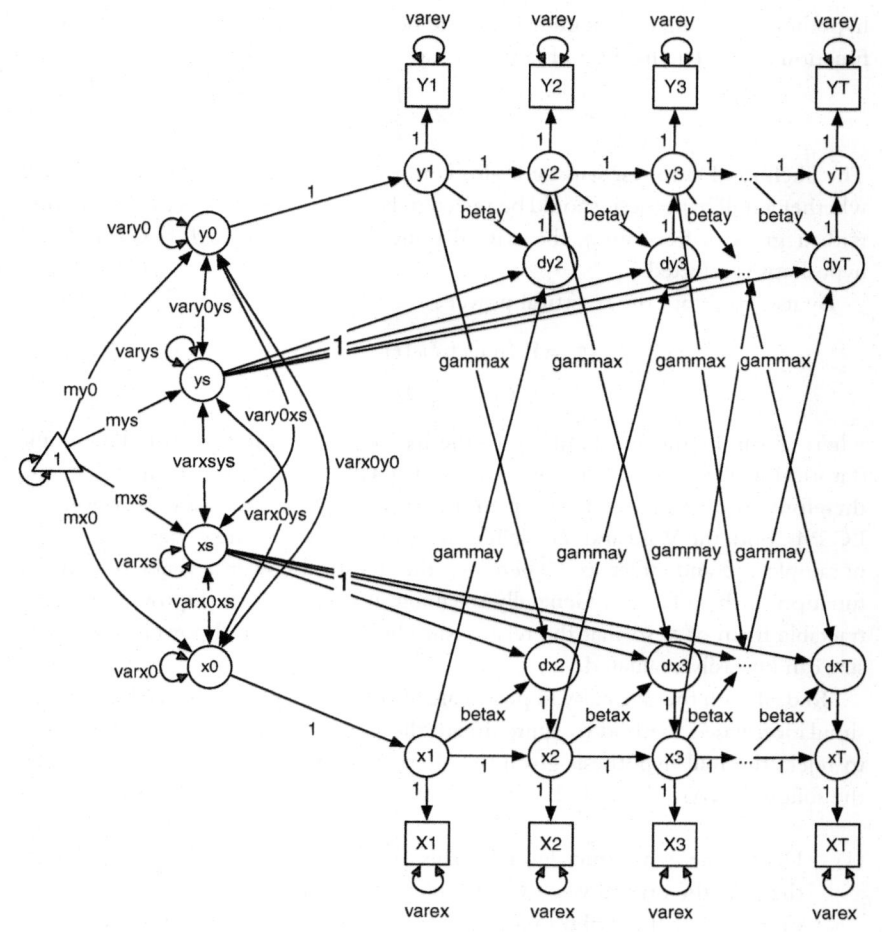

FIGURE 9.3 The path diagram for a bivariate latent change score model.

where $\hat{\tau}$ is the parameter estimates in $\hat{\theta}$ corresponding to τ and $\hat{\Phi}$ is the covariance matrix of $\hat{\tau}$. The Wald test statistic can be compared to a critical value C_α under the null hypothesis. If $T > C_\alpha$, the null hypothesis is rejected. Under the null hypothesis and the typical normality assumption, the Wald statistic asymptotically follows a chi-square distribution (χ_q^2) with the degrees of freedom q, where q is the number of parameters in τ. Then, the critical value at the significance level α is $C_\alpha = \chi_q^2(1 - \alpha)$. Note that when working with a single parameter, the Wald test is the square of a Z test.

The likelihood ratio test works in the similar manner. In the likelihood ratio test, one first estimates the model under the alternative hypothesis to get the value of the likelihood function at L_1. Then, one can estimate the model under the null hypothesis by fixing the parameters in γ to be γ_0 to get the value of the likelihood function at L_0. The likelihood ratio test statistic is defined as

$$T = -2\ln\frac{L_0}{L_1}. \tag{9.16}$$

The likelihood ratio test statistic is also compared to a critical value C_α to decide whether a null hypothesis should be rejected. If T follows a chi-square distribution with degrees of freedom q, the critical value is $\chi_q^2(1 - \alpha)$. If $T > C_\alpha$, the null hypothesis is rejected.

By its definition, the statistical power is

$$\pi = \Pr(\text{reject } H_0 | H_1 \text{ is true})$$
$$= \Pr(T > C_\alpha | H_1 \text{ is true}), \tag{9.17}$$

where T can be the Wald statistic or the likelihood ratio test statistic. For simple statistical analysis such as a t-test, one can obtain an analytical form for π and therefore power and sample size planning can be conducted easily. However, for LCSMs, both the Wald and the likelihood ratio test statistics are complex functions of sample size and effect size. Therefore, the statistical power π is also a complex function of these factors. Generally speaking, it is difficult or impossible to get a tractable form of π so that the relationship between statistical power and sample size can be easily evaluated.

To deal with the difficulty in power analysis for LCSMs, we use a Monte Carlo simulation based method to approximate the power using the relative frequency to reject the null hypothesis given the alternative hypothesis is true. Specifically, the following procedure can be used.

(1) Decide the significance level. Usually, the default 0.05 can be used. Based on that, get the critical value C_α. If only one parameter is tested, the C_α based on the normal distribution is 1.96 for a z-test and 3.84 for the chi-squared distribution for the Wald test.
(2) Specify a LCSM M_1 under H_1 with the hypothesized population parameter values (θ).
(3) Generate a set of data with the sample size N and the number of measurement occasions T from the model using random number generation techniques.
(4) Fit Models M_1 and M_0, the model by setting $\tau = \tau_0$, to the generated data and obtain the Wald statistic using Equation (9.15) and/or the likelihood ratio statistic using Equation (9.16).
(5) If the test statistic $T > C_\alpha$, the null hypothesis H_0 is rejected.
(6) Repeat Steps (2)–(5) for a total of $R(R \geq 1000)$ times.
(7) Suppose that out of the R replications, the null hypothesis H_0 is rejected r times. Then the statistical power with the sample size n is estimated by $\hat{\pi} = \frac{r}{R}$.

(8) For sample size planning, if $\hat{\pi}$ is smaller than the desired power, say 0.8, one can increase the sample size or the number of measurement occasions to repeat Steps (2) and (7) to recalculate the power. Otherwise, the sample size or the number of measurement occasions can be set to a smaller value.

The above Monte Carlo simulation based method for statistical power analysis has been widely used in the literature for mediation analysis and SEM (e.g., Muthén & Muthén, 2002; Thoemmes, MacKinnon & Reiser, 2010; Zhang & Wang, 2009; Zhang, 2014). This procedure is especially effective for complex models. For example, Muthén and Muthén (2002) illustrated how to use Mplus to conduct statistical power analysis for structural equation models using such a procedure. Zhang and Wang (2009) focused on how to conduct statistical power analysis for growth curve models with and without missing data. Thoemmes et al. (2010) discussed how to apply the procedure in mediation analysis. Zhang (2014) extended Theommes et al. for the analysis of missing data and non-normal data.

For a typical power analysis for LCSM, a single parameter is often of interest. For example, one may be only interested in the parameter β in the model. In this case, the power can be calculated using the above procedure based on the Z test. Since Monte Carlo simulation is conducted, when estimating the power for one parameter, power for all the other parameters can also be calculated without much extra effort. Therefore, in our software, we output the power for all parameters in a LCSM model as we will show in our examples.

Software for Power Analysis for Latent Change Score Models

Although the idea of Monte Carlo simulation based power analysis is straightforward, it would still need the software to implement it to make it useful. Recently, Zhang et al. (2015) developed the R package RAMpath that can estimate both univariate and bivariate LCSMs. We expanded RAMpath so that it can carry out power analysis for LCSMs. To further simplify power analysis for researchers who might not be familiar with R, we also developed online software based on RAMpath.

R Package

The R package RAMpath is now on CRAN and therefore it can be installed directly within R as a typical package. For example, to install it, use the R code `install.packages("RAMpath")`. To use the package within R, use `library("RAMpath")`. There are three functions in the package for power analysis: `powerLCS`, `powerBLCS`, and `plot`.

The function `powerLCS` is used to conduct power analysis for univariate LCSMs. The basic usage of the function is given below:

```
powerLCS(N = 100, T = 5, R = 1000, betay = 0, my0 = 0,
```

```
mys = 0, varey = 1, vary0 = 1, varys = 1,
vary0ys = 0,alpha = 0.05, ...)
```

In the function, N is the sample size and T is the number of measurement occasions. Both of them can be a single value or a vector. For example, using N=c(100,200,500) will calculate power for the three provided sample sizes. R is the number of Monte Carlo simulation used to estimate the power. A larger R will provide more accurate power estimation but also take more computing time. As a rule of thumb, at least 1,000 should be used. alpha is the significance level for testing the hypothesis of the model parameters. The default value is 0.05.

To obtain statistical power, the population parameter values have to be provided. Such values can be decided based on literature review, pilot study, expert opinions, etc. By default, all the mean, intercept, and covariance parameters are set at 0 and all the variance parameters are set at 1. Those values typically have to be changed in real power analysis. Note that the name of each parameter corresponds to that used in the path diagram in Figure 9.2. In addition to the basic input, for advanced users, other information can be provided to control the parameter and standard error estimation methods. For example, the options used in Lavaan to control model estimation can be used directly within the function. More information can be found in the help document of the R package.

The output of the R function includes four main pieces of information for each parameter in the model. The first is the Monte Carlo estimate (mc.est). It is calculated as the mean of the R sets of parameter estimates from the simulated data. Note that the Monte Carlo estimates should be close to the population parameter values used in the model. The second is the Monte Carlo standard deviation (mc.sd), which is calculated as the standard deviation of the R sets of parameter estimates. The third is the Monte Carlo standard error (mc.se), which is obtained as the average of the R sets of standard error estimates of the parameter estimates. Last, mc.power is the statistical power for each parameter.

The function powerBLCS is used to conduct power analysis for bivariate LCSMs. The basic usage of the function is given below. It is the same as for the univariate LCSMs.

```
powerBLCS(N=100, T=5, R=1000, betay=0, my0=0, mys=0,
    varey=1, vary0=1, varys=1, vary0ys=0, betax=0, mx0=0,
    mxs=0, varex=1, varx0=1, varxs=1, varx0xs=0,
    varx0y0=0, varx0ys=0, vary0xs=0, varxsys=0, gammax=0,
    gammay=0, alpha=0.05, ...)
```

The function plot is used to generate a power curve, which has the form plot(x, parameter, ...). The first input of the function, x, is the output from either powerLCS or powerBLCS. In the input of the function for power analysis, either the sample size N or the number of occasions T should be a vector. The second input is the name of a parameter to plot its power curve. Since there are multiple parameters in a LCSM, one can generate a plot for each model parameter. The name of a parameter should match the one in `powerLCS` or `powerBLCS`. This function will generate one or multiple line plots in which power is shown on the y-axis and sample size or the number of occasions is shown on the x-axis.

Online Interface

In order to help researchers who are not familiar with R, we also provide a Web-based interface for power analysis for LCSMs. The URL for the univariate LCSMs is http://psychstat.org/lcsm and for the bivariate LCSMs is http://psychstat.org/blcsm.

The Web interface for the univariate LCSMs is shown in Figure 9.4. Since the interface is built on the R function shown earlier, it requires the same input information and gives the same output. For both sample size and number of occasions, multiple values can be provided in two ways to calculate power for each given value. We discuss this using the sample size as an example since the same method is used for the number of occasions. First, multiple sample sizes can be provided and separated by spaces. For example, inputting 100 150 200 will

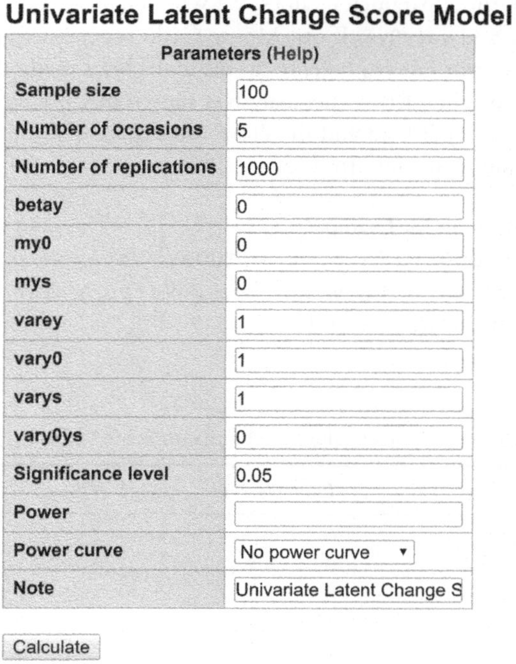

Univariate Latent Change Score Model

Parameters (Help)	
Sample size	100
Number of occasions	5
Number of replications	1000
betay	0
my0	0
mys	0
varey	1
vary0	1
varys	1
vary0ys	0
Significance level	0.05
Power	
Power curve	No power curve ▾
Note	Univariate Latent Change S

Calculate

FIGURE 9.4 The online interface for power analysis for univariate latent change score models. http://psychstat.org/lcsm.

calculate power for the three sample sizes 100, 150, and 200. Second, a sequence of sample sizes can be generated using the method *s:e:i* with *s* denoting the starting sample size, *e* as the ending sample size, and *i* as the interval. Note that the values are separated by a colon ":". For example, 100:150:10 will generate a sequence of sample sizes: 100 110 120 130 140 150.

The interface for the bivariate LCSMs is similar and is not provided here for the sake of space.

Examples

In this section, we show how to carry out power analysis for both univariate and bivariate LCSMs through several examples.

Example 9.1: Type I Error Rate Investigation for a Univariate LCSM

Note that if the null hypothesis is true, the Monte Carlo procedure will yield the type I error rate. For example, suppose the parameter $\beta_y = 0$ in the population. Then the estimated power for it should be the same as the significance level, typically 0.05. For illustration, we set the population parameter values to those shown in the second column of Table 9.1. Therefore, if we conduct a power analysis based on those parameter values, we will obtain the type I error rates for `betay`, `my0`, `mys`, and `vary0ys`. If our Monte Carlo procedure performs well, we expect the type I error rates to be close to the alpha level used.

The R code for conducting the analysis is shown in Code 9.1. Note that the significance level is set at 0.05 and therefore, we expect that the estimated values in the power column are close to 0.05.

Code 9.1 R input script for Example 9.1.

```
powerLCS(N = 100, T = 5, R = 1000, betay = 0, my0 = 0,
   mys = 0, varey = 1, vary0 = 1, varys = 1,
   vary0ys = 0,alpha = 0.05)
```

TABLE 9.1 Population parameter values used in Examples 9.1 to 9.4.

	Example 9.1	*Example 9.2*
betay	0	0.1
my0	0	20
mys	0	1.5
varey	1	9
vary0	1	2.5
varys	1	0.05
vary0ys	0	0

The output of the R code is given in Code 9.2. First, the estimate for each parameter is very close to the true population parameter values, as can be seen in the column named `mc.est`. This indicates that the power calculation procedure runs well. Second, the Monte Carlo standard errors are close to the corresponding Monte Carlo standard deviations, another indicator that the power calculation is trustworthy. Third, as expected, the power for `betay`, `my0`, `mys`, and `vary0ys` is close to 0.05, the nominal type I error rate. Overall, this suggests that the Monte Carlo based method can provide well-controlled type I error rate.

Code 9.2 Type I error rate and power for parameters in Example 9.1.

	pop.par	mc.est	mc.sd	mc.se	mc.power	N	T
betay	0	0.001	0.056	0.056	0.046	100	5
my0	0	0.001	0.129	0.126	0.056	100	5
mys	0	0.002	0.105	0.105	0.044	100	5
varey	1	0.994	0.083	0.081	1.000	100	5
vary0	1	0.990	0.236	0.230	1.000	100	5
vary0ys	0	-0.005	0.136	0.136	0.044	100	5
varys	1	1.006	0.227	0.227	1.000	100	5

Example 9.2: Power Analysis for a Univariate LCSM

To conduct a power analysis, one has to specify the population parameter values for the model. Zhang et al. (2015) included an example on using a univariate LCSM model to analyze the WISC data (see McArdle & Nesselroade, 2014). In order to plan a future study with the sample size 100 and 5 measurement occasions, we use the estimates as our population parameter values. Column 3 in Table 9.1 shows the roundup parameter estimates being used in our example.

The R code for conducting the analysis is shown in Code 9.3 and the output of the R code is given in Code 9.4. From the output, we can see that the power to detect the parameter `betay` to be significant with a sample size 100 and a number of measurement occasions 5 is about 0.664. The power for another parameter, the constant change `mys`, is 0.274. Since often one hopes to get a power at least 0.8, a larger sample size is needed for this study. In addition, for studying power for different parameters, different sample sizes are often required.

Code 9.3 R input script for Example 9.2.
```
powerLCS(N = 100, T = 5, R = 1000, betay = 0.1,
  my0 = 20, mys = 1.5, varey = 9, vary0 = 2.5,
  varys = .05, vary0ys = 0, alpha = 0.05)
```

Code 9.4 Power for parameters in Example 9.2.

	pop.par	mc.est	mc.sd	mc.se	mc.power	N	T
betay	0.10	0.103	0.043	0.044	0.664	100	5

```
my0          20.00 19.999 0.324 0.319    1.000 100 5
mys           1.50  1.418 1.106 1.120    0.274 100 5
varey         9.00  8.961 0.724 0.732    1.000 100 5
vary0         2.50  2.463 1.151 1.139    0.583 100 5
vary0ys       0.00 -0.004 0.408 0.403    0.048 100 5
varys         0.05  0.053 0.173 0.175    0.050 100 5
```

Example 9.3: Generate a Power Curve for Different Sample Sizes for a Univariate LCSM

Example 9.2 above showed that a larger sample size was needed in order to get sufficient power for parameters betay and mys. Although one can try a difference sample size greater than 100, for convenience, we can generate a power curve with different sample sizes. For example, Figure 9.5 shows the power curves for the two parameters betay and mys with sample sizes ranging from 100 to 200 with an interval 10. From the plot, we can easily see that to get a power 0.8 for the parameter betay, a sample size about 150 is needed. On the other hand, a sample size larger than 200 is needed for the parameter mys to have a power 0.8, with the exact number undecided based on the plot.

The R code for generating the power curve is shown in Code 9.5. Note that in the plot function, we refer to a specific parameter directly using its name. In the input, seq(100, 200, 10) generate a sequence of sample sizes and in the output, power for each sample size is provided. Code 9.6 shows the output when the sample sizes are 100 and 200 only to save space.

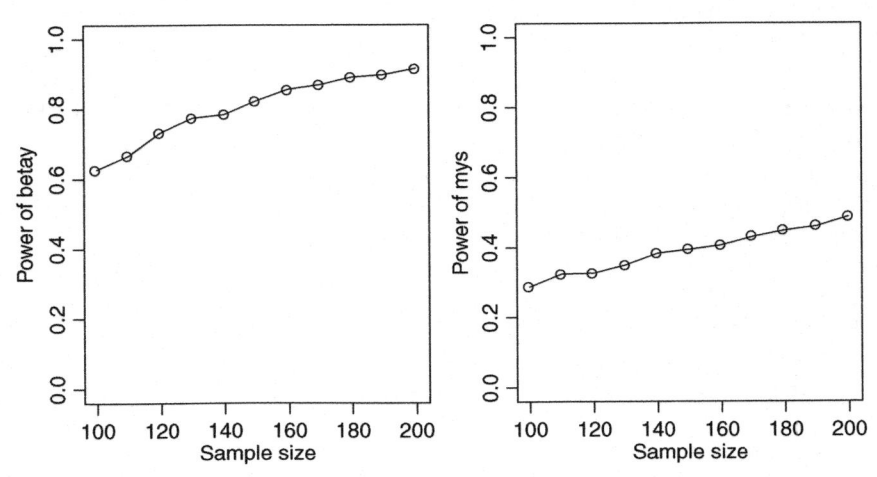

FIGURE 9.5 Power curve for betay (left plot) and mys (right plot) along with the sample size in the univariate latent change score model.

Code 9.5 R input script for power curve in Example 9.3.

```
res <- powerLCS(N = seq(100, 200, 10), T = 5,
    R = 1000, betay = 0.1, my0 = 20, mys = 1.5,
    varey = 9, vary0 = 2.5, varys = .05, vary0ys = 0,
    alpha = 0.05)
plot(res, 'betay')
plot(res, 'mys')
```

Code 9.6 Output for generating power curves in Example 9.3.

`$`N100-T5``

	pop.par	mc.est	mc.sd	mc.se	mc.power	N	T
betay	0.10	0.100	0.044	0.044	0.627	100	5
my0	20.00	20.002	0.331	0.319	1.000	100	5
mys	1.50	1.505	1.136	1.119	0.287	100	5
varey	9.00	8.970	0.744	0.732	1.000	100	5
vary0	2.50	2.489	1.218	1.146	0.599	100	5
vary0ys	0.00	-0.009	0.413	0.403	0.059	100	5
varys	0.05	0.054	0.176	0.175	0.050	100	5

. . . .

`$`N200-T5``

	pop.par	mc.est	mc.sd	mc.se	mc.power	N	T
betay	0.10	0.100	0.031	0.031	0.915	200	5
my0	20.00	20.002	0.225	0.226	1.000	200	5
mys	1.50	1.505	0.790	0.791	0.487	200	5
varey	9.00	8.971	0.532	0.518	1.000	200	5
vary0	2.50	2.480	0.803	0.808	0.904	200	5
vary0ys	0.00	0.005	0.283	0.283	0.049	200	5
varys	0.05	0.051	0.125	0.122	0.054	200	5

Example 9.4: Generate a Power Curve for Different Number of Occasions for a Univariate LCSM

For LCSMs, power is not only related to the sample size but also the number of measurement occasions. With the increase of the number of occasions, one would expect the increase of power. For example, Figure 9.6 shows the power curves for the two parameters betay and mys with the number of occasions ranging from 4 to 10 with an interval 1 and with the fixed sample size 100. From the plot, we can easily see that the power increases along with the number of measurement occasions. For example, for the same sample size 100, the power is less than 0.2 with 4 occasions of data but increases to more than 0.8 with 7 occasions of data

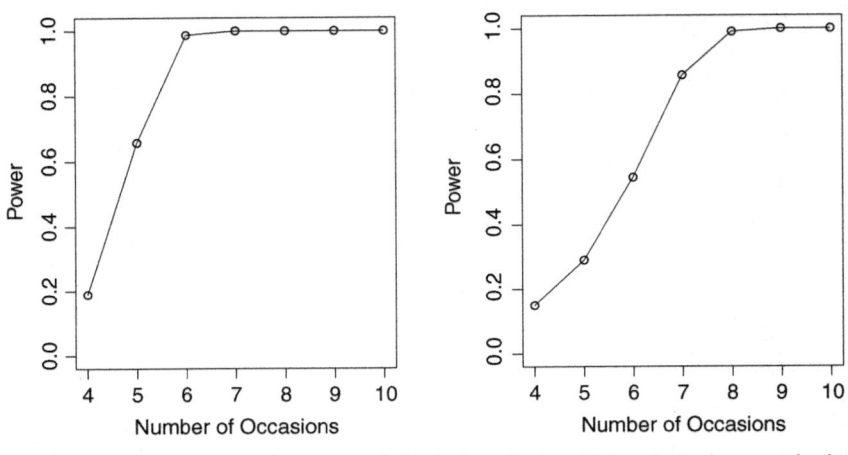

FIGURE 9.6 Power curve for `betay` (left plot) and `mys` (right plot) along with the number of measurement occasions in the univariate latent change score model.

for the parameter `mys`. The R code for generating the power curve is shown in Code 9.7.

Code 9.7 R input script for power curve with the number of occasions in Example 9.4.

```
res <- powerLCS(N = 100, T = 4:10, R = 1000,
    betay = 0.1, my0 = 20, mys = 1.5, varey = 9,
    vary0 = 2.5, varys = .05, vary0ys = 0,
    alpha = 0.05)
plot(res, 'betay')
plot(res, 'mys')
```

Example 9.5: Power Analysis for a Bivariate LCSM

Power analysis can be similarly conducted for bivariate LCSMs. As an example, we use the parameter estimates from a bivariate latent change score model in Zhang et al. (2015) with some modification as population parameter values (see Table 9.2).

The script in Code 9.8 shows the R code for power analysis for the bivariate LCSM with the sample size 100. From the output in Code 9.9, we can see that the parameter estimates are not very accurate. This is because the bivariate LCSM requires a much larger sample size to provide accurate parameter estimates. In this case, the statistical power obtained might not be accurate either.

Code 9.8 R input script for power analysis for bivariate latent change score model in Example 9.5.

TABLE 9.2 Population parameter values used in Example 9.5.

Parameter	value	Parameter	value
betay	0.08	betax	0.2
gammax	0	gammay	−0.1
my0	20	mx0	20
Mys	1.5	mxs	5
varey	9	varex	9
vary0	3	varx0	3
varys	0.05	varxs	0.6
vary0ys	0	varx0xs	0
varx0y0	1		
vayx0ys	0		
vary0xs	0		
varxsys	0		

```
powerBLCS(N=100, T=5, R=1000, betay=0.08, my0=20,
        mys=1.5, varey=9, vary0=3, varys=1,
        vary0ys=0, alpha=0.05, betax=0.2, mx0=20,
        mxs=5, varex=9, varx0=3, varxs=1, varx0xs=0,
        varx0y0=1, varx0ys=0, vary0xs=0, varxsys=0,
        gammax=0, gammay=-.1)
```

Code 9.9 Output for power analysis in Example 9.5.

```
         pop.par mc.est mc.sd mc.se mc.power   N  T
betax       0.20   0.230  0.260  0.187    0.241 100  5
betay       0.08   0.164  0.572  0.435    0.081 100  5
gammax      0.00  -0.033  0.234  0.178    0.112 100  5
gammay     -0.10  -0.175  0.641  0.458    0.075 100  5
mx0        20.00  20.004  0.336  0.326    1.000 100  5
mxs         5.00   5.933  7.848  5.615    0.167 100  5
my0        20.00  20.019  0.346  0.326    1.000 100  5
mys         1.50   0.451  6.933  5.321    0.156 100  5
varex       9.00   8.941  0.744  0.732    1.000 100  5
varey       9.00   8.939  0.749  0.720    1.000 100  5
varx0       3.00   3.029  1.243  1.222    0.739 100  5
varx0xs     0.00  -0.210  0.768  0.767    0.030 100  5
varx0y0     1.00   1.052  0.840  0.835    0.226 100  5
varx0ys     0.00  -0.012  0.668  0.601    0.017 100  5
varxs       0.60   2.343  6.805  2.687    0.090 100  5
varxsys     0.00   0.072  3.559  1.740    0.019 100  5
vary0       3.00   2.951  1.423  1.245    0.684 100  5
vary0xs     0.00   0.198  2.263  1.629    0.031 100  5
```

vary0ys	0.00	-0.371	1.970	1.511	0.106	100 5
varys	0.05	1.415	3.730	2.096	0.024	100 5

Increasing the sample size will lead to more accurate results as shown in Code 9.10 where the sample size is 500. In planning the sample size for LCSM models, one should pay attention to the parameter estimates to make sure they are accurate enough for power calculation. Specifically for the coupling parameters gammax and gammay, the power and type I error are 0.057 and 0.271, respectively.

Code 9.10 Output for power analysis in Example 9.5 when the sample size is 500.

	pop.par	mc.est	mc.sd	mc.se	mc.power	N	T
betax	0.20	0.2009	0.031	0.031	1.000	500	5
betay	0.08	0.0830	0.070	0.068	0.199	500	5
gammax	0.00	-0.0014	0.030	0.029	0.057	500	5
gammay	-0.10	-0.1022	0.072	0.073	0.271	500	5
mx0	20.00	19.9911	0.145	0.145	1.000	500	5
mxs	5.00	5.0308	0.939	0.942	1.000	500	5
my0	20.00	19.9999	0.143	0.146	1.000	500	5
mys	1.50	1.4684	0.889	0.885	0.420	500	5
varex	9.00	8.9836	0.340	0.328	1.000	500	5
varey	9.00	8.9961	0.341	0.328	1.000	500	5
varx0	3.00	3.0052	0.524	0.523	1.000	500	5
varx0xs	0.00	-0.0144	0.222	0.230	0.047	500	5
varx0y0	1.00	1.0064	0.360	0.360	0.808	500	5
varx0ys	0.00	-0.0012	0.199	0.201	0.051	500	5
varxs	1.00	1.0312	0.180	0.189	1.000	500	5
varxsys	0.00	0.0028	0.161	0.163	0.045	500	5
vary0	3.00	2.9777	0.519	0.547	1.000	500	5
vary0xs	0.00	0.0072	0.286	0.294	0.035	500	5
vary0ys	0.00	-0.0135	0.252	0.257	0.043	500	5
varys	1.00	1.0246	0.260	0.253	0.999	500	5

Discussion and Future Directions

To complement the research on LCSMs, in this chapter, we discuss how to plan the sample size and the number of measurement occasions for both univariate and bivariate LCSMs. Specifically, we illustrate how to calculate power for each individual model parameter of interest. Since the analytical solution to power is intractable, we used a Monte Carlo based method. We also provided an R package RAMpath and an online interface to carry out the power analysis procedure.

In calculating power, we need the information on the population parameter values. Each value can be viewed as the unstandardized effect size for the parameter of interest. We did not define the standardized effect size such as

Cohen's d (Cohen, 1988) for several reasons. First, given the complexity of LCSMs, it is difficult to define a standardized effect size. Second, in general, it is easier to specify the unstandardized effect size because when conducting a literature review, one can simply adopt the parameter estimates directly from the published results. Third, if a researcher is interested in standardized measures, he/she can use the standardized coefficients as the population parameter values in conducting power analysis.

One way to streamline the specification of the population parameters is to use the R-squared. For example, in a bivariate LCSM, the variance of the change score is from three sources – the constant change, the own level score, and the level score of the other variable. By changing the parameter values, one can quantify the portion of variance explained by each source. On the other hand, depending on the expected variance explained, one can set the parameter values. Using this method, one can take advantage of the existing effect size cutoffs for R-squared, namely, 0.02 for small, 0.13 for medium, and 0.26 for large effect sizes.

The current study can be improved in many ways in the future. First, in this chapter, we have focused on the power analysis of a single model parameter, as this is the most common situation. If a researcher wants to test multiple parameters simultaneously, a procedure based on the likelihood ratio test can be developed as for the growth curve analysis in Zhang & Wang (2009).

Second, in the current study, we have focused on the basic univariate and bivariate LCSMs. Since their invention, the basic univariate and bivariate LCSMs have been extended in many ways. For example, Hamagami and McArdle (2007b) expanded the traditional specifications of univariate and bivariate LCSMs to the parallel process change score model and the second-order LCSMs. Grimm, An, McArdle, Zonderman, & Resnick (2012) extended latent difference scores to allow for testing hypotheses where recent changes, as opposed to recent levels, are a primary predictor of subsequent changes. The Monte Carlo procedure used in this study can be flexibly extended to the more advanced models.

Third, the current study has assumed that the collected data will be complete. However, in practice, missing data are almost not avoidable in longitudinal studies. For example, Puma, Olsen, Bell, & Price (2009) found that student achievement outcomes are often missing for 10–20% in studies funded by the National Center for Education Evaluation and Regional Assistance. Missing data reduce power and without careful consideration, a well-planned study can become under-powered; taking into consideration that missing data in power calculation requires the specification of missing data generating mechanism that can be used in the data generation step in our Monte Carlo method.

Fourth, in our Monte Carlo method, we have assumed that our data are normally distributed. However, practical data often deviate from a normal distribution. For example, Micceri (1989) evaluated 440 distributions of large-sample achievement and psychometric measures and found that all of them were non-normal. More recently, Blanca, Arnau, López-Montiel, Bono, & Bendayan

(2013) evaluated non-normality using the skewness and kurtosis of 693 small samples and found that 94.5 % of them violated the normality assumption. In addition, Cain, Zhang, & Yuan (2016) reviewed 254 multivariate distributions of data used in Psychological Science and the American Education Research Journal and found that 68% multivariate distributions deviated from normal distributions. Therefore, in the future, the influence of non-normal data should be considered when estimating power.

Finally, the Monte Carlo based method can be very computationally intensive because of the involvement of the Monte Carlo simulation. For example, it took about 10 minutes on a modern desktop to complete the power analysis in Example 9.4. At the same time, the Monte Carlo method can be easily parallelized to take advantage of modern hardware such as multi-core processors (e.g., Zhang, 2014). In the future, the R package RAMpath can be improved with the capacity of parallelization.

Note

1 The study was supported by a grant from the Department of Education (R305D140037). However, the contents of WebPower do not necessarily represent the policy of the Department of Education, and you should not assume endorsement by the Federal Government.

References

Blanca, M. J., Arnau, J., López-Montiel, D., Bono, R., & Bendayan, R. (2013). Skewness and kurtosis in real data samples. *Methodology, 9*(2), 78–84.

Boker, S. M., McArdle, J. J., & Neale, M. C. (2002). An algorithm for the hierarchical organization of path diagrams and calculation of components of covariance between variables. *Structural Equation Modeling, 9*(2), 174–194.

Boker, S. M., Neale, M., Maes, H., Wilde, M., Spiegel, M., Brick, T., ... et al. (2011). Openmx: an open source extended structural equation modeling framework. *Psychometrika, 76*(2), 306–317.

Browne, M. W. (1993). Structured latent curve models. In C. M. Cuadras & C. R. Rao (Eds.), *Multivariate analysis: Future directions 2* (pp. 171–198). Amsterdam: North-Holland.

Cain, M. K., Zhang, Z., & Yuan, K.-H. (2017). Univariate and multivariate skewness and kurtosis for measuring nonnormality: Prevalence, influence and estimation. *Behavior Research Methods, 49*(5), 1716–1735.

Cohen, J. (1988). *Statistical power analysis for the behavioral sciences* (2nd ed.). Hillsdale, NJ: Lawrence Ehrlbaum Associates.

Enders, C. K. (2011). Missing not at random models for latent growth curve analyses. *Psychological methods, 16*(1), 1–16.

Fox, J. (2006). Structural equation modeling with the sem package in R. *Structural Equation Modeling, 13*, 465–486.

Gerstorf, D., Lövdén, M., Röcke, C., Smith, J., & Lindenberger, U. (2007). Well-being affects changes in perceptual speed in advanced old age: Longitudinal evidence for a dynamic link. *Developmental psychology, 43*(3), 705.

Ghisletta, P. & Lindenberger, U. (2005). Exploring the structural dynamics of the link between sensory and cognitive functioning in old age: Longitudinal evidence from the Berlin aging study. *Intelligence, 33*, 555–587.

Ghisletta, P. & McArdle, J. J. (2012). Latent curve models and latent change score models estimated in R. *Structural Equation Modeling: A multidisciplinary Journal, 19*(4), 651–682.

Grimm, K. J., An, Y., McArdle, J. J., Zonderman, A. B., & Resnick, S. M. (2012). Recent changes leading to subsequent changes: Extensions of multivariate latent difference score models. *Structural Equation Modeling: A multidisciplinary Journal, 19*(2), 268–292.

Grimm, K. J., Ram, N., & Estabrook, R. (2016). *Growth modeling: Structural equation and multilevel modeling approaches.* New York: Guilford Publications.

Grimm, K. J., Ram, N., & Hamagami, F. (2011). Nonlinear growth curves in developmental research. *Child Development, 82*(5), 1357–1371.

Hamagami, F. & McArdle, J. J. (2007a). Dynamic extensions of latent difference score models. In S. M. Boker & M. J. Wenger (Eds.), *Data analytic techniques for dynamical systems* (pp. 47–86). Mahwah, NJ: Lawrence Erlbaum Associates.

Hamagami, F. & McArdle, J. J. (2007b). Dynamic extensions of latent difference score models. In S. M. Boker & Wenger (Eds.), *Data analytic techniques for dynamical systems* (pp. 47–85). Mahwah, NJ: Lawrence Erlbaum Associates.

Hamagami, F., Zhang, Z., & McArdle, J. J. (2010). Bayesian discrete dynamic system by latent difference score structural equations models for multivariate repeated measures data. In S.-M. Chow, E. Ferrer, & F. Hsieh (Eds.), *Statistical methods for modeling human dynamics: An interdisciplinary dialogue* (pp. 319–348). New York: RoutledgeTaylor & Francis Group.

Hedges, L. V. & Rhoads, C. (2010). Statistical power analysis in education research. ncser 2010-3006. *National Center for Special Education Research.*

King, L. A., King, D. W., McArdle, J. J., Saxe, G. N., Doron-LaMarca, S., & Orazem, R. J. (2006). Latent difference score approach to longitudinal trauma research. *Journal of Traumatic Stress, 19*(6), 771–785.

Lu, Z. L., Zhang, Z., & Cohen, A. (2013). Bayesian methods and model selection for latent growth curve models with missing data. In *New developments in quantitative psychology* (pp. 275–304). Springer.

McArdle, J. J. (1986). Latent variable growth within behavior genetic models. *Behavior Genetics, 16*, 163–200.

McArdle, J. J. (1998). Modeling longitudinal data by latent growth curve methods. In G. Marcoulides (Ed.), *Modern methods for business research* (pp. 359–406). Mahwah, NJ: Lawrence Erlbaum Associates.

McArdle, J. J. (2000). A latent difference score approach to longitudinal dynamic structural analyses. In R. Cudeck, S. du Toit, & D. Sorbom (Eds.), *Structural equation modeling: Present and future* (pp. 342–380). Lincolnwood, IL: Scientific Software International.

McArdle, J. J. (2009). Latent variable modeling of differences and changes with longitudinal data. *Annual Review of Psychology, 60*, 577–605.

McArdle, J. J., & Anderson, E. (1990). Latent variable growth models for research on aging. In J. E. Birren & K. W. Schaie (Eds.), *Handbook of the psychology aging* (p. 21–44). New York: Academic Press.

McArdle, J. J., & Bell, R. Q. (1998). Recent trends in modeling longitudinal data by latent growth curve methods. In T. D. Little, K. U. Schnabel, & J. Baumert (Eds.), *Modeling longitudinal and multiple-group data: Practical issues, applied approaches, and scientific examples* (p. 69–107). Mahwah, NJ: Lawrence Erlbaum Associates.

McArdle, J. J. & Boker, S. M. (1990). *Rampath*. Hillsdale, NJ: Lawrence Erlbaum Associates.

McArdle, J. J. & Epstein, D. (1987). Latent growth curves within developmental structural equation models. *Child Psychology, 58*, 110–133.

McArdle, J. J. & Hamagami, F. (1992). Modeling incomplete longitudinal and cross-sectional data using latent growth structural models. *Experimental Aging Research, 18*(3), 145–166.

McArdle, J. J. & Hamagami, F. (2001). Latent difference score structural models for linear dynamic analyses with incomplete longitudinal data. In L. M. Collins & A. G. Sayer (Eds.), *New methods for the analysis of change* (pp. 139–175). Washington, DC: American Psychological Association.

McArdle, J. J. & Nesselroade, J. R. (1994). Using multivariate data to structure developmental change. In S. H. Cohen & H. W. Reese (Eds.), *Life-span developmental psychology: Methodological contributions* (pp. 223–267). Hillsdale, NJ: Lawrence Erlbaum Associates.

McArdle, J. J. & Nesselroade, J. R. (2014). *Longitudinal data analysis using structural equation models.* Washington, DC: American Psychological Association.

Micceri, T. (1989). The unicorn, the normal curve, and other improbable creatures. *Psychological Bulletin, 105*(1), 156–166.

Muthén, L. K. & Muthén, B. O. (2002). How to use a Monte Carlo study to decide on sample size and determine power. *Structural Equation Modeling, 9*(4), 599–620.

Myors, B. & Wolach, A. (2014). *Statistical power analysis: A simple and general model for traditional and modern hypothesis tests.* Mahwah, NJ: Lawrence Erlbaum Associates.

Neale, M. C. & McArdle, J. J. (2000). Structured latent growth curves for twin data. *Twin Research, 3*, 165–177.

Puma, M. J., Olsen, R. B., Bell, S. H., & Price, C. (2009). What to do when data are missing in group randomized controlled trials. 2009–0049. *National Center for Education Evaluation and Regional Assistance.*

Raz, N., Lindenberger, U., Ghisletta, P., Rodrigue, K. M., Kennedy, K. M., & Acker, J. D. (2008). Neuroanatomical correlates of fluid intelligence in healthy adults and persons with vascular risk factors. *Cerebral Cortex, 18*(3), 718–726.

Rosseel, Y. (2012). lavaan: An R package for structural equation modeling. *Journal of Statistical Software, 48*, 1–36.

Shadish, W. R., Cook, T. D., & Campbell, D. T. (2002). *Experimental and quasi-experimental designs for generalized causal inference.* Boston, MA: Wadsworth Cengage learning.

Thoemmes, F., MacKinnon, D. P., & Reiser, M. R. (2010). Power analysis for complex mediational designs using monte carlo methods. *Structural Equation Modeling, 17*, 510–534.

Wang, L. & McArdle, J. J. (2008). A simulation study comparison of Bayesian estimation with conventional methods for estimating unknown change points. *Structural Equation Modeling, 15*, 52–74.

Yuan, K.-H. & Zhang, Z. (2012). Robust structural equation modeling with missing data and auxiliary variables. *Psychometrika, 77*, 803–826.

Zhang, Z. (2013). Bayesian growth curve models with the generalized error distribution. *Journal of Applied Statistics, 40*, 1779–1795.

Zhang, Z. (2014). Monte Carlo based statistical power analysis for mediation models: Methods and software. *Behavior Research Methods, 46*(4), 1184–1198.

Zhang, Z., Hamagami, F., Grimm, K. J., & McArdle, J. J. (2015). Using R package RAM-path for tracing SEM path diagrams and conducting complex longitudinal data analysis. *Structural Equation Modeling: A Multidisciplinary Journal, 22*(1), 132–147.

Zhang, Z., Lai, K., Lu, Z., & Tong, X. (2013). Bayesian inference and application of robust growth curve models using Student's t distribution. *Structural Equation Modeling, 20*, 47–78.

Zhang, Z. & Wang, L. (2009). Statistical power analysis for growth curve models using SAS. *Behavior Research Methods, 41*, 1083–1094.

10

INVESTIGATING THE PERFORMANCE OF cart- AND RANDOM FOREST-BASED PROCEDURES FOR DEALING WITH LONGITUDINAL DROPOUT IN SMALL SAMPLE DESIGNS UNDER mnar MISSING DATA

Timothy Hayes

Quantitative researchers have begun to consider ways of utilizing exploratory data mining techniques to address missing data. Although many algorithms could conceivably prove useful for this goal, Classification and Regression Trees (CART; Breiman, Friedman, Olshen, & Stone, 1984) and Random Forests (Breiman, 2001) seem particularly promising, based on their ability to model complex, nonlinear, interactive relationships amongst missing data correlates (for accessible introductions to CART and random forests, see Berk, 20009; James, Witten, Hastie, & Tibshirami, 2013; Strobl, Malley, & Tutz, 2009). Recently, two strategies have been proposed for using CART and random forests to address missing data. The first strategy uses CART to predict whom in a dataset is most likely to go missing, with the goal of creating inverse data weights (Hayes, Usami, Jacobucci, & McArdle, 2015; McArdle, 2013). The second strategy uses CART to predict people's scores on missing outcome variables, with the goal of generating multiple imputations (Doove, van Buuren, & Dusseldorp, 2014; Shah, Bartlett, Carpenter, Nicholas, & Hemingway, 2014; van Buuren, 2012). This chapter provides a brief overview of these two missing data methods and describes a simulation designed to assess whether CART-based weights and CART-based multiple imputations can provide relief in small sample studies with outcome–dependent (Missing Not at Random, or MNAR) missing data (Rubin, 1976). The next section provides brief conceptual overview of the aspects of these techniques most relevant to addressing missing data. I then describe how CART and random forests can be utilized to address missing data.

Introduction to CART and Random Forests

The goal of a CART analysis is to use the values of a set of observed predictors to split the dataset into homogeneous (or more *pure/less impure*) subgroups with respect to a single outcome variable, y (Breiman et al., 1984). A homogeneous group could either be a group in which the majority of group members share the same category membership on a categorical outcome, or a group in which the majority of members share similar scores on a continuous outcome, such that their scores are tightly clustered around the group's mean. The results of a CART analysis are visualized as a tree diagram, as displayed in Figure 10.1. Here, the subgroups created by CART are depicted as the *terminal nodes* at the bottom of the tree.

Two aspects of this picture are worth noting. First, because each successive split in the tree depends on the split that came before it, CART trees are fundamentally interactive and nonlinear. Thus, on the left-hand side of the diagram we see a moderated effect in which the prediction for age among people younger than 65 depends upon whether they fall above or below a cutoff on a depression measure. On the right-hand side of the diagram, we see a nonlinear effect, in which the prediction for age is not constant across levels of the variable, but differs by subgroup.

The second aspect to note about Figure 10.1 is that each terminal node receives a predicted value which can be applied to each person in the group. If y is continuous, the predicted value is simply the average value in the node – the group mean, $\bar{y}_{Node_j}$. If y is categorical, however, the predicted value could either be a predicted probability of being classified as a given class, simply defined as the proportion of people in the node who are members of that class, or it could be a predicted class membership that is defined by majority vote as the class with the most members in the node. Thus, if three-quarters of the members of Node 1 are

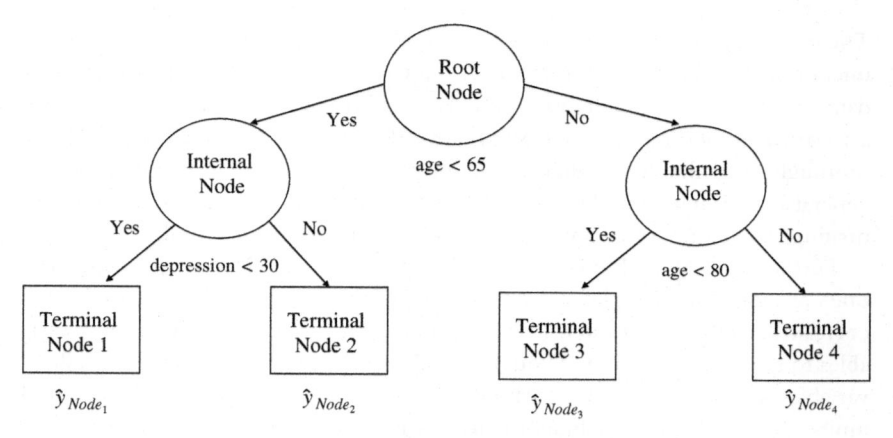

FIGURE 10.1 Hypothetical tree diagram from a CART analysis.

classified as $class_k$, the predicted probability of being $class_k$ is equal to .75 and the predicted class in the node is $class_k$.

Left unchecked, CART analyses tend to result in large, unstable trees with very small subgroups that tend to *overfit* the data (Hastie, Tibshirani, & Friedman, 2009). Two extensions of CART address this shortcoming and improve the method's predictive accuracy. *Cost-complexity pruning* uses cross-validation methods to identify a complexity parameter that imposes a penalty on larger trees. Thus, pruned CART results in smaller, more stable subtrees with better predictive accuracy in new samples.

A second extension of CART improves its predictive accuracy by using bootstrapping (Efron & Tibshirani, 1993). The earliest method, *bagging* (short for "bootstrap aggregation," Breiman (1996) boostraps the dataset many times, fits a large CART tree to each bootstrapped dataset, and averages across the results. For continuous outcomes, a case's predicted value is simply the mean of the predicted values given to that case across the bootstrapped samples. For categorical outcomes, a case's predicted probability of being classified as $class_k$ is simply the proportion of times the case was classified as $class_k$ across the bootstrap samples, whereas the case's predicted class is simply the class assigned in the majority of bootstrap trees.[1]

The *random forests* algorithm (Breiman, 2001) is similar to bagging in that it uses bootstrapping to estimate a "forest" of many trees. However, random forest analysis adds a twist: at each split, only a random subset of the predictors is used for consideration as splitting variables. In this way, over the course of many bootstrap samples, highly correlated predictors each get a chance to contribute to the prediction at each split. Thus, random forests not only bootstraps but also addresses potential collinearity among the predictors.

Using CART and Random Forests to Address Missing Data

The intuitive appeal of CART-based methods in handling missing data rests on the uncomfortable reality that, in practice, the true causal model predicting missing data is unknown. Although most researchers (at least ideally) hold well-developed, a priori hypotheses about their substantive data analysis models, few hold such thorough, well-developed theories about the causal mechanism responsible for generating missing data. Thus, in the absence of concrete, a priori predictions, turning to exploratory data mining methods carries intuitive appeal.

Furthermore, though it is useful to incorporate so-called *auxiliary variables* into one's analysis (for example, as predictors in an imputation model, or as saturated correlates, Graham & Schafer, 1999), it is unclear in advance which auxiliary variables to select for inclusion. Though including more, rather than fewer, auxiliary variables seems only to aid estimation (Collins, Schafer, & Kam, 2001), practical limits exist on the identifiability of analysis and imputation models (for example, as in regular OLS regression, regression-based imputation methods cannot include more predictors than cases in the analysis). CART-based methods obviate this difficulty by incorporating potentially large sets of (auxiliary) predictor variables into a single analysis, generating a single set of predicted values.

Finally, the literature on missing data has long-emphasized the importance of employing missing data models that are congenial to the true missing data generating model (Meng, 1994). Crucially, this means not only including all relevant variables in the missing data model, but all relevant interactions and nonlinear terms as well. Because CART-based methods automatically detect complex interactive and nonlinear relationships, these methods stand poised to capture complex relationships amongst sets of auxiliary variables that other techniques (such as using logistic regression to predict missing data indicator variables) might potentially miss.

Although missing data methods, such as the use of surrogate split variables, exist for handling missing data on predictor variables within a CART analysis (cf. Berk, 2009; see also the `rfImpute()` method employed in the `randomForest` R package; Liaw & Wiener, 2002), recent proposals have suggested two ways that CART and random forests might be employed to address missing data in a variety of other (non-CART) analysis models. The first method uses CART and random forests to predict a binary response (or return) indicator in which missing observations (e.g., dropouts from the study) are coded 0 and non-missing observations (e.g., people who returned to the study and provided responses) are coded 1. This analysis serves to split the data into groups of participants whose responses are either mostly missing (mostly 0s) or mostly non-missing (mostly 1s). The resulting predicted probabilities of returning to the study and providing data (i.e., of receiving a 1) can then be inverted to form data weights that serve to up-weight individuals in terminal nodes with a low probability of returning to the study and down-weight individuals in terminal nodes where they have a high probability of returning (Potthoff, Woodbury, & Manton, 1992; Stapleton, 2002). Weights are typically rescaled to sum to the relative sample size (see e.g., Kish, 1995; Potthoff et al., 1992). Weighted structural equation modeling analyses are then conducted using pseudo-maximum likelihood estimation, typically maximum likelihood with robust standard errors (MLR: for details, se Asparouhov, 2005; Hayes et al., 2015; McArdle, 2013).

The second method uses CART and random forests to predict the missing outcome variable, itself (rather than a response indicator), in order to group together participants who share similar scores and generate imputations for the missing cases (Doove et al., 2014; Shah et al., 2014). Although it would be easy to simply use the predicted value (e.g., majority class or node mean) from a CART analysis to serve as an imputed value, this would lead to inadequate variability, analogous to omitting the stochastic error term in standard regression imputation. To address variability more appropriately, instead of simply using the predicted value in a given node, the algorithm implemented in the `mice` package (van Buuren & Groothuis-Oudshoorn, 2011) in R chooses imputed values by randomly sampling from the non-missing observations falling in the same terminal node as a given missing case (for more concrete details of the algorithms use for CART and random forest imputations, see Doove et al. 2014; van Buuren, 2012). Random forest imputation extends this procedure by randomly sampling from the set of all non-missing observations that fall in the same terminal node as a given missing data point in any of the bootstrap trees (Doove et al., 2014; Shah et al., 2014; van Buuren, 2012). After the imputation phase is complete, the analysis and pooling phases follow standard procedures (Enders, 2010; Little & Rubin, 1987; van Buuren, 2012).

Thus far, little research has investigated the performance of these CART-based missing data methods. Initial simulations suggest that CART-based weighting methods exhibit strong performance in identifying true selection model variables and in reducing parameter bias, even in small sample datasets (Hayes & McArdle, 2017). Additionally, two sets of simulations demonstrated that, in terms of bias, efficiency, confidence interval width, and coverage, CART-based multiple imputation methods outperformed traditional multiple imputation when estimating interaction terms and performed nearly as well in estimating main effects in regression and survival models (Doove et al., 2014; Shah et al., 2014). However, these studies only simulated large sample datasets ($N = 1,000$ and $N = 2,000$). Thus, the performance of CART-based multiple imputation in small sample settings remains unknown.

The Present Research

In the present research, I used statistical simulation methods to assess the performance of CART-based weighting methods and CART-based multiple imputation methods in small sample, randomized clinical trial settings. Randomized clinical trials provide an interesting context for studying the missing data methods described in this chapter for at least two reasons. First, researchers conducting clinical trials often face practical constraints on the number of individuals available to participate in their studies. This is because clinical trials often target participants from specialized populations, such as those with specific mental health diagnoses, who may be difficult to recruit in large numbers.

Second, clinical trials face a very real threat of attrition based on individuals' scores on the outcome under study. For example, it is possible that the most depressed individuals – those whose values on the dependent variable fail to improve or worsen over time – might plausibly become discouraged by their lack of improvement in the trial and ultimately drop out of the study. Alternatively, it is possible that those individuals who improve the most as a result of treatment might feel so much better that they fail to return to the trial because they feel that they no longer need help. In either case, the distribution of scores on the dependent variable will be fundamentally altered (truncated at either the top or the bottom, in a pattern that will be differential by treatment group, with the most depressed patients likely being control patients and the most improved patients presumably being treatment group patients).[2]

Such Missing Not at Random (MNAR; Rubin, 1976) mechanisms are amongst the most deleterious and difficult-to-address forms of missing data (Enders, 2010; Yang & Maxwell, 2014). To my knowledge, no prior research has assessed the performance of CART-based weighting and CART-based under MNAR missing data. It is well-established that auxiliary variables can help provide at least some relief under MNAR, so long as these variables are highly correlated with y (see Collins et al. 2001, study 3). Building on this logic, I suspected that these tree-based, greedy algorithms might be particularly well-suited for identifying patterns in the data that might relate to the MNAR mechanism and ultimately provide relief from parameter bias.

For these reasons, the present research investigates the performance of CART and random forest methods for dealing with missing data under small sample-sizes and a variety of MNAR missing data mechanisms. In the simulation presented below, I employ a growth model designed to mirror a randomized longitudinal clinical trial and included auxiliary variables that were either moderately correlated or highly correlated with y at the time of dropout. I conducted the simulation using R statistical software (R Core Team, 2013).

Method

Data Generation Model

For each cell of the simulation, I generated 200 datasets based on the template model displayed in Figure 10.2. Here, *Group* indicates a dummy-coded

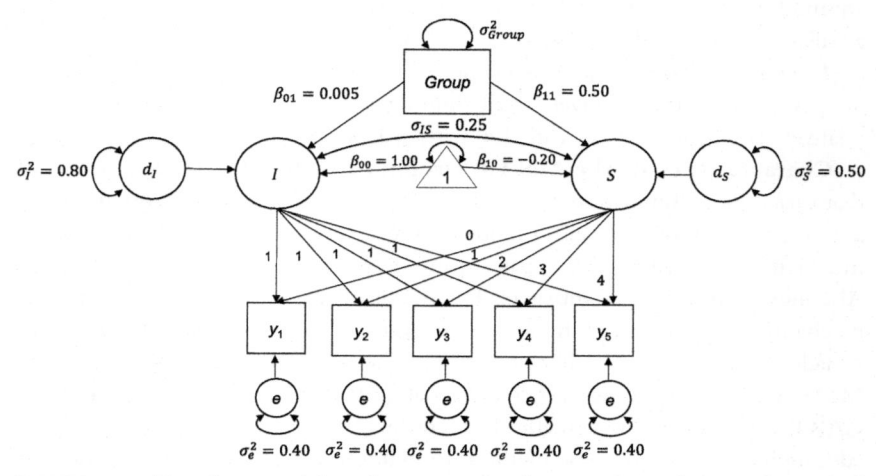

FIGURE 10.2 Template model and parameter values used in the simulation (all unlabeled paths are equal to 1).

experimental grouping variable where $0 =$ "control" and $1 =$ "treatment" in our fictional clinical trial. Three features of this template model deserve brief mention. First, the influence of *Group* on individuals' starting levels (random intercepts, I) is set to 0.005 in the model. This is to indicate an influence that is near zero, in line with our assumption that treatment group should have zero influence at baseline before the treatment is administered. Second, the mean intercept, β_{00}, is set equal to 1.00.[3] I chose a starting level of 1 rather than a standardized starting level of 0, in order to avoid division by zero and facilitate calculations of standardized parameter bias, as described below.

Finally, the mean slope value is set to $\beta_{10} = -0.20$, indicating a negative trajectory over time amongst control group participants (coded 0 on the dummy coded *Group*). For experimental group participants coded 1 on *Group*, however, their expected simple slopes were $\beta_{10} + \beta_{11} Group = -0.20 + 0.50 \times 1 = 0.30$. Thus, whereas average control group members in this model follow a decreasing linear expected trajectory in which their scores on y decrease from a starting level of 1 by 0.20 between each consecutive time point, average treatment group members in the model follow a positive linear expected trajectory in which their scores on y increase from the starting level of 1 by 0.30 between each consecutive time point. In addition to the model variables pictured in Figure 10.2, I also simulated three auxiliary variables, arbitrarily labeled x, v, and w, that were set to either highly correlate with y at time 1 or highly correlate with y at time 2, as described below.

Factors Manipulated in the Simulation

I varied four main factors in the simulation: sample size, type of MNAR mechanism, functional form of MNAR mechanism, and correlation between the auxiliary variables and y. I discuss each of these factors in turn.

1. Sample size. I simulated two sample sizes: $N = \{60, 200\}$. This was designed to approximate either relatively small clinical trials with 30 participants per cell or relatively large clinical trials with 100 participants per cell.

Characteristics of the MNAR Dropout Mechanism. The main factors that varied in the simulation concerned the nature of the MNAR dropout mechanism. Across simulation cells, I modeled a relatively simple dropout mechanism, in which approximately 30% of participants dropped out at the second time point. Although critical and attentive readers might correctly note that this dropout mechanism is quite simplistic and unlikely to occur in real longitudinal data, I made this choice for a deliberate reason. The weighting methods proposed by McArdle (2013) and assessed by Hayes et al. (2015) are aimed at using univariate CART and random forests methods to create a single set of inverse data weights. Although extensions of these methods to multivariate missing data situations can be readily imagined (e.g. by employing multivariate CART or survival CART and extensions of these techniques, such as those proposed by Brodley & Utgoff,

1995; De'ath, 2002; Larsen & Speckman, 2004), as an initial step in assessing the performance of these weighting techniques, I felt it was important to assess these methods under straightforward, well-controlled conditions, in order to obtain a useful benchmark for their performance under ideal conditions.[4] Although the time point of univariate dropout was held constant at time 2 throughout all simulation cells, I experimentally varied both the type of MNAR mechanism and the functional form of the MNAR mechanism used to induce attrition. All dropout mechanisms described below led to approximately a 30% dropout rate.

2. Type of MNAR mechanism. Following Yang and Maxwell (2014), I induced missing data using either *outcome-dependent MNAR*, in which dropout depended upon individuals' scores on y at the time of dropout (time 2 in the present simulation) or *slope-dependent MNAR*, in which dropout dependent upon individuals' scores on the latent slope factor.

3. Functional form of MNAR mechanism. For both types of MNAR attrition, I induced dropout using one of two tree diagrams. Specifically, I simulated dropout according to either a tree with a single split at the 50th percentile of the simulated variable, depicted in Figure 10.3 panel (a), or a tree with two splits, at the 25th and 75th percentiles, as depicted in Figure 10.3 panel (b). Conceptually, the one-split tree represents a situation in which the majority of participants with the lowest scores or the lowest random slopes on the outcome variable dropped out of the study (e.g., the most depressed individuals do not come back). The two-split tree represents a situation in which both the highest and lowest participants on y (or the random slope of y) dropped out of the study.

Within any simulation cell, I first used these tree-based models in concert with the `rbinom()` function in R to simulate a return indicator in which participants coded 0 dropped out of the study and participants coded 1 returned to the study. I then induced missing values for scores on all y variables occurring at *time* ≥ 2 for simulated participants who received a 0 on the return indicator.

4. Correlation between each auxiliary variable and y. Beyond small sample sizes and MNAR missing data, randomized longitudinal clinical trials present an additional challenge. The types of auxiliary variables typically used to help address missing data (cf. Collins et al., 2001), are often baseline measures assessed at the first time point (e.g., demographic measures, scores on psychological inventories taken at time 1, etc.). If all time 1 measures are baseline assessments – that is, assessments taken before the treatment is administered or before the treatment is thought to take effect – then any correlation between the time 1 outcome variables and other baseline auxiliary variables will necessarily become increasingly different over time as the experimental treatment begins to take effect.

Thus, the final factor that I varied in the simulations was the correlation between each auxiliary variable and y. I simulated two scenarios. In the first scenario, each auxiliary variable had a .80 correlation with y at baseline. Because of the treatment effect modeled in the study, however, the correlation between each auxiliary variable and y by time 2 was only approximately $r = 0.51$ and this

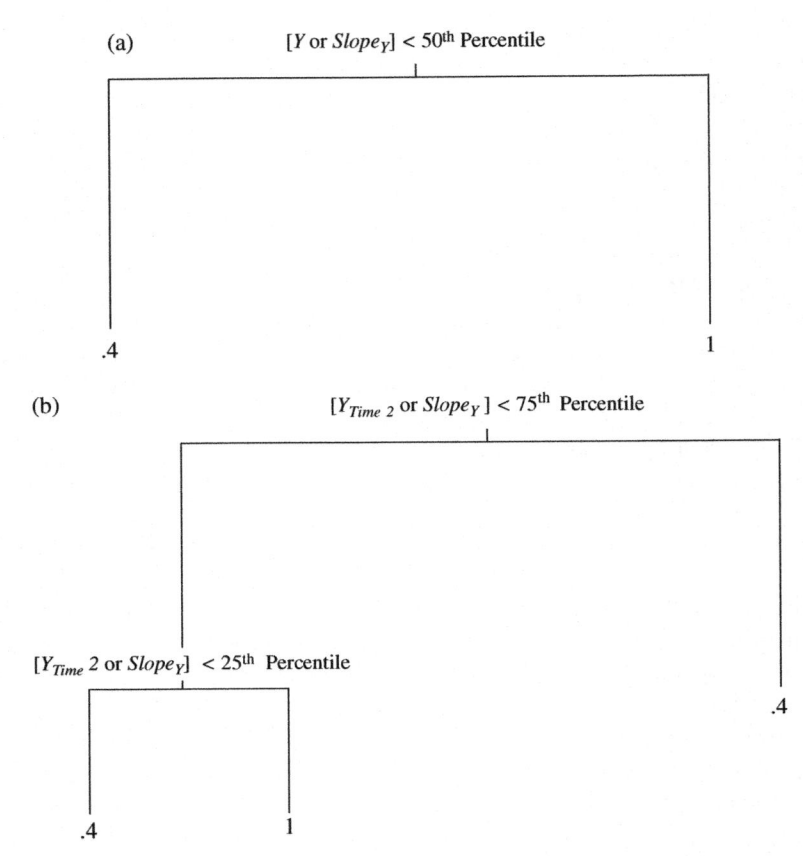

FIGURE 10.3 Tree structures used to induce dropout in the simulation study. (a) depicts the one-split condition, while (b) depicts the two-split condition. Predicted probabilities for terminal nodes represent participants' probability of returning to the study.

correlation decreased over time, ultimately reaching approximately $r = 0.41$ by the end of the study. This scenario models the realistic condition in which baseline measurements are correlated with auxiliary variables in a manner that may not persist across the experimental trial.

In the second scenario, each auxiliary variable had a .80 correlation with y at time 2. Under these conditions, this artificially induced-correlation remained high (between 0.72 and 0.74) throughout the remaining time points. However, due to the nature of the model expectations, in this scenario, each auxiliary variable was only correlated with y at baseline at approximately $r = 0.57$. This scenario models a situation closer to the ideal situation of highly correlated auxiliary and outcome variables assessed in prior research (Collins et al., 2001). The average observed correlations amongst the auxiliary variables and y variables in the simulation are displayed in Table 10.1.

TABLE 10.1 Average correlations between covariates and y variables in the simulation.

	x	w	v	y_1	y_2	y_3	y_4	y_5
$r_{xy2} \approx .5$								
x	1.00	0.65	0.65	0.81	0.51	0.45	0.41	0.38
v	0.65	1.00	0.65	0.81	0.51	0.45	0.41	0.38
w	0.65	0.65	1.00	0.81	0.51	0.45	0.41	0.38
$r_{xy2} \approx .8$								
x	1.00	0.78	0.78	0.56	0.88	0.74	0.73	0.72
v	0.78	1.00	0.78	0.56	0.88	0.74	0.73	0.72
w	0.78	0.78	1.00	0.56	0.88	0.74	0.73	0.72

Note: results are averaged across sample sizes.

Overall simulation design. Varying these four factors, the overall simulation design was a 2 ($N = 60$ vs. 200) $\times$ 2 (MNAR mechanism = y-dependent vs. slope-dependent) $\times$ 2 (functional form of MNAR mechanism = 1 split tree vs. 2 split tree) $\times$ 2 (correlation of auxiliary variables with y at time 2 = .5 vs .8) design. This led to 16 unique simulation cells and $2 \times 2 \times 2 \times 2 \times 200 = 1,600$ simulated datasets.

Analyses Conducted on Each Simulated Dataset

I analyzed each simulated dataset using 11 different analyses of interest. All analyses specified the correct linear growth model structure, as depicted in Figures 10.2 and 10.3 (that is, the simulation only assessed accuracy and error that resulted from the missing data techniques being evaluated and did not introduce additional error that would result from model misspecification). I conducted all SEM analyses of our template model using the lavaan package in R (Rosseel, 2012). The 11 analyses conducted in the simulation can be grouped into 3 categories: baseline comparison analyses, inverse weighting analyses, and multiple imputation analyses.

Baseline comparison analyses. Three analyses provided initial baseline measures of performance. First, I analyzed each simulated dataset prior to injecting missing data, thus providing a measure of how far the simulated data fell from the true population parameters simply due to the small sample sizes used in the simulation. Next, I analyzed each dataset with missing data using listwise deletion in order to provide a baseline measure of how harmful each MNAR mechanism was to the parameter estimates when participants who dropped out of the study were simply ignored and thrown out of the analysis. Finally, I also analyzed each dataset using standard Full Information Maximum Likelihood (FIML, with the missing = "fiml" argument in lavaan), providing a baseline measure of performance for this default, commonly used missing data method. It should be noted that this basic FIML condition did not include the auxiliary covariates (x, v, and

w), since the purpose of the condition was to mirror what I suspected many applied researchers would actually do in practice.

Inverse weighting analyses. After conducting the baseline analyses mentioned above, I conducted a number of weighted analyses. I first transformed all weights into relative weights before conducting weighted analyses using the package `lavaan.survey` (Oberski, 2014) in R with the estimator in the `sem()` function in `lavaan` set to MLR (maximum likelihood with robust standard errors, as recommended by Asparouhov, 2005; and as specified in Hayes et al. 2015).

Before testing the performance of logistic regression and tree-based approaches for forming inverse weights, I sought a general measure of the performance of inverse probability weights under ideal conditions. Toward this aim, in each simulation cell I formed an initial set of inverse weights from the true population probabilities used to generate attrition in the simulated data (as depicted in panels a and b of Figure 10.3) and analyzed each dataset using these true population weights. Although these true population probabilities of attrition would never actually be known to analysts, the initial analyses of the datasets using these population weights provide a useful benchmark for the performance of weighting methods, in general. Thus, in all tables of results presented below, the true weighted analyses conceptually represent the best possible performance of weighting methods, if all population probabilities of dropout were perfectly estimated.

Following this initial weighted analysis, I formed weights using the predicted probabilities generated by (a) logistic regression, (b) CART analysis, (c) pruned CART, and (d) random forests. All analyses predicted a missing data indicator coded 0 = dropout, 1 = return and included all covariates (x, v, and w) as well as y at time 1 (in this way, all analyses predicted dropout at time 2 using all complete variables that occurred prior to time 2). The logistic regression analysis modeled main effects only, which I believed would be the most common approach to logistic regression taken by applied researchers with no a priori hypotheses concerning interactions among the four variables. Random forest analyses used the R package `randomForest` (Liaw & Wiener, 2002). CART and pruned CART analyses used the package `rpart` (Themeau, Atkinson, & Ripley, 2014) with the same settings described in Hayes et al. (2015).

Multiple imputation analyses. I tested three multiple imputation analyses in the simulation using the `mice` package in R (van Buuren & Groothuis-Oudshoom, 2011) using all variables, including the model variables as well as the covariates x, w, and v in the imputation models. First, I used standard Bayesian regression imputation by using the `method = ''norm''` argument in the `mice()` function[5]. Additionally, I assessed the performance of single-tree CART and random forest multiple imputation methods using the `method = ''cart''` and `method = ''rf''` arguments. In all cases, I set the number of imputations equal to 20, rather than the default 5, in order to give the imputation methods the best chance to perform well in the simulation. I also set the argument `maxiter` equal to 20. Otherwise, I used default settings for all `mice` methods. Since, by default, `mice` does not include analysis and pooling functions for SEM analyses, the simulation included custom code to fit the SEM growth model on each imputed dataset using `lavaan` and pool the estimates and standard errors using Rubin's rules (Little & Rubin, 1987; Rubin, 1976, 1987).

Outcomes Measured in the Simulation

I assessed each missing data method in terms of its bias and efficiency in returning accurate growth model parameter estimates. Following previous work (Enders & Bandalos, 2001; Hayes et al., 2015), I assessed percent bias for each estimate by computing

$$\%Bias = \left[\frac{\hat{\theta} - \theta}{\theta} \right] * 100 \tag{10.1}$$

where $\hat{\theta}$ is the value of the parameter estimate returned by a given analysis of a given simulated dataset and θ is the true population parameter. I note that values greater than 15% are considered problematic (Muthén, Kaplan, & Hollis, 1987). I calculated efficiency as the empirical standard deviation of each growth model parameter estimate across the 200 simulated trials in each cell.

Results

In the next sections, I present the results of each measure (bias, efficiency) in turn. I start with percent bias. Note that, across tables of results, I omit parameter β_{01} from Figure 10.2, since this parameter was functionally set to be zero in the simulation.

Percent Bias

The primary results of the simulation concern the average percent bias observed in the parameter estimates of the growth model from Figures 10.1 and 10.3. These results are displayed in Tables 10.2 to 10.5 for the $N = 60, cor_{xy_2} \approx .5$, $N = 60, cor_{xy_2} \approx .8$, $N = 200, cor_{xy_2} \approx .5$, and $N = 200, cor_{xy_2} \approx .8$ conditions, respectively[6]. Several trends in these tables are worth mentioning. First, examining the columns corresponding to listwise deletion, it is clear that the MNAR mechanisms used in the simulation cells were quite harmful, as indicated by levels of bias that were often far above 15%. The harmful effects of the missing data mechanisms are confirmed by examination of the FIML columns, where it is easy to see that, in the absence of further information, standard FIML estimation was unable to remedy the sometimes-dramatic levels of bias induced by the MNAR dropout (see, for example, the cells corresponding to the fixed slope β_{10}

TABLE 10.2 Percent bias for missing data methods under $N = 60$, $r_{xy_2} \approx .5$ conditions.

	Complete	Listwise	FIML	Inverse weighting methods					Multiple imputation methods		
				True	Log	CART	Prune	RF	Norm	CART	RF
β_{00}											
1 split γ	0.17	28.07	4.95	0.68	4.76	10.64	11.52	0.68	8.43	11.67	9.52
2 splits γ	1.39	7.51	2.52	4.72	7.13	8.07	7.97	8.16	3.52	2.79	2.87
1 split S	−1.05	10.00	−0.07	−1.08	0.66	1.82	1.81	−3.91	0.76	2.07	1.52
2 splits S	−0.81	0.71	−0.65	0.85	0.72	1.49	1.42	0.19	−0.28	−0.55	−0.28
β_{10}											
1 split γ	−2.64	−88.90	−75.30	−8.88	−72.83	−75.54	−77.32	−65.17	−94.07	−158.36	−115.82
2 splits γ	3.56	−9.38	−9.06	2.28	−9.73	−7.76	−8.78	−6.42	−15.62	−43.38	−37.10
1 split S	3.40	−114.42	−108.56	1.62	−109.20	−106.65	−106.23	−104.14	−121.07	−161.13	−142.26
2 splits S	1.97	4.93	5.97	5.99	5.28	5.87	6.92	8.67	1.42	−31.70	−23.71
β_{11}											
1 split γ	1.60	−3.57	−3.62	−1.64	−1.79	−4.16	−4.17	−3.68	−10.12	−33.04	−26.35
2 splits γ	−3.68	−13.90	−13.56	−5.34	−14.22	−12.28	−13.00	−12.45	−18.03	−39.54	−35.08
1 split S	−0.01	2.61	1.93	4.37	3.29	4.79	5.09	4.56	−4.16	−28.05	−22.00
2 splits S	0.84	1.36	1.69	2.82	1.94	4.45	4.58	4.72	−0.79	−28.85	−21.60
σ_I^2											
1 split γ	−3.79	−13.92	−4.52	−8.02	−4.06	−8.28	−8.34	−7.23	−11.83	−31.49	−37.29
2 splits γ	−0.92	−31.88	−10.30	−7.10	−31.82	−24.71	−25.85	−13.78	−19.79	−36.92	−43.32
1 split S	−3.82	−8.32	−4.43	−9.41	−5.46	−8.32	−7.99	0.20	−9.26	−27.80	−32.63
2 splits S	−3.22	−13.62	−5.76	−11.67	−12.60	−10.55	−10.36	−1.58	−10.22	−27.45	−30.57
σ_S^2											
1 split γ	−3.22	−9.52	−9.12	−6.73	−10.65	−10.34	−10.11	−10.65	4.41	−0.38	−18.83
2 splits γ	−4.78	−22.39	−21.84	−10.38	−23.17	−23.13	−23.41	−23.00	−8.83	−15.84	−30.62

1 split S	−3.46	−16.84	−16.72	−6.92	−17.00	−17.04	−17.10	−16.03	−4.22	−8.04	−24.67
2 splits S	−3.73	−41.56	−41.38	−11.64	−42.71	−42.87	−42.40	−43.93	−31.36	−32.71	−47.86
σ_{IS}											
1 split γ	−1.75	−18.22	−14.69	−1.75	−10.17	−11.14	−11.69	−7.02	−18.67	−42.94	−10.67
2 splits γ	−2.17	−58.37	−57.67	−9.35	−58.57	−57.35	−57.54	−51.34	−58.18	−81.69	−58.05
1 split S	−2.45	−12.74	−11.54	−3.10	−12.75	−13.83	−13.24	−7.40	−14.19	−33.43	−8.96
2 splits S	2.11	−39.07	−36.94	−8.54	−40.11	−38.03	−37.68	−35.38	−36.04	−57.33	−36.76
σ_e^2											
1 split γ	−0.53	−0.54	−0.42	−0.84	1.26	0.75	0.75	2.27	20.68	57.85	105.49
2 splits γ	−0.32	−1.82	−0.90	−0.32	−2.75	−2.12	−1.98	−0.79	19.58	47.16	88.66
1 split S	0.22	1.11	1.13	0.11	0.11	0.95	0.95	1.14	21.03	57.59	99.22
2 splits S	−0.21	−0.12	0.12	−1.48	−0.56	−0.17	−0.13	1.56	21.08	48.93	79.34

Note: norm = Bayesian regression imputation in mice. γ indicates the dependent variable. S indicates latent slope.

TABLE 10.3 Percent bias for missing data methods under $N = 60$, $r_{xy2} \approx .8$ conditions.

	Complete	Listwise	FIML	Inverse weighting methods					Multiple imputation methods		
				True	Log	CART	Prune	RF	Norm	CART	RF
β_{00}											
1 split γ	−0.18	30.55	4.43	3.53	−13.05	6.22	6.57	−8.95	0.65	−0.23	3.78
2 splits γ	1.55	4.92	2.05	0.16	5.82	1.86	2.17	−3.19	1.61	0.12	1.26
1 split S	2.00	14.88	3.45	3.15	−3.19	−2.13	−1.57	−9.78	−1.90	−3.29	−0.16
2 splits S	0.67	−0.52	0.66	−0.07	−0.39	0.40	0.41	−2.11	0.74	−0.31	−0.02
β_{10}											
1 split γ	0.20	−82.75	−65.23	−1.16	37.34	−17.36	−18.00	24.10	−20.33	−145.22	−57.58
2 splits γ	−4.42	−12.91	−12.28	5.39	−15.49	−3.70	−5.15	15.09	−4.42	−43.41	−27.21
1 split S	1.22	−117.01	−109.79	−3.38	−53.91	−73.29	−73.61	−47.45	−67.45	−161.53	−101.18
2 splits S	5.19	10.51	9.73	16.89	10.26	9.30	9.26	9.85	5.21	−25.36	−18.01
β_{11}											
1 split γ	1.39	−0.10	1.11	4.81	18.14	4.72	4.14	1.99	−1.95	−30.16	−19.36
2 splits γ	−1.25	−11.03	−10.62	2.21	−12.78	−2.61	−4.42	9.05	−3.44	−37.47	−23.31
1 split S	1.02	4.41	4.91	4.47	5.83	4.45	5.23	5.82	3.58	−26.18	−16.62
2 splits S	1.47	3.80	3.34	7.67	4.50	5.09	4.60	5.41	1.63	−26.36	−17.83
σ_I^2											
1 split γ	1.38	−13.28	0.17	−5.34	8.54	−3.06	−3.48	−8.05	−3.33	−17.42	−32.28
2 splits γ	−5.55	−36.12	−15.08	−12.28	−36.46	−18.91	−22.82	−5.02	−12.76	−26.67	−43.45
1 split S	−3.32	−5.77	−3.07	−6.28	−0.89	−3.35	−3.07	−1.75	−4.70	−17.76	−30.50
2 splits S	−4.20	−10.50	−5.72	−8.76	−9.68	−2.05	−3.32	8.88	−3.83	−16.61	−25.80
σ_S^2											
1 split γ	−4.31	−10.86	−10.16	−7.51	−4.13	−7.07	−7.33	−11.50	1.65	2.54	−17.30
2 splits γ	−1.98	−18.50	−17.91	−5.88	−18.61	−9.05	−10.93	−4.85	1.96	−9.32	−24.66

1 split S	−4.16	−17.37	−17.34	−6.88	−7.55	−10.82	−11.27	−10.75	−6.91	−5.20	−22.41
2 splits S	−3.58	−40.09	−39.99	−10.08	−40.70	−38.36	−38.49	−34.61	−28.9	−29.04	−43.84
σ_{IS}											
1 split γ	0.73	−18.76	−13.21	−2.02	26.75	3.00	2.03	3.60	−6.11	−65.54	−1.29
2 splits γ	−0.47	−56.58	−54.50	−8.26	−55.47	−21.25	−28.96	6.20	−18.70	−94.82	−29.84
1 split S	−4.36	−16.75	−16.35	−6.53	1.53	−6.64	−5.89	−3.23	−12.03	−60.73	−5.55
2 splits S	−2.74	−39.31	−38.20	−9.93	−38.59	−28.93	−29.47	−14.36	−24.41	−71.39	−25.88
σ_e^2											
1 split γ	−1.50	−1.95	−1.74	−1.91	−1.56	−1.59	−1.86	−3.12	15.77	71.41	102.03
2 splits γ	0.81	−1.26	−0.28	−0.52	−1.72	−1.05	−1.32	0.53	19.19	56.99	89.92
1 split S	0.65	0.42	0.41	−1.24	1.53	0.95	1.21	2.01	19.57	68.07	93.59
2 splits S	−1.71	−1.26	−1.12	−2.12	−1.94	−1.27	−1.10	−0.73	18.22	55.82	71.39

Note: norm = Bayesian regression imputation in mice. γ indicates the dependent variable. S indicates latent slope.

TABLE 10.4 Percent bias for missing data methods under $N = 200$, $r_{xy_2} \approx .5$ conditions.

	Complete	Listwise	FIML	Inverse weighting methods					Multiple imputation methods		
				True	Log	CART	Prune	RF	Norm	CART	RF
β_{00}											
1 split γ	−0.40	28.83	4.49	0.17	1.75	8.80	9.80	0.43	7.76	9.21	8.46
2 splits γ	−0.70	4.76	0.45	0.18	4.59	3.71	4.57	1.43	1.22	0.81	0.82
1 split S	0.03	12.79	1.25	0.91	1.96	3.53	3.67	−0.91	2.15	2.87	2.42
2 splits S	0.62	1.15	0.79	1.41	1.28	1.35	1.36	1.24	1.01	0.79	0.72
β_{10}											
1 split γ	−4.69	−90.76	−74.67	−4.80	−68.90	−74.38	−74.65	−67.9	−92.02	−139.20	−108.97
2 splits γ	3.10	−10.82	−9.94	3.22	−10.75	−8.59	−9.36	−8.51	−15.26	−40.61	−32.65
1 split S	−2.66	−125.61	−117.98	−7.12	−118.75	−118.9	−118.8	−116.41	−128.92	−162.61	−146.30
2 splits S	3.80	2.72	2.83	3.52	2.41	4.21	3.18	4.03	−0.62	−29.98	−20.56
β_{11}											
1 split γ	−1.73	−4.99	−4.06	−0.44	−2.28	−2.94	−2.65	−3.03	−9.96	−31.21	−25.20
2 splits γ	0.31	−11.66	−11.04	−0.44	−11.62	−10.18	−10.37	−10.25	−15.2	−35.95	−29.30
1 split S	−1.81	−1.79	−1.52	−1.99	−1.82	−1.38	−1.48	−1.51	−6.95	−28.55	−22.28
2 splits S	2.54	1.91	1.98	2.79	1.66	2.52	2.25	2.20	−1.20	−25.24	−17.23
σ_I^2											
1 split γ	−1.46	−11.22	−2.34	−1.47	7.77	−3.37	−2.30	2.08	−8.41	−16.26	−23.42
2 splits γ	0.11	−30.47	−10.12	−2.65	−30.20	−15.69	−19.66	−5.82	−16.63	−26.40	−33.10
1 split S	−0.68	−2.23	−0.49	−0.86	1.21	−1.46	−0.11	3.68	−2.97	−10.67	−17.19
2 splits S	−2.30	−8.07	−3.18	−2.77	−7.89	−5.29	−5.03	0.84	−5.12	−12.64	−18.62
σ_S^2											
1 split γ	−0.59	−6.98	−6.68	−2.14	−4.12	−5.12	−5.25	−5.03	−4.37	3.36	−12.74
2 splits γ	−0.95	−18.90	−18.75	−3.89	−19.11	−18.72	−18.54	−17.86	−15.95	−10.70	−25.25

1 split S	−0.38	−13.55	−13.48	−2.58	−12.71	−13.06	−12.66	−12.34	−10.88	−3.98	−19.65
2 splits S	−0.69	−36.58	−36.50	−0.88	−36.58	−36.81	−36.62	−36.18	−34.34	−28.27	−41.39
σ_{IS}											
1 split y	0.13	−17.78	−13.92	−0.25	−2.21	−9.84	−9.94	−6.07	−22.82	−35.24	−10.00
2 splits y	1.26	−56.28	−53.57	−2.49	−56.20	−51.57	−51.98	−47.33	−58.68	−72.99	−54.32
1 split S	−0.33	−13.32	−12.54	−1.96	−11.75	−12.82	−11.55	−10.74	−19.04	−29.37	−11.94
2 splits S	0.61	−35.65	−34.17	−0.84	−35.61	−33.60	−33.97	−32.40	−37.14	−45.00	−33.94
σ_e^2											
1 split y	−0.27	−0.27	−0.19	−0.99	1.16	0.52	0.44	1.18	5.83	20.24	63.52
2 splits y	0.09	−1.62	−0.72	−0.42	−1.87	−0.73	−1.02	0.72	4.52	17.36	55.36
1 split S	0.41	0.24	0.23	−0.15	0.20	−0.21	−0.08	0.42	5.17	16.40	56.23
2 splits S	−0.42	−0.62	−0.44	−1.07	−0.85	−0.15	−0.19	−0.30	4.17	15.65	47.94

Note: norm = Bayesian regression imputation in mice. y indicates the dependent variable. S indicates latent slope.

TABLE 10.5 Percent bias for missing data methods under $N = 200$, $r_{xy_2} \approx .8$ conditions.

	Complete	Listwise	FIML	Inverse weighting methods					Multiple imputation methods		
				True	Log	CART	Prune	RF	Norm	CART	RF
β_{00}											
1 split γ	−0.98	28.24	3.91	−0.66	−27.38	2.41	3.31	−9.71	−0.23	−2.79	0.93
2 splits γ	−0.05	5.13	0.77	0.28	5.16	0.86	1.00	−3.23	−0.04	−1.52	−0.52
1 split S	−0.90	10.94	0.10	−0.75	−7.26	−3.99	−3.43	−12.30	−4.70	−6.60	−4.21
2 splits S	−0.80	−1.38	−1.05	−1.72	−0.80	−3.27	−3.15	−4.42	−1.07	−2.46	−2.03
β_{10}											
1 split γ	2.34	−83.34	−67.81	0.48	65.50	−10.45	−12.05	18.75	−13.91	−94.44	−37.67
2 splits γ	2.46	−16.65	−16.09	−4.02	−15.67	−6.64	−6.20	4.80	−4.70	−35.33	−24.52
1 split S	0.79	−120.09	−112.48	−0.28	−52.82	−67.11	−71.72	−47.03	−69.92	−128.66	−91.24
2 splits S	2.97	3.18	2.86	5.16	2.66	6.72	5.41	8.95	2.14	−24.92	−18.11
β_{11}											
1 split γ	0.84	−4.34	−3.47	−1.07	18.16	1.42	1.01	2.66	−0.78	−27.03	−15.81
2 splits γ	−1.47	−15.15	−14.55	−3.77	−15.15	−5.16	−6.49	1.91	−6.61	−32.09	−21.81
1 split S	−0.15	1.29	1.24	1.42	1.49	3.93	3.26	3.82	−1.25	−23.82	−15.73
2 splits S	2.96	2.52	2.57	3.55	2.73	6.73	6.10	8.85	2.48	−19.79	−13.96
σ_I^2											
1 split γ	−1.81	−12.02	−2.68	−2.46	35.89	1.87	1.11	−0.07	−3.35	−7.56	−20.28
2 splits γ	−1.33	−31.84	−11.85	−4.63	−31.84	−7.02	−12.86	7.65	−5.21	−10.43	−27.60
1 split S	−0.89	−3.30	−1.18	−1.97	5.23	0.50	1.44	4.12	−0.73	−5.86	−17.23
2 splits S	−1.92	−9.22	−2.93	−4.35	−8.91	3.32	−0.19	13.27	1.90	−4.89	−14.81
σ_S^2											
1 split γ	−1.83	−7.27	−7.01	−3.07	11.54	−0.55	−1.17	−1.21	−2.78	−0.19	−10.36
2 splits γ	−1.26	−16.65	−16.53	−1.12	−16.73	−5.60	−8.27	−0.18	−4.94	−9.62	−16.11

1 split S	0.15	−12.20	−12.08	−0.85	0.74	−5.24	−4.79	−3.01	−8.30	−3.29	−13.58
2 splits S	−1.69	−37.90	−37.83	−3.58	−37.72	−32.50	−33.67	−28.78	−32.24	−29.28	−38.27
σ_{IS}											
1 split γ	−1.41	−18.49	−14.81	−1.21	62.49	5.07	4.85	5.86	−6.39	−43.70	1.51
2 splits γ	−2.11	−58.63	−56.57	−4.83	−58.44	−14.33	−25.09	9.45	−18.26	−72.96	−20.55
1 split S	1.12	−11.62	−10.44	0.36	15.03	0.50	1.33	4.97	−4.50	−37.83	1.09
2 splits S	0.21	−37.00	−35.38	−2.50	−36.70	−19.55	−23.72	−7.83	−19.52	−48.30	−20.54
σ_e^2											
1 split γ	−0.59	−0.43	−0.33	−0.54	1.31	−0.49	−0.61	−0.8	3.56	26.77	56.59
2 splits γ	−0.05	−0.94	0.00	0.72	−1.06	0.02	−0.44	0.12	4.27	27.03	61.25
1 split S	−0.31	−0.44	−0.42	−0.98	0.79	0.28	0.13	0.73	4.68	23.13	52.33
2 splits S	0.00	−0.15	0.09	0.08	−0.25	0.48	0.22	0.96	5.46	23.13	46.56

Note: norm = Bayesian regression imputation in mice. γ indicates the dependent variable. S indicates latent slope.

under a 1 split S MNAR mechanism, which exhibits bias well over 100% in all simulation cells).

A second interesting, and somewhat surprising, initial observation was the strong performance of the true population probability weights in all cells of the simulation. Whereas the estimated probability weights from logistic regression, CART, pruned CART, and random forests still struggled in absolute terms in a variety of conditions, the true probability weights provided more consistent, accurate corrections to the parameter estimates than any other missing data method. This assuages concerns that might be raised about ceiling effects that could exist for the performance of weighting methods. At least under the conditions studied here, inverse weights seem to have the potential to perform extremely well when the selection probabilities are accurately modeled. Continuing to examine standard and baseline measures, it is instructive to look at the results for Bayesian regression imputation across cells of the simulation (labeled **norm** in the tables, corresponding to its label in the `mice` package). Consistent with expectations, standard Bayesian regression imputation performed admirably well in a variety of simulation cells, although MNAR still created substantial bias under a variety of conditions.

One of the most surprising results is that, across cells, the performance of both CART and random forest imputation methods was quite poor when compared with the other methods. Although random forest imputation appeared to fare a bit better than single tree CART imputation, in general, both of these methods performed substantially worse than standard Bayesian regression imputation and also performed worse than the various weighting methods assessed across the majority of simulation cells.

Comparing results of weighted analyses based on CART, pruned CART, and random forest methods, with few exceptions random forest analysis seemed to most consistently provide the largest reductions in bias across simulation cells, and this was especially evident in the cells with the most bias. For one strong example, see the coefficient β_1, "1 split, S" cells of Table 10.3 ($N = 60$, $r_{xy_2} \approx .8$). FIML estimates displayed an average bias of -109.79. Bayesian regression imputation improves upon this considerably, returning estimates with an average bias of -67.45. Finally, random forest weights produce the greatest improvement, clocking in with -47.45. This number is, admittedly, still extremely troubling in absolute terms, but represents over a 50% improvement upon FIML and a 10% improvement upon Bayesian regression imputation. Similar patterns are found in other problematic cells throughout the simulation.

Finally, how did random forest weights compare to weights generated from logistic regression? In general, random forest weights tended to perform either similarly to, or in some cases much better than, logistic regression weights in terms of bias, with the greatest improvements occurring when the correlations between the auxiliary variables and $y_2 - y_5$ were higher. For some examples, examine Table 10.5. Estimating the same fixed β_{10} coefficient in the 1 split y

condition, logistic regression weights were 65.50% biased on average compared to only 18.75% bias observed for random forest weights. Similarly, when estimating the fixed β_{11} coefficient in the 1 split γ and 2 split γ conditions, logistic regression analysis produced average bias of 18.16% and −15.15%, respectively, compared to only 2.66 and 1.91 for random forest weights.

Efficiency

Table 10.6 displays the results for efficiency of each estimate in the $N = 60$ and $N = 200$ conditions, respectively, collapsed over covariate correlations and MNAR mechanisms. Although the empirical standard deviations of each estimate were quite similar across most analyses, it is worth pointing out that, by their nature, the weighted analyses were a bit less efficient, in general, than full-information approaches such as FIML and MI. The most pronounced differences in efficiency were found in the $N = 60$ cells of the simulation. Although weighted estimates were still slightly less efficient in the $N = 200$, the differences overall were smaller in these larger samples size conditions.

Discussion

In this simulation, inverse data weights formed from decision tree analyses – particularly random forest analysis – were able to substantially alleviate bias in parameter estimates of the simulated growth curve model, although absolute levels of bias under the MNAR mechanisms remained problematic in many conditions. The fact that bias was not completely (or even close to completely) eradicated in this simulation is owed to the extreme MNAR missing data mechanism employed. MNAR, in general, presents formidable (if not intractable) challenges, and the particular implementation used here, involving total dropout at time 2 (the first post-treatment measurement), was particularly pernicious.

Of particular interest, analyses that used inverse weights formed using the true selection probabilities from the simulation performed strikingly well, even in the lowest sample size conditions used in the study ($N = 60$). Although throwing out data and only using available cases via listwise deletion, several harmed the growth curve parameter estimates, reweighting those same available cases using the true population probabilities of return to the study provided a surprising amount of relief. This suggests that if the population probabilities are modeled accurately, then inverse weighting could plausibly be a very effective method for dealing with missing data even under extremely deleterious selection mechanisms.

The best-performing methods in the simulation were random forest weights, closely followed by Bayesian regression imputation and logistic regression weights. In many conditions, the levels of bias produced by these methods tracked quite closely, but when the auxiliary variables were more highly correlated with the outcome variables (y_2-y_5), random forest weights tended to provide greater relief

TABLE 10.6 Efficiency for missing data methods.

	Complete	Listwise	FIML	Inverse weighting methods					Multiple imputation methods		
				True	Log	CART	Prune	RF	Norm	CART	RF
$N = 60$											
β_{00}	0.19	0.25	0.19	0.26	0.27	0.26	0.25	0.32	0.20	0.20	0.19
β_{10}	0.14	0.19	0.18	0.19	0.20	0.20	0.19	0.22	0.18	0.20	0.17
β_{11}	0.19	0.21	0.21	0.27	0.26	0.25	0.25	0.29	0.21	0.16	0.17
σ_I^2	0.19	0.23	0.20	0.26	0.28	0.26	0.26	0.29	0.21	0.20	0.20
σ_S^2	0.10	0.12	0.12	0.13	0.14	0.14	0.14	0.15	0.13	0.13	0.11
σ_{IS}	0.10	0.11	0.12	0.13	0.14	0.13	0.13	0.15	0.11	0.11	0.11
σ_e^2	0.04	0.05	0.05	0.05	0.06	0.06	0.06	0.07	0.06	0.13	0.14
$N = 200$											
β_{00}	0.11	0.17	0.11	0.15	0.20	0.14	0.14	0.17	0.11	0.12	0.11
β_{10}	0.08	0.14	0.13	0.11	0.15	0.13	0.13	0.14	0.13	0.14	0.12
β_{11}	0.11	0.12	0.12	0.15	0.16	0.14	0.14	0.15	0.11	0.10	0.10
σ_I^2	0.10	0.14	0.11	0.14	0.24	0.15	0.15	0.17	0.12	0.12	0.12
σ_S^2	0.05	0.08	0.08	0.07	0.11	0.09	0.09	0.10	0.08	0.09	0.08
σ_{IS}	0.05	0.07	0.08	0.08	0.13	0.09	0.08	0.10	0.07	0.08	0.07
σ_e^2	0.02	0.03	0.03	0.03	0.03	0.03	0.03	0.03	0.03	0.05	0.06

Note: norm = Bayesian regression imputation in mice.

than the other methods. These improvements in bias did come at the cost of slightly lower efficiency than other methods, particularly in the case of random forest weights, however, although the level of inefficiency did not seem severe in the present study.

In addition to providing a broad evaluation of these missing data techniques under small sample sizes and MNAR attrition, this simulation provided an important insight into the nature of covariate-outcome correlations at baseline in randomized longitudinal clinical trials. As shown in Table 10.1, when the simulated covariates were highly correlated with y at baseline, these correlations quickly dissipated over subsequent measurement occasions as the experimental treatment took effect, leading the treatment and control groups to diverge. Under these conditions, none of the missing data methods performed optimally. It was only when the covariates were artificially simulated to be highly correlated with y at the time of dropout that the missing data techniques provided the greatest relief.

One surprising result of the simulation was the poor performance of CART and random forest imputation under the conditions studied, compared to the other methods under study. Although traditional Bayesian regression imputation performed relatively well, even under the low sample size conditions modeled here, the CART and random forest imputation methods produced the most bias out of all of the methods assessed. This seems to suggest that it is not imputation, per se, that suffers under low sample sizes, but these particular extensions of multiple imputation.

It is unclear why these methods failed to perform well in the simulation, relatively speaking, but one potential explanation is that at very low sample sizes there may not be adequate variability amongst complete cases falling in terminal nodes of CART trees fit to the data. Because CART and random forest trees generate imputed values by randomly sampling the observed values from the complete cases falling in each terminal node, if the number of such complete cases is trivially small (e.g., only a few observations), this might not provide enough variability to generate realistic imputed values. The results of the weighted analyses provide a potential counterargument to this theory, however. These methods simply reweighted the complete cases in the data and returned substantially improved results, suggesting that the variability in the complete data was not wholly inadequate for providing more accurate estimates.

It is important for future studies to assess the performance of CART and random forest imputation under multivariate attrition with similar sample sizes and missing data mechanisms. These approaches still have much to recommend them, and one benefit of the chained equations imputation framework is the ease with which successive univariate CART and random forest analyses can be employed to generate imputations for any number of variables with missing data. Multivariate extensions of the CART and random forest weighting methods are not as obvious, however, since these methods must ultimately produce a single set of probabilities that can be inverted to form weights. The most promising approach to this problem involves assessing discrete and continuous time versions of survival CART and survival forests which, as their names imply, bridge decision tree approaches with survival analysis for censored data (see Zhou & McArdle, 2015 for an accessible and thorough introduction to survival trees and ensembles).

Furthermore, future research is needed to assess how best to address missing data on CART predictor variables when the goal of CART is to predict or impute missing data. With respect to imputation methods, the current approach is to populate all variables with an initial set of random imputations based on the observed values of each variable, iteratively updating these predictions with each (CART-based) imputation. With respected to predicting dropout probabilities and forming weights, an open question remains as to whether it is preferable to use existing surrogate-split methods to deal with missing data on CART predictors, or rely on more conventional imputation methods to fill in these variables prior to performing the CART analysis (or a set of CART analyses, from which the predicted probabilities might be pooled).

What recommendations can this simulation provide for applied researchers conducting clinical trials similar to the ones described here? First, it seems that random forest weights are a sensible choice for scenarios like the one depicted here, even when sample sizes are quite low, while Bayesian regression imputation appears to be another very solid choice. However, all of the methods studied were most helpful when the auxiliary covariates were highly correlated with the missing outcome variables. Therefore, researchers conducting small sample, experimental research should be cautious in assuming that variables highly correlated with y at baseline will necessarily remain highly correlated with successive measurements of y as the experimental treatment begins to create group differences.

Notes

1 A clever modification of this approach recognizes that, on average, about one-third of cases will be left out of each bootstrapped sample. These unsampled cases are termed *out-of-bag (OOB) estimates*. To increase the predictive accuracy of bagging analyses, the predicted values for each case can be calculated using only these OOB observations.

2 As a reviewer of this manuscript correctly points out, the root causes of MNAR missing data patterns are in no way limited to voluntary dropout. In clinical trial research, for example, the progression of a patient's depressive symptoms may lead to medication prescriptions that contraindicate or preclude continued participation in the study. In such a scenario, missing data would be inextricably linked to the study outcome, but non-voluntary. Though this and other more complex scenarios present intriguing complications for missing data analysis, these are outside the scope of the present chapter.

3 Technically, the intercept for the control group (dummy-coded 0) is equal to 1.00, whereas the intercept for the treatment group (dummy-coded 1) is equal to $1.00 + 0.005 = 1.005$.

4 In the absence of such benchmark results, if these CART-based weighting methods were applied directly to multivariate missing data problems and encountered performance problems, it would be difficult to ascertain whether the issues resulted from flaws in

the basic methods or flaws in the generalization of these univariate procedures to the multivariate case. For these reasons, then, I chose to prioritize experimental control over ecological realism in the present, initial simulation.

5 Knowledgeable readers may wonder why I used Bayesian regression imputation (method = "norm" in mice) instead of the default predicted mean matching (method = "pmm" in mice). I used the norm imputation both because this represents a standard approach to multiple imputation, generally, and because this method outperformed pmm in initial simulations. Therefore, I chose to present the norm imputation results instead, to demonstrate the stronger performance of this standard imputation technique.

6 Because all covariates, x, w, and v, were simulated in exactly the same way, the notation cor_{xy_2} indicates the correlation between any of the interchangeable covariates and y_2.

References

Asparouhov, T. (2005). Sampling weights in latent variable modeling. *Structural Equation Modeling: A Multidisciplinary Journal, 12*(3), 411–434. https://doi.org/10.1207/s15328007sem1203_4

Berk, R. A. (2009). *Statistical learning from a regression perspective*. New York: Springer.

Breiman, L. (1996). Bagging predictors. *Machine Learning, 24*(2), 123–140. https://doi.org/10.1007/BF00058655

Breiman, L. (2001). Random Forests. *Machine Learning, 45*(1), 5–32. https://doi.org/10.1023/A:1010933404324

Breiman, L., Friedman, J. H., Olshen, R. A., & Stone, C. J. (1984). *Classification and regression trees*. Pacific Grove, CA: Wadsworth.

Brodley, C. E. & Utgoff, P. E. (1995). Multivariate decision trees. *Machine Learning, 19*(1), 45–77. https://doi.org/10.1007/BF00994660

Collins, L. M., Schafer, J. L., & Kam, C. M. (2001). A comparison of inclusive and restrictive strategies in modern missing data procedures. *Psychological Methods, 6*(4), 330–351. https://doi.org/10.1037/1082-989X.6.4.330

De'ath, G. (2002). Multivariate regression trees: A new technique for modeling species–environment relationships. *Ecology, 83*(4), 1105–1117. https://doi.org/10.1890/0012-9658(2002)083[1105:MRTANT]2.0.CO;2

Doove, L. L., van Buuren, S., & Dusseldorp, E. (2014). Recursive partitioning for missing data imputation in the presence of interaction effects. *Computational Statistics & Data Analysis, 72*, 92–104. https://doi.org/10.1016/j.csda.2013.10.025

Efron, B. & Tibshirani, R. (1993). *An Introduction to the bootstrap*. New York: Chapman & Hall.

Enders, C. K. (2010). *Applied missing data analysis*. New York: Guilford Press.

Enders, C. K. (2011). Missing Not at Random models for latent growth curve analyses. *Psychological Methods, 16*(1), 1–16. Retrieved from http://dx.doi.org/10.1037/a0022640

Enders, C. K. & Bandalos, D. L. (2001). The relative performance of full information maximum likelihood estimation for missing data in structural equation models. *Structural Equation Modeling: A Multidisciplinary Journal, 8*(3), 430–457. https://doi.org/10.1207/S15328007SEM0803_5

Graham, J. W. & Schafer, J. L. (1999). On the performance of multiple imputation for multivariate data with small sample size. In R. H. Hoyle (Ed.), *Statistical strategies for small sample research* (pp. 1–27). Thousand Oaks, CA: Sage.

Hastie, T., Tibshirani, R., & Friedman, J. H. (2009). *The elements of statistical learning*. New York: Springer-Verlag.

Hayes, T., Usami, S., Jacobucci, R., & McArdle, J. J. (2015). Using Classification and Regression Trees (CART) and random forests to analyze attrition: Results from two simulations. *Psychology and Aging, 30*(4), 911–929. https://doi.org/10.1037/pag0000046

James, G., Witten, D., Hastie, T., & Tibshirani, R. (2013). *An introduction to statistical learning with applications in R*. New York: Springer.

Kish, L. (1995). Methods for design effects. *Journal of Official Statistics, 11*(1), 55–77. Retrieved from www.jos.nu/Articles/abstract.asp?article=11155

Larsen, D. R. & Speckman, P. L. (2004). Multivariate regression trees for analysis of abundance data. *Biometrics, 60*(2), 543–9. https://doi.org/10.1111/j.0006-341X.2004.00202.x

Liaw, A. & Wiener, M. (2002). Classification and regression by randomForest. *R News, 2*(3), 12–22.

Little, R. J. A. & Rubin, D. B. (1987). *Statistical analysis with missing data*. New York: Wiley.

McArdle, J. J. (2013). Dealing with longitudinal attrition using logistic regression and decision tree analyses. In *Contemporary issues in exploratory data mining in the behavioral sciences* (pp. 282–311). New York: Routledge.

Meng, X. (1994). Multiple-imputation inferences with uncongenial sources of input. *Statistical Science, 9*(4), 538–558.

Muthén, B., Kaplan, D., & Hollis, M. (1987). On structural equation modeling with data that are not missing completely at random. *Psychometrika, 52*(3), 431–462. https://doi.org/10.1007/BF02294365

Oberski, D. (2014). lavaan.survey: An R package for complex survey analysis of structural equation models. *Journal of Statistical Software, 57*(1), 1–27. https://doi.org/10.18637/jss.v057.i01

Potthoff, R. F., Woodbury, M. A., & Manton, K. G. (1992). "Equivalent sample size" and "equivalent degrees of freedom" refinements for inference using survey weights under superpopulation models. *Journal of the American Statistical Association, 87*(418), 383–396. https://doi.org/10.1080/01621459.1992.10475218

R Core Team. (2013). R: A language and environment for statistical computing. Vienna, Austria: R Foundation for Statistical Computing. Retrieved from http://r-project.org/

Rosseel, Y. (2012). lavaan: An R package for structural equation modeling. *Journal of Statistical Software, 48*(2), 1–36. https://doi.org/10.18637/jss.v048.i02

Rubin, D. B. (1976). Inference and missing data. *Biometrika, 63*(3), 581–592. https://doi.org/10.2307/2335739

Rubin, D. B. (1987). *Multiple imputation for nonresponse in surveys*. New York: Wiley.

Shah, A. D., Bartlett, J. W., Carpenter, J., Nicholas, O., & Hemingway, H. (2014). Comparison of random forest and parametric imputation models for imputing missing data using MICE: A CALIBER study. *American Journal of Epidemiology, 179*(6), 764–774. https://doi.org/10.1093/aje/kwt312

Stapleton, L. M. (2002). The incorporation of sample weights into multilevel structural equation models. *Structural Equation Modeling: A Multidisciplinary Journal, 9*(4), 475–502. https://doi.org/10.1207/S15328007SEM0904_2

Strobl, C., Malley, J., & Tutz, G. (2009). An introduction to recursive partitioning: Rationale, application, and characteristics of classification and regression trees, bagging, and random forests. *Psychological Methods, 14*(4), 323–348. https://doi.org/http://dx.doi.org/10.1037/a0016973

Therneau, T., Atkinson, B., & Ripley, B. (2014). rpart: Recursive Partitioning and Regression Trees. Retrieved from https://cran.r-project.org/package=rpart

van Buuren, S. (2012). *Flexible imputation of missing data*. Boca Raton, FL: Chapman & Hall/CRC.

van Buuren, S. & Groothuis-Oudshoorn, K. (2011). MICE: Multivariate imputation by chained equations in R. *Journal of Statistical Software, 45*(3), 1–67. https://doi.org/10. 18637/jss.v045.i03

Yang, M. & Maxwell, S. E. (2014). Treatment effects in randomized longitudinal trials with different types of nonignorable dropout. *Psychological Methods, 19*(2), 188–210. Retrieved from http://dx.doi.org/10.1037/a0033804

Zhou, Y. & McArdle, J. J. (2015). Rationale and applications of survival tree and survival ensemble methods. *Psychometrika, 80*(3), 811–833. https://doi.org/10.1007/s11336-014-9413-1

11

FROM FACTORS OF CURVES TO FACTORS OF CHANGE

Ryne Estabrook

Introduction

It is difficult to overstate the importance or utility of longitudinal data. Not only does longitudinal data provide more information than cross-sectional data, but measuring people more than once allows us to answer questions we otherwise cannot answer. Baltes and Nesselroade (1979) identified five rationales for longitudinal research, centered around the level, variability, and associations around how people change. Too often we discuss these benefits in abstract terms, failing to capture the importance of this line of research. The presence of longitudinal data allows us to differentiate between a student's current performance and their improvement, which is the difference between current aptitude and learning. It allows us to distinguish between a patient's current state of health and disease progression or treatment response, which is crucial for studying chronic disorders and treatment efficacy. The union of longitudinal data and sophisticated longitudinal modeling allows us to move from describing someone's current state to attributing that state to an ongoing process or system, the two of which are conflated when individuals are only observed once.

Nowhere is this ability to separate otherwise indistinguishable concepts as important as in measurement and measurement evaluation. In any single observation, it can be difficult or impossible to tell whether two variables measure the same construct or measure separate but correlated constructs. More complex measurement structures, like those that include residual correlations or residual factors accounting for method or other variance (e.g., bifactor and mutli-trait multi-method models), further exacerbate these problems. Longitudinal data can address these problems by separating level and change at the item or manifest variable level. Latent variable approaches all assume that common traits underlie and cause variation in observed items and variables. If test items change in different ways, then this assumption cannot hold, as there is no way for changes in a unidimensional latent variable to cause discrepant changes in the items it predicts. Unfortunately, most approaches to measurement evaluation rely on a single occasion of measurement, or treat repeated measures as unrelated independent or conditionally independent samples from a distribution, ignoring this rich source of information. Not only is this a missed opportunity, it allows researchers to think that people are not changing over time because some of the items on a scale increase whilst others decrease.

Part of this problem is the inability to easily combine longitudinal data and measurement modeling, particularly with ordinal data. Many measures in psychology and behavioral science use categorical responses. Item response modeling provides a set of techniques for measurement evaluation with categorical responses, but is employed nearly exclusively to cross-sectional data. However, item response models and factor models are strongly related to the point where they can often be transformed into one another (Kamata & Bauer, 2008), and the measurement principles and estimation techniques used in item response models can make longitudinal extensions of factor analytic measurement useful and efficient. When invariance of threshold parameters is assumed, ordinal data can be used for growth curve modeling (Mehta, Neale, & Flay, 2004). Similar combinations of ordinal data and longitudinal techniques can be implemented to answer questions related to measurement structures. Unless these branches of research can be connected in an accessible and implementable way, we will not be able to evaluate the measurement structure of dynamic constructs measured with ordinal variables.

The purpose of this chapter is to argue for a focus on item-level change when we build measures. When we compare a one-factor model to a two-factor model or a model with a residual correlation to a model with a residual factor, we may find few if any changes in fit or in interpretation. However, these types of modeling decisions greatly change the predictions made and tested in subsequent longitudinal modeling. If cross-sectional measurement evaluation can be oversimplified as testing whether a set of variables are sufficiently intercorrelated to create a construct, longitudinal measurement evaluation can be similarly reduced to testing whether those variables change together. When we build measures that cannot accurately account for how variables change, any longitudinal model fitted on top of that measure will contain and possibly exacerbate that misfit.

Latent Variable Measurement, Indeterminacy, and Model Equivalence

Measurement in psychological science often focuses on some form of latent trait measurement. Under such approaches, a set of observed or manifest variables are hypothesized to indicate one or more unmeasured continuous variables, commonly referred to as latent variables, factors, or traits. The existence of these latent variables is presumed based on the fit of some form of factor analysis or item response model, with the latent variables predicting the manifest variables thus explaining their covariation. Such reflective models, named for the fact that the manifest variables reflect the latent variables that cause them (Edwards & Bagozzi, 2000), predict that the covariances between k items can be explained by k regressions on a (unidimensional) common factor. If this model can accurately predict the $\frac{k(k-1)}{2}$ covariances between observed items, then a k-dimensional set of observed variables and their covariances can be more parsimoniously accounted for by a single unmeasured variable. A rich literature of work on latent variable models has grown this relatively simple idea into a robust set of methods that make much of behavioral science possible.

A common problem in latent variable models in general, and factor models specifically, is the issue of indeterminacy. Factor indeterminacy takes many forms, but they all center around the fact that there is always more than one equivalent way to fit or draw a factor model. Factor score indeterminacy is one of the oldest critiques, reflecting the fact that there is an infinite number of possible factor scores due to the fact that there are always more latent factors (common and residual/specific) than observed variables (Wilson, 1928). More simply, for any factor model and associated set of possible scores on common factor(s), it is possible to pick values for the residual factors that perfectly reproduce any dataset. The effects of indeterminacy have been quantified (Guttman, 1955), and a variety of factor score estimation methods yield useful scores that acknowledge and account for the issue of indeterminacy (Acito & Anderson, 1986; Estabrook & Neale, 2013; Grice, 2001a, 2001b; Tucker, 1971).

More pertinent to this discussion is one of rotational indeterminacy, and related issues in model equivalence. Factor models can be rotated, or multiplied by a transformation matrix that rescales factor loadings, variances, and covariances to yield some desired characteristics. This does not change the fit of the model, but can take a difficult to interpret model and transform it into an equivalent but more understandable alternative. Exploratory factor models and some item response models use rotation to enforce things like simple structure or to generate oblique factor solutions from orthogonal extraction methods. Specific rotation methods are beyond the scope of this chapter, but there exist countless methods that span foundational factor analytic techniques (Browne, 2001; Kaiser, 1958, 1960) and emerging areas of psychometric research (Jennrich & Bentler, 2012; Mansolf & Reise, 2016; Yamamoto & Jennrich, 2013).

In confirmatory factor models, this indeterminacy manifests through the related concept of model equivalence. Factor analysis and structural equation modeling are incredibly flexible techniques that are centered around reproducing an observed covariance matrix, or equivalently, maximizing the likelihood of raw continuous or categorical data under and expected covariance structure. Any two models that yield the same expected covariance matrix and expected means and thresholds are equivalent, regardless of how they are drawn. This means that any given cross-sectional factor or structural equation model can be redrawn in such a way as to make different predictions when extended longitudinally.

Figure 11.1 shows two versions of the factor model that differ in their presentation in two ways that frequently occur. First, these two models have different numbers of factors. The model on the left contains only a single factor, while the model on the right contains two correlated factors with simple structure. When the factor correlation in the rightmost diagram is set equal to 1.0, these two models are equivalent. It is further worth mentioning that these two models may be statistically indistinguishable when the factor correlation is lower than 1.0 but still high. One- and two-factor models will make different predictions when the factor correlation is not 1.0, but small sample sizes, ordinal data, missing data, or complex factor structures may make it difficult to detect these differences with sufficient power. Second, these models differ in how they present residual structures. The model on the left contains a residual correlation between items y and z, whereas the model on the right predicts that same bivariate relationship using a residual factor (labeled θ_{yz}). Provided only one free parameter is estimated between the loadings and variance terms for θ_{yz}, these models are exactly equivalent. This equivalence carries over to residual factors predicting three items, as they describe three residual covariances with three factor loading parameters[1].

These two example cases are important because they represent ways that the same expected covariance cannot only be represented differently, but interpreted differently. Differing numbers of common factors may provide similar fit, but connote different predictions about individual differences and developmental change. Comparing one- and two-factor models is a classic comparison, but this problem shows up in more complex ways when additional common factors

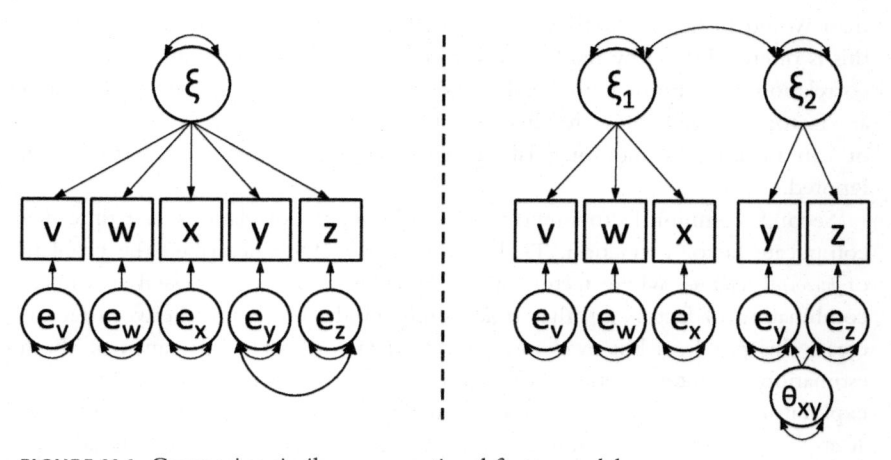

FIGURE 11.1 Comparing similar cross–sectional factor models.

are possibly present. For example, there are many existing methods for testing unidimensionality and thus ruling out the presence of a second factor (e.g., eigenvalue ratio tests, Ahn & Horenstein, 2013), but distinguishing between three or four common factors or between second-order factor structures is much more difficult and features the same problems of interpretation. Similarly, residual correlations and residual factor structures are more often equivalent, but plagued by the same interpretation factors. A residual correlation can be considered as a nuisance parameter meant to account for comparable wording in items, whereas a residual factor represents potentially stable method variance.

Longitudinal data provide a unique way to distinguish among equivalent or near-equivalent hypotheses. Common factors, residual and method factors, and correlations all come with specific connotations about how they change over time. Common factors are typically thought to contain some degree of stable traits, and thus autocorrelate with themselves over time. Residual factors are typically uncorrelated with all common factors and other residual factors at a given timepoint. Residual factors representing method variance may be stable across time, or have simple autocorrelative structures that are uncorrelated with all other processes. The specifics of these predictions are up to individual researchers and will vary by construct and measure, but the point is that these parameterizations make differential longitudinal predictions, and using this information can answer previously unanswerable questions.

Problems with Longitudinal Measurement Modeling

Despite the utility of extending measurement evaluation into longitudinal data, several statistical issues prevent a researcher from simply throwing repeated measurements into a standard exploratory factor analysis program. First, it is common to find that the same measure or variable has stronger correlations with itself than would be expected from the latent trait alone. In confirmatory models, this is often achieved by method factors and residual structures, including autocorrelations and more complex longitudinal models. When longitudinal data are factor analyzed, these residual structures either require explicit parameters or can manifest as additional latent factors or bias in parameter estimates if ignored.

Second, common factors tend to have a high autocorrelations over time that complicate factor extraction. Tisak & Meredith (1989) described the problem of *factorial collapse*, where factors at one timepoint can be expressed as a linear combination of factors at other time points. High correlations between factors create this problem, but even lower levels of factor correlation can make both estimation and interpretation difficult. Absent constraints on factor loadings, and exploratory factor models are free to let items at one time point load on to factors at any other timepoint, leading to uninterpretable factors that indicate within-item longitudinal associations rather than common constructs.

Even if the above problems were solved with method or residual factors, corrections for factorial collapse, and constraints to enforce temporal simple structure, these methods would still have fitting and interpretation problems. If there are differences in the structures of between- and within-person differences, the between-person differences will be easy to spot whilst within-person structures will be distributed across all parts of the model. Molenaar (2004) has pointed out that the equivalence between between- and within-person structures is a strong assumption, and one that is rarely tested and often violated in psychology and related fields.

If we want to know something about the structure of change, then we must directly discuss change. Such a method would require that we eschew traditional approaches that first evaluate each time point individually in favor of direct analysis of change scores. The challenge of such an approach is to correctly parameterize change in such a way as to avoid creating additional problems.

Factor of Curves Model

While a focus on change is not the norm in measurement evaluation, combining dynamic modeling and latent variable measurement has been around for decades. McArdle's (1988) Factor of Curves or FOCUS model takes a set of longitudinally measured items or constructs and fits a two-level model. In the first level, each item or construct is fitted with a latent growth curve model, describing each of them through individual differences in level and slope(s). In the second, the set of latent intercepts and slopes are fitted by a multidimensional factor model. In his (1988) chapter, McArdle outlined the importance and utility of this approach, and contrasted it with alternative multivariate longitudinal techniques.

The FOCUS model can be described via path diagrams, or via matrix or multilevel specifications, but all are equivalent. An item (X) is measured on person i, at time t, each of which vary across individuals (i) and constructs (k). Each person has one intercept and one slope for each of the k constructs, which is shown in Equation 11.1, and on construct k, and can be decomposed into latent intercepts (I_{ik}) and slopes $(S_{ik})^2$. The intercepts are then fitted by a common intercept factor or factors (ξ_I), just as though they were observed scores in any cross-sectional factor model. The slopes are also fitted with a common slope factor or factors (ξ_S). The equations for these factor models are given in Equations 11.2 and 11.3. This yields the direct projection of common factors on items shown in Equation 11.4.

$$X_{itk} = I_{ik} + S_{ik}t_{itk} + \epsilon_{itk} \tag{11.1}$$

$$I_{ik} = \mu_{I_k} + \xi_{I_i}\lambda_I + \theta_{I_{ik}} \tag{11.2}$$

$$S_{ik} = \mu_{S_k} + \xi_{S_i}\lambda_S + \theta_{S_{ik}} \tag{11.3}$$

$$X_{itk} = (\mu_{I_k} + \xi_{I_i}\lambda_I + \theta_{I_{ik}}) + (\mu_{S_k} + \xi_{S_i}\lambda_S + \theta_{S_{ik}})t_{itk} + \epsilon_{itk} \tag{11.4}$$

Equation 11.4 provides direct substitution of Equations 11.2 and 11.3 into Equation 11.1, but is difficult to read and interpret. It can be regrouped into three parts, as shown in Equation 11.5. First, observed scores are modeled as a function of common intercept and slope factors that predict all items, and items load onto these second order factors via the product of common factor loadings (λ_I and λ_S for intercepts and slopes) and growth curve loadings (omitted constant ones for intercepts, t_{itk} for slopes). Second, residual longitudinal associations between the same item over time are modeled by the individually varying intercept and slope residuals ($\theta_{I_{ik}}$ and $\theta_{S_{ik}}$), which are the part of each item's intercept and slope that are not accounted for by ξ_{I_i} and ξ_{S_i}. Finally, item means and residual variances are governed by growth curve means and a residual term. In the simplest language possible, the FOCUS model predicts that longitudinally-measured items be predicted by a common factor representing level, a second common factor representing change, and a residual structure that allows the same item to autocorrelate consistent with a latent growth curve.

$$X_{itk} = (\xi_{I_i}\lambda_I + \xi_{S_i}\lambda_S t_{itk}) + (\theta_{I_{ik}} + \theta_{S_{ik}} t_{itk}) + (\mu_{I_k} + \mu_{S_k} t_{itk} + \epsilon_{itk}) \tag{11.5}$$

The FOCUS model is closely related to both the Curve of Factors model and differential R-technique factor analysis. The Curve of Factors or CUFFS model (McArdle, 1988) was introduced as a companion to the FOCUS model, flipping the model structure such that latent variable models were fit at each time point underneath subsequent latent growth curve modeling. If Equations 11.1 to 11.5 were respecified under the CUFFS model, observed scores X_{itk} would be fitted first with common factors at each time point (ξ_{it}), which would in turn be fitted by common intercept and slope factors (I_i and S_i). Both models feature a relationship between the common second order factors and the observed items equivalent to the product of growth factor basis coefficients and the factor loadings λ. These models differ in their structure of residual correlations: under the FOCUS model, items covary with other items measuring the same construct over time, whereas the CUFFS model predicts that items covary with other items measured at the same time. These are two different hypotheses about residual structures, which McArdle (1988) compares theoretically and empirically in his chapter.

The FOCUS model is also related to differential R-technique factor analysis (Cattell, 1963; Nesselroade & Cable, 1974), which is a factor analysis of two-occasion difference scores. This can be extended into a "factor of difference scores," which simultaneously fits latent factors to difference scores and to a first-occasion score (McArdle & Nesselroade, 1994). This approach directly applies to the measurement structure of change. McArdle (2007) stated "if metric invariance does not fit both the starting point factors and difference factors, then the factorial interpretation of the changes can be interpreted from these difference loadings."

These models directly assess the measurement structure of change, both on its own and in comparison to an intercept (FOCUS) or first occasion score (factor of difference scores). Factor loading equivalence between intercept and change factors can be interpreted as (weak) factorial invariance, and through that, arguments can be constructed about the congruence of the structures of between-person and within-person differences.

If there are weaknesses in these approaches, they are in the strong longitudinal hypotheses that are implied by model structure. The FOCUS model presumes that all items and processes are not only fit by a latent growth curve, but all items or constructs under investigation are well characterized by the *same* latent growth curve. There is no version of the FOCUS model that allows for some items to have linear relationships with time, while other have non-linear processes. Furthermore, the model cannot distinguish between longitudinal and measurement misfit: if the FOCUS model fits poorly, it is not clear whether this is a problem with the longitudinal modeling (i.e., a missed autocorrelation or quadratic slope) or measurement modeling (wrong number of factors or an invalid invariance constraint). As the factor of difference scores is simply the FOCUS model constrained to two occasions, it maintains all the same weaknesses, with the added drawback that more than two occasions may be necessary to capture the dynamics of some processes.

For a FOCUS-like modeling approach to be broadly applicable, it needs to have ways of accounting for longitudinal misfit that cannot be misconstrued as measurement misfit. Ideally, it would allow maximal flexibility in the longitudinal portion of the model, allowing for application to a wide array of potential constructs and any number of measurement occasions. It would also yield interpretable change scores just as FOCUS does via intercepts and slopes. The FOCUS model provides a framework for a factor model of item-level change: the remainder of this chapter will be devoted to an extension of this method that attempts to address some of these weaknesses.

Measurement Model of Derivatives

The Measurement Model of Derivatives (MMOD; Estabrook, 2015) is an alternative approach that attempts to address the inherent problems with assessing the structure of within-person change. The model consists of two parts: a data transformation and a multidimensional factor model fit to the transformed data. The data transformation is designed to rotate observed data into a set of change variables, with each new variable representing a different possible pattern of within-person change. The key to this model is the nature of the data transformation: each set of longitudinally measured items is transformed into an equal-rank set of orthogonal item-level derivatives. The transformation and multidimensional measurement modeling can be completed and discussed separately.

Derivative Estimation

As the name would suggest, the Measurement Model of Derivatives fits a model to the derivatives of each item on a measure with respect to time. The reason we use derivatives rather than other methods of assessing change is that derivatives are, by definition, a flexible method for describing any pattern of change. Each order of derivative represents a different and interpretable relationship between a given variable and time. Derivatives are typically addressed via ordinal numbers (0th, 1st, 2nd) and written mathematically either through the more verbose Leibniz's notation (x, $\frac{dx}{dt}$, $\frac{d^2x}{dt^2}$) or the simpler Newtonian notation (x, $\dot{x}$, $\ddot{x}$).

The method for estimating these derivatives is an orthogonal extension of generalized local linear approximation (GLLA; Boker & Nesselroade, 2002; Boker, 2001; Boker, Deboeck, Edler, & Keel, 2010) proposed by DeBoeck (2010a). While methods like functional data analysis might make an effort to fit and differentiate a time series to yield derivatives (Trail, Collins, Rivera, Li, Piper, & Baker 2009), GLLA uses simple linear combinations of observed data to estimate local rates of change around a given measurement occasion. Much like the basis coefficients that define the loadings of longitudinal items on intercept and slope factors, GLLA uses fixed loadings or transformations to turn longitudinal items into either derivative scores or latent derivatives. At their simplest, GLLA derivatives are weighted sum scores that use data around time t to estimate derivatives at time t. The weights for these sum scores can then be compiled into factor loading or transformation matrices. This model uses generalized orthogonal local derivatives (GOLD; Deboeck, 2010), an alternative method that adjusts and smooths these weights over a block of longitudinal data and minimize spurious associations between derivatives.

The above discussion is theoretical, and does not do justice to the simplicity and utility of this method. To demonstrate this utility, I will briefly describe the meaning and estimation of GOLD derivatives assuming three time points of data. In this example, x_1, x_2, and x_3 will be transformed into x, $\dot{x}$, and $\ddot{x}$.

The simplest possible derivative is the zeroth derivative, which is commonly referred to as location or position. The zeroth derivative of x at time t is x_t. It is simply a restatement of the current value of a variable, either in its raw form or as a predicted or smoothed value. While some methods will simply take the middle timepoint, GOLD smooths derivatives to some degree and uses essentially a sum score for three occasion data. GOLD uses weights of 0.333, 0.333, and 0.333 to estimate the zeroth derivative of x as the sum of x_1, x_2, and x_3. The rationale for this smoothing is described in greater detail elsewhere (Deboeck, 2010; Estabrook, Sadler, & McGue, 2015).

The most commonly-used derivative is the first derivative, also termed velocity. It is the rate of change of x with respect to time. This is, to put it in more common psychological terms, a slope. The first derivative or velocity is just how fast a person is increasing or decreasing. Under a three-occasion GOLD estimation, the weights are -0.5, 0 and 0.5, yielding a first derivative defined as $\frac{x_3-x_1}{2}$. In growth curve terms, this is a linear slope. In factor of difference scores (McArdle & Nesselroade, 1994) terms, this is a difference or change score. With four or more timepoints, this extends to include more than two scores, but is always essentially a slope.

The second derivative or acceleration is the first derivative of velocity, and reflects how much a score is speeding up or slowing down. Under GOLD and other LLA methods, this is most commonly done for three-dimensional transformations by calculating two first derivatives. First, one calculates the first derivative at the beginning $(x_2 - x_1)$ and end $(x_3 - x_2)$ of the set, then calculating change over the entire interval $\left(\frac{(x_3 - x_2) - (x_2 - x_1)}{2} = \frac{x_3 - 2x_2 + x)1}{2} \right)$. This yields weights of 0.5, -1, and 0.5, which is proportional to a centered quadratic slope from a growth curve.

Put together, the three sets of derivative estimation weights can make a transformation matrix like the one shown in Equation 11.6. Three occasions of data may be transformed by this matrix, as shown in Equation 11.7.

$$W_{GOLD} = \begin{bmatrix} 0.333 & -0.5 & 0.5 \\ 0.333 & 0 & -1 \\ 0.333 & 0.5 & 0.5 \end{bmatrix} \tag{11.6}$$

$$\begin{bmatrix} x_1 & x_2 & x_3 \end{bmatrix} W_{GOLD} = \begin{bmatrix} x & \dot{x} & \ddot{x} \end{bmatrix} \tag{11.7}$$

These GOLD weights and other LLA methods are very similar to the basis coefficients used in growth curve modeling. However, the weights themselves and their application in MMOD have several characteristics that make them well-suited to measurement evaluation.

Full Dimensionality

One of the problems with fitting item-level growth curve models prior to measurement evaluation is that models by definition incur misfit. A linear growth curve model fit to k longitudinal observations will describe k observed means with two latent means and $\frac{k(k-1)}{2}$ observed covariances from three latent variance/covariance terms that propagate down through basis coefficients. This creates a more parsimonious explanation of the observed data, ideally describing most of the observed relationships with many fewer parameters. However, no model fits perfectly, and even in the best case scenarios this model creates some degree of misfit. When the goal of the FOCUS and MMOD approaches is to evaluate the structure of the construct, any longitudinal misfit can be misconstrued as a measurement problem.

GOLD derivatives and MMOD get around this by using a fully saturated longitudinal model. Three time points of data are represented as three derivatives. Larger number of time points yields a larger number of derivatives. There are no manifest variable error terms, because all manifest variable information is transmitted up into the derivatives. As there is no misfit generated by the longitudinal model, any misfit found in the model can be attributed to measurement structures, and the model can thus be changed to better account for the measurement structure of the items. This is a very different approach from many other longitudinal latent variable models, as all manifest variable error is transmitted to the latent derivatives.

Scalable

Part of the need for a FOCUS or MMOD-like approach is that longitudinal data does not have any inherent number of timepoints. A process of change may be measured densely, with many measurements, or sparsely with only one or two. Derivatives can be extended to any number of timepoints: two occasion versions reduce to a version of the factor of difference scores, but can theoretically scale up to dozens or hundreds of time points. If too many orders of derivative are calculated, this can be handled in the measurement portion of the model, and higher-order terms can have little or no variance, which obviates the need to do variable-specific tests of the shape of longitudinal effects.

Orthogonal

GOLD derivatives are orthogonalized such that the weights of each order of derivative are independent of all other sets of weights. Each column of W_{GOLD} (Equation 11.6) is column-wise orthogonal to all others, yielding a set of weights that are independent, just as planned contrasts in regression and ANOVA are independent. This underlies the main goal of this approach: not to ascertain the longitudinal structure of the construct, but rather to restate the item-level longitudinal structure so that it can be used to ascertain the dimensionality and measurement structure of the items prior to subsequent confirmatory modeling of a validated measure.

Interpretable

Derivatives have an inherent scale and analogues to physical systems. Position, velocity, and acceleration have real-world meanings, and their relationships are thus interpretable. If position and velocity are positively correlated, it means that higher scores are associated with more positive growth rates. A negative correlation between position and acceleration means that the higher your score, the more you decelerate and start changing back toward the mean. Dynamical systems approaches are broadly concerned with these types of associations, which can be stated as relationships between level and changes relative to an equilibrium state that is most simply defined as a within-person mean. They can be extended into higher terms, each differentiating the one below it. Alternatively, GOLD derivatives map on well to the polynomial terms common in growth curve modeling.

Multidimensional Measurement Modeling

Once derivatives are estimated, MMOD progresses very similarly to FOCUS or other multidimensional factor models. If the sampling weights W_{GOLD} are used to create observed derivative scores, then this model is a conventional multidimensional factor model, and can be fitted using any available SEM software. Instead of factors at the first time point predicting items at the first time point, zeroth derivative factors predict zeroth derivative items, and so on.

However, manifest derivative transformation requires continuous and complete data, which can be a problem for measurement and longitudinal models respectively. The derivatives may be estimated in latent space, with the weight matrix inverted into a loading matrix L, where $L = W^{-1}$. Instead of the data multiplied by W_{GOLD} yielding derivatives, derivatives are multiplied by L ($L = W_{GOLD}^{-1}$) to yield observed data. Equation 11.8 shows this relationship, where observed data X_{itk} for each person (i), timepoint (t) and variable or item (k) are made up of an equal rank set of latent derivatives (d_{ijk}) for each person (i), order of derivative (j) and variable or item (k), with these two matrices linked by post-multiplication of a weight matrix L'. These derivatives are then fitted by common factors that vary across individuals (i) and order of derivatives (j, replacing t). Unidimensional models have common traits ξ_{ij}, while multidimensional extensions add another dimension ξ_{ijq} to express multiple factors per order of derivative. This can be drawn as shown in Figure 11.2, which differs from the FOCUS model in the pattern of basis coefficients, the saturation

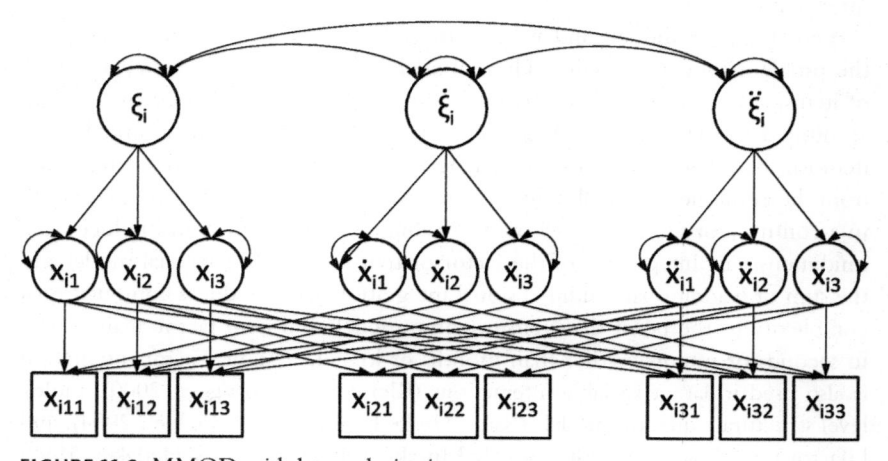

FIGURE 11.2 MMOD with latent derivatives.
Note: Path diagram for three-occasion Measurement Model of Derivatives fit to three longitudinally measured items. First-order loadings of manifest variables on latent derivatives fixed to the values of L. Second-order loadings of latent derivatives on common factors (η_i, $\dot{\eta}_i$, and $\ddot{\eta}_i$) are freely estimated.

of the first-order of the model, and the removal of manifest variable residual terms.

$$X_{itk} = d_{ijk}L' \tag{11.8}$$

$$d_{ijk} = \mu_{jk} + \xi_{ijq}\lambda + \epsilon_{ijk} \tag{11.9}$$

This model can then be fit via conventional structural equation modeling software. Item derivatives on derivative factors can be treated as though they were items at time points for the purposes of longitudinal invariance testing. Levels of factorial invariance can be tested by making constraints on the parameters at each order of derivative: weak factorial invariance can be tested by constraining factor loadings, while strong and strict invariance require additional research due to scaling differences across orders of derivatives[3].

Redefining MMOD for Item-Level Data

A weakness of this approach and any covariance-based factor analysis is its reliance on high dimensional integration when ordinal data is used. MMOD generates an expected covariance matrix, just as any other confirmatory factor model fit to continuous data. When extended to ordinal or binary data, fitting MMOD requires integrating that expected covariance matrix to obtain expected probabilities of endorsement for each category of each categorical variable. Such high-dimensional integration is incredibly computationally expensive, due to both the nature of integration methods and the size of the data required for longitudinal measurement evaluation.

Item response models and item factor analyses get around this by restating the problem they are solving. These models assume conditional independence of items, such that items are uncorrelated once the common factor or traits are accounted for. If scores on these factors or traits are known or assumed, each item can be integrated or solved separately, and the fit of the model determined from the combined fit of all items [4]. What would be a k-dimensional integration in a confirmatory factor model, with k being the number of items, reduces to a unidimensional integration of the factor or trait in a unidimensional model and the sum of k additional unidimensional integrations. This reduces computational complexity to the point that item response models and item factor analyses run in seconds or minutes rather than months or longer, if at all. Factor integration is also used in latent variable interactions (Klein & Moosbrugger, 2000), multi-level structural equation models (Rabe-Hesketh, Skrondal, & Pickles, 2004), and bifactor modeling (Bock, Gibbons, & Muraki, 1988; Gibbons & Hedeker, 1992; Reise, 2012).

This is unfortunately not an option for MMOD or related approaches, as MMOD relies on estimating latent item-level derivatives. If the data to be analyzed have $k \star t$ items (k items at t timepoints), there will be $k \star t$ latent derivative variables. If there are as many latent variables as there are observed variables to be replaced, then latent variable integration does not provide any computational or time savings for this method. More traditional applications such as integrating only the common factors provide no savings, as the item-level derivatives must still be dealt with either via integration or the creation of a covariance matrix.

Item response modeling has dealt with similar problems in different ways. One of these ways is via the bifactor model, an extension of two-level factor analysis that specifically gets around the need for high-dimensional integration (Bock, Gibbons, & Muraki, 1988; Gibbons & Hedeker, 1992; Reise, 2012). Item response models are incredibly efficient for unidimensional traits, but that efficiency suffers with multidimensional traits to the point that models have to be adapted when more than a constructs underlie a set of items (McDonald, 2000; Reckase, 2009). Bifactor models restate a multidimensional factor model as a two-level factor model, using a unidimensional second-order factor to predict the first-order factors and explain their intercorrelation. This yields a second-order common factor that predicts all items and a set of residualized first-order factors that predict sets of items. As the first-order residualized factors are by definition uncorrelated with the second-order factor, the bifactor model restates a high number of correlated factors into a set uncorrelated factors. This means the factors can be integrated independently, greatly speeding estimation.

The bifactor model may provide the same solution to MMOD. MMOD is a higher-order factor model: a small number of common second-order factors predict a larger number of first-order factors, which in turn predict observed variables. MMOD has an uncommonly high number of first-order latent variables, structured factor loadings for those variables, and a lack of residual variance terms. The bifactor model was proposed as a simplification of these types of second-order factor models. First-order factors are separated into a dummy factor (perfectly predicted by the common traits, thus having no residual variance) and a residual or specific factor, uncorrelated with all other traits. The dummy factors can be omitted and the items they predict projected onto the common traits, thus yielding a model. Hill (2006b) and Cai (2010) have proposed such two-level item factor models for longitudinal data.

Applying this transformation and two-level approach could be carried out by substituting MMOD into the two-level FOCUS specification first shown in Equation 11.5. Equation 11.10 shows this substitution, where observed responses for a given variable X_{itk} (person i, time t, item k) can be expressed as a function of a set of common derivative factors ξ_{ij} (person i, derivative order j, assuming unidimensionality) and residual derivative factors ϵ_{ijk}. The common factors load on the observed items directly through the product of the two loading matrices, with Λ consisting of the estimated regressions of item derivatives on traits, and L' made up of fixed loadings defining the relationship between observed items and latent derivatives.

$$X_{itk} = \mu_{jk}L' + \xi_{ij}\Lambda L' + \epsilon_{ijk}L' \tag{11.10}$$

The common and specific traits ξ_{ij} and ϵ_{ijk} can be leveraged to create an item response model. There are many papers that show the equivalencies between item factor models and both binary and polytomous item response models (Kamata & Bauer, 2008; McDonald, 1967, 1985; Muthén, 1984; Widaman & Reise, 1997). This equivalence is further used in Cai's (2010) two-level item factor model. Applying this notation to a dichotomous response bifactor model yields the model in Equation 11.11.

$$P_{X_{itk}} = 1(\xi_{ij}, \epsilon_{ijk}) = \frac{1}{1 + \exp[-[\alpha + \Lambda L' \xi_{ij} + L' \epsilon_{ijk}]]} \tag{11.11}$$

The product term $\Lambda L'$ replaces the discrimination term for the common traits, while L' replaces the discrimination term for specific traits. The resulting model provides a marginal increase in complexity for the common trait due to the addition of the product term, but the fact that one of those terms is fixed mitigates this complexity. Furthermore, the specific factors have no estimated loadings, easing the computational burden of this portion of the model.

Defining Residual Dynamic Structure

The last remaining challenge for fitting a bifactor MMOD model is defining the specific factors so that they capture the residual dynamic structure present in any single item measured longitudinally. MMOD contains as manny derivative factors as their are items. This greatly complicates integration and trait score estimation, as there will be more traits than there are variables, thus making the model undefined. The absence of variable-specific residual terms further breaks the transformations that connect item response and item factor models, like those described by McDonald (1967, 1985) and others.

However, the residual dynamics terms defined in MMOD are nuisance parameters: they exist to explain the residual dynamics of each item and flexibly account for unique longitudinal change without imposing a restrictive model that could contribute misfit. This can theoretically be accomplished with any number of latent variables, provided appropriate constraints are made. A more flexible approach could even improve fit: the original specification of MMOD had the common factors explain all item-level associations between all orders of derivatives, which is inherently restrictive. Specifically, MMOD specified that all associations between zeroth and first derivatives were accounted for by the common factors, relying on the orthogonalized derivative loading matrix L to remove any other sources of association. This is a restrictive assumption, and one that can be more easily freed than enforced in a bifactor MMOD.

If we shift the goal from matching MMOD's full rank set of derivative factors to a set of factors that account for residual dynamics without misfit, then two- and three-occasion bifactor MMODs become trivially easy. Two occasion models simply require a residual correlation, as all that can be modeled is an association between the two time points or, equivalently, an association between zeroth and first derivatives or level and change. This can be accomplished by a single residual or specific factor, though such duplet factors traditionally require an additional identification constraint.

Three occasion extensions are even easier: they require that the three residual correlations (r_{12}, r_{13}, and r_{23}) be described by three parameters. Factors predicting three variables without additional constraints create a fully saturated model that completely accounts for these three correlations. This residual correlation matrix can in turn be transformed into a two-dimensional dynamical system using the same local linear approximation methods used in MMOD (Boker & Nesselroade, 2000; Deboeck, 2010). Four or more occasions cannot be described with a single residual factor, but could be identified with small numbers of factors with sufficient identification constraints.

Put together, this creates a simpler version of a bifactor MMOD that removes the constraints on the specific factors. Equation 11.12 shows a two- or three-occasion version of this model. It differs from Equation 11.11 by replacing the set of derivative factors ϵ_{ijk} with a single residual factor θ_{ik}, and freely estimating the discriminations β_S. It differs from Hill's (2006a) longitudinal bifactor model by replacing the common factor discriminations with the product term $\Lambda L'$ that projects the common factor discriminations on all occasions.

$$P_{X_{itk}=1}(\xi_{ij}, \theta ik) = \frac{1}{1 + \exp[-[\alpha + \Lambda L'\xi_{ij} + \beta_S \theta ik]]} \tag{11.12}$$

Estimation of such a model should be a relatively straightforward addition above and beyond other bifactor models. Cai (2010) outlines marginal maximum likelihood estimation of such two-level models (see Section 3.4, pages 589–590). The use of the product discrimination term appears to make estimation more complex. However, same L term appears as part the common factor term and is the entirety of the specific factor term. Therefore, these two terms are proportional and satisfy the restrictions of the testlet model (Bradlow, Wainer, & Wang, 1999). Rijmen (2010) points out the flexibility of estimating such bifactor models under full-information maximum likelihood and the E-M algorithm (Gibbons & Hedeker, 1992).

Discussion

The purpose of this chapter is jointly to argue for the importance of longitudinal data in measurement evaluation and show how we can build on McArdle's FOCUS model into a dynamic measurement evaluation paradigm that spans factor analysis and item response modeling. Longitudinal data have a number of characteristics that make conventional measurement approaches difficult to fit and interpret. The FOCUS model provides a template for thinking about broadly defined change variables and how they relate to one another. MMOD builds on this template, yielding orthogonal change scores that avoid some of the pitfalls of longitudinal modeling. The rest of the chapter gleaned insight from bifactor modeling to make an ordinal MMOD model possible, with reinterpretation of specific factors to account for residual dynamics. I wish to close with a longer discussions of two issues related to the merging of longitudinal measurement models with bifactor modeling, and make recommendations for future work.

Parameterizing Residual Dynamics

The novelty of an item-level MMOD is in having a complete but estimable parameterization of residual dynamic structures. On three occasions, the bifactor model provides an equivalent fit to the types of dynamical relationships hypothesized under MMOD. Higher-dimensional data will require more complex parameterizations. Whilst it is theoretically important that the residual autocorrelative structure be fully saturated to avoid misfit, future extensions to many time points may require a more parsimonious method.

Deciding which residual dynamics specification is best is an empirical question. Few dynamical systems approaches either within or outside psychology make hypotheses that require large numbers of derivatives. Autoregressive processes can be restated in dynamical systems terms, and most multilevel packages allow for constrained residual structures including autoregressive or AR processes of varying degrees.

FOCUS, CUFFS, and Cross-Classified Data

McArdle (1988) compared and contrasted the FOCUS and CUFFS models, finding that they differed in their handling of residual covariance structures, as shown in Equation 11.5 and the surrounding text. While the CUFFS model and most other multivariate approaches fit factors to time points (and thus fit residual structures at each occasion), FOCUS and MMOD assume that items are the first level of nesting and allow for structured residual correlations within items across time.

Both modeling paradigms and multivariate longitudinal data itself should be viewed as clustered or multilevel data. Multiple level 1 observations are nested within each level 2 unit. Most multilevel modeling applications deal exclusively with hierarchical clustering of this type. However, it is also possible for data to be cross-classified, breaking this hierarchical structure by having level 1 observations assigned to more than one level 2 unit. This can occur in two different ways. If there is only one dimension of level 2 units, level 1 observations can be assigned to more than one of them. For example, students (level 1) can be nested within teachers or classrooms (level 2), but students can move between classrooms or be assigned to more than one. More relevant to this measurement issue is the possibility of more than one level 2 dimension. Observed items at any time point are assigned to both their time point and to the person that completed them.

It should be possible to further extend the models described above to multiple orthogonal specific factors for both time points and items. Multi-trait multi-method models already distinguish between common and specific factors cross-sectionally, and can be extended longitudinally (Grimm, Pianta, & Konold, 2009; Geiser, Eid, Nussbeck, Courvoisier, & Cole, 2010). A model with sets of specific factors for each time point and item would combine the residual structures of the FOCUS and CUFFS models, but has additional estimation difficulties that would need to be addressed prior to use.

Closing

Longitudinal measurement evaluation is vitally important and larger than any one model or modeling approach. If we are going to make inferences about how people change on a given construct, we must verify that our measure is a reliable and valid measure of that construct. This chapter argues for a specific modeling approach, which should further be extended to include testing, empirical example, and software development.

However, the real goal of this line of research is not a model or software product, but an expansion of measurement principles to include change. Reliable measures should not only have internal consistency, but should reliably measure within-person change. Valid measures should demonstrate longitudinal convergent and divergent validity, showing coincident changes with constructs that should change together and no relationship with constructs that should not be related. Thinking about how items and measures should change will strengthen measurement, longitudinal modeling, and behavioral science in general.

Notes

1 These two- and three-item factors are special cases. In the two-item case, the item (residual) correlation is equal to the product of the residual factor variance and the two factor loadings. Two constraints must be made for identification. For three-item factors with an assumed unit variance, any residual covariance can be estimated as the product of those items' residual factor loadings.

2 In Equations 11.1 to 11.5, t_{itk} is meant to represent the time at which X_{ijk} is observed. Most growth curve approaches allow for individually varying times of observation.

3 Zeroth derivatives are means in raw units, first derivatives are change per unit time, second derivatives per unit squared time, etc. Measurement error in the observed variables are transmitted to all orders of derivatives, but not necessarily equally or proportional to units. As such, restrictions on means and variances central to tests of strong and strict invariance require additional testing prior to use. However, weak factorial invariance only requires invariant factor loadings.

4 If these models are fit via maximum likelihood, model fit is determined by the product of all of the item likelihoods, or equivalently by the sum of all item log likelihoods.

References

Acito, F. & Anderson, R. D. (1986). A simulation study of factor score indeterminacy. *Journal of Marketing Research*, *23*(2), 111–118.

Ahn, S. C. & Horenstein, A. R. (2013). Eigenvalue Ratio Test for the number of factors. *Econometrica*, *81*(3), 1203–1227. Retrieved from http://onlinelibrary.wiley.com/doi/10.3982/ECTA8968/abstract

Baltes, P. B. & Nesselroade, J. R. (1979). History and rationale of longitudinal research. In J. R. Nesselroade & P. B. Baltes (Eds.), *Longitudinal research in the study of behavior and development* (pp. 1–39). New York: Academic Press.

Bock, R. D., Gibbons, R., & Muraki, E. (1988). Full-information item factor analysis. *Applied Psychological Measurement*, *12*(3), 261–280.

Boker, S. M. (2001). Differential structural modeling of intraindividual variability. In L. Collins and A. Sayer (Eds.), *New methods for the analysis of change* (pp. 3–28). Washington, DC: American Psychological Association.

Boker, S. M., Deboeck, P. R., Edler, C. & Keel, P. K. (2010). Generalized local linear approximation of derivatives from time series. In E. F. &. F. H. S.–M. Chow (Ed.), *Statistical methods for modeling human dynamics: An interdisciplinary dialogue* (pp. 161–178). New York: Taylor & Francis.

Boker, S. M. & Nesselroade, J. R. (2000). *Multilevel modeling of dynamical systems: Random coefficients and order parameters*. Cologne: International Sociological Association.

Boker, S. M. & Nesselroade, J. R. (2002). A method for modeling the intrinsic dynamics of intraindividual variability: {R}ecovering the parameters of simulated oscillators in multi–wave data. *Multivariate Behavioral Research*, *37*, 127–160.

Bradlow, E. T., Wainer, H., & Wang, X. (1999). A Bayesian random effects model for testlets. *Psychometrika*, *64*(2), 153–168.

Browne, M. W. (2001). An overview of analytic rotation in exploratory factor analysis. *Multivariate Behavioral Research*, *36*(1), 111–150. Retrieved from www.tandfonline.com/doi/abs/10.1207/S15327906MBR3601_05

Cai, L. (2010). A two-tier full-information item factor analysis model with applications. *Psychometrika*, *75*(4), 581–612.

Cattell, R. B. (1963). The interaction of hereditary and environmental influences. *The British Journal of Statistical Psychology*, *16*, 191–210.

Deboeck, P. R. (2010). Estimating dynamical systems: Derivative estimation hints from Sir Ronald A. Fisher. *Multivariate Behavioral Research*, *45*(4), 725–745.

Edwards, J. R. & Bagozzi, R. P. (2000). On the nature and direction of relationships between constructs and measures. *Psychological methods*, *5*(2), 155–74. Retrieved from www.ncbi.nlm.nih.gov/pubmed/10937327

Estabrook, R. (2015). Evaluating measurement of dynamic constructs: Defining a measurement model of derivatives. *Psychological Methods*, *20*(1), 117. Retrieved from www.ncbi.nlm.nih.gov/pubmed/24364383

Estabrook, R. & Neale, M. (2013). A comparison of factor score estimation methods in the presence of missing data: Reliability and an application to nicotine dependence. *Multivariate Behavioral Research*, *48*(1), 1–27. Retrieved from /pmc/articles/PMC3773873/?report=abstract

Estabrook, R., Sadler, M. E., & McGue, M. (2015). *Differential item functioning in the Cambridge Mental Disorders in the Elderly (CAMDEX) Depression Scale across middle age and late life*. *27*, 4. Washington, DC: American Psychological Association.

Geiser, C., Eid, M., Nussbeck, F. W., Courvoisier, D. S., & Cole, Q. A. (2010). Analyzing true change in longitudinal multitrait-multimethod studies: application of a multimethod change model to depression and anxiety in children. *Developmental Psychology, 46*(1), 29–45.

Gibbons, R. D. & Hedeker, D. R. (1992). Full-information item bi-factor analysis. *Psychometrika, 57*(3), 423–436.

Grice, J. W. (2001a). A comparison of factor scores under conditions of factor obiquity. *Psychological Methods, 6*(1), 67–83.

Grice, J. W. (2001b). Computing and evaluating factor scores. *Psychological Methods, 6*(4), 430–450.

Grimm, K. J., Pianta, R. C., & Konold, T. (2009). Longitudinal Multitrait-Multimethod Models for developmental research. *Multivariate Behavioral Research, 44*(2), 233–258.

Guttman, L. (1955). The determinacy of factor score matrices, with implications for five other basic problems of common-factor theory. *British Journal of Statistical Psychology, 8*, 65–81.

Hill, C. (2006a). *Two models for longitudinal item response data.* Unpublished doctoral dissertation, University of North Carolina.

Hill, C. (2006b). *Two models for Longitudinal Item Response Modeling.* Unpublished doctoral dissertation, University of North Carolina at Chapel Hill.

Jennrich, R. I. & Bentler, P. M. (2012). Exploratory Bi-factor Analysis: The oblique case. *Psychometrika, 77*(3), 442–454.

Kaiser, H. F. (1958). The varimax criterion for analytic rotation in factor analysis. *Psychometrika, 23*(3), 187–200.

Kaiser, H. F. (1960). The application of electronic computers to factor analysis. *Educational and Psychological Measurement, 20*(1), 141–151. Retrieved from http://journals.sagepub.com/doi/10.1177/001316446002000116

Kamata, A. & Bauer, D. J. (2008). A note on the relation between factor analytic and item response theory models. *Structural Equation Modeling, 15*(1), 136–153.

Klein, A. & Moosbrugger, H. (2000). Maximum likelihood estimation of latent interaction effects with the LMS method. *Psychometrika, 65*(4), 457–474.

Mansolf, M. & Reise, S. P. (2016). Exploratory Bifactor Analysis: The Schmid-Leiman Orthogonalization and Jennrich-Bentler Analytic Rotations. *Multivariate Behavioral Research, 51*(5), 698–717.

McArdle, J. J. (1988). Dynamic but structural equation modeling of repeated measures data. In J. R. Nesselroade & R. B. Cattell (Eds.), *The handbook of multivariate experimental psychology, Vol. 2* (pp. 561–614). New York: Plenum Press.

McArdle, J. J. (2007). Five steps in the structural factor analysis of longitudinal data. In S. H. Cohen & H. W. Reese (Eds.), *Factor analysis at 100: {H}istorical developments and future directionsistorical developments and future directions. mahwah, nj, us: Lawrence erlbaum associates publishers, xiii, 381 pp.* (pp. 99–130). Hillsdale, NJ: Lawrence Erlbaum Associates.

McArdle, J. J. & Nesselroade, J. R. (1994). Using multivariate data to structure developmental change. In S. H. Cohen and H. W. Reese (Eds.), *Life-span developmental psychology: {M}ethodological contributions* (pp. 223–267). Hillsdale, NJ: Lawrence Erlbaum Associates.

McDonald, R. P. (1967). Factor interaction in nonlinear factor analysis. *British Journal of Mathematical and Statistical Psychology, 20*(2), 205–215.

McDonald, R. P. (1985). *Factor analysis and related methods.* Hillsdale, NJ: Lawrence Ehrlbaum Associates.

McDonald, R. P. (2000). A basis for multidimensional item response theory. *Applied Psychological Measurement, 24*(2), 99–114.

Mehta, P. D., Neale, M. C., & Flay, B. R. (2004). Squeezing interval change from ordinal panel data: latent growth curves with ordinal outcomes. *Psychological Methods, 9*(3), 301–333.

Molenaar, P. C. M. (2004). A manifesto on psychology as idiographic science: Bringing the person back into scientific psychology – This time forever. *Measurement: Interdisciplinary Research and Perspectives, 2*, 201–218.

Muthén, B. (1984). A general structual equation model with dichotomous, ordered categorical and continuous latent variables indicators. *Psychometrika, 49*, 115–132.

Nesselroade, J. R. & Cable, D. G. (1974). "Sometimes it's okay to factor difference scores" – The separation of state and trait anxiety. *Multivariate Behavioral Research, 9*, 273–282.

Rabe-Hesketh, S., Skrondal, A., & Pickles, A. (2004). Generalized Multilevel Structural Equation Modeling. *PsychometriKa, 69*(2), 167–190.

Reckase, M. (2009). *Multidimensional Item Response Theory*. Retrieved from www.springerlink.com/index/10.1007/978-0-387-89976-3

Reise, S. P. (2012). The rediscovery of bifactor measurement models. *Multivariate behavioral research, 47*(5), 667–696. Retrieved from www.tandfonline.com/doi/abs/10.1080/00273171.2012.715555#.VaSREflVhBc

Rijmen, F. (2010). Formal relations and an empirical comparison among the bi-factor, the testlet, and a second-order multidimensional IRT model. *Journal of Educational Measurement, 47*(3), 361–372.

Tisak, J. & Meredith, W. (1989). Exploratory longitudinal factor analysis in multiple populations. *Psychometrika, 54*(2), 261–281.

Trail, J. B., Collins, L. M., Rivera, D. E., Li, R., Piper, M. E., & Baker, T. B. (2009). Functional data analysis for dynamical system identification of behavioral processes. *Psychological Methods, 27*(52), 175–187.

Tucker, L. R. (1971). Relations of Factor Score Estimates to their use. *Psychometrika, 4*(36), 427–435.

Widaman, K. F. & Reise, S. P. (1997). Exploring the measurement invariance of psychological instruments: Applications in the substance use domain. In K. J. Bryant, M. Windle, & S. G. West (Eds.), *The science of prevention: Methodological advances from alcohol and substance abuse research.* (pp. 281–324). Washington, DC: American Psychological Association.

Wilson, E. (1928). On heirarchical correlational systems. *Proceedings of the National Academy of Science, 14*, 283–291.

Yamamoto, M. & Jennrich, R. I. (2013). A cluster-based factor rotation. *British Journal of Mathematical and Statistical Psychology, 66*(3), 488–502.

Novel Applications of Multivariate Longitudinal Methodology

SECTION II

Novel Applications of
Multivariate Optimization
Methodology

12

THE ROLE OF INTERVAL MEASUREMENT IN DEVELOPMENTAL STUDIES

Ryan P. Bowles

Measurement is the way scientists assign "numerals to events or objects according to rule" to reflect some attribute, according to Stevens' (1959, p. 25) classic definition of measurement. Measurement is the essence underlying all quantitative analyses in the sciences; almost all statistical analyses are based on numerical data. Measurement is particularly important for understanding development using sophisticated longitudinal methods, many of which were developed in part by Jack McArdle, such as latent change score models (McArdle, 2001, 2009). In most scientific studies, successful measurement is assumed with minimal evidence: many empirical articles report only an estimate of reliability such as coefficient alpha as the sole psychometric property, and any additional evidence is one or more correlations with scores from other instruments. This lack of concern about measurement should be surprising because the validity of conclusions from quantitative analyses depends crucially on the success of the measurement process that leads to the numbers being analyzed. If the meaning of the measurement units changes as an individual develops, then no quantitative conclusions can be made; if an individual is 40 units tall at time 1, measured in inches, and 60 units tall at time 2, measured in centimeters, claiming the individual grew 20 units is meaningless (in fact, this individual actually shrunk 14 centimeters, so even the direction of change is invalid). Even worse is if the attribute being measured changes; if an individual is 5 units at time 1, measured in apples, and the 7 units at time 2, measured in oranges, then the change of 2 units is utterly meaningless. In this chapter, I will first describe what is meant by successful measurement and why it is particularly important for understanding development. I will then describe and critique three methods for establishing successful measurement. Finally, I will emphasize the need for pragmatism as well as progress in measurement in longitudinal studies, highlighting Jack McArdle's contributions on one of our coauthored articles (McArdle, Grimm, Hamagami, Bowles, & Meredith, 2009), and offer recommendations for further efforts on measurement in developmental studies.

Validity

At the heart of successful measurement is the concern of validity: do the assigned numbers measure what is intended to be measured (Borsboom, Mellenbergh, & van Heerden, 2004)? Concerns with validity have a long history in the social sciences (Newton & Shaw, 2014), and arguments about the nature of validity continue (Markus & Borsboom, 2013). There is general consensus that validity is not simply a yes or no question, but rather an accumulation of evidence (Kane, 1992, 2013). However, what constitutes evidence of validity is an ongoing area of discussion in psychometric literature. For example, there remains disagreement as to whether validity is exclusively about whether the assigned numbers – the scores – measure what is intended to be measured, or whether the interpretation and use of the scores are also relevant for validity (Bachman, 2005).

One critical concern for measurement that is rarely acknowledged is whether the assigned numbers work in the intended way. Measurement philosophers generally agree that most measurement in the social sciences is *representational* (see Hand, 1996; Markus & Borsboom, 2013, ch. 2; and Michel, 1990, ch. 1 for good discussions of the philosophical basis of measurement). Under representational measurement, objects of measurement (e.g., people) have attributes (e.g., depression, vocabulary knowledge), and measurement is assigning numbers to represent the attributes of interest to the scientist or other person interested in the measurement. In addition, the attributes have properties that are represented by relations among the numbers. For example, an attribute may have the property of equality: two individuals can have the same level of depression or vocabulary knowledge. In this case, equality will typically be represented by the number relation of equality: the two individuals should be assigned the same number. Similarly, the attribute may have the property of order: one individual can have *more* depression or vocabulary knowledge. To represent order, the individual with the higher level of the attribute should be assigned a higher number.

Perhaps the most important property for most developmental analyses is interval scaling (Michel, 1990). An attribute may have the property of intervals, which means that the differences between two individuals on the attribute can be described not just by direction (i.e., order), but also by amount. More formally, suppose there are two children, each of which has the attribute of height. Suppose the height of the first child is assigned the number A, and the height of the second child is assigned the number B. Suppose each child grows, yielding new heights A′ and B′. If a judgment can be made about whether the first child grew more than the second child, regardless of any differences in the initial height of the two children, then height has the property of intervals. If the numbers A, A′, B, and B′ are assigned so that the difference between A and A′

is correspondingly greater than the difference between the numbers assigned to B and B', then the property of intervals is represented by intervals or differences among the numbers assigned to the children. A process of assigning numbers that represents intervals is commonly called *interval scaling*. Interval scaling implies a stable measurement unit; that is, the meaning of a change of one unit remains the same for any level of the scale, regardless of the starting point. Put another way, a centimeter is a centimeter whether starting from something 1 meter tall or 100 meters tall.

Validity under representational measurement is therefore not simply if the assigned numbers measure what is intended to be measured; a validity argument must also address whether the properties of the assigned numbers represent the properties of the attributes. Note that this is a one directional process – formally called a homomorphism; all relevant properties of the attributes such as order or intervals must be represented by properties of the numbers, but the numbers having a certain property does imply that this property represents a property of the attribute. For example, a classic example is temperature measured in centigrade. An object with a temperature of 40°C does not have twice as much heat as an object with a temperature of 20°C even though the number 40 is twice as large as the number 20; the numbers can be expressed in terms of ratios, but this does not imply ratios of heat (cf. the Kelvin scale). However, the difference in heat between these two objects is the same as the differences in heat between two objects assigned the numbers 30 and 50; intervals of heat are represented by intervals of temperature in centigrade.

Importance of Interval Scaling

Nearly all commonly used statistical procedures assume or require interval scaling. Any descriptive or inferential statistic that involves addition or subtraction requires intervals with a stable unit, including means, variances, and covariances and any statistical method that uses these summary statistics. These methods include most forms of ANOVA, regression, multilevel modeling, and structural equation modeling. Any form of measurement invalidity in which the attribute's intervals are not successfully represented by number intervals will result in invalid conclusions from these statistical techniques.

However, not all methods are equally sensitive to violations of interval representation. In general, methods that describe the level of an individual's attribute with a single number will be relatively robust to typical levels of imperfect interval representation. Such methods include between-individual analyses such as independent samples t-tests and regressions. On the other hand, methods that describe individuals with differences or change can be quite sensitive, including methods such as dependent samples t-tests or longitudinal analyses.

Demonstration. To demonstrate the potential impact of invalidity associated with intervals, I ran a simulation based on the simple example shown in Figure 12.1,

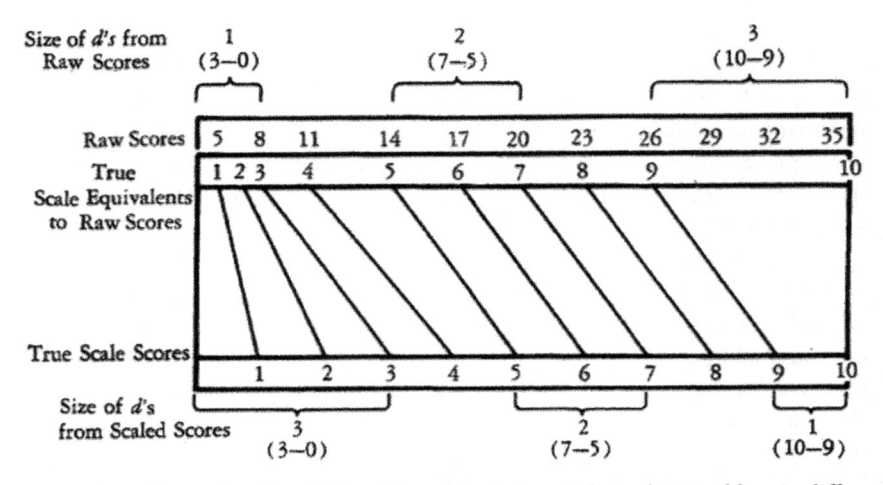

FIGURE 12.1 Example of invalidity of intervals. *Source*: "The scaling problem in difference scores contrasted with absolute single occasion scores", by R. B. Cattell, p. 366. Copyright 1966 by McNally.

taken from Cattell (1966). Along the bottom are "true scores", or the true level of an individual's attribute. Along the top are raw scores from an instrument intended to measure the attribute. In this hypothetical, the raw scores are the numbers assigned to the individuals and are intended to represent equality, order, and intervals in the attribute. However, while equality and order are successfully represented by the raw scores, intervals are imperfectly represented. The diagonal lines map the true scores to the observed scale scores. For example, a true score of 1 shows up as an observed score of 5 on the instrument, a true score of 4 as 11, and a true score of 9 as 26. Such a number assignment system can easily arise when a total score on an instrument is used, and the instruments has many difficult items but few easy items.

I simulated 10,000 individuals under this number assignment system to examine the impact of the invalidity. Each simulee was observed two times. At time 1, simulees were assigned a true score from 0 to 10, with each score equally likely. Simulees were then assigned an integer level of change from time 1 to time 2 ranging from 0 to 3, with each amount of change equally likely, and the change score was added to the time 1 score to yield the time 2 score. Simulated change scores that yielded a time 2 scores above 10 were constrained to yield a time 2 score of 10. I then calculated the observed score for each true score, as well as an observed change score equal to the difference between the time 2 and time 1 observed scores. Results indicated that this invalidity would have almost no impact on conclusions from statistical analyses based on only time 1 or time 2 scores. The correlation between the true score at time 1 and the observed score at time 1 was .99; for time 2, the correlation was .98. However, conclusions about change could be seriously compromised; the correlation between the true change and the observed change was only .52. Note that there is no measurement error in this system; all invalidity results from mistakes in the rule for number assignment and are not related to the well-known issues with difference score unreliability (Lord, 1956; Rogosa, Brandt, & Zimowski, 1982).

Methods for Valid Measurement

Given the need for valid measurement in order to make valid conclusions, particularly in developmental studies, it is necessary to identify methods that allow for strong arguments of representational measurement, especially interval measurement. Methods for arguing that the assigned numbers measure what they are supposed to measure are well-established. These methods include procedures for ensuring the appropriate content of an instrument through test blueprints, expert review, and other methods described in the AERA/APA/NCME standards (2014). The scores can also be compared to scores from other instruments using multitrait-multimethod analyses, structural equation modeling, or factor analyses, collectively called methods for examining nomothetic span (Embretson, 1983).

Methods for arguing that the assigned numbers measure the attribute in the intended way, that is, representation of the properties of the attribute, are less well-established. In this section, I briefly review three relatively well-known approaches, highlighting some advantages and challenges: mechanistic modeling, latent variable modeling, and Rasch measurement. It is important to note from the first, however, that none of these approaches offers a particularly satisfying general approach, but may offer some incomplete evidence of interval measurement.

Mechanistic Modeling

Mechanistic modeling is predicated on the standard theory-to-model approach most common in statistical analysis, particularly in fields like cognitive psychology that aim to describe mechanisms or processes that lead to observed outcomes. In this paradigm, a researcher considers a theory that focuses on how one or more independent variables *cause* one or more dependent variables. For example, attachment theory posits that a mother's withdrawing behaviors will cause a child's pattern of attachment, which will then cause differences in later outcomes such as referrals to clinical psychologists (Lyons-Ruth, Bureau, Easterbrooks, Obsuth, Hennighausen, & Vulliez-Coady, 2013). To more fully specific the theory, the researcher then identifies how the variables in the theory are related through some statistical model. The statistical model is applied to data from a sample to make inferences about the validity of the theory in light of the statistical results.

In the measurement context, mechanistic modeling involves developing a theory for how the object of measurement, typically a person, interacts with an item from a measurement instrument to yield an observable item response. Typically, the person is described by one or more latent traits, and measurement of the latent trait(s) is the goal of the measurement process. Likewise, the items are described by one or more latent variables defining properties of the items. Finally, a causal statistical model is hypothesized linking the person traits with the item properties to yield a probabilitistic distribution of expected item responses. For example, a researcher may hypothesize that individuals with greater math skills will be more likely to respond correctly to a math problem; math skills cause responses to math problems. Here, the latent trait being measured is math skills. This theory, however, is underspecified. The theory does not state how differences among the math problems can affect the responses, for example, through differences in item difficulty. Furthermore, the theory does not include any specific statistical model about *how* differences in math skills will affect the probability of a correct response. It is possible that higher math skills will always lead to (monotonic) increases in the likelihood of a correct response, or there could be stages of math skills, so that the likelihood of a correct response stays the same, unless the child moves to the next stage.

In mechanistic modeling, the latent traits associated with the person are typically assumed to have the property of intervals, and fit of the model is treated as support for this assumption, allowing for developmental analyses that require interval measurement like McArdle's latent change score models. However, there are well-known problems with fit as evidence of the correctness of a theory, such as long-standing concerns with the appropriateness of standard cutoffs for fit statistics to conclude that the fit is "good enough" (e.g., Fan & Sivo, 2005, 2007; Hu & Bentler, 1999; Yuan, 2005). Furthermore, statistical models reflecting very different mechanistic theories can nonetheless have equivalent fit to any data (Hershberger, 2006), so that inferring the validity of the mechanistic theory from model fit is not automatic. Finally, concluding that an assumption of interval measurement is justified because of model fit requires a long series of logical statements: fit of the data to the model implies the model is approximately correct, which implies the theory is approximately correct, which implies the assumptions of the theory including interval measurement are correct. This distance between the assumption of interval measurement and the evidence of model fit should lead researchers to have no more than weak confidence in support of the assumption.

In practice, the mechanistic modeling approach is even weaker. There are few theories that provide strong theoretical mechanisms about how persons interact with items to yield item responses. Some work on individual differences in the item response mechanism has been done, particularly in the cognitive components literature of the 1980s (e.g., Embretson & Wetzel, 1987; Mulholland, Pellegrino, & Glaser, 1980). Furthermore, some statistical models have been developed to understand the mechanisms (Bockenholt, 2017; Fischer, 1973). However, neither of these research directions have had a major impact on the development of strong psychological theories of the response interaction. Rather, most measurement analyses use popular statistical models without any claim of an underlying causal theory.

Latent Variable Modeling

The latent variable modeling approach to measurement applies an existing statistical model to parsimoniously describe patterns of relations amongst item responses, and includes techniques such as item factor analysis (IFA; Wirth & Edwards, 2007), structural equation modeling (SEM) with categorical outcomes, and item response theory (IRT). Almost all of these models include at least one latent factor associated with the object of measurement to explain the pattern of relations, and often the latent factor based on the statistical model is interpreted as representing a "real" attribute of the object of measurement. In contrast to mechanistic modeling, latent variable modeling starts from the premise of using existing useful models to analyze the data, and fit of the model offers support for the existence of the latent trait but no claim of a causal mechanism for the item responses themselves.

The link between results from latent variable modeling and interval measurement is tenuous at best. Although the models typically include a latent factor with assumed interval measurement, there is no direct test of this assumption, and if fit is examined, the data–model fit is considered holistically and not at the level of individual item responses. For example, typical practice in IFA is to focus on the number of latent dimensions, with limited concern on overall fit of the model and no concern for fit of the model for individual items. In practice, many applications of latent variable modeling do not consider fit at all. Most uses of IRT models involve applying the model with no consideration of whether the model adequately described the data, although such fit statistics are available (Orlando & Thissen, 2000, 2003). Thus, any conclusion about interval measurement with latent variable modeling is generally based on weak or limited evidence, and sometimes no evidence at all. For that reason, the term measurement is often inappropriate with latent variable modeling; for example, some psychometricians refer to IRT as a scaling method rather than a measurement approach.

Rasch Measurement

Rasch measurement offers the strongest justification for a claim of interval measurement, but also has the most limited usefulness. The basic Rasch model (Rasch, 1960/1980) for a single latent trait with dichotomous outcomes is a probabilistic version of additive conjoint measurement (Perline, Wright, & Wainer, 1979), which is a form of axiomatic measurement in which interval measurement can be inferred if certain properties of the item responses are met (Luce & Tukey, 1964). Thus, perfect fit to a Rasch model is strong evidence of interval measurement (although see Karabatsos, 2001). Perfect fit is impossible, of course, so standard practice is to examine a series of fit statistics to determine if the fit is good enough. Guidelines for acceptable fit are available and commonly used (Wright & Linacre, 1994), but there are strong arguments for more stringent criteria and alternative fit statistics (Glas & Verhelst, 1995; Smith & Suh, 2003). Furthermore, standard Rasch fit statistics do not directly test the properties necessary for additive conjoint measurement; more direct tests exist but are rarely implemented (Domingue, 2014).

The link between additive conjoint measurement and extensions of the Rasch model such as the Partial Credit Model (Masters, 1982) or multidimensional Rasch model (Adams, Wilson, & Wang, 1997) is less clear. As Georg Rasch identified in his seminal work developing the Rasch model (Rasch, 1960/1980; Rost, 2001), the fundamental property of models in the Rasch family is specific objectivity: objects of measurement can be compared independently of the particular items used to assess them. Specific objectivity is related to, but not equivalent to, additive conjoint measurement (Fischer, 1995). Thus, fit to extensions of the Rasch model offers some support for interval measurement, but in the absence of more direct psychometric research on the relation between additive conjoint measurement and specific extensions of the Rasch model, the support can only be considered indirect and incomplete.

Need for Pragmatism

The requirement of interval measurement and sensitivity to violations should lead developmental researchers to give greater attention to measurement in order to reach valid conclusions from developmental studies. The lack of strong methods for justifying a claim of interval measurement may lead researchers to conclude that good developmental research is virtually impossible. I do not hold that view, but instead call for improvements in measurement methods and developmental research methodology. In a developmental study, perhaps strong justification of intervals is not feasible, but acknowledgement of the challenges and pragmatic approaches to dealing with them can lead to *more* valid conclusions, if still with caveats. Researchers and peer reviewers should not lose the good to achieve the perfect.

To demonstrate measurement pragmatism in a remarkable longitudinal study, I present the approach taken by Jack McArdle and colleagues (including me) to examine the development of vocabulary knowledge across nearly the entire lifespan (McArdle et al., 2009). The data were combined from three classic studies on intellectual abilities started in the late 1920s and early 1930s and continued through the 1990s; 419 individuals participated in up to 16 waves of data collection starting as early as age 2 and continuing as late as age 72. The particular assessments used changed regularly throughout the studies as intellectual abilities batteries were revised, such as from the original Wechsler Adult Intelligence Scale (WAIS; Wechsler, 1955) to the revised version (WAIS-R; Wechsler, 1981), or because more theoretically and psychometrically justified batteries were developed, such as the Woodcock-Johnson-Revised (WJ-R; Woodcock & Johnson, 1989).

Using the vocabulary scores from each test battery would certainly not have met the requirement of interval measurement, since each is on a separate scale. Understanding the development of vocabulary knowledge therefore required careful attention to how every item response reflected an individual's vocabulary knowledge at any age. We used common–item and common–person linking at the item response level to attempt to put all individuals at all time points on a common scale with the same origin or zero-point and the same unit; that is, to achieve interval measurement. Common–item linking occurred because the same item was used on multiple versions of the same test battery; for example, 33 vocabulary items are common to both the WAIS and the WAIS-R. Common-person linking occurred because the same person took multiple test batteries at the same measurement occasion; for example, the WAIS and the WJ-R were both administered at two occasions in one of the constituent longitudinal studies. Still, one test battery, the Wechsler-Bellevue (Wechsler, 1941), could not be linked with the others because its items were unique and it was never administered with another battery. We dealt with this issue without losing valuable data by including items from the Information subscales of the Wechsler-Bellevue, WAIS, and WAIS-R, which had substantial common-item overlap, and the Information and Vocabulary subscales tend to be highly correlated ($r > .8$). As some of the items were scored right/wrong and others were scored on a 3-point partial credit rating scale, the item responses were analyzed using a hybrid Rasch/Partial Credit Model to yield estimated levels of the latent trait of vocabulary knowledge at every age. The resulting spaghetti plot is in Figure 12.2.

Although we used Rasch modeling, the sparse data matrix made examination of fit infeasible. Our approach was closer to latent variable modeling with no consideration of fit, and therefore it is difficult to justify a claim of interval measurement. It is important, however, to recognize that longitudinal curves spanning 70 years of age are likely unique in psychological research, so the results of this study are potentially of major consequence for understanding development. Instead of rejecting the results because of concerns with interval measurement, the challenges should be acknowledged and suggestions for improvement raised and addressed. For example, McArdle et al. (2009) noted that there was no way to test whether the way vocabulary knowledge was measured changed over the long time period of the study or over the lifespan (i.e., metric factorial invariance); it is possible that some vocabulary words became easier over time (e.g., an item asking for the definition of computer) or more difficult (e.g., an item asking for

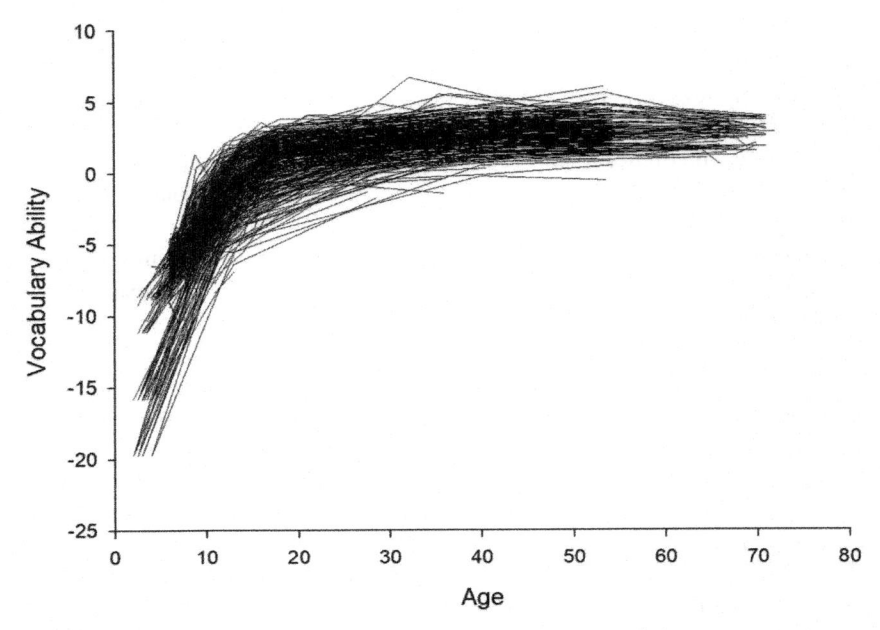

FIGURE 12.2 Individual longitudinal plots of vocabulary knowledge.

Source: Adapted from "Modeling life-span growth curves of cognition using longitudinal data with multiple samples and changing scales of measurement," by J. J. McArdle, K. J. Grimm, F. Hamagami, R. P. Bowles, & W. Meredith, 2009, p. 137. Copyright 2009 by the American Psychological Association.

identification of a picture of a buggy whip). The authors also made several suggestions for the design of future longitudinal research studies that could both yield improved conclusions and capitalize on methods employed in the study.

Recommendations

As a conclusion to this chapter, I offer several recommendations for measurement in developmental studies. Perhaps the most important is that researchers should pay close attention to issues of measurement *before* a longitudinal study begins. Longitudinal studies require a huge investment of time and resources to complete successfully, so an initial investment in examining measurement with proposed instruments will lead to large returns in the validity of conclusions. For example, consideration of item overlap before data collection would have prevented McArdle et al.'s (2009) need for the ad hoc solution of including the Information items. Likewise, careful selection of assessment instruments is needed before the start of a longitudinal study. Some instruments already have strong evidence of interval measurement, such as the WJ-R and its more recent revisions, which used a Rasch measurement approach. Using Woodcock-Johnson tests rather than instruments with poorly understood or unestablished psychometric properties would lead to more valid conclusions from developmental studies.

Once data is collected, offering multiple sources of evidence for an assumption of interval measurement is critical, even if no particular source offers strong evidence (Kane, 1992). Although item factor analysis, for example, offers limited support for interval measurement, establishing the factor structure of a measurement instrument is a necessary precursor step; after all, if the attribute being measured does not exist, then interval measurement is meaningless. As another example, polytomous Rasch models have the property of specific objectivity, which is related to but not equivalent to additive conjoint measurement. Fit to a polytomous Rasch model offers evidence of interval measurement, but more indirectly than dichotomous models. Analyzing item responses with both item factor analysis and polytomous Rasch models can offer two important but incomplete sources of evidence of interval measurement, so both analyses together offer more accumulating evidence of validity than either alone.

Another possible source of evidence of interval measurement may come from collateral information outside the main measurement data. Such collateral information could be within the study, as with the Information items, which allowed all vocabulary items to be put on a common scale. The collateral information could also be from other studies, such as studies that examine the same instruments. For example, Bowles and Salthouse (2008) examined multiple vocabulary assessments, including some used in McArdle et al. (2009) and identified differences in relations between age and scores on the assessment. This finding would suggest that treating all vocabulary items as equally representative of the latent trait of vocabulary knowledge is incorrect, and an adjustment to the Rasch analysis in McArdle et al. may be needed, such as including residual relations among items with the same format. Another option for collateral information is conducting targeted research studies that address the extent to which an instrument yields interval measurement. For example, McArdle et al. could have conducted a study after the main data collection was completed, in which individuals responded to vocabulary items from both the Wechsler-Bellevue and other test batteries in order to make the missing link. Such a study would have required assumptions about the stability of item functioning over time, but could at the least have potentially offered converging evidence with the results.

Finally, I offer some recommendations to the field of measurement. First, latent variable modeling offers the weakest evidence for interval measurement, so this approach should be avoided. The blind application of popular models without consideration of how measurement can be justified is much too common. Second, Rasch modeling offers strong evidence of interval measurement, but this evidence is only available in full when there is one latent trait and dichotomous item responses. Other forms of Rasch modeling, such as models for polytomous item responses or multidimensionality, offer evidence of interval measurement, but the evidence is less direct because of a more tenuous relation to additive conjoint measurement. Thus, further development of the field is needed to establish under what conditions additive conjoint measurement also applies to multidimensionality and polytomous item responses. Additionally, more research on fit statistics is needed to establish how departures from perfect fit are associated with departures from additive conjoint measurement.

Mechanistic modeling seems to be the most fruitful direction for further methodological innovations, as it is a general approach appropriate for many measurement situations. Mechanistic modeling is a standard theory-to-model approach, so there are well-established methods: families of models with well-known behavior (e.g., factor analysis with categorical outcomes) and extensive research on model-theory evaluation (e.g., the behavior of fit indices). What is lacking is strong psychological theories of the response interaction that can be tested against item response data to justify a claim of interval measurement. Thus, I encourage further development of such theories, as well as models that reflect those theories. Developmental researchers should not limit their theories to the level of latent traits, but instead consider the level of item responses, the most fine-grained observable variables in most research studies. This approach has the potential to yield more valid conclusions from developmental studies.

References

Adams, R. J., Wilson, M., & Wang, W. (1997). The multidimensional random coefficients multinomial logit model. *Applied Psychological Measurement, 21,* 1–23.

American Educational Research Association, American Psychological Association, and National Council on Measurement in Education, and Joint Committee on Standards for Educational and Psychological Testing (2014). *Standards for educational and psychological testing.* Washington, DC: AERA.

Bachman, L. F. (2005). Building and supporting a case for test use. *Language Assessment Quarterly, 2,* 1–34.

Bockenholt, U. (2017). Measuring response styles in Likert items. *Psychological Methods, 22,* 69–83.

Borsboom, D., Mellenbergh, G. J., & van Heerden, J. (2004). The concept of validity. *Psychological Review, 111,* 1061–1071.

Bowles, R. P. & Salthouse, T. A. (2008). Vocabulary test format and differential relations to age. *Psychology and Aging, 23,* 366–376.

Cattell, R. B. (1966). Pattern of change: Measurement in relation to state-dimension, trait change, lability, and process concepts. In R. B. Cattell (Ed.), *Handbook of multivariate experimental psychology* (pp. 355–402). Chicago: Rand McNally.

Domingue, B. W. (2014). Evaluating the equal-interval hypothesis with test score scales. *Psychometrika, 79,* 1–19.

Embretson, S. E. (1983). Construct validity: Construct representation versus nomothetic span. *Psychological Bulletin, 93,* 179–197.

Embretson, S. & Wetzel, C. D. (1987). Component latent trait models for paragraph comprehension tests. *Applied Psychological Measurement, 11,* 175–193.

Fan, X. & Sivo, S. A. (2005). Sensitivity of fit indexes to misspecified structural or measurement model components: Rationale of two-index strategy revisited. *Structural Equation Modeling: A Multidisciplinary Journal, 12*, 343–367.

Fan, X. & Sivo, S. A. (2007). Sensitivity of fit indices to model misspecification and model types. *Multivariate Behavioral Research, 42*, 509–529.

Fischer, G. H. (1973). The linear logistic test model as an instrument in educational research. *Acta Psychologica, 37*, 359–374.

Fischer, G. H. (1995). Derivations of the Rasch model. In G. H. Fischer & I. W. Molenaar (Eds.), *Rasch models: Foundations, recent developments, and applications* (pp. 15–38). New York: Springer.

Glas, C. A. W. & Verhelst, N. D. (1995). Testing the Rasch model. In G. H. Fischer & I. W. Molenaar (Eds.), *Rasch models: Foundations, recent developments, and applications* (pp. 67–95). New York: Springer.

Hand, D. J. (1996). Statistics and the theory of measurement. *Journal of the Royal Statistical Society, Series A, 159*, 445–492.

Hershberger, S. L. (2006). The problem of equivalent structural models. In G. R. Hancock & R. O. Mueller (Eds.), *Structural equation modeling: A second course* (pp. 13–41). Greenwich, CT: Information Age.

Hu., L. & Bentler, P. M. (1999). Cutoff criteria for fit indexes in covariance structure analysis: Conventional criteria versus new alternatives. *Structural Equation Modeling, 6*, 1–55.

Kane, M. T. (1992). An argument-based approach to validation. *Psychological Bulletin, 112*, 527–535.

Kane, M. T. (2013). Validating the interpretations and uses of test scores. *Journal of Educational Measurement, 50*, 1–73.

Karabatsos, G. (2001). The Rasch model, additive conjoint measurement, and new models of probabilistic measurement theory. *Journal of Applied Measurement, 2*, 389–423.

Lord, F. M. (1956). The measurement of growth. *Educational and Psychological Measurement, 16*, 421–437.

Luce, R. D. & Tukey, J. W. (1964). Simultaneous conjoint measurement: A new scale type of fundamental measurement. *Journal of Mathematical Psychology, 1*, 1–27.

Lyons-Ruth, K., Bureau, J.-F., Easterbrooks, M. A., Obsuth, I., Hennighausen, K., & Vulliez-Coady, L. (2013). Parsing the construct of maternal insensitivity: Distinct longitudinal pathways associated with early maternal withdrawal. *Attachment and Human Development, 15*, 562–582.

Markus, K. A. & Borsboom, D. (2013). Frontiers of test validity theory: Measurement, causation, and meaning. New York, NY: Routledge.

Masters, G. N. (1982). A Rasch model for partial credit scoring. *Psychometrika, 47*, 149–174.

McArdle, J. J. (2001). A latent difference score approach to longitudinal dynamic structural analyses. In R. Cudeck, S. duToit, & D. Sorbom (Eds.), *Structural equation modeling: Present and future* (pp. 342–380). Lincolnwood, IL: Scientific Software International.

McArdle, J. J. (2009). Latent variable modeling of differences and changes with longitudinal data. *Annual Review of Psychology, 60*, 577–605.

McArdle, J. J., Grimm, K. J., Hamagami, F., Bowles, R. P., & Meredith, W. (2009). Modeling life-span growth curves of cognition using longitudinal data with multiple samples and changing scales of measurement. *Psychological Methods, 14*, 126–149.

Michel, J. (1990). *An introduction to the logic of psychological measurement.* Hillsdale, NJ: Erlbaum.

Mulholland, T. M., Pellegrino, J. W., & Glaser, R. (1980). Components of geometric analogy solution. *Cognitive Psychology, 12,* 252–284.

Newton, P. E., and Shaw, S. D. (2014). *Validity in educational and psychological assessment.* Washington, DC: Sage.

Orlando, M. & Thissen, D. (2000). New item fit indices for dichotomous item response theory models. *Applied Psychological Measurement, 24,* 50–64.

Orlando, M. & Thissen, D. (2003). Further investigation of the performance of S-χ^2: An item fit index for use with dichotomous item response theory models. *Applied Psychological Measurement, 27,* 289–298.

Perline, R., Wright, B. D., & Wainer, H. (1979). The Rasch model as additive conjoint measurement. *Applied Psychological Measurement, 3,* 237–255.

Rasch, G. (1980). *Probabilistic models for some intelligence and attainments tests (Expanded edition).* Chicago: University of Chicago Press. (Original work published 1960).

Rogosa, D. R., Brandt, D., & Zimowski, M. (1982). A growth curve approach to the measurement of change. *Psychological Bulletin, 90,* 726–748.

Rost, J. (2001). The growing family of Rasch models. In A. Boomsma, M. A. J. van Duijn, & T. A. B. Snijders (Eds.), *Essays on Item Response Theory* (pp. 25–42). New York: Springer.

Smith, R. M. & Suh, K. K. (2003). Rasch fit statistics as a test of the invariance of item parameter estimates. *Journal of Applied Measurement, 4,* 153–163.

Stevens, S. S. (1959). Measurement, psychophysics and utility. In C. W. Churchman & P. Ratoosh (Eds.), *Measurement: Definitions and theories* (pp. 18–63). New York: Wiley.

Wechsler, D. (1941). *The measurement of adult intelligence* (2nd ed.). Baltimore: Williams & Wilkins.

Wechsler, D. (1955). *Manual for the Wechsler Adult Intelligence Scale.* New York: Psychological Corporation.

Wechsler, D. (1981). *WAIS-R: Wechsler Adult Intelligence Scale Revised.* New York: Harcourt Brace Jovanovich.

Wirth, R. J. & Edwards, M. C. (2007). Item factor analysis: Current approaches and future directions. *Psychological Methods, 12,* 58–79.

Woodcock, R. W. & Johnson, M. B. (1989). *Woodcock–Johnson Psycho-Educational Battery—Revised.* Allen, TX: DLM Teaching Resources.

Wright, B. D. & Linacre, J. M. (1994). Reasonable mean-square fit values. *Rasch Measurement Transactions, 8,* 370.

Yuan, K. (2005). Fit indices versus test statistics. *Multivariate Behavioral Research, 40*(1), 115–148.

13

GROWTH MODELING USING THE DIFFERENTIAL FORM[1]

Translations from Study of Fish Growth

Nilam Ram & Xiao Yang

Growth Modeling using the Differential Form: Translations from Study of Fish Growth

Theories of development all promote the idea that human functioning proceeds simultaneously on multiple levels (e.g., cells to society) and time-scales (e.g., seconds to decades). Meta-theoretical frameworks (Baltes, Lindenberger, & Staudinger, 2006; Bronfenbrenner & Morris, 2006; Ford & Lerner, 1992; Gottlieb, 2007, Overton & Lerner, 2012) highlight the importance of understanding how, when, and why individuals change (see also Li, 2003). Domain specific theories too suggest how, when, and why particular attributes, abilities, and characteristics change with time and/or age and in relation to specific biological, psychological, social, and environmental factors. To deal with the complexities involved in studying developmental processes, methodologists have advanced a wide variety of longitudinal methods for accurately charting how individuals and, more generally, "entities" (since we will be looking at models of fish growth) change across time. Innovations in longitudinal study design continually push forward researchers' ability to discover and explain *intraindividual change* processes and the *interindividual differences* therein (see McArdle & Nesselroade, 2014).

Cohort sequential, longitudinal panel, and accelerated longitudinal studies – wherein multiple reports are obtained from multiple individuals at regular intervals – have enhanced our capability to describe and test hypotheses about within-person change (Hertzog & Nesselroade, 2003; McArdle & Anderson, 1990; McArdle & Bell, 2000). Data from these types of studies are typically analyzed using some variant of *growth modeling* (McArdle & Nesselroade, 2003). Certainly, and in large part following McArdle's innovations, growth modeling has emerged as the primary method for examination of developmental processes. McArdle's extensions for modeling of multivariate change and latent change (differences or differentials) are at the forefront of current possibility. Celebrating Jack McArdle's continual push for better and more robust models, we use this opportunity to explore recent and classic ecological literature on growth modeling and develop some nascent ideas about how the models in use there may be applied in study of human development. In the sections that follow, we review the benefits of considering growth models as *change process models* and explore the mathematical and theoretical connections between growth models used in ecology for study of fish growth and models of development in humans. We finish the chapter with some notes on implementation and some suggestions for what the future may bring.

Reformulating Growth Models in the Differential Form

In the past few years we have attempted to organize our work on growth modeling with respect to the goals of longitudinal research, issues surrounding practical implementation in both SEM and MLM frameworks dealing with nonlinearity (both with respect to time and to the model parameters and random coefficients), and how various models are used to examine qualitative and quantitative interindividual differences and intraindividual changes in features of growth trajectories (e.g., growth mixture and/or age-conditioned growth models). Along the way we are continually wrestling with how growth models and, more generally, longitudinal models provide an interface for reconciling theory and data. McArdle pushed us to consider the theoretical model of change – and, in particular, forwarded the latent change score framework that allows for more precise articulation of theory and representation of longitudinal data. Our current exploration follows hints we found on an *n*th reading of McArdle's classic chapter in the *Handbook of Multivariate Experimental Psychology* (McArdle, 1988).

In brief, growth models are used to describe individuals' longitudinal trajectories and the between-person differences in those trajectories. Specific mathematical functions (e.g., linear, quadratic, exponential, sigmoid, sinusoidal) are used to describe the observed *output* of a latent change process. For example, the linear growth model describes the observed outputs, y_{it}, as a linear function of time,

$$y_{it} = \beta_{0i} + \beta_{1i}(time_{it}) + r_{it} \tag{13.1}$$

where β_{0i} is a person-specific *intercept* (predicted value of y) located at $time = 0$, β_{1i} is a person-specific *slope* that is interpreted as the rate of linear change in y for a one unit change in *time*, and r_{it} are time-specific residuals. Pushing for more explicit rendering of the *change process* that is producing the observed output, McArdle and Hamagami (2001) presented a formulation of the standard latent growth model that is based on successive changes. In general form, this (univariate) *change score model* can be written as

$$y_{it} = [\beta_{0i}] + \left(\sum\nolimits_{t=2}^{t} \Delta y_{it}\right) + r_{it} \tag{13.2}$$

where individual i's score at occasion t, y_{it}, is the sum of an initial score, β_{0i} (interpreted as an intercept or baseline score) and all of the subsequent changes that have accrued up to that time (sum of Δy_{it} from $t = 2$ to t). This (re-)rendering of the basic growth model makes the underlying change process explicit. Specifically, we see that, to obtain equivalence between Equations 13.1 and 13.2 (i.e., the standard linear growth model and the latent change rendition of the model), the model for all the successive changes must be

$$\frac{\Delta y_i}{\Delta t} = \beta_{1i} \qquad (13.3)$$

where β_{1i} is a person-specific rate of change. This *difference equation*, then, is an explicit rendering of the change process underlying the linear growth model – and serves as the *theory of change* that can be tested against repeated measures data.

Portending the presentation of models for fish growth that will come later, we highlight that the contrast McArdle makes between the models used to describe *outputs* (traditional regression-based model for y_{it}) and models used to describe the *change process* (difference equation model for Δy_{it}) has also emerged in recent discussions of fish growth (Enberg, Jørgensen, Dunlop, Varpe, Boukal, Baulie, Eliassen, & Heino, 2012). In particular, a contrast is made between fish *size*, which characterizes an individual's state, and fish *growth*, which is a process that leads to that state. Models of the growth process are formulated as difference or differential equations and derived from bioenergetic and behavioral principles, and the models of size measurements (e.g., length, weight, mass) are integral solutions of those change process equations.

When presenting the change score models, McArdle and colleagues have mostly been working with repeated measures data with between 2 and 20 measurement occasions obtained at monthly, yearly, or longer intervals – data from longitudinal panel studies. Representations of the *time* variable in these applications are usually *discrete*, in that the number of measurements is conceived as finite. The discrete representation of time has been particularly useful in SEM implementations, where the measurements for a given time period can be invoked as a unique factor loading and/or variable. Outside the SEM framework, representations of the time variable are often continuous (e.g., chronological age), in that the number of (potential) measurements is conceived as infinite. Continuous representations of time have been particularly useful, because they explicitly invoke notions of organismic continuity that sit at the core of many developmental and process-oriented theories. Although mostly a semantic nuance in practice, continuous time models support straightforward description of changes over spans of time while discrete time models support description of changes between moments in time (see Ram & Reeves, 2018). In practice, growth modelers are fluidly moving between discrete and continuous time with ease – invoking discrete or continuous interpretations of the time variables wherever convenient. For example, the change process described by Equation 13.3, which is a discrete time *difference equation* where the time variable spans a sequence of integer values, $t = 1, 2, 3, \ldots T$, is easily rewritten as a continuous time *differential equation* where the time variable spans the entire real number line (see e.g., Boker, 2001),

$$\frac{dy}{dt} = \beta_{1i} \tag{13.4}$$

Once made explicit as a difference or differential equation, the simplicity of this particular theory of change is clear. We see clearly that the linear growth model implies that the intraindividual change processes can be entirely described by a single number, β_{1i}, that does not vary over time, is not related to where an individual is in the change process (e.g., level of y_{it}), and is not related to any aspect of context. As such, the linear growth model seems at odds with key tenets of most developmental theories. The re-rendering of the model as a difference or differential equation makes this explicit – and thus brings us closer to the actual phenomena of interest: *change processes* (see McArdle, 1988, 2009).

More generally, the explicit descriptions of the underlying change process afforded by difference and differential equations prompt consideration and testing of more precise, appropriate, and complex hypotheses about behavioral change. Most theories of human behavior suggest that people are dynamic, and that the change processes that drive their development are probably not constant. A few simple extensions can illustrate how working directly with the differential equation models facilitates articulation and construction of more complex and realistic theories of change. For example, we may theorize that there is endogenous dependence in the growth process. That is, the progression of the process depends on the level of output or ability already achieved,

$$\frac{dy}{dt} = ky_t \tag{13.5}$$

Also, we can incorporate the idea that growth is bounded by endogenous or exogenous constraints. Incorporating an upper bound or *carrying capacity*, Y_∞, into Equation 13.5, we get the change process model that will be the focus of our discussion through the rest of the chapter,

$$\frac{dy}{dt} = k\left(Y_\infty - y_t\right). \tag{13.6}$$

This model indicates that the closer y_t is to the carrying capacity, the smaller the rate of change. The general idea is that translating theoretical propositions into differential equations is much more straightforward than working directly with the analytical equations that are actually fit to the data. The "lingua-franca" of differential equations provides for straightforward articulation of knowledge about change processes, highlights the potential inadequacy of currently popular models (e.g., linear growth), and opens up a wide range of possibilities for articulating the complexities of behavioral change.

Translating Models from Ecology to Developmental Science

A wide variety of growth models are being used to study change processes in many fields, including agronomy, biology, chemistry, ecology, economics, engineering, forestry, ichthyology, medicine, psychology, sociology, and zoology. Indeed, general books on growth modeling are filled with long lists of potential models – differential equations that describe many types of change processes. For instance, Panik (2014) lists 20 or so "mainstream" models for change (linear, logistic, Gompertz, Weibull, von Bertalanffy, Chapman-Richards, Janoshek, Morgan-Mercer-Flodin, etc.). As far as we know, only a handful of these models have made their way into the developmental and psychological literature (see reviews in Preacher & Hancock, 2015; Wood, Steinley, & Jackson, 2015). Our overall view is that uptake might be hastened when these models are recast in ways that facilitate mapping to theoretical models of change. McArdle (1988) has long suggested that this is where the *differential equation* formulations can be quite useful.

In our exploration of how differential equation models are used to examine change, we noted (as others have) that naturally occurring processes that underlie many self-organizing phenomena, including pattern formation and self-regulation, may be described using relatively simple *activator+inhibitor* models (Ram, Gatzke-Kopp, Gerstorf, Coccia, Morack, & Molenaar, 2015). In brief, these two-component systems consist of an activator that stimulates its own production as well as the production of the inhibitor, which in turn represses production of the activator (e.g., Geier & Meinhardt, 1972). The utility of the models is particularly evident in systems biology, where similar two-component "competing processes" models afford description of a wide variety of qualitative and quantitative interindividual differences in change processes (Murray, 2003; Turing, 1952). In our search for recent innovations in growth modeling, we delved into the ecology literature and found work (see special issue of *Fisheries Research* on growth; Maunder, Crone, Punt, Valero, & Semmens, 2016) that, when consumed alongside McArdle's (1988) treatise, inspired us to consider further how models used in biology may be useful in our study of human development and behavioral change. Here, we draw on a model that is at the core of many fishery applications – the von Bertalanffy (1956) model. Similar to the *activator+inhibitor* model, this *anabolism–catabolism* model also affords theoretical and empirical description of a wide variety of qualitative and quantitative interindividual differences in intraindividual change.

In the sections that follow, we approach the model in three ways. First, we present the familiar integrated mathematical form used to describe observed repeated measures data – traditional regression-based model of *outputs* (i.e., size). Plots of prototypical trajectories illustrate how the parameters of the model map to specific features of the growth trajectory. Second, we outline how theoretical propositions about the processes driving intraindividual change are formalized in the differential form – differential equation model of the *change process*. Simulations are used to illustrate the flexibility in development afforded by the anabolism–catabolism "competing processes" model. Finally, we highlight some of the ways the von Bertalanffy growth model is being adapted and extended to accommodate plasticity in growth, interindividual (or interspecies) differences and the role specific biological and environmental factors play in growth. In doing so we attempt to discern how innovations forwarded in study of fisheries (and other animal and plant populations) may be applied in the study of human development.

A von Bertalanffy Growth Model for Fish Growth: The Integral Form

The von Bertalanffy growth function is widely used in study and management of fish populations (Quinn & Deriso, 1999). The model is often written as

$$L_t = L_\infty \left(1 - e^{-K(t-t_0)}\right) \qquad (13.7)$$

where L_t, the length of the fish at time t, is modeled as a nonlinear function of the asymptotic length L_∞, the growth rate K, and the time (or age) t_0 at which the fish has a length of zero. A representative trajectory is shown in Figure 13.1, with the parameterized features of the trajectory highlighted: $L_\infty = 100$, $K = 0.046$,

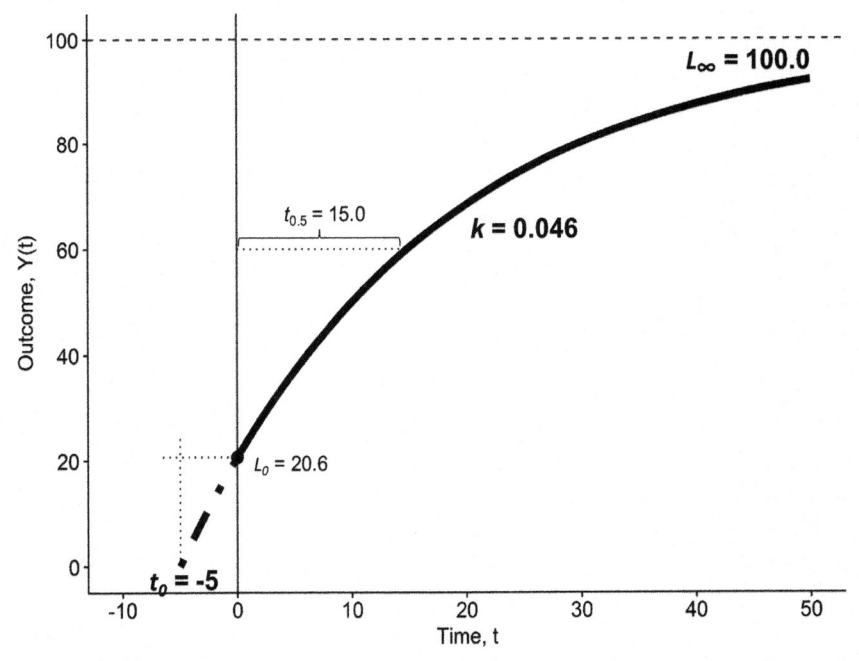

FIGURE 13.1 Illustration of the von Bertalanffy growth model. Trajectory for L_t, the length of a fish at time t, is modeled as a nonlinear function of asymptotic length L_∞, growth rate K, and the time (or age) t_0 at which the fish has a length of zero.

and $t_0 = -5.0$. An *equivalent* specification that trades t_0 (the constant indicating the timing of $L_t = 0$) for an L_0 intercept (indicating expected length at $t = 0$),

$$L_t = L_0 e^{-Kt} + L_\infty \left(1 - e^{-Kt}\right), \tag{13.8}$$

may be useful in some empirical situations. The trajectory in Figure 13.1 provides the classic depiction of growth in fish length, an asymptotic curve progressing from birth length of $L_0 = 20.62$ with continually declining growth rate toward an asymptote. As may be noted mathematically or visually, this 3-parameter von Bertalanffy model is functionally equivalent to the negative exponential model used by McArdle to describe age-related change across the life span in individuals' intellectual ability (e.g., McArdle, Grimm, Hamagrami, Bowles, & Meredith, 2009), and is similar to many other nonlinear trajectory models, including the Logistic, Gompertz, Richards and Schnute models that the McArdle group has used in recent years. In-depth discussion of the connections amongst all of these models can be found in Banks (1994) and Panik (2014).

For examination of interindividual differences in intraindividual change, the model is easily cast as a nonlinear growth model in either the multilevel or SEM framework and used to simulate and/or describe individual trajectories (Grimm, Ram, & Estabrook, 2017; McArdle & Nesselroade, 2014). For example, expanding the model to accommodate interindividual differences in all three parameters and presence of measurement/residual error, we can generate a collection of individual trajectories using the multilevel model

$$L_{it} = L_{\infty i} \left(1 - e^{-K_i(t-t_{0i})}\right) + r_{it} \tag{13.9}$$

where L_{it}, the observed outcome for fish i at time t, is modeled as a function of fish-specific coefficients for the upper asymptote, growth rate, and horizontal shift features, $L_{\infty i}$, K_i, and t_{0i}, which are in turn modeled as

$$L_{\infty i} = \pi_{00} + \cdots + u_{0i} \tag{13.10}$$

$$K_i = \pi_{10} + \cdots + u_{1i} \tag{13.11}$$

$$t_{0i} = \pi_{20} + \cdots + u_{2i} \tag{13.12}$$

where the πs are sample-level parameters that describe the trajectory of the "prototypical fish", and the us describe between-fish differences in the features of the trajectories. Interindividual differences (that are assumed multivariate normally distributed) in the parameterized features are shown in the panels of Figure 13.2. The top left panel, for instance, isolates differences in the upper asymptote ($L_{\infty i}$). Similarly, the middle left panel isolates differences in growth rate (K_i), and the lower left panel isolates initial length or "launch time" (L_{0i} or t_{0i}).

Setting up a later point of discussion, we note here how the growth rate parameter may be transformed for additional interpretive value. The rate parameter K_i has units of reciprocal time. Transformation of K_i into a *doubling time* or *half-life*

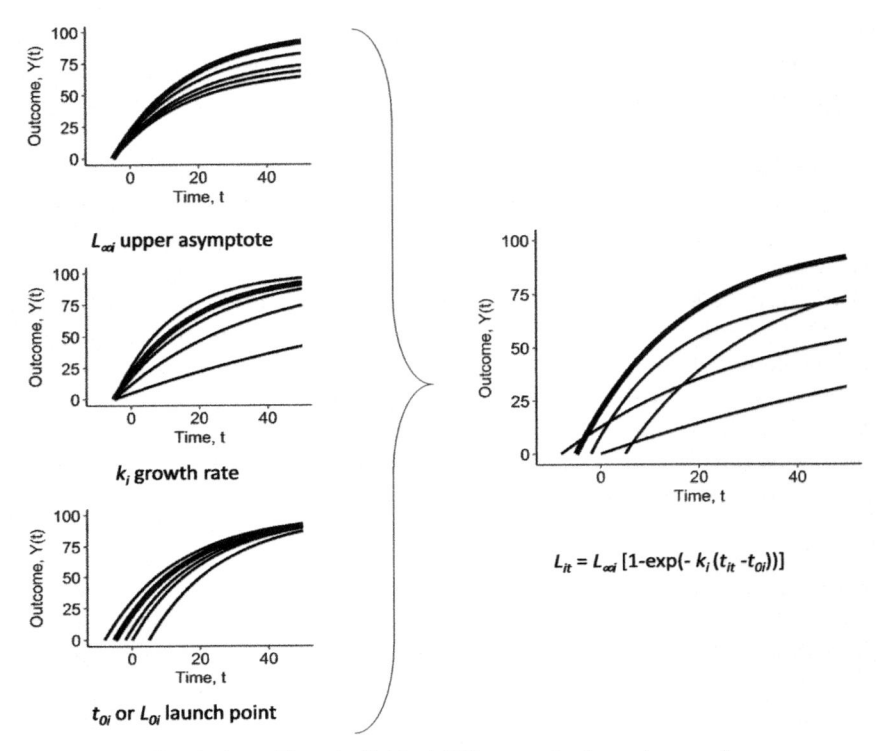

FIGURE 13.2 Depiction of interindividual differences in the trajectory features parameterized in the integral form of the von Bertalanffy growth model. The top left panel isolates differences in the upper asymptote ($L_{\infty i}$), the middle left panel isolates differences in growth rate (K_i), and the lower left panel isolates initial length or "launch time" (L_{0i} or t_{0i}). The right panel collects the differences in all three parameters to illustrate the range of potential interindividual differences in intraindividual change captured by the model.

parameter that is scaled in units of time facilitates discussion of the characteristic time-scale of the growth process, and the interindividual differences therein. Specifically, we use the equation

$$t_x = \frac{1}{K} \ln \left(\frac{L_\infty - L_0}{L_\infty (1 - x)} \right) \tag{13.13}$$

to calculate the half-life for each individual as $t_{0.5i} = \frac{1}{K_i} \ln 2$. For example, the time it takes to travel half the distance between $L_0 = 20.6$ and $L_\infty = 100$ in Figure 13.1 is calculated from $K = 0.046$ years^{-1} as $t_{0.5} = 15$ years. The same transformation can also be used to calculate a so-called *longevity estimate* that is conceptualized as the time it takes to reach a specific fraction x of L_∞, Fish classics (Fabens, 1965; Ricker, 1979) suggest interpretation of $t_{0.95}$ or $t_{0.99}$ (see Calliet, Smith, Mollet, & Goldman, 2006).

Bringing the three sets of coefficients together, the right panel of Figure 13.2 provides an overview of the range of interindividual differences in intraindividual change covered by this model. As with other nonlinear models, the von Bertalanffy model expands the possibilities for describing meaningful heterogeneity far beyond what can be captured by the linear growth model. Although not written out explicitly here, explanatory predictors can be added to explain both the growth process and the interindividual differences therein (see Ghisletta, Cantoni, & Jacot, 2015). We will touch on some of those extensions later. The main message we want to convey at this juncture is that the von Bertalanffy growth model is similar in structure and layout to other growth models being used in study of development (McArdle & Nesselroade, 2003; Ram & Grimm, 2015).

Bioenergetic Determinants of Growth: The Differential Form

In our attempt to better understand the ways in which theoretical models can be mapped to difference and differential equation models of change, the von Bertalanffy growth model has been particularly useful, in part because it was formulated from a very general bioenergetics model – i.e., from basic theoretical propositions. Both the initial development of the model, and the more recent extensions, are attempts to articulate specific physiological phenomena in a mathematical terminology that provides precise mapping of theoretical concepts to model parameters and longitudinal data.

In brief, individual organisms are considered analogous to reacting chemical systems that obey the laws of mass action (i.e., that the rate of a given chemical reaction is proportional to the activities or concentration of the reactants). The physiological processes responsible for the changes in mass of an organism are classified into two broad categories, *anabolism* (e.g., the synthesis or building up of body materials and the structures that support ability) and *catabolism* (e.g., the breaking down or maintenance of body materials and structures supporting ability). The basic von Bertalanffy growth model is then developed from the idea that growth is the net result of the antagonistic interplay of *anabolism* and *catabolism*. Simplistically,

$$growth \ = \ anabolism \ - \ catabolism$$

or restated in bioenergetic terms, *growth = energy assimilation – energy loss*. In line with basic tenets of lifespan development, the model explicitly acknowledges that during any given span of time, there is *both* gain and loss (Baltes et al., 2006).

Formalizing the propositions into mathematical form, the change process is described by the differential equation

$$\frac{dW}{dt} = HW^d - mW^n \tag{13.14}$$

where H and m are coefficients of anabolism and catabolism respectively, and the exponents d and n indicate how the two processes scale with organism size, W.

Conceptually, the exponent for anabolism, d, may be thought of as the proportion of the organism that can convert inputs into energy (i.e., "effective resorbing surface"; how much of the organism's body material can be restructured). In parallel, the catabolism exponent, n, may be thought of as the proportion of the organism that uses energy (i.e., is engaged in metabolism). In fish populations, for instance, early empirical evidence suggested that the acquisition of resources, anabolism, is proportional to body surface and thus scales with $d = 2/3$. In contrast, the catabolic costs of maintenance (e.g., basal metabolism and reproductive investment) are assumed directly proportional to body mass and thus scale with $n = 1$. The differential scaling of anabolism and catabolism suggest that as the fish grows larger, more and more of the available energy will be used for maintenance, so that growth slows down and eventually stops – as depicted by the nonlinear trajectory in Figure 13.1.

The size-dependent change in the rate of growth has parallels in human development. Indeed, many lifespan developmental theories highlight the importance of ontogenetic changes in the relative allocation of resources to growth versus maintenance (Baltes et al., 2006). For instance, socioemotional selectivity theory (Carstensen, Isaacowitz, & Charles, 1999) suggests that as people age their motivational priorities gradually shift from information seeking (analogous to anabolism) toward emotion regulation and maintenance (analogous to catabolism). Similarly, motivational theory of lifespan development (Heckhausen, Wrosch, & Schulz, 2010) suggests that personal growth is facilitated through interplay of primary control processes directed at changing the world to bring the environment into line with one's wishes (enacting goals) and secondary control processes directed at changing the self to bring oneself into line with environmental forces (e.g., giving up goals). Trajectories of successful aging thus might also be explicitly modeled with respect to individuals' selective allocation of resources to primary control and secondary control processes using a von Bertalanffy model. Individual differences in allocations to each category of processes (e.g., differences in H and m) or contextual differences in opportunity to exert control (e.g., sociodemographic differences in d) provide for heterogeneity in individuals' life course trajectories. Growth in intellectual ability may also be simultaneously driven by anabolic and catabolic processes. For example, changes in ability may be the outcome of interplay between neurogenesis and neural pruning (Stiles & Jernigan, 2010). In sum, the "competing processes" model invoked by the allometric relations in Equation 13.14 provides a general framework for articulating a variety of developmental theories.

Noting the parallels between bioenergetic principles and propositions forwarded in lifespan developmental theory, we explored further how differences in the coefficients and exponents in the change process model in Equation 13.14 may invoke differential development. To do so we built a simulation engine that allowed us to generate synthetic data for a range of coefficient values. Specifically, we simulated data from the differential equation model across many parameter combinations (varying H, m, and d, and assuming $n = 1$) using a feed-forward procedure to track and plot how both the change process (growth, dW/dt) and the outcome of the change process (size, W) evolved over time. Data were generated iteratively from $t = 0$ to 50 with a step-size of $dt = 1.0$, starting with an initial value for $W_t = 0.01$. A select set of the resulting change process data, for parameter combinations where $H \in [0.75, 0.85, 0.95]$, $m \in [0.25, 0.35, 0.45]$ and $d \in [0.62, 0.67, 0.72]$, are shown in Figure 13.3.

As seen throughout the array the *growth rate* curves (dW/dt on the y-axis and *time* on the x-axis) generated from the von Bertalanffy model are generally characterized by an inverted-U shape where the growth rate increases and then

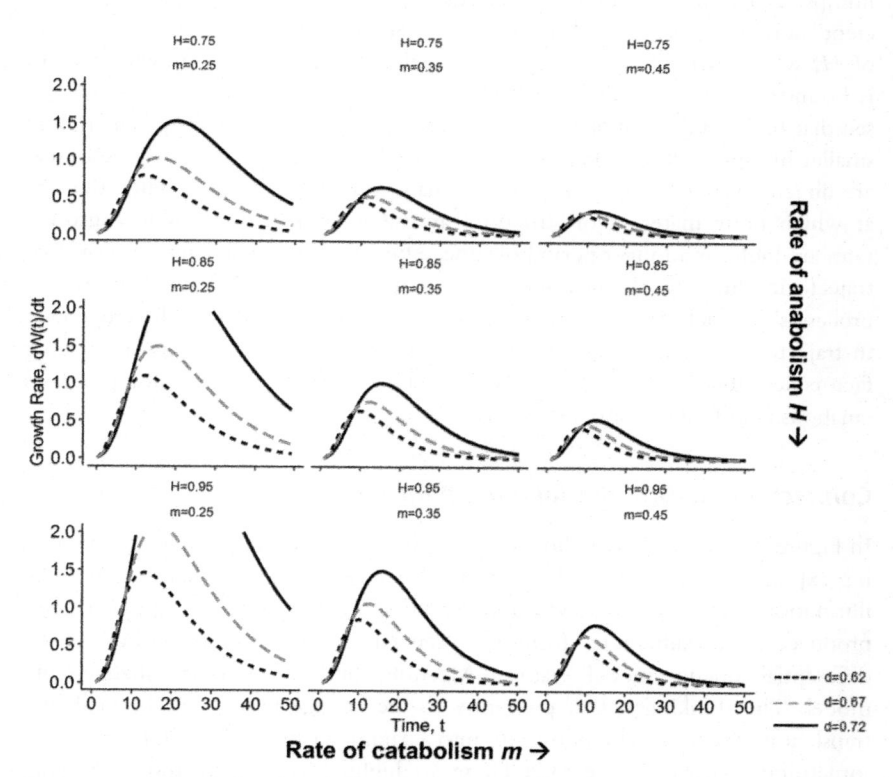

FIGURE 13.3 Simulation-based depiction of how different values of the allometric coefficients and scaling exponents in the differential form of the von Bertalanffy growth model produce different growth rate (dW/dt) curves. As the rate of anabolism (H) increases across panels, top to bottom of the figure, the asymptotes are higher. As rate of catabolism (m) increases across the panels, left to right, the asymptotes are reached earlier. Within a given panel, when the anabolic scaling factor is higher (high d), the asymptotes are higher and reached later.

decreases over time. Patterns across the grid are instructive about how the allometric relations surrounding anabolism and catabolism influence the growth process. Starting with how anabolism scales with mass, we see that larger values of d produce larger and longer lasting growth. For example, looking within any specific panel, we see that the peak of the solid line (high $d = .72$) is both higher and arrives later than the peak for the darker dashed line (low $d = .62$). Indeed, it makes sense that when a greater proportion of mass is available as an effective resorbing surface, more of the assimilated energy is available for growth. The anabolic processes are able to contribute more to growth before they are "overtaken" or "overwhelmed" by the catabolic processes. Similarly, looking across panels vertically, we see that higher values of H are also associated with larger humps. When anabolic processes are being directed toward growth in an "efficient" way (large H), growth rates are generally larger. In contrast, at low values of H, when anabolic processes are not being directed toward growth, growth is bounded or never really gets started. Looking across panels horizontally we see that higher values of m are associated with lower growth rates generally, and smaller humps. Indeed, when the rate of metabolism is high (large m), resources are directed toward maintenance rather than growth. In contrast, when the rate at which body materials or structures are being broken down is low, growth rates are high for a longer period of time. Altogether, the collection of simulated trajectories illustrates the flexibility in growth patterns afforded by a "competing processes" model like the von Bertalanffy model, and how the heterogeneity in trajectories is tethered to systematic variation in the coefficients and scaling factors describing the allometric relations between specific physiological processes (anabolism and catabolism) and growth.

Connecting the Differential and Integral Forms

In Figure 13.3 we examined how variation in the allometric coefficients and scaling exponents in Equation 13.14 produced a variety of growth rate curves. The illustration demonstrates individual differences in the *growth process* (i.e., changes) produced by the differential form. Our general push has been toward use of the differential equation model – same as McArdle's push for use of the change score model. The thinking is that proximity to the change process model facilitates translation of theoretical propositions into a parameter space. We did, however, do something similar in Figure 13.2. There, we highlighted how the model provides for description of interindividual differences in the three *features* of the trajectories (upper asymptote, shape, launch point) parameterized in Equation 13.7. For continuity, the array of *size* trajectories that are produced by the array growth processes displayed in Figure 13.3 are shown in Figure 13.4. Thus, one can see visually how the specific patterns of growth manifest in the outputs. Looking vertically across the panels in Figure 13.4, as the rate of anabolism (H) increases, the asymptotes are higher. Looking horizontally across panels, as rate of catabolism (m)

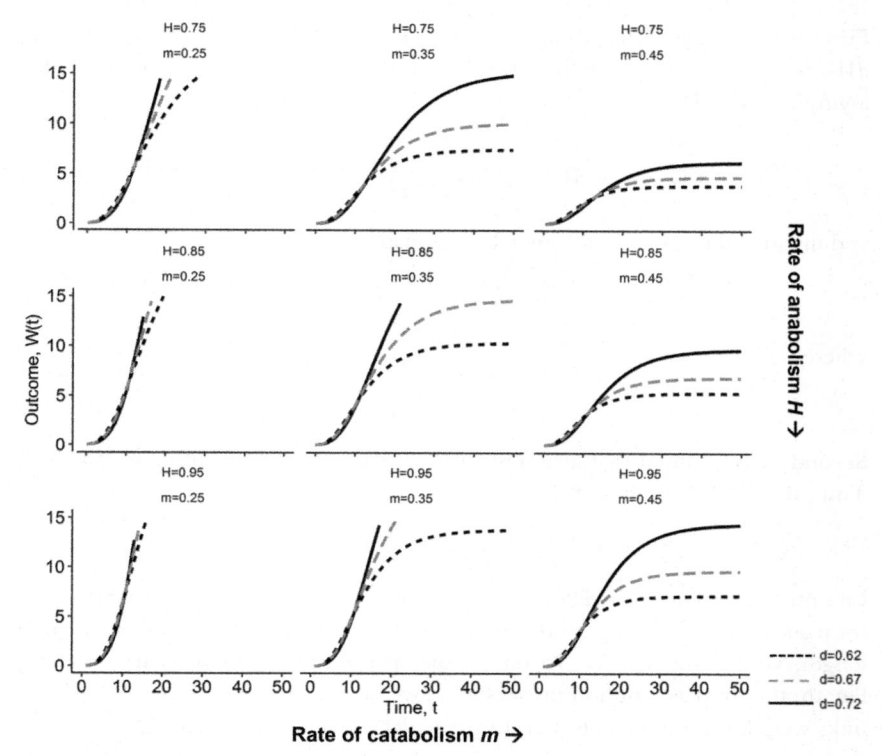

FIGURE 13.4 Simulation-based depiction of how different values of the allometric coefficients and scaling exponents in the differential form of the von Bertalanffy growth model produce different trajectories for size (W_t).

increases, the lower asymptotes are reached earlier. Looking within a panel, when the anabolic scaling factor is higher (solid line = high d) the asymptotes are higher and reached later. Most notable is that the asymptote changes in relation to all three parameters being varied. Building from the visual illustration, the mathematical relations illustrate more formally how the parameters (H, m, d, n) in the differential equation model (which map to theoretical principles) are linked to the three parameters (Y_∞, K, and t_0) in the integral equation model (which map to visual features of the size trajectories).

von Bertalanffy used three assumptions to obtain the model for length, Equation 13.7, from the differential model in Equation 13.14 (see van Poorten, 2016). Notably, although these assumptions have both a theoretical and empirical basis, they also happen to be mathematically convenient. The bioenergetics model for growth is formulated specifically in units of mass (i.e., weight, W),

$$\frac{dW}{dt} = HW^d - mW^n \tag{13.15}$$

First, it is assumed that catabolism varies directly with mass, $n = 1$. Setting $dW/dt = 0$ and $n = 1$, Equation 13.15 can then be rearranged to solve for asymptotic weight as

$$W_\infty = \lim_{t \to \infty} W_t = \left(\frac{H}{m}\right)^{\frac{1}{1-d}} \tag{13.16}$$

and integrated to obtain the generalized equation for weight

$$W_t = W_\infty \left(1 - e^{-K(t-t_0)}\right)^{\frac{1}{1-d}} \tag{13.17}$$

where

$$K = m(1 - d). \tag{13.18}$$

Second, it is assumed that anabolism varies as the 2/3 power of mass, $d = 2/3$. Thus, the model simplifies to

$$W_t = W_\infty \left(1 - e^{-K(t-t_0)}\right)^3. \tag{13.19}$$

Of note, and a point we will come back to later, the cubic exponent in the model for mass indicates that this model exists in a 3-dimensional world where fish have length, width, and height. To obtain the specialized 1-dimensional model for length, the third assumption invokes what we would call a *measurement model* that links weight (W) and length (L). In particular, the relation is assumed as

$$W = aL^b \tag{13.20}$$

with $b = 3$ (for fish exhibiting isometric growth). Applying the assumptions that $n = 1$, $d = 2/3$, and $b = 3$ (and $a = 1$), the equations simplify to the model used for Figures 13.1 and 13.2,

$$L_t = L_\infty \left(1 - e^{-K(t-t_0)}\right). \tag{13.21}$$

Three important implications for study of individual differences in growth become apparent when examining the relations between the parameters of the differential equation model for change and the parameters of the integrated model for length: (13.1) The growth parameter K is proportional to the catabolic parameter, $K = m/3$ (from Equation 13.18). This means that, in the 3-parameter von Bertalanffy model, the rate at which an individual moves toward the asymptote is *only* related to rate of catabolism, and not to anabolism. Thus, the external factors related to interindividual differences in K_i may be interpreted as factors that influence catabolic processes. (13.2) The asymptote L_∞, is a scaled ratio of mass-specific consumption and metabolic costs (H and m)

$$L_\infty = \left(\frac{H}{m}\right) a^{-\frac{1}{3}}. \tag{13.22}$$

That is, the asymptotic size is related to *both* anabolism and catabolism. Thus, external factors related to interindividual differences in $L_{\infty i}$ may be interpreted as factors that influence anabolic *and/or* catabolic processes. Lack of association with $L_{\infty i}$, however, should not be interpreted as lack of influence because factors that influence both consumption and metabolic costs may cancel out. For example, temperature exponentially increases both fishes' basal metabolism and their feeding rate. The (lack of) relation between temperature and asymptotic length misses the influence on the underlying metabolic processes driving growth. (13.3) Because K and L_∞ are both directly related to m, interindividual differences in the rate of growth and asymptote will be correlated. As such, it is very likely that external factors that are related to $L_{\infty i}$ will also be related to K_i. Thus, it is the differential relations that may be particularly useful for parsing which factors act on which underlying processes. In summary, when selecting and examining predictors of interindividual differences in growth (i.e., in Equations 13.10 to 13.12), researchers should carefully consider how each feature of the trajectory is related to the underlying (anabolic and catabolic) processes driving intraindividual change.

Example Extensions

The von Bertalanffy growth model is, of course, too simple and based on questionable assumptions. Indeed, ecologists are continually discussing and developing extensions that might accommodate additional biological considerations (e.g., investment in reproductive tissues) and the wide variety of (fish) population demographic and environmental factors known to influence growth (e.g., age-structure and density of population, spatial variation in availability of prey, behavioral changes induced by predators, temperature, oxygen concentration). With an interest in how the modeling extensions are conceived and constructed in ecology, we highlight two variants of the von Bertalanffy growth model that have emerged to accommodate variation in growth related to biological investment in reproduction and seasonal changes in environment.

Biphasic growth. A pervasive concern in the application of the von Bertalanffy growth model is that the model often describes growth of adult fish much better than growth of juveniles (Jones, 2002). Extrapolation to younger or older ages is often unrealistic. The root cause of these concerns is the assumption that the allometries of anabolism and catabolism are invariant over age. Contrary to the assumption, there are ontogenetic shifts in diet, activity, and energy allocation. As fish grow, so too does cruising speed, size of spatial range, attack rate, gape size, and visual acuity – all of which have important implications for consumption and metabolism, and thus growth. Of particular importance in the management of fisheries, for example, is the increased allocation of resources to reproductive tissue and behavior around the time of maturation.

A variety of models have emerged to account for reproductive investment. Generally, these models accommodate the possibility that one or more parameters shift over time. For example, the typical von Bertalanffy model can be supplemented with a time-varying factor A_t that modifies the growth rate as a function of time (Soriano et al., 1992). The model becomes

$$L_t = L_\infty \left[1 - e^{-KA_t(t-t_0)} \right] \tag{13.23}$$

where the function given by

$$A_t = 1 - \frac{h}{(t - t_h)^2 + 1} \tag{13.24}$$

introduces two new parameters: t_h defines the time (i.e., age) at which the transition between the two growth phases occurs, and h determines the magnitude of the maximum difference between the functions for Phase 1 and Phase 2. Depictions of a few trajectories are shown in Figure 13.5A, with values of the t_h and h parameters specifically chosen to highlight possibility of identifying differences in timing of the phase-switch and the extent of the switch.

Similar in layout to the Preece-Baines model for human growth (Preece & Baines, 1978; see notational similarity with example in Grimm, Ram &

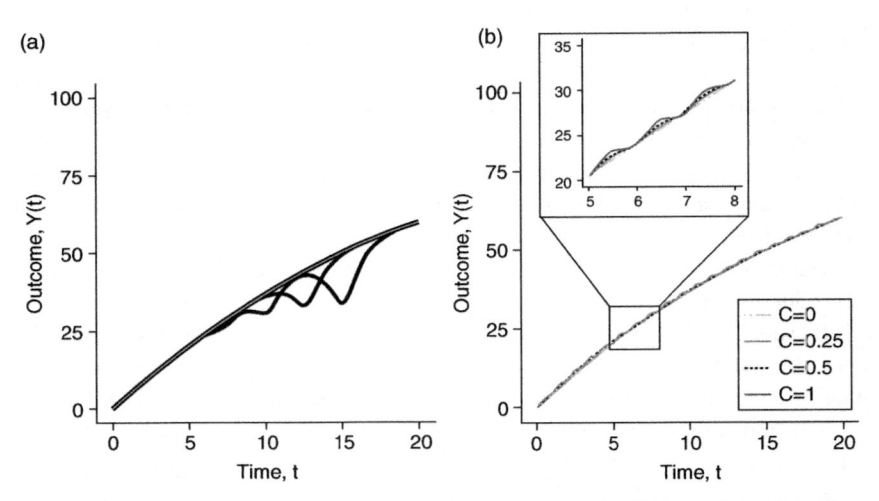

FIGURE 13.5 Depictions of two extensions of the von Bertalanffy growth model. Output of the typical model is shown as a white line. Panel (a) depicts outputs from the biphasic model, with variations in the extent of difference between phases, h, and timing of the phase-switch, t_h, illustrated by the four lines. Panel (b) depicts outputs from the seasonal model, with variations in amplitude illustrated by the three types of lines – shown most prominently within the zoomed section.

Hamagami, 2011), the biphasic von Bertalanffy model provides for examination of interindividual differences in some additional features of individuals' change trajectories. Although the A_t factor was not derived from bioenergetics principles, the modification does provide for a more precise empirical description of observed growth patterns and is considered a reasonable approximation of how age-related diversion of resources toward reproductive processes affects growth. In this regard, we are immediately struck by the possibility of using the model to examine physical and behavioral changes that accompany puberty and adolescence. For example, a number of developmental theories suggest that the dual-processes governing individuals' self-regulation may be mismatched during adolescence (Steinberg, 2010). Considering that the interplay between *bottom-up processes* associated with temptations and impulses and *top-down processes* involved in deliberative evaluation can be mapped to anabolism and catabolism, and that the developmental mismatch between these two processes occurs around puberty, it seems reasonable that a biphasic model meant to accommodate reproductive investment may be useful for describing lifespan developmental changes in self-regulation. Indeed, the "dips" seen in Figure 13.5A propel the possibility of using this variant of the von Bertalanffy model for precise and parsimonious description of the psychological and social changes that manifest specifically in adolescence.

Sinusoidal growth. To accommodate some of the changes in environment that are systematically organized with respect to the Earth's rotation, the von Bertalanffy growth function has also been expanded to include a sinusoidal component. Specifically (following Somers, 1988), the seasonal von Bertalanffy model for annual cycles becomes

$$L_t = L_\infty \left[1 - e^{-K(t-t_0) - S_t + S_{t0}} \right] \tag{13.25}$$

with

$$S_t = \left(\frac{CK}{2\pi} \right) \sin \left[2\pi \left(t - t_s \right) \right] \tag{13.26}$$

where C modulates the amplitude of the growth oscillations, the period of the cycle $= 1$ (see Quinn & Deriso, 1999 for generalization to cycles of any length period), t_s is a phase shift parameter that locates the cycle in time (i.e., defines the "wintering point" $= t_s + 0.5$), and L_∞, K, and t_0 are as above. When $C = 1$ growth is completely stopped at the "wintering point" each year, and when $C = 0$, there is no seasonality to growth. Depictions of some seasonally oscillating trajectories are shown in Figure 13.5B. In particular, we see that when C gets larger the seasonality variability increases (amplitude) Different values of t_s would shift the location of the "wintering" when size is stable. Of note for interpretation, the assumption embedded in this model is that the biotic or environmental factors related to C induce sinusoidal variation in the growth rate K, which is related to seasonal changes in the environment. As such, interindividual differences or intraindividual changes in C may describe, as noted in the earlier temperature example, factors influencing both anabolism and catabolism. Importantly, investigation of seasonal growth requires that time (e.g., age) be recorded on a fine enough scale to define the seasonal variation. For example, if seasonal growth is driven by an annual cycle, it may be necessary to locate the repeated measures with weekly or even daily precision (see Ram & Reeves, 2018). In studies of human development, application of seasonal growth models to multi-year school achievement data and examination of the "forgetting" that accompanies summer holidays should be straightforward when weekly or monthly repeated measures are available.

The biphasic and sinusoidal extensions illustrate just two ways that time-varying biological and environmental factors are being incorporated into the von Bertalanffy model. On-going discussions about how to best incorporate the cost of reproduction (Minte-Vera, Maunder, Casselman, 2016) while remaining connected to the bioenergetic principles from which the models are derived (van Poorten & Walters, 2016), and about the various ways to model the plasticity of fish growth, are provoking consideration of many interesting models (Lorenzen, 2016). Notable, for instance, is consideration of how the whole framework can be recast into stochastic differential equation models that accommodate the wide variety of unknown spatially and temporally varying factors that influence growth and change at multiple time scales (Román-Román, Romero, & Torres-Ruiz, 2010; Russo, Baldi, Parisi, Magnifico, Mariani, & Cataudella, 2009). Developmental researchers will likely be able to make use of all of these extensions in their attempts to better understand humans' physical, psychological, and social growth.

Future Directions

Our intent aim in this chapter was to explore recent and classic ecological literature on growth modeling and to develop some nascent ideas about how the models in use there may be applied to our study of human development. In that literature, we happened upon rich discussions and widespread use of the von Bertalanffy growth model, and learned that fish growth is generally conceptualized as the net result of the antagonistic processes of anabolism (the building up of body materials) and catabolism (the breaking down of body materials). As analysts looking for efficient models, we find the description of univariate change as a "dual-process" model non- parsimonious. Indeed, identification constraints (or additional assumptions) are needed to find a solution for the differential equation and actually fit the model to data. However, as developmentalists looking for representations of growth process, we find that the "dual-process" interplay between anabolism and catabolism provides the flexibility organisms need as they respond to and transact with an ever-changing environment. Indeed, the range of behaviors and trajectories we often see in our data may actually be much better represented in multivariate space than in the univariate space in which the measures were conceived and obtained.

Multivariate Growth and Measurement Models. Let us consider again the "measurement model" that was embedded in the derivation of the von Bertalanffy model for length, $W = aL^b$. In that derivation, it was mathematically convenient to take $b = 3$ in order that some exponents would cancel out in the move from a construct that exists in a 3-dimensional space (weight indicative of volume) to a construct that exists in a 1-dimensional space, length. The relation of body proportions, however, can be either simple or complex. When body proportions remain the same, the ratio of body depth to body length or head length to body length remains constant. In many species, the fish's biomass is a cubic function of their length, $W = aL^3$, and the fishes exhibit what is called *isometric* growth. The isometric measurement model provides for straightforward data reduction and reduced data collection costs. We need only measure and model changes in fish size in one dimension, $L =$ length. In contrast, when one body part grows faster or slower than another, growth is referred to as allometric. For fish that exhibit allometric growth, biomass generally follows a power function of length, $W = aL^b$. Usually, b is taken as invariant over time or age, but there are some species where it is necessary that the size allometry is allowed to be age-specific, $b(t)$ to accommodate, for example, substantial differences in the growth ratios among body parts for juveniles and adults (Jones, 2002).

McArdle (1988) introduced two models for multivariate growth. In a *curve-of-factors* model, where the multivariate repeated measures are modeled as indicators of a common factor that changes over time (i.e., also labelled 2nd-order growth models, Hancock, Kuo, & Lawrence, 2001). The measurement model establishing the common factor must be invariant. As in isometric growth of fish, a single change function defines how change proceeds in all dimensions. Changes in length or the common factor are directly proportional (*a* can be interpreted as a factor loading) to the changes in girth, or any of the indicator variables. That is, the *b* exponent is the same for all variables. By analogy, we can imagine growth of a cube. In the simple version of the curve-of-factors and isometric growth models, all the three dimensions of the cube (length, width, height) grow at the same rate, so that the cube maintains equivalence of shape over time. Changes in volume of the cube can be inferred from repeated measurement of any one dimension. Alternatively, in a *factor-of-curves* model, the repeated measures of each dimension are modeled using separate growth functions, with the parameters governing change driven by a common cause. This model is in principle like models for allometric growth, where *b* differs across variables (e.g., Griffiths & Sandland, 1984). The dimensions of the cube may grow at different scales. Over time, the cube with equal length sides transforms into a cuboid with unequal lengthed sides. While our and others' implementations of the *curve-of-factors* and *factor-of-curves* models have been almost entirely focused on linear measurement models and linear change models, our hunch is that more detailed elaboration of how McArdle's models merge with the von Bertalanffy frameworks used in biology will open up new possibilities for investigation of multivariate growth.

Time-scales and Study Design. In our scan through empirical studies of fish growth, we noted the precision with which the time-scale of growth is known and discussed. In part, this is because patterns of growth and timing of reproductive investment are extremely important in management of fisheries. Indeed, our ability to have salmon or tilapia for dinner in central Pennsylvania, or even for Jack in Hawaii, depends on knowledge of when and at what ages fish can be harvested in a profitable and sustainable way. Widespread use of the *half-life* (or doubling-time) and longevity metrics (calculated as shown in Equation 13.13) makes it very easy to locate the time-scales at which different fish grow and to plan for various interventions (e.g., temperature, food resources). In the same way that measures of *periodicity* (i.e., frequency) quantify the time-scale at which different oscillatory process manifests, measures of *half-life* quantify the time-scale at which different growth process manifest (Newell, Liu, & Meyer-Kress, 2001). We underscore this possibility because knowledge of half-life has important implications for design of longitudinal panel studies. When studying oscillatory processes, we know how to choose the measurement interval. The Nyquist-Shannon sampling theorem provides an algorithmic framework for considering how often to sample. In basic form, the sampling theorem states that the continuous signal (i.e., pattern of change) can be fully reconstructed from discrete samples obtained at a sampling frequency that is at least twice the maximum relevant bandwidth. For example, study of heart beat activity that manifests at between 0.5 and 100 Hz requires electrocardiogram sampling of at least 200 Hz. When studying incremental change processes, however, we have not been able to make such clear recommendations about when to obtain the repeated measurements. We usually wing it. When the half-life is known (or there is a clear hypothesis), however, it may be possible to make some more specific recommendations (see also Timmons & Preacher 2015). Indeed, in pharmacology, there is a body of work on optimal sampling for description of drugs' pharmacokinetic profiles (i.e., decay curves). The algorithms all seem to make use of initial knowledge of a drug's half-life (e.g., Reed, 1999; Schumacher, 1984). Although not immediately clear how this work translates to design of longitudinal panel studies of developmental processes, it is clear that quantifications or hypotheses of half-life can inform selection of sampling interval. To this end, we note that calculation of half-life requires *non-linearity*. Linear growth, which extends forever, has no discernable half-life, and the parameters used to describe straight lines are not sufficient for use in Equation 13.13. In sum, informed selection of sampling interval requires consideration of non-linear growth models, the differential forms and simulations of which facilitate construction of theoretically driven hypotheses.

Epilogue

For as long as we have known, Jack has ebulliently encouraged efforts to incorporate the use of differential equations into the analysis of behavioral change. As he often notes (e.g., McArdle, 1988, 2009), the "lingua-franca" of differential equations provides for straightforward articulation of knowledge about change processes, highlights the simplicity and potential value of models used in other fields, and opens up a wide range of possibilities for articulating the complexities of behavioral change.

In this chapter, our engagement with the differential equation models used in the study of fish growth has expanded both the vocabulary we can now use to describe change processes and our understanding of how nonlinear growth models work. As illustrated above, the differential equations are particularly useful in connecting theory to data, because they provide for direct translation of theoretical propositions about the change process into mathematical form. Given their location in a theory to method to data research process (process-oriented theoretical model → differential equation model of change process → growth model of change outputs → empirical observations of change outputs), these models can greatly facilitate progression of knowledge about developmental and other change processes. Our general conclusion from this excursion into the fisheries literature is that many basic process models (e.g., reaction–diffusion, activator–inhibitor, anabolism–catabolism) have been worked out (also as apparent in chemistry, biology, engineering etc.). The mathematical, physical, and biological tractability of these "dual-process" models is known. Where we can see parallels between human behavior and physical and biological systems, we should make use of and/or adapt those models. Jack has always encouraged us to fish (even more strongly recently, McArdle & Ritschard, 2013 :-) — "Just try it out and see what happens." We are always happy we did!

Note

1 We gratefully acknowledge the support provided by the National Institute on Health (R01 HD076994, P2C HD041025, and UL1 TR002014), the National Science Foundation I/UCRC Center for Healthcare Organization Transformation (#1624727), and the Penn State Social Science Research Institute. We thank Jack McArdle for sharing his love of longitudinal data analysis, and for his unending support.

References

Baltes, P. B., Lindenberger, U., & Staudinger, U. M. (2006). Lifespan theory in developmental psychology. In W. Damon & R. M. Lerner (Series Ed.) & R. M. Lerner (Vol. Ed.), *Handbook of child psychology: Vol. 1. Theoretical models of human development*, 6th edn., (pp. 569–664). Hoboken, NJ: Wiley.

Banks, R. B. (1994). *Growth and diffusion phenomena*. New York: Springer.

Boker, S. (2001). Differential structural equation models of intraindividual variability. In L. M. Collins & A. G. Sayer (Eds.), *New methods for the analysis of change* (pp. 5–27). Washington, DC: American Psychological Association.

Bronfenbrenner, U. & Morris, P. A. (2006). The bioecological model of human development. In W. Damon & R. M. Lerner (Series Ed.) & R. M. Lerner (Vol. Ed.), *Handbook of child psychology: Vol. 1. Theoretical models of human development* 6th ed., (pp. 793–828). Hoboken, NJ: Wiley.

Cailliet, G. M., Smith, W. D., Mollet, H. F., & Goldman, K. J. (2006). Age and growth studies of chondrichthyan fishes: the need for consistency in terminology, verification, validation, and growth function fitting. *Environmental Biology of Fishes, 77*, 211–228.

Carstensen, L. L., Isaacowitz, D. M., & Charles, S. T. (1999). Taking time seriously: A theory of socioemotional selectivity. *American Psychologist, 54*, 165–181.

Enberg, K., Jørgensen, C., Dunlop, E. S., Varpe, Ø., Boukal, D. S., Baulier, L., Eliassen, S. and Heino, M. (2012), Fishing-induced evolution of growth: concepts, mechanisms and the empirical evidence. *Marine Ecology, 33*, 1–25.

Fabens, A. (1965). Properties and fitting of the von Bertalanffy growth curve. *Growth, 29*, 265–289.

Ford, D. H. & Lerner, R.M. (1992). *Developmental Systems Theory: An integrative approach.* Newbury Park, CA: Sage.

Ghisletta, P., Cantoni, E., & Jacot, N. (2015). Nonlinear growth curve models. In M. Stemmler, A., von Eye, & W., Wiedermann. (Eds.), *Dependent data in social sciences research: Forms, issues, and methods of analysis.* Springer Proceedings in Mathematics & Statistics, *145*, 47–66.

Gierer, A. & Meinhardt, H. (1972). A theory of biological pattern formation. *Kybernetik, 12*, 30–39.

Gottlieb, G. (2007). Probabilistic epigenesis. *Developmental Science, 10*, 1–11.

Griffiths D. & Sandland, R. (1984). Fitting generalized allometric models to multivariate growth data. *Biometrics, 40*, 139–150.

Grimm, K. J., Ram, N., & Hamagami, F. (2011). Nonlinear growth curves in developmental research. *Child Development, 82*, 1357–1371.

Grimm, K. J., Ram, N., & Estabrook, R. (2017). *Growth modeling: Structural equation and multilevel modeling approaches.* New York: Guilford.

Hancock, G. R., Kuo, W.-L., & Lawrence, F. R. (2001). An illustration of second-order latent growth models. *Structural Equation Modeling: A Multidisciplinary Journal, 8*, 470–483.

Heckhausen, J., Wrosch, C., & Schulz, R. (2010). A motivational theory of life-span development. *Psychological Review, 117*, 32–60.

Hertzog, C. & Nesselroade, J. R. (2003). Assessing psychological change in adulthood: An overview of methodological issues. *Psychology and Aging, 18*, 639–657.

Jones, C. M. (2002). Age and growth. In L. A. Fuiman & R. G. Werner (Eds.) *Fishery science: The unique contributions of early life stages* (pp. 33–63). Malden, MA: Blackwell Science.

Li, S.-C. (2003). Biocultural orchestration of developmental plasticity across levels: The interplay of biology and culture in shaping the mind and behavior across the lifespan. *Psychological Bulletin, 129*, 171–194.

Lorenzen, K. (2016). Toward a new paradigm for growth modeling in fisheries stock assessments: Embracing plasticity and its consequences. *Fishery Research, 80*, 4–22.

Maunder, M. N., Crone, P. R, Punt, A. E., Valero, J. L., & Semmens, B. X. (2016). Growth: Theory, estimation, and application in fishery stock assessment models. *Fisheries Research, 180*, 1–3.

McArdle, J. J. (1988). Dynamic but structural equation modeling of repeated measures data. In J. R. Nesselroade & R. B. Cattell (Eds.), *Handbook of multivariate experimental psychology.* (vol. 2, pp. 561–614). New York: Plenum Press.

McArdle, J. J. (2009). Latent variable modeling of differences and changes with longitudinal data. *Annual Review of Psychology, 60*, 577–605.

McArdle, J. J. & Anderson, E. (1990). Latent variable growth models for research on aging. In J. E. Birren & K. W. Schaie (Eds.), *The handbook of the psychology of aging* (pp. 21–43). New York: Plenum Press.

McArdle, J. J. & Bell, R. Q. (2000). An introduction to latent growth models for developmental data analysis. In T. D. Little & K. U. Schnabel (Eds.), *Modeling longitudinal and multilevel data: Practical issues, applied approaches, and specific examples* (pp. 69–107). Mahwah, NJ: Erlbaum.

McArdle, J. J. & Nesselroade, J. R. (2003). Growth curve analysis in contemporary psychological research. In J. Schinka & W. Velicer (Eds.), *Comprehensive handbook of psychology: Volume II. Research methods in psychology* (pp. 447–480). New York: Pergamon.

McArdle, J. J. & Nesselroade, J. R. (2014). *Longitudinal data analysis using structural equation models.* Washington, DC: American Psychological Association.

McArdle, J. J. & Ritschard, G. (Eds.). (2013). *Contemporary issues in exploratory data mining in the behavioral sciences.* New York: Routledge.

McArdle, J. J., Grimm, K. J., Hamagami, F., Bowles, R. P., & Meredith, W. (2009). Modeling life-span growth curves of cognition using longitudinal data with multiple samples and changing scales of measurement. *Psychological Methods, 14*, 126.

McArdle, J. J. & Hamagami, F. (2001). Latent difference score structural models for linear dynamic analyses with incomplete longitudinal data. In L. M. Collins and A. G. Sayer (Eds.). *New methods for the analysis of change* (pp. 139–175). Washington, DC: American Psychological Association.

McArdle, J. J. & Nesselroade, J. R. (2003). Growth curve analysis in contemporary psychological research. In Schinka, J. A., & Velicer, W. F. (Eds.) *Handbook of psychology. Volume II: Research methods in psychology* (pp. 447–480). New York: John Wiley & Sons.

Minte-Vera, C., Maunder, M. N., & Casselman, J. M. (2016). Growth functions that incorporate the cost of reproduction. *Fishery Research, 180*, 31–44.

Murray, J. D. (2003). *Mathematical biology.* New York: Springer-Verlag.

Newell, K. M., Liu, Y. T., & Meyer-Kress, G. (2001). Time-scales in motor learning and development. *Psychological Review, 108*, 57–82.

Overton, W. F. & Lerner, R. M. (2012). Relational developmental systems: A paradigm for developmental science in the post-genomic era. *Behavioral and Brain Sciences, 35*, 375–376.

Panik (2014). *Growth curve modeling: Theory and applications.* Hoboken, NJ: Wiley.

Poorten, B. T. & Waters, C. J. (2016). How can bioenergetics help us predict changes in fish growth patterns? *Fishery Research, 180*, 23–30.

Preacher, K. J. & Hancock, G. R. (2015). Meaningful aspects of change as novel random coefficients: A general method for reparameterizing longitudinal models. *Psychological Methods, 20*, 84–101.

Preece, M. A. & Baines, M. I. (1978). A new family of mathematical models describing the human growth curve. *Annals of Human Biology, 5*, 1–24.

Quinn, T. J. & Deriso, R. B. (1999). *Quantitative fish dynamics.* Oxford, UK: Oxford University Press.

Ram, N., Gatzke-Kopp, L., Gerstorf, D., Coccia, M., Morack, J., & Molenaar, P. C. M. (2015). Intraindividual variabiity across the life span: Moving toward computational develpmental science. In M. Diehl, K. Hooker, & M. J. Sliwinski (Eds), *Handbook of Intraindivdiaul Variability Across Life Span* (pp. 16–34). New York: Routledge.

Ram, N. & Grimm, K. (2015). Growth curve modeling and longitudinal factor analysis. In W. Damon & R. M. Lerner (Series Ed.) & P. C. M. Molenaar (Vol. Ed.), *Handbook of child psychology: Vol. 1. Theoretical models of human development* (7th ed.). Hoboken, NJ: Wiley.

Ram, N. & Reeves, B. (2018). Time sampling. M. H. Bornstein, M. E., Arterberry, K. L. Fingerman, & J. E. Lansford (Eds.), *The SAGE encyclopedia of lifespan human development* (pp. 2247–2248). Thousand Oaks, CA: Sage.

Reed, M. D. (1999). Optimal sampling theory: an overview of its application to pharmacokinetic studies in infants and children. *Pediatrics*, 104(Supplement 3), 627–632.

Ricker, W. E. (1979) Growth rates and models. In W. Hoar, S. Hoar, D. J. Randall, & J. R. Brett (Eds.), *Fish Physiology, III, Bioenergetics and growth* (pp 677–743). New York: Academic Press.

Román-Román, P., Romero, D., & Torres-Ruiz, F. (2010). A diffusion process to model generalized von Bertalanffy growth patterns: Fitting to real data. *Journal of Theoretical Biology, 263*, 59–69.

Russo, T., Baldi, P., Parisi, A., Magnifico, G., Mariani, S., & Cataudella, S. (2009). Lévy processes and stochastic von Bertalanffy models of growth, with application to fish population analysis. *Journal of Theoretical Biology, 258*, 521–529.

Schumacher, G. E. (1984). Choosing optimal sampling times for therapeutic drug monitoring. *Clinical Pharmacy, 4*, 84–92.

Somers, I. F. (1988). On a seasonally oscillating growth function. *Fishbyte, 6*, 8–11.

Soriano, M., Moreau, J., Hoenig, J. M., & Pauly, D. (1992). New functions for the anlaysis of two-phase growth of juvenile and adult fishes, with application to Nile perch. *Transactions of the American Fisheries Society, 121*: 486–493.

Steinberg, L. (2010). A dual systems model of adolescent risk-taking. *Developmental Psychobiology, 52*, 216–224.

Stiles, J. & Jernigan, T. L. (2010). The basics of brain development. *Neuropsychology Review, 20*, 327–348.

Timmons, A. C. & Preacher, K. J. (2015). The importance of temporal design: How do measurement intervals affect the accuracy and efficiency of parameter estimates in longitudinal research? *Multivariate Behavioral Research, 50*, 41–55.

Turing, A. (1952). The chemical basis of morphogenesis. *Philosophical Transactions of the Royal Society of London. Series B, Biological Sciences, 237*, 37–72.

von Bertalanffy, L. (1956). General Systems Theory. *General Systems, I*, 1–10.

Wood, P. K., Steinley, D., & Jackson, K. M. (2015) Right-sizing statistical models for longitudinal data. *Psychological Methods, 20*, 470–488.

14

MODELING CHANGE WITH DATA COLLECTED FROM RELATIVES[1]

Michael C. Neale

Introduction

I first met Jack McArdle in the cafeteria of the Institute of Psychiatry at King's College in London, when I was a graduate student with David Fulker. Jack had visited in part to discuss modeling of data from twins and their parents, which was to become a central part of my PhD thesis. We considered a path diagram of genetic and cultural transmission from parents to their twin children, to which Jack added an auto-correlation path to represent residual variation in the child's genotype. This tweak to the diagram seemed rather trivial and insignificant at the time; Fulker and I exchanged skeptical glances and may have smirked a bit. Jack was in fact giving us a lesson in precise specification of a structural equation model via a mathematically complete path diagram. Little did I realize that I was going to become one of its most ardent devotees. It took some years, and my move to the United States before I fully understood the value of a mathematically complete path diagram of a structural equation model. Early in the 1990s, while actively collaborating with Jack, I developed the program Mx (Neale, 1991). Its graphical interface, with which users could directly specify and fit models to data, would not have existed without the influence of McArdle on myself and our mutual friend and colleague Steve Boker. Today, the same method underwrites graphical modeling software such as Onyx (von Oertzen, Brandmaier, & Tsang, 2017) or Amos (Arbuckle, 1995). In practice, diagram-based modeling is a valuable teaching tool, and useful for small- to medium-sized models. Larger models are usually more efficiently programmed via matrix algebra or purpose-built functions that specify the data, model type and optimizer or other options.

Assortative Mating

My first publication with Jack concerned resemblance between spouses (Neale & McArdle, 1990), which can arise from assortative mating, i.e., like marrying like. Marital resemblance is weak or absent for many personality traits, but is very substantial for educational attainment, political affiliation, and substance use. It is significant in genetic epidemiology because the genotypes of the parents become correlated, which in turn increases the genetic variance and covariances between siblings in the next generation. We had figured out a way to represent the assortative mating model in LISREL (Joreskog & Sorbom, 1996) and published it. The model involved multivariate path analysis (Vogler, 1985), in which each variable in a path diagram may represent a vector of (latent or observed) variables, and the paths between them consist of matrices. Subsequently, we experimented with specifying the model with the RAMPATH software he co-developed with Steve Boker. The software found a simpler drawing that avoided paths crossing as they do in Figure 14.1 of the 1990 paper. These diagrams are shown in Figure 14.1. My original diagram was drawn with the idea of keeping all the husbands' variables on one side of the figure, and all the wives' variables on the other. However, it had the disadvantage that two paths crossed each other; RAMPATH's automatic drawing avoided this intersection. Being taught such simple things by a computer program can be rewarding for any user; for developers there is the additional sense of completing the circle one began by teaching the computer to do new things.

Psychometric and Biometric Factor Models

Data collected from relatives such as monozygotic (MZ) and dizygotic (DZ) twins permit partitioning of trait variation into components associated with genetic and environmental factors. The value of this natural experiment was appreciated in the nineteen century by Sir Francis Galton (1875), and the comparison of MZ and DZ pairs' similarities was developed by Merriman (1924). However, despite the development of path analysis by Sewall Wright (1921) many years would pass before structural equation modeling software capable of fitting models simultaneously to multiple groups would be developed and it was not until the 1990s that SEM became the method of choice for analyzing data from twins and other relatives.

   McArdle and Goldsmith (1990) recognized that multivariate data from twins could be analyzed by extending a factor model in two ways. The "Psychometric Factor" model (a.k.a. the Common Pathway model) takes the usual single factor model and partitions all the latent variables (i.e., the random effects) into additive genetic (A), common environment (C; shared by twins) and non-shared environment (E) components. Figure 14.2 shows a path diagram of this model when there are three orthogonal factors: F1, F2, and F3. A popular alternative to this model is to impose restrictions such that the latent factors'

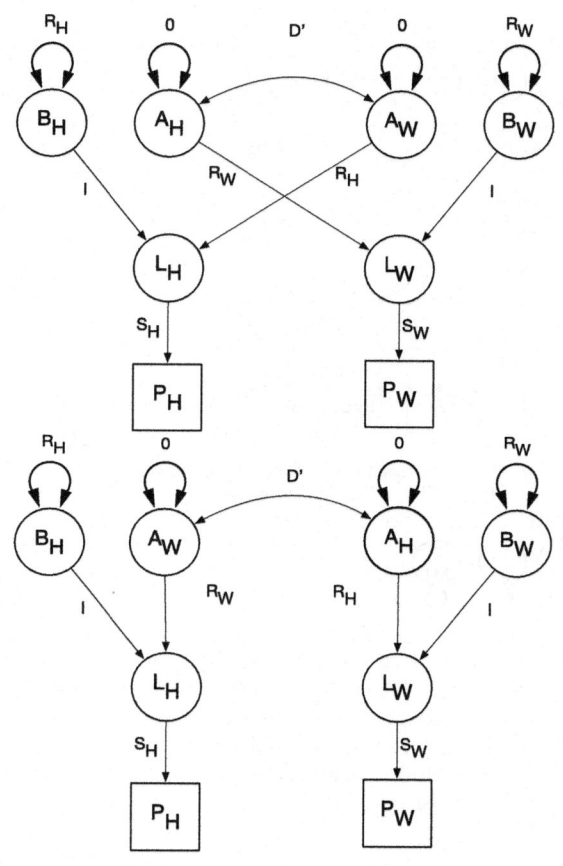

FIGURE 14.1 Multivariate path diagrams for modeling marital resemblance for multiple traits. Left: diagram designed by human being (MCN); Right: diagram designed by intelligent software (RAMPATH). The zero variance-covariance matrices atop the A_H and A_W variables generate covariance between spouses' phenotypes (P_H and P_W), but do not affect their variances.

variance is assumed to be composed of entirely one type of variation, A, C, or E. This second 'Biometric Factor' model (a.k.a. the Independent Pathway model) is shown in Figure 14.3; it has six fewer free parameters than the three-factor psychometric model. To identify the model, the latent factor variances are typically constrained to equal unity, so effectively the models differ by just three unconstrained parameters. Many applications of these two models have sadly compared only the single psychometric factor model (Figure 14.2 without F2 or F3), to the three-factor biometric one, and found the latter to fit much better. Those with experience in analyses of unrelated persons will divine that a single factor model often fits worse than a three-factor one, and that exactly the same type of data are represented in the within-person covariances of the individual twins. Failure to specify enough within-person factors is poor rationale

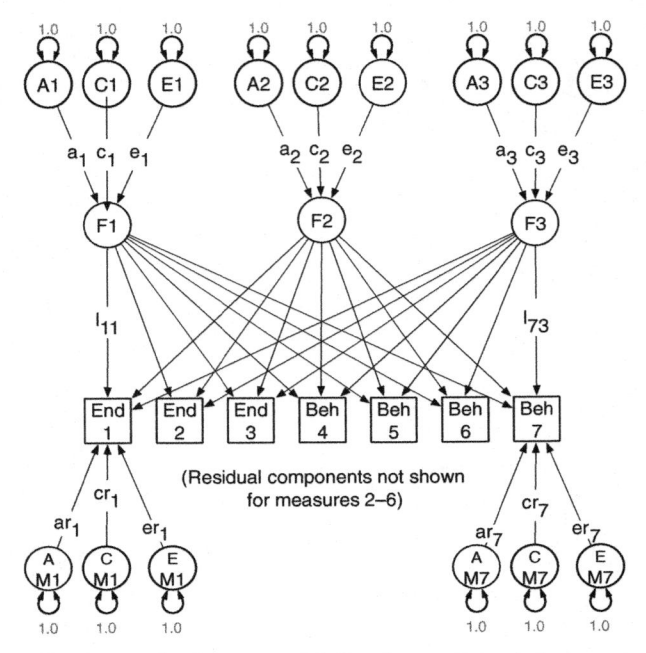

FIGURE 14.2 Psychometric factor model for data collected from twins or other relatives. Latent factors F1, F2, and F3 influence seven measured variables M1–M7. Variation in the latent factor and the residual, variable-specific components are partitioned into additive genetic, shared and unique environment components (A, C, and E, respectively). Model identification requires two types of relative, with differences in the degree of covariation between the relatives' A and C variance components.

to favor the biometric factor model over the single-factor psychometric one. A reviewer requested examples of this pattern, of which there are many in *Behavior Genetics* and similar journals. It seems best to identify a few publications that I myself co-authored before realizing the oversight (Kendler, Neale, Kesslier, Heath, & Eaves, 1992; Kendler, Walters, Neale, KIesslier, Heath, & Eaves, 1995). Indeed, I seemed to be comfortable with that approach in Kendler (1995), in which we stated "the common pathway model was rejected, suggesting that the genetic and environmental risk factors for these disorders are not influencing comorbidity in the same manner." (Kendler, Walters, Neale, Kessler, Heath, & Eaves, 1995). While that conclusion may be correct, fitting "the" common pathway model (as if there is only one, the single factor variety) is insufficient for it to be drawn. Here I note that both types of model may be extended by adding either psychometric or biometric factors, and that this could be done *ex hypothesi* for confirmatory work, or automatically using, for example, a loop in R. The resulting long list of models might be summarized by model-averaging. However, it is the opinion of this author that the biometric factor model is intrinsically less plausible for most (and perhaps all) complex

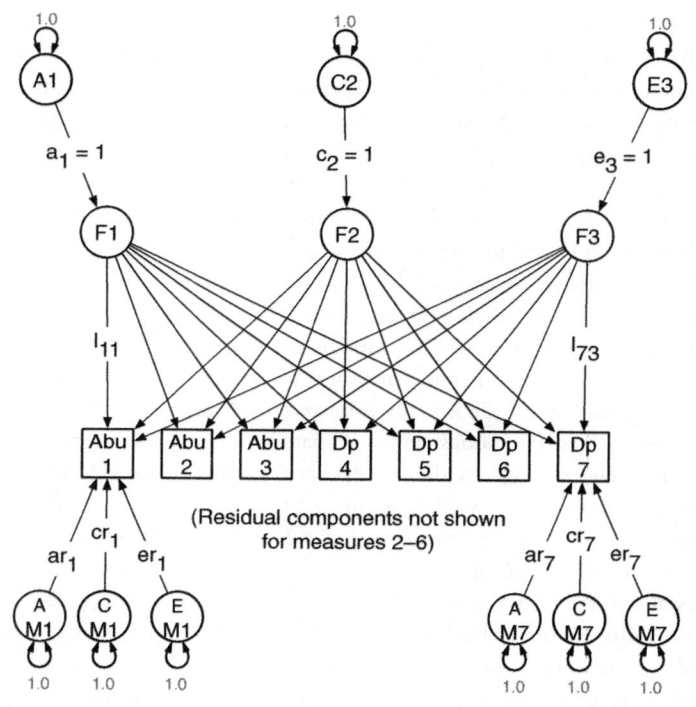

FIGURE 14.3 Biometric factor model for data collected from twins or other relatives. Latent factors F1, F2, and F3 influence seven measured variables M1–M7. Variation in latent factor F1 is specified as entirely additive genetic, that in F2 is entirely common environment, and F3 is exclusively unique environment. Model identification requires two types of relative, with differences in the degree of covariation between the relatives' A and C variance components.

behavioral traits. Genetic and environmental influences seem likely to act together on the structure and function of the brain or other physiological systems en route to affecting variation in behavioral and psychological traits. That is, so-called endophenotypes – such as size or connectivity of brain regions – likely combine genetic and environmental influences during their development prior to affecting, e.g., psychiatric, psychological, and behavioral traits that are often the primary outcomes of interest (Meyer-Lindenberg & Weinberger, 2006). Therefore, McArdle's psychometric factor model seems optimal for this area of research – with more than one factor if the data so warrant. This is an empirical question that was not often addressed in the past; I hope that future analyses will do so.

Latent Growth Modeling

Dr McArdle has also made great contributions to the genetic modeling of longitudinal, repeated measures data. He is credited with adapting growth curve models such as that of Meredith and Tisak (1984) and Browne (1993) for application to data with twins. His 1986 paper partitioned latent factors into A and E components alone, although there was no impediment to including shared environmental variance components McArdle, (1986). Similarly, with Aki Hamagami, he added biometric components to latent change score models (MArdle & Hamagami, 2003), enabling dynamical systems perspective on genetic and environmental factors in development. Here I focus on the latent growth curve approach, on which he and I collaborated to develop in the early 1990s, although it was not until the turn of the century that these methods were finally published. To publish original material some six years later than planned is a luxury afforded to those, such as Jack, who are many years ahead of the field.

Most latent growth curve (LGC) models use two or more factors to represent level, linear (and possibly quadratic or other) growth by fixing the factor loadings to particular values. McArdle initially followed the Meredith and Tisak approach, in which some factor loadings were estimated as free parameters. Since then, growth curve factors have, with rare exception, used the fixed factor loadings approach; loadings for the level factor are all set to 1.0, those for the linear growth factor are set to increasing integers (0, 1, 2...), and those for the quadratic are the square of the linear. This polynomial approach is suitable for growth processes about which we have little knowledge or theory to guide curve type selection. Although the polynomial model may provide a good fit to data over a limited developmental period, it is often poor when the measurement window is extended. This is true, even of the less widely-applied growth curve models that include quadratic components: asymptotic behavior is difficult to approximate with a small number of polynomial factors. Human height, for example, follows two periods of accelerated development, which the Preece-Baines curve closely models (Beunen, Thomis, Maes, Loos, Malina, Claessens, & Vlietinck, 2000), with asymptotic behavior that matches the leveling off of human height in adulthood. Accordingly, I now consider factor modeling of growth with particular functional forms, i.e., a parametric growth curve (PGC) approach.

In our 2000 paper, McArdle and I showed how Gompertz, Logistic and Exponential family curves could be specified and fitted to data from MZ and DZ twin pairs (Neals & McArdle, 2000). Fitting such growth curves seems rational for many ongoing studies. For example, the Adolescent Behavioral and Cognitive Development (ABCD, 2017) study, which is currently collecting longitudinal data on brain development and cognition from 11,500 9 to 10-year-old youths, including 800 pairs of twins. This is but one example of Jack's contributions to the study of development, which will surely benefit research studies long into the future. The 2000 treatment used classic Mx (Neale, Bokrer, Xie, & Maes, 2003) to fit models to summary statistics consisting of means and covariance matrices, but this software is no longer supported since it was superseded by OpenMx (Boker, Neale, Maes, Wilde, Spiegel, Brick, Spies, Estabrook, Kenny, Bstes, Mehta, & Fox, 2011); Neale, Hunter, Pritikin, Zahery, Brick, Kirkpatrick, Estabrook, Bates, Maes, & Boker, (2016). Endel Tulving remarked "a Festschrift frequently enough also serves as a convenient place in which those who are invited to contribute find a permanent resting place for their otherwise unpublishable or at least difficult-to-publish papers" (Tulving, 2007). It therefore seems appropriate to revisit the growth curve models of the 2000 paper, using modern analytical methods. Open source software increases reliability and reproducibility of findings, and safeguards its legacy, so implementation in OpenMx seems worthwhile. Here we have an opportunity to self-examine; if the original researcher cannot reproduce their own results, it seems unlikely that others would.

Modeling growth curves such as those that arise from differential equations is a more complex task than is usual for structural equation modeling. Effectively, the factor loadings are neither constants nor free parameters, but complex functions obtained as the partial derivatives of the growth curve function with respect to its free parameters. The expected means are obtained directly from the growth curve function itself, but these too may involve non-trivial algebra. In our 2000 paper, Jack and I tabulated these derivatives for the Logistic, Gompertz and Exponential growth curve forms (Neale & McArdle, 2000). Here, for illustration, I reproduce the equations for the Gompertz curve in Table 14.1. Figures 14.4 and 14.5 respectively show path diagrams for the conventional level, slope, and quadratic polynomial component LGC model, and a parametric structured curve model. The primary difference between the figures is that in the LGC model the factor loadings are fixed to constant values, whereas in the PGC model the loadings are complicated algebraic functions of the free parameters of the growth curve being fitted.

Some interesting things happened in the attempted reproduction of the results using OpenMx instead of classic Mx. Translating the script was straightforward, but the original data files could not be found. The covariance matrices and means were, however, published in Jack's 1986 paper, so they were re-entered (McArdle, 1986). Fitting the models anew, the results were similar but not identical to those of the original article. The number of estimated parameters were the same in OpenMx and classic, but the chi-squared fit of all the models had deteriorated by some 20 units. To identify the source of this issue, the models were refitted using the Mx version 1.69, which generated very similar values for model fit and parameter estimates to those obtained by OpenMx. This agreement increased once the sample sizes for Mx were increased from 75 to 76, because OpenMx's fit function uses N rather than N-1 when fitting to summary statistics, to be consistent with its full information maximum likelihood fit function. With one exception, the remaining differences in model fit between OpenMx and Mx were less than a single unit of chi-squared, and likely due to differences in numerical precision and orders of operation when evaluating the log-likelihood. Optimization can be sensitive to relatively slight changes in numerical precision, although both programs appear satisfied that they have arrived at a strong local, and possibly global minimum. The single exception is that the effect of dropping all the occasion-specific familial components, A_s and C_s, is approximately 4.6 chi-squared units greater with Mx than with OpenMx. This appears to be an

TABLE 14.1 Parametric growth curve functions F_x for Gompertz ($x = G$), Exponential ($x = E$) and Logistic ($x = L$) curves, and their partial derivatives $\frac{dF_x}{d\theta}$ with respect to the elements of the free parameter vector θ for asymptote (a), initial (i), and rate (r), as a function of time t. The partial derivative vectors for $t = 1 \ldots T$ are used as the factor loadings (e.g., dy/da) shown in Figure 14.5. Further details are given in Neale and McArdle (2000), on which this table was based.

Gompertz

$$F_G = a\exp\left[\log[\frac{i}{a}]\exp[-(t-1)r]\right] \tag{14.1}$$

$$\frac{dF_G}{da} = [1 - \exp[-(t-1)r]]\exp\left[\log[\frac{i}{a}]\exp[-(t-1)r]\right] \tag{14.2}$$

$$\frac{dF_G}{di} = \frac{a}{i}\exp\left[-(t-1)r + \log[\frac{i}{a}]\exp[-(t-1)r]\right] \tag{14.3}$$

$$\frac{dF_G}{dr} = -a\log[\frac{i}{a}](t-1)\exp\left[-(t-1)r + \log[\frac{i}{a}]\exp[-(t-1)r]\right] \tag{14.4}$$

Exponential

$$F_E = a - (a-i)\exp[-(t-1)r] \tag{14.5}$$

$$\frac{dF_E}{da} = 1 - \exp[-(t-1)r] \tag{14.6}$$

$$\frac{dF_E}{di} = \exp[-(t-1)r] \tag{14.7}$$

$$\frac{dF_E}{dr} = (a-i)(t-1)\exp[-(t-1)r] \tag{14.8}$$

Logistic

$$F_L = \frac{ai}{i + (a-i)\exp[-(t-1)r]} \tag{14.9}$$

$$\frac{dF_L}{da} = \frac{i - \exp[-(t-1)r]F_L}{i + (a-i)\exp[-(t-1)r]} \tag{14.10}$$

$$\frac{dF_L}{di} = \frac{a - \left(1 - \exp[-(t-1)r]\right)F_L}{i + (a-i)\exp[-(t-1)r]} \tag{14.11}$$

$$\frac{dF_L}{dr} = \frac{(a-i)(t-1)\exp[-(t-1)r]F_L}{i + (a-i)\exp[-(t-1)r]} \tag{14.12}$$

optimization failure on behalf of the older software, possibly due to the order in which the models were fitted. Eliminating variance components that account for a substantial proportion of variance can make for poor starting values for subsequent model fitting attempts, a general point to be aware of when using model-fitting software.

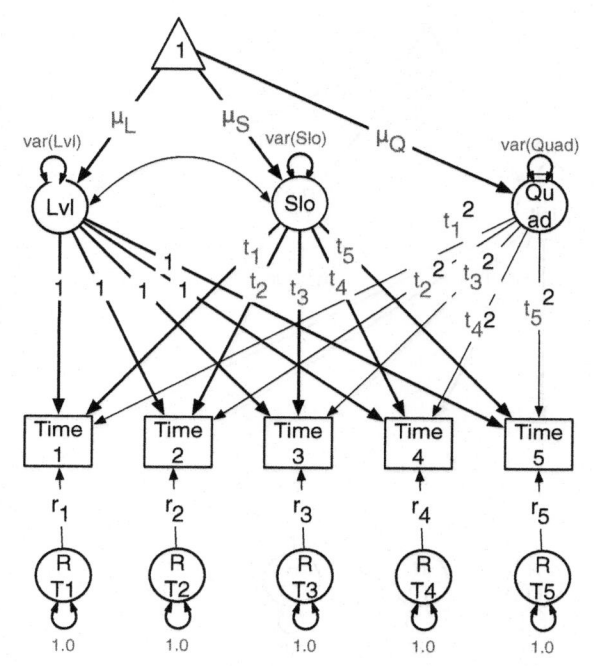

FIGURE 14.4 Latent Growth Curve Model with Level (Lvl), Slope (Slo) and Quadratic (Quad) variance components. These factors have means μ_L, μ_S and μ_Q. Typically, values of the factor loadings $t_1, t_2 \ldots t_5$ are fixed to integer values such as $1, 2 \ldots 5$. In practice, individuals may differ with respect to age at assessment, and may be substituted with individuals' ages at measurement on a casewise basis using, e.g., definition variables in OpenMx.

Table 14.2 shows parameter estimates from fitting the logistic, exponential, and Gompertz growth curves to the Bayley Infant Mental Development data, in the same format as Table 14.2 in Neale and McArdle (2000). Goodness–of–fit statistics of the three models and a set of seven submodels are shown in Table 14.3. The bad news is that neither the goodness–of–fit statistics nor the parameter estimates agree 100% with those from the original article. However, the main substantive conclusions have **not** changed; much of the variation in the random components of the growth curves is associated with shared environmental factors, there remains substantial (residual) variation not associated with the growth curve factors, and some of the residual, time-specific variation is shared between the members of the twin pair. The origin of the disparities between this description and that of Neale and McArdle (2000) seems to be the data files; using the new data shows close, but not perfect agreement between classic Mx and its successor. A further point to note is that the sample size and number of occasions of measurement are both relatively small for the intended purpose of estimating latent growth curves. These limitations make optimization more difficult, because the fit function may change

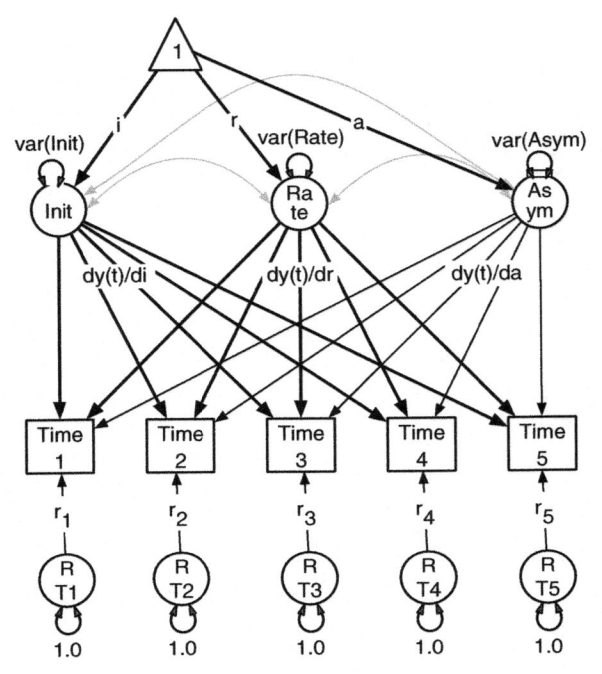

FIGURE 14.5 Structural Model for Functional Latent Growth Curves featuring asymptote (*A*), initial (*I*), and rate (*R*) variance components, which generate variation in the observed measures on occasions (Time 1 ... 5. The factor loadings denoted, e.g., $dy(t)/di$, are partial derivatives of the growth curve function with respect to its initial (*i*), rate (*r*) and asymptote (*a*) parameters; these parameters are also the estimated means of the latent factors.

little in response to a change in parameter value, i.e., the gradients, being the partial derivatives of the fit function with respect to the parameters are almost flat.

The scripts and data files used in this article can be found on the following website: http://somewhere.suggested.by.editor?. These, we hope, will facilitate future uses of the method of fitting structured latent growth curves to data from relatives. The scripts can also be used to fit models to data from unrelated persons, but the genetic and shared environmental variance components at both the factor and residual levels should be set to zero. In effect, the model becomes one of random, individual-specific effects, which, to a behavioral geneticist, seems a strong assumption. It is important for researchers from all disciplines to recognize that variance components at both the factor and occasion-specific (residual) levels may include reliable and familial components of variance.

Conclusions

This chapter embarked on a reproducibility exercise, using entirely different software (to create OpenMx no code was 'borrowed' from Mx – all code was

TABLE 14.2 Parameter estimates for three growth curve models fitted to Bayley Infant Mental Development data on MZ and DZ twins assessed at four occasions. Variance in the growth curve components $a, i,$ and r due to genetic (G_f), common environment (C_f) and specific environment (E_f) factors are shown on the diagonal of matrices, with covariances below and correlations above. Variance due to occasion-specific genetic and environmental factors $A_s, C_s,$ and E_s are shown for the four occasions t_1 to t_4.

Parameter		Exponential				Model Logistic				Gompertz		
a		116.98				84.75				93.64		
i		39.90				40.11				39.99		
r		0.11				0.37				0.24		
		a	i	r		a	i	r		a	i	r
G_f	a	528.48	−18.85	−1.14	a	5.21	−2.05	−0.11	a	43.08	−5.61	−0.32
	i	−18.85	0.67	0.04	i	−2.05	0.80	0.04	i	−5.61	0.73	0.04
	r	−1.14	0.04	0.00	r	−0.11	0.04	0.00	r	−0.32	0.04	0.00
		a	i	r		a	i	r		a	i	r
C_f	a	6726.92	−49.58	−9.70	a	382.38	−5.37	−1.17	a	1013.65	−13.34	−2.84
	i	−49.58	10.25	0.07	i	−5.37	9.85	−0.03	i	−13.34	10.05	0.02
	r	−9.70	0.07	0.01	r	−1.17	−0.03	0.00	r	−2.84	0.02	0.01
		a	i	r		a	i	r		a	i	r
E_f	a	1035.26	20.57	−1.63	a	77.61	5.51	−0.40	a	180.93	8.51	−0.65
	i	20.57	0.41	−0.03	i	5.51	0.39	−0.03	i	8.51	0.40	−0.03
	r	−1.63	−0.03	0.00	r	−0.40	−0.03	0.00	r	−0.65	−0.03	0.00
	t_1	t_2	t_3	t_4	t_1	t_2	t_3	t_4	t_1	t_2	t_3	t_4
A_s	2.31	1.28	2.12	0.00	2.33	1.24	2.11	0.00	2.31	1.28	2.12	0.00
C_s	1.03	0.00	0.00	0.00	1.06	0.00	0.25	0.00	1.05	0.00	0.00	0.00
E_s	2.04	1.96	1.80	1.91	2.04	1.95	1.80	1.89	2.04	1.96	1.80	1.90

TABLE 14.3 Fit statistics obtained for Growth curve models and submodels applied to Bayley Infant Mental Development data on MZ and DZ twins.

	Fit Statistic			Difference χ^2		
Model	χ^2	d.f.	AIC	χ^2	d.f.	p
Exponential						
Full	148.90	55	38.90	—	—	—
Orthogonal	163.28	64	35.28	14.38	9	0.11
No A	157.37	61	35.37	8.47	6	0.21
No C	190.86	61	68.86	41.96	6	0.00
No E	159.86	61	37.86	10.96	6	0.09
No A_s,C_s	187.72	63	61.72	38.82	8	0.00
No A_s	158.44	59	40.44	9.54	4	0.05
No C_s	149.02	59	31.02	0.12	4	1.00
Logistic						
Full	157.55	55	47.55	—	—	—
Orthogonal	168.54	64	40.54	10.99	9	0.28
No A	165.58	61	43.58	8.03	6	0.24
No C	198.63	61	76.63	41.08	6	0.00
No E	168.39	61	46.39	10.84	6	0.09
No A_s, C_s	202.17	63	76.17	44.62	8	0.00
No A_s	167.20	59	49.20	9.65	4	0.05
No C_s	157.70	59	39.70	0.15	4	1.00
Gompertz						
Full	151.88	55	41.88	—	—	—
Orthogonal	164.46	64	36.46	12.58	9	0.18
No A	160.17	61	38.17	8.29	6	0.22
No C	193.45	61	71.45	41.57	6	0.00
No E	162.78	61	40.78	10.91	6	0.09
No A_s, C_s	192.77	63	66.77	40.89	8	0.00
No A_s	161.38	59	43.38	9.51	4	0.05
No C_s	152.01	59	34.01	0.14	4	1.00

freshly developed). Encouragingly, only modest differences were found between the two implementations of extended structural equation modeling, and no change in substantive conclusions was warranted. The one exception shows better optimization performance with OpenMx than with Mx, which indicates progress. It should be noted that OpenMx offers several different optimization algorithms – with more planned for future releases – although the same optimizer, NPSOL (Gill, Murray, Saunders, & Wright, 1986), was used in both packages for this illustration.

Finally, I have tremendous respect for Professor McArdle and his many contributions to behavioral science generally, and to multivariate and developmental behavioral genetics in particular. His influence on my own career was quite profound. In the early days of developing Mx, Jack recommended that I not join others who were selling their structural equation modeling software. This advice proved crucial; I have not had to trouble myself with running a business as well as a research team at VCU. I also feel that having obtained tax payer money to develop the software, it would be immoral to charge users for purchase or license fees, because the same tax payer would likely have to foot the bill for them. Indeed, Jack's insight foreshadowed the rise of open source software and open science – principles with which I whole-heartedly agree. For science, anything other than open source software should be considered unfit for purpose. One approach to validating a model-fitting program is to feed it data simulated using known parameter values to see if its parameter estimates do not depart from them for reasons other than sampling error. However, this method is analogous to a Turing test for artificial vs. human intelligence. The concept is to feed questions in through a letterbox, on the other side of which is either a human or a machine, which responds without directly revealing its mechanism. With a series of such questions, a Turing test may establish with some degree of confidence whether the room contains a human being or a computer. This confidence is typically much less than would be obtained if one could look inside the room and examine its contents. Open source software puts the researcher in the position of being able to examine the contents of the room. Indeed, a user of closed source software should really run simulation tests on every model being used, to ensure that no "corner case" bug exists. Even then, the best that can be achieved outside the black box is support for the hypothesis that it is doing the right thing. While keeping the source code secret may be good from the perspective of maintaining an economic advantage over one's competitors, it seems poor for the purposes of reproducible scientific research. Structural equation modeling, and especially the field of behavioral genetics, are indebted to Dr McArdle for his prescient wisdom in recommending free and open source software for scientific research.

Note

1 This study was supported by NIDA grants R01DA-018673 and R25DA-26119.

References

ABCD (2017). The adolescent study of cognitive development http://abcdstudy.org. Technical report, University of San Diego, http://abcdstudy.org

Arbuckle, J. L. (1995). *AMOS for Windows. Analysis of moment structures (Version 3.5)*. Chicago, IL: SmallWaters.

Beunen, G, Thomis, M., Maes, H. H., Loos, R., Malina, R. M., Claessens, A. L., & Vlietinck, R. (2000). Genetic variance of adolescent growth in stature. *Annals of Human Biology, 27*(2), 173–186.

Baker, S., Neale, M., Maes, H. H., Wilde, M., Spiegel, M., Brick, T. R., Spies, J., Estabrook, R., Kenny, S., Bates, T., Mehta, P., & Fox J. (2011). OpenMx: An open source extended structural equation modeling framework. *Psychometrika, 76*(2), 306–11.

Browne, M. W. (1993). Structured latent curve models. In C M Cuadras and C R Rao, editors, *Multivariate analysis: Future directions 2*, pages 171–198. Amsterdam: North-Holland Publishing Co.

Galton, F. (1875). The history of twins, as a criterion of the relative powers of nature and nurture. *Fraser's Magazine, 12*: (pp. 566–576).

Gill, P. E., Murray, W., Saunders, M. A., and Wright, M. H. (1986). User's guide for npsol (version 4.0): A FORTRAN package for nonlinear programming. Technical Report SOL 86–2, Department of Operations Research, Stanford University, Stanford.

Jöreskog, K. G. and Sörbom, D. (1996). *LISREL 8 User's Reference Guide*. Mooresville, IN: Scientific Software, Inc.

Kendler, K. S., Neale, M. C., Kessler, R. C., Heath, A. C., and Eaves, L. J. (1992). The genetic epidemiology of phobias in women. the interrelationship of agoraphobia, social phobia, situational phobia, and simple phobia. *Arch Gen Psychiatry, 49*(4), 273–81.

Kendler, K. S., Walters, E. E., Neale, M. C., Kessler, R. C., Heath, A. C., & Eaves, L. J. (1995). The structure of the genetic and environmental risk factors for six major psychiatric disorders in women. phobia, generalized anxiety disorder, panic disorder, bulimia, major depression, and alcoholism. *Arch Gen Psychiatry, 52*(5), 374–83.

McArdle, J. J. (1986). Latent variable growth within behavior genetic models. *Behavioral Genetics, 16*(1), 163–200.

McArdle, J. J. & Goldsmith, H. H. (1990). Alternative common-factor models for multivariate biometric analyses. *Behavioral Genetics, 20*, 569–608.

McArdle, J. J. & Hamagami, F. (2003). Structural equation models for evaluating dynamic concepts within longitudinal twin analyses. *Behavioral Genetics, 33*(2), 137–159.

Meredith, W. & Tisak, J. (1984). Tuckerizing curves. *Paper presented at Psychometric Society Annual Meeting, Santa Barbara CA.*

Merriman, C. (1924). The intellectual resemblance of twins. *Psychological Monographs, 33*, 1–58.

Meyer-Lindenberg, A. & Weinberger, D. R. (2006). Intermediate phenotypes and genetic mechanisms of psychiatric disorders. *Nat Rev Neurosci, 7*(10), 818–27.

Neale, M. C. (1991). *Mx: Statistical Modeling*. Box 710 MCV, Richmond, VA 23298: Department of Human Genetics.

Neale, M. C. & McArdle, J. J. (1990). The analysis of assortative mating: a lisrel model. *Behavioral Genetics, 20*(2), 287–96.

Neale, M. C. & McArdle, J. J. (2000). Structured latent growth curves for twin data. *Twin Research, 3*, 165–77.

Neale, M. C., Boker, S. M., Xie, G., & Maes, H. H. (2003). *Mx: Statistical Modeling*. Department of Psychiatry, Virginia Commonwealth University, Box 980126 Richmond VA, 6th edition.

Neale, M. C., Hunter, M. D., Pritikin, J. N., Zahery, M., Brick, T. R., Kirkpatrick, R. M., Estabrook, R., Bates, T. C., Maes, H. H. M., & Boker, S. M. (2016). OpenMx 2.0: Extended structural equation and statistical modeling. *Psychometrika, 81*(2), 535–49.

Tulving, E. (2007). Are there 256 different kinds of memory? In James, S. Nairne (Ed.). *The foundations of remembering: Essays in honor of Henry L. Roediger III*, page 39. New York: Psychology Press.

Vogler, G. P. (1985). Multivariate path analysis of familial resemblance. *Genetic Epidemiology, 2*, 35–53.

von Oertzen, T., Brandmaier, A. M., & Tsang, S. (2015). Structural equation modeling with onyx. *Structural Equation Modeling: A Multidisciplinary Journal, 22*(1), 148–161.

Wright, S. (1921). Correlation and causation. *Journal of Agricultural Research, 20*, 557–585.

15

MAKING THE CUT

How a Quantitative Psychologist Changed College Sports

Todd A. Petr & Thomas S. Paskus

There are currently about 500,000 college student-athletes at schools within the National Collegiate Athletic Association (NCAA) and it is unlikely any of them know the name Jack McArdle. There are tens of thousands of famous and not-so-famous coaches at NCAA colleges and only a few might be familiar with McArdle. There are countless athletics administrators, faculty and presidents on campus who have never heard of him. Yet, virtually every one of these athletes, coaches, and administrators intersects with Jack McArdle's NCAA legacy on a daily basis.

Other chapters in this volume have described the marvelous technical and scientific research contributions that McArdle made over his long and distinguished career. But, many readers may not know about his research program within college athletics. It is fair to say that McArdle had a profound effect on the world of intercollegiate athletics that continues to this day. His work with the NCAA also serves as an excellent example of how to develop research programs that can best impact real-world policies.

Jack McArdle's association with the NCAA began in the late 1980s when the NCAA Director of Research at the time, Ursula Walsh, reached out to John Nesselroade to identify a quantitative psychologist who could analyze data from a new study of the educational outcomes of NCAA Division I student-athletes. John recommended Jack and it was love at first sight for both McArdle and his NCAA colleagues.

McArdle was initially hired by the NCAA to conduct analyses related to what are called "initial eligibility" rules. These are the academic standards that determine whether a college recruit will be allowed to compete in intercollegiate athletics at the Division I level as a freshman. In the early 1980s, after decades of debate and a series of high-profile academic scandals (see Crowley, 2006), the

NCAA had significantly increased the minimum initial eligibility standards. The new benchmarks (commonly referred to as Proposition 48 or "Prop 48") included minimum scores on the ACT or SAT and a minimum grade-point average (GPA) in a prescribed set of high school core curriculum courses. The goal at that time was to ensure that all NCAA athletes were capable of succeeding in college-level classes and eventually graduating. And, even though the legislation had the imprimatur of organizations like the American Council on Education (ACE), the standards were created in an environment that was "remarkably free of empirical analysis" as Dr. Walsh liked to say. That is, no one really knew whether these specific high school academic benchmarks were predictive of college academic success.

When Prop 48 was passed by the NCAA membership in 1983, there was not even a mechanism in place to collect high school or college academic data for student-athletes. Recognizing this, the NCAA brought together educational experts from within its membership to design an Academic Performance Study (APS) that McArdle would later use to assess the impacts of the new rules. Division I colleges were asked to compile data on high school academic preparation and college academic outcomes on a specific entering class of student-athletes. The cohorts were spread over a 5-year period from 1984 through 1988, with the members of each cohort collecting up to six years of college academic outcomes on an entering class of student-athletes. Since the new academic benchmarks did not go into effect until the fall of 1986, McArdle was later able to compare data from two cohorts of student-athletes who entered before the increased standards with three cohorts that entered after the regulations were implemented (e.g., see McArdle & Hamagami, 1994).

McArdle's analysis of data from the Academic Performance Study (APS) yielded some surprising results for NCAA policy makers. In particular, Prop 48 was shown to be a problem. The benchmarks for the ACT and SAT were set too high relative to the minimum acceptable high school grades. In addition, McArdle showed that a compensatory rule (cut-score set on an algebraic combination of GPA and test scores) could produce decisions that were more accurate and fairer than those from a conjunctive rule like Prop 48 (hard minimum cut-scores set on both GPA and test). However, great research met strong resistance from various NCAA policy makers who were not accustomed to trusting research data over their gut instincts. It took a number of years meeting with NCAA committees and college athletics leaders to convince them that regression analyses, utility curves, and invariance models should guide policies impacting college football and basketball teams.

In that process, McArdle and his research colleagues at the NCAA learned some valuable lessons that were applied throughout a 25-year partnership. Those lessons were applied not only in modifying academic initial eligibility standards, but also academic progress-toward-degree standards that boosted student-athlete graduation rates. They were applied during the process of creating improved academic outcome metrics like the Graduation Success Rate (GSR) and Academic Progress Rate (APR). They have also led to enhancing the lives of student-athletes on and off the playing field, by ingraining the importance of survey research into the DNA of the NCAA. It is not our purpose here to run down the litany of policy changes that were informed by McArdle's work – those are detailed thoroughly in two articles in the *Journal of Intercollegiate Sport* (Paskus, 2012; Petr & McArdle, 2012). Rather, it is to describe a few bedrock principles that Jack McArdle instilled in the NCAA as it relates to making science and data an integral component of creating policy.

Research Can't Answer Every Question

At first, that may not seem like a principle Jack McArdle would espouse. We can answer any question if we collect enough data and conduct enough analyses, right? Part of McArdle's brilliance in the NCAA policy debates was understanding exactly how to draw the line for decision makers between what was indisputable from the research and what was their call.

The discussions on initial eligibility standards that followed McArdle's work on the APS study provides a perfect example of this tenet. The research clearly showed that the best academic predictor of college success was an equally-weighted combination of SAT/ACT score and core-course GPA. No form of a conjunctive rule (minimum cut-score on each component rather than setting a cut on the composite) could match the accuracy of decisions nor the minimization of adverse impacts possible with a compensatory standard. Armed with stacks of analyses, McArdle encouraged us to stand firm on the principle that the test score cut was generally unsupportable. He endured years of questions and criticism from those who felt you could not have a reasonable standard without a test-score floor, but he held firm in defense of the research and its conclusions.

At the same time that he was promoting a specific research-based strategy for combining variables, McArdle told the NCAA membership that the research could not support a "correct answer" for what cut-score should be chosen on the composite. We could provide ample data showing projected GPAs and graduation rates associated with various cut-scores. He would also show how any choice of cut-score would lead to test selection biases that impacted prospective student-athletes from racial/ethnic minority groups (McArdle, 1998). If the NCAA raised the cut-score, academic success rates would increase, but so would adverse impacts. Many researchers might have simply suggested a cut-score based on their own values of how success and impact should be balanced, but McArdle chose a very different approach. He employed utility theory to show various decision makers how the optimal cut-score on the composite varied as a function of how much one valued the correct identification of eventual graduates relative to the perceived costs of failing to make eligible somebody who had sufficient academic preparation to earn a college degree if given the opportunity. He even took the novel approach of working backwards and confronting NCAA policy makers with the utility weights inferred by the cut-scores they were supporting (Paskus, 2013).

The resulting cut-score discussions were not at all free of data – there were many meetings where utility weights and false positives/negatives were center stage. But, McArdle made it clear that decisions on a cut-score would eventually have to come down to judgments about how correct and incorrect decisions were valued by the schools of the NCAA. Research could always inform in this setting, but Jack McArdle was adept at knowing the limits of even the most sophisticated analyses.

Understand Your Audience

In the early days of our efforts to illuminate NCAA policy makers, we would structure presentations like one would at an academic conference. There would be a robust discussion of the scientific questions, followed by minutiae on the methods used for the study, and then a detailed look at the statistical results. Only after all that would we get around to discussing the implications to the NCAA of what the analysis had uncovered. As we all came to find out quickly, policy-making bodies are very different from academic audiences. While these NCAA committees are typically comprised of bright and accomplished people (university presidents, faculty, athletics administrators, coaches, etc.) very few of them are experts in research methods or statistics. Thus, when we presented in the academic style, most of the room was lost or asleep somewhere between the analysis of response rates and the description of logistic regression models.

It quickly became evident to McArdle that even the most sophisticated research program would be ineffective in enhancing policies if we did not tailor our presentations differently to each audience. It did not mean that the underlying work was any less robust, but some groups simply wanted the bottom line and perhaps a few take-home statistics that coaches and media could understand. Others would test the researchers and question the methods and analytic details. McArdle stressed that to accomplish the goal of informing policy, research staff members had to be adept at moving seamlessly from audience to audience, sometimes within a single presentation. We found that providing less detail at the appropriate times was making our work more impactful, with McArdle serving as the master communicator. Having worked with many academic researchers, we can guarantee you that this is not a skill that most possess. As time went on, it was clear that committee members were becoming more engaged, more informed, and much more willing to use our data to make decisions.

Eventually, this led to significant changes in the NCAA itself. Historically the NCAA, like many other organizations, made policy too often based upon anecdote and experiences. Thus, there was some natural resistance to our efforts to introduce data into the discussion (including once being referred to dismissively as "science boy" by a high-ranking committee member). In the early 1990s, data analysts waited outside many NCAA committee meeting rooms until being summoned for a 15-minute audience and summarily dismissed. Over time, though, McArdle's expertise and ability to make the data interesting and relevant began to get the research staff more exposure to these committees. By the early 2000s, the Division I Board of Directors was scheduling full-day sessions devoted to a review and discussion of data and its policy implications. The change was so profound that when the NCAA's strategic plan was developed in 2004, one of the five pillars on which the plan was built was "Data-Driven Decision Making." That would not have occurred without Jack McArdle's influence. Today, research staff members are considered integral liaisons to every NCAA committee.

You Need More and Better Data

When Jack McArdle was first hired to work on the APS, the NCAA research staff was very proud of the scope of that study. They had collected 5-year longitudinal academic data on a representative sample of over 12,000 student-athletes. McArdle's reaction when he first started his work was something to the effect of "Yeah, this is great, but wouldn't it be better if there was a lot more?" McArdle and his colleagues did some remarkable work with those early APS data, but Jack had visions of how much more could be done with additional information.

In the mid-1990s, McArdle helped design a larger study called the Academic Performance Census (APC). In this study, every Division I school was asked to participate by providing academic data for all their student-athletes for a 6-year period. Most schools participated, and tens of thousands of records were being obtained each year. The analyses that McArdle and the NCAA research staff conducted on these data (for e.g., see McArdle, Paskus, & Boker, 2013) led to fundamental changes in the way that the NCAA viewed and implemented academic regulations for student-athletes once they were admitted to college. These data were also used to develop the Academic Progress Rate (APR), which is a real-time assessment of team-level academic progress that is predictive of eventual graduation rates. Even after all this work and positive change, McArdle's assessment of the data that were used was something like: "But wouldn't it be great if we could get data on everyone?"

In the early 2000s, that wish would come to fruition. When the APR was adopted, it required that data be collected on the term-by-term academic eligibility and retention of every student-athlete in Division I. The NCAA Division I Board of Directors, understanding how important and impactful the previously collected academic data had been, extended the data collection mandate to include a wide range of other academic variables like cumulative GPA, credit hours attempted and earned, academic major and many others. These

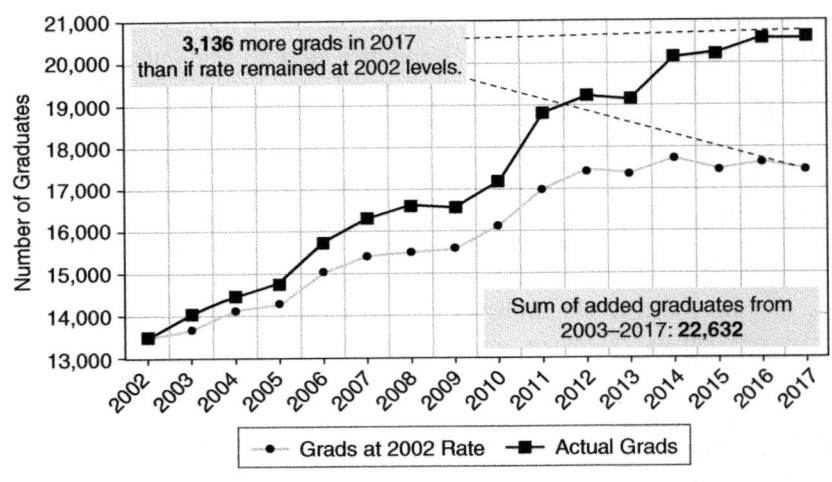

FIGURE 15.1 NCAA Division I actual graduates by year vs. number projected to earn degree if graduation rate remained at 2002 level.

college-level longitudinal data are matched directly with required high school transcript data that are collected for review by the NCAA Eligibility Center. This allows the NCAA to study the academic trajectories through high school and college of over 100,000 Division I student-athletes per year. The NCAA's Division II now follows suit in collecting academic data, and to date, there are several million academic records for Division I and II student-athletes stored in the NCAA database, making it the most comprehensive data collection on secondary and postsecondary education in the country (Petr & Paskus, 2009).

But, all along, McArdle was after a much wider range of variables on these student-athletes. In the 1990s, Jack, John Nesselroade, and James Jackson created the NCAA Basic Academic Skills Study (BASS), which provided a wide-range of experiential and cognitive data on a large sample of student-athletes. This allowed researchers to describe other factors beyond GPAs and test scores that related to whether a student graduated from college or not. BASS led to the NCAA Growth, Opportunities, Aspirations and Learning of Students in college (GOALS) study. The GOALS survey has now been used multiple times over the past decade to obtain information directly from student-athletes (20,000 per administration) related to their experiences whilst on campus. These include their academic, athletic, and social experiences; an accounting of their daily time commitments to academics and athletics; experiences around physical/mental health and well-being; descriptions of their relationships with coaches and faculty, and many other variables. Surveys on other topics are now administered annually by the NCAA. McArdle also helped develop the Study of College Outcomes and Recent Experiences (SCORE). This study targeted former student-athletes when they were about 30 years old, and asked them about their educational and job trajectories, as well as their current and past daily life experiences.

In 25 years, the NCAA shifted from an organization that did not collect or use much educational data to one of the primary national voices on the educational experiences of college students.

Quantifying a Legacy

It is very difficult to put Jack McArdle's legacy to the NCAA in simple numeric terms as he, we are sure, would want to do. Obviously, his impact on the research and policy-making efforts of the NCAA is substantial and appears to defy quantification. There is one telling number, though, that begins to describe in human terms (another research principle McArdle promoted) the impact that his efforts had on NCAA student-athletes. In 2002, when we began to collect the Graduation Success Rate (GSR) for Division I student-athletes, the overall rate was 74%. Since that time, which was interspersed with policy changes ushered in by the research program McArdle developed, the overall GSR at the Division I level has risen to 87%. Figure 15.1 illustrates how many student-athletes would have graduated had the overall rate not changed, versus the number who graduated under the new academic policies. In that timeframe, nearly 23,000 more student-athletes graduated than would have without the change in rates. That is 23,000 lives enhanced in part due to McArdle's efforts. And like the 500,000 current student-athletes mentioned at the beginning of this chapter, none of the 23,000 has probably ever heard the name Jack McArdle. No matter, Jack just wanted to use the data to help others make good decisions that would provide student-athletes with a chance to graduate. That is a legacy of which anyone should be proud.

References

Crowley, J. N. (2006). *In the arena: The NCAA's first century.* Indianapolis, IN: NCAA.

McArdle, J. J. (1998). Contemporary statistical models for examining test bias. In J. J. McArdle & R. W. Woodcock (Eds.), *Human cognitive abilities in theory and practice* (pp. 157–195). Mahwah, NJ: Erlbaum.

McArdle, J. J. & Hamagami, F. (1994). Logit and multilevel logit modeling of college graduation for 1984/1985 freshman student-athletes. *Journal of the American Statistical Association, 89,* 1107–1123.

McArdle, J. J., Paskus, T. S., & Boker, S. M. (2013). A multilevel multivariate analysis of academic performances in college based on NCAA student-athletes. *Multivariate Behavioral Research, 48,* 57–95.

Paskus, T. S. (2012). A summary and commentary on the quantitative results of current NCAA academic reforms. *Journal of Intercollegiate Sport, 5,* 41–53.

Paskus, T. S. (2013). Using exploratory data mining to identify academic risk among college student-athletes in the United States. In J. J. McArdle & G. Ritschard (Eds.), *Contemporary issues in exploratory data mining in the behavioral sciences* (pp. 345–370). New York: Routledge.

Petr, T. A. & McArdle, J. J. (2012). Academic research and reform: A history of the empirical basis for NCAA academic policy. *Journal of Intercollegiate Sport, 5*, 27–40.

Petr, T. A. & Paskus, T. S. (2009). The collection and use of academic outcomes data by the NCAA. In J. Hoffman, J. Antony & D. Alfaro (Eds.), *Data-driven decision making in intercollegiate athletics* (pp. 77–92). San Francisco, CA: Jossey-Bass.

16

A SUCCESSFUL CONSULTATION "TEAM" MODEL APPLYING CONTEMPORARY ADVANCED STATISTICS TO MINORITY RESEARCH CENTERS

Earl S. Hishinuma, Deborah A. Goebert, Naleen N. Andrade, Jane M. M. Onoye, Jeanelle J. Sugimoto-Matsuda, Junji Takeshita, & Stephanie T. Nishimura

Introduction

Jack's Impressive Academic Accomplishments

Dr John ("Jack") McArdle has advanced our science extensively, including the application of contemporary advanced statistics to the fields of psychometrics (McArdle, Grimm, Hamagami, Bowles, & Meredith, 2009), multi-level methodologies (McArdle, Hamagami, Bautista, Onoye, Hishinuma, Prescott, Takeshita, Zonderman, & Johnson, 2013), longitudinal designs (McArdle & Nesselroade, 2014), and data-mining techniques (McArdle & Ritschard, 2014). He has also tackled perplexing psychological and neurocognitive issues, including in the area of cognitive measurement, development, and aging (McArdle & Woodcock, 1998).

Jack's Successful Team-Approach in Working with Minority Researchers and Organizations

What is much less well-known by reading his academic publications, however, is Jack's more *personal* and professional ability to connect with and support clinical and applied minority researchers who are planning, conducting, and disseminating critically important research. In particular, the development and maintenance of an academic core conducting innovative minority research within a clinical department in the middle of the Pacific Ocean requires a successful partnership with an expert who complements the endeavor in just the right way – frankly, by readily adapting to the minority organization's "culture," and by sacrificing his time and effort needed to build minority research centers.

Jack has done just this for the Research Division of the Department of Psychiatry, John A. Burns School of Medicine, University of Hawai'i at Mānoa. He first started working with the Department of Psychiatry in 1990 – over a quarter-century ago. Prior to 1990, Dr Ronald C. Johnson, former Chair of the Department of Psychology, University of Hawai'i at Mānoa, had worked closely with Dr Naleen N. Andrade, who, at the time, was the Associate Chair of the Department of Psychiatry. Dr Johnson began working with Jack, including on the Hawai'i Family Study of Cognition – a large cohort from the early 1970s (see below) – and introduced Jack to Dr Andrade in 1990. At that time, Dr Andrade was spearheading a National Institutes of Health, Selective Excellence in Health-Related Research Supplement for Research Center in Minority Institutions (RCMI) to establish a Native Hawaiian mental health center that would conduct epidemiological studies on community and clinical samples of Native Hawaiians.

Fast-forward to the present, and looking back, Jack has had a profound and lasting impact on the Department of Psychiatry. Collectively, we have been successful because of Jack's approach of: (1) readily adapting to our organizational "culture"; (2) establishing relationships and a team; (3) providing technical training and application; and (4) strategically planning for the long-term. We elaborate and discuss this approach below, and also delineate some of the major outcomes. We also argue that such a model is much less common than the more traditional, short-term "consultation," but Jack's model is so direly needed; yet, it is antithetical to the relatively short-term extramural funding cycles. We specifically used quotations around "consultation," because we do not feel Jack is a "consultant" to us, but rather, part of our team.

Readily Adapting to Our Organizational "Culture"

Individualism

America's western culture values individualism and productivity – that is, independence, self-reliance, individual achievement, timeliness, competition, and having only one winner. In general, embedded within this broader culture, academia reflects these values, for example, by the conventions of having only one first-author on peer-reviewed journal articles and having only one Principal Investigator on extramural grants. This one person receives the bulk of the credit, at times, even when indispensable teams are involved. Further, the argument has been made with ample support that academic psychologists are trained, to some degree, to be individualistic – to stand out from everyone else and make names for themselves – even by "reinventing the wheel" and calling the same psychological construct something else to promote their own recognition (Staats, 1983). These oftentimes implicit, and sometimes explicit, tides have greatly worked against minority academicians, including minority researchers trying to conduct high-quality research in psychology, psychiatry, and mental health.

Collectivism

For the cultures of Native Hawaiians, Pacific Peoples, and Asian Americans, there is much more value and emphasis on inter-dependence, reliance on one another and on a team, group competition, team achievements, and process (rather than on only productivity). The Department of Psychiatry at the University of Hawai'i at Mānoa is the most ethnically diverse in the US regarding Native Hawaiian, Pacific People, and Asian-American faculty and residents. In its history, the Department of Psychiatry has had only four leaders: Dr Walter F. Char of Chinese ancestry, Dr John F. McDermott of European American heritage, Dr Naleen N. Andrade of Native Hawaiian and Portuguese ancestry, and Dr Anthony P. S. Guerrero of Filipino heritage (Guerrero, 2015).

Therefore, contrary to the individualistic view, a more team- and harmony-oriented approach is needed (Merkin, 2015). In this regard, Jack readily embraced the more collectivistic perspective with a personality conducive to "going with the flow" (as opposed to "my way or the highway" for some consultation models). Thus, he quickly adapted to our more collectivistic organizational culture. For example, at first, Jack appeared to be more used to wearing formal "East Coast" attire (e.g., neck tie), starting meetings and trainings exactly on time and going immediately into the content, not eating during meetings, and not having more informal "play time." He soon learned to expect meetings and trainings to start on "local time" – that is, only after people have arrived and gotten their food, had an opportunity to greet each other, and catch up, because for the Native Hawaiian culture, relationships, and not time, define the focus and completion of a set of complex tasks. And hence, activities, such as sharing a meal, are the most effective means of getting people around a common table to begin the work of building a cohesive team. And he learned to also "play" both during meetings and trainings with the Department of Psychiatry (e.g., what we call "talk-story," which is an informal discussion, but is an important way to establish relationships) and outside of these events (e.g., enjoying dinners, going to the movies, visiting Hawaiian historical sites). The cultural context of the importance of relationships and building interpersonal trust, even within an academic environment, was and still remains a large part of how collaborations and partnerships are formed and sustained in Hawai'i. An even more subtle distinction can be made between "vertical" vs. "horizontal" collectivism (Singelis, Triandis, Bhawuk, & Gelfand, 1995). Vertical collectivism involves perceiving being part of the collective, but accepting inequalities within. Horizontal collectivism involves perceiving being part of the collective and seeing all members as the same. Despite Jack clearly possessing advanced skills in contemporary statistics, he always conveys horizontal collectivism to our team.

In addition to adapting to our organizational culture, Jack also readily adapted the content and level of his trainings to the applications that we needed at the time and to those who were in the audience, including clinical psychiatrists who had virtually no background in statistics – let alone contemporary advanced statistics.

Further, the content that we studied was directly on the role of Native Hawaiian ethnicity and culture on mental health. The readers may not be aware, but Native Hawaiians, the indigenous people of the Hawaiian Islands, were devastated by Western contact. Although there are different estimates of the population of the Hawaiian Islands prior to Western contact, one source estimated that there were approximately 1 million Native Hawaiians when Captain James Cook arrived in 1778 (Stannard, 1988). Primarily through disease and marginalization, there were only 6,000 full Native Hawaiians and 34,000 mixed Native Hawaiians by 1893 – the time of the overthrow of the Hawaiian Monarchy – a decrease of 96% in just 115 years (Blaisdell, 1989). Added to this cultural complexity was the flow of immigrants into Hawai'i for religious, political, and economic reasons (Andrade & Bell, 2011; McDermott & Andrade, 2011). Given this context, Jack also displayed the sensitivity, humility, and respect needed for someone supporting first-hand the analysis and interpretation of the results involving Native Hawaiian culture and the indigenous response to devastating historical loss and trauma of their people and nation to Euro-American colonization.

In this process, Jack was no longer viewed as a "consultant," but one of the "team." In Hawai'i, he blended in as a "local"; someone with the values of collectivism and respect of diverse cultures.

Establishing Relationships and a Team

Trusting Relationships

One important component of collectivism is inter-dependence. Implicit in the term is not just the assembly of people with the right academic skill set – this is sometimes the easy part; however, this alone can be disastrous. Implicit in the term is people genuinely getting along and *trusting* one another. To no surprise, this takes both good people and a lot of time – years.

Since 1990, Jack's relationship with the Department of Psychiatry blossomed. He routinely provided the Department of Psychiatry annual, if not more frequent, trainings and collaborations – initially as a visiting professor and consultant, and subsequently, as an invaluable team member helping us year-round. Jack also reciprocated in inviting several of the Department of Psychiatry's faculty and staff to the University of Virginia when he was there, and to the University of Southern California.

We have also trusted Jack to have our best interests in mind and have seen him as a mentor and advisor to the research development within our Native Hawaiian research endeavors. And when new ideas surface, Jack is always thinking about how to partner to maximize benefit to others.

Team

Part of collectivism is forming a competent, cohesive, and trusting team. The team consists of Department of Psychiatry faculty, residents, researchers, students, and administrators. In addition to Jack joining our team, he also brought in two important contributors: Dr Carol Prescott and Dr Fumiaki ("Aki") Hamagami. Dr Prescott is a Clinical Psychologist and Professor of Psychology at the University of Southern California. Prior to this appointment, she was a faculty member in the Department of Psychiatry at Virginia Commonwealth University. Her clinical psychology training, mental health research expertise, extramural experience, and background in a Department of Psychiatry are invaluable. Dr Hamagami earned his PhD in psychology from the University of Virginia, and is an expert in advanced statistical analyses and cross-cultural issues. He continues to support our efforts in tackling sophisticated data analyses for our large-scale epidemiologic observational studies. Both Dr Prescott and Dr Hamagami are part of the team and well-known to the Research Division of the Department of Psychiatry.

Providing Technical Training and Application

Training Approach

Jack's training approach is: (1) "down to Earth"; (2) adapted to be directly relevant; (3) hands-on; and (4) quality-driven. We have heard it many times – Jack just has a way of explaining complicated statistics in such simple and understandable terms – this coming from psychiatrists and others who have little or no background in statistics and research. And when you have questions, he always makes you feel that your questions are important, no matter how rudimentary they may be.

Jack adapts the content and instructional format to meet the needs of the audience, including topics as varied as psychometrics, prevalence differences across minority groups, and longitudinal observational designs.

His trainings are "hands-on." We apply the training on the spot with the goal of actually submitting the manuscript shortly thereafter. And luckily for us, with the advent of various ways to communicate using technology, he supports our efforts, in actuality, throughout the year.

Jack also sides with "quality over quantity" when it comes to analyses and dissemination. He nudges us to take the time and energy to analyze data using contemporary advanced statistical techniques, even if it takes longer, with the goal of disseminating and publishing quality research. Such an approach is also contagious and has spread to all of our research efforts.

Jack's principles in technical training and application apply not only to the projects that he supports (see below), but also individual graduate-level research projects. He and his team have assisted and advised several graduate-level doctoral dissertations (e.g., Dr Deborah Goebert, Dr 'Iwalani Else, Dr Stephanie Nishimura, Dr Janice Y. Chang, Dr Jane Chung-Do, and Dr Mapuana Antonio), all involving Native Hawaiian, Pacific People, and/or Asian American populations, enabling them to utilize contemporary advanced statistics.

Projects

Although Jack has provided support to many of our studies, including having scheduled one-to-one and small-group meetings with psychiatry faculty and researchers, he has provided enormous support to three major research programs: (1) *National Center on Indigenous Hawaiian Behavioral Health (NCIHBH)*; (2) *Hawai'i Family Study of Cognition* (HFSC); and (3) *Asian/Pacific Islander Youth Violence Prevention Center* (APIYVPC).

National Center on Indigenous Hawaiian Behavioral Health. The *National Center on Indigenous Hawaiian Behavioral Health* (NCIHBH; formerly the Native Hawaiian Mental Health Research Development Program) was first established by Dr Naleen Andrade, with guidance, collaboration, and mentorship from several experts: Jack, Dr Ronald Johnson (former Chair of the Department of Psychology), Dr John McDermott, Jr. (child-adolescent psychiatrist, and at the time, Chair of the Department of Psychiatry), Dr Spero Manson (expert in American Indian/Alaska Native mental health research), Dr James (Jim) Shore (at the time, Chair of the Department of Psychiatry, University of Colorado, Denver), and Dr Fredrick (Fred) Greenwood (at the time, head of the Research Centers in Minority Institutions, University of Hawai'i at Mānoa). One of the primary aims of the program was to develop an epidemiologic map of Native Hawaiian adolescent mental health. The program was first funded by the Research Centers in Minority Institutions (RCMI) Supplement, National Institutes of Health (NIH; RR0361-06S1), and subsequently funded by two National Institute of Mental Health (NIMH) minority training and research grants (i.e., Native Hawaiian Mental Health Research Development Program, R24 MH5015-01; Pacific People Mental Health Research Support Program; R24 MH57079-A1). The empirical research centerpieces were two large, ethnically diverse, longitudinal cross-sequential epidemiologic data sets: (1) 1992–1996 Hawaiian High Schools Health Survey (HHSHS; $N = 7,317$, number of completed surveys $= 12,284$) and Diagnostic Interview Schedule for Children (DISC, $N = 619$), 9th–12th graders from 5 high schools across 3 of the Hawaiian Islands (Andrade, Hishinuma, McDermott, Johnson, Goebert, Makini, Nahulu, Yuen, McArdle, Bell, Carlton, Miyamoto, Nishimura, Else, Guerrero, Darmal, Yates, & Waldron, 2006); and (2) 2001–2005 Hawai'i Adolescent Behavioral Survey (HABS; $N > 1,000$), Diagnostic Interview Schedule for Children, Diagnostic Interview Schedule, Wechsler Intelligence Scale for Children 3rd ed. (WISC-III), and Wechsler Adult Intelligence Scale 3rd ed. (WAIS-III), 8th graders followed to 10th grade from 6 middle schools, and 12th graders followed through adulthood from 6 high schools (Else & Andrade, 2008; Native Hawaiian Mental Health Research Development Program, 1998).

Hawai'i Family Study of Cognition. The *Hawai'i Family Study of Cognition* (HFSC) was established by Dr Johnson and several of his colleagues, with the aim of assessing the genetic and environmental bases of cognitive abilities and how these were modified by cultural context. The program was funded by the National Science Foundation (NSF GB-34720) and National Institutes of Health (NICHD HD-06669). The original cohort consisted of over 6,500 individuals from over 1,800 families living on O'ahu, Hawai'i, from 1972–1976 (DeFries et al., 1976; Onoye, Hishinuma, McArdle, Zonderman, Bumanglag, & Takeshita, 2014). The advantages of this database are the ethnic diversity, measurement and linkage of parent-child cognitive abilities, and subsequently, longitudinal follow-ups.

Asian/Pacific Islander Youth Violence Prevention Center. The *Asian/Pacific Islander Youth Violence Prevention Center* (APIYVPC) was first established in 2000 by Dr Gregory Mark, formerly of the University of Hawai'i at Mānoa, in collaboration with the National Council on Crime and Delinquency (NCCD) of California. The APIYVPC was renewed in 2005 with Dr Hishinuma as the Principal Investigator. Both five-year grant periods were funded by the Centers for Disease Control and Prevention (CDC; R49/CCR918619-05, U49/CE000749-01, respectively). In addition to this program including ethnically diverse epidemiologic data sets (e.g., Mayeda, Hishinuma, Nishimura, Garcia-Santiago, & Mark, 2006), Jack's contributions were in the multitude of trainings and advice that he provided as a Scientific Advisory Committee member and research methodologist-statistician consultant to the entire APIYVPC.

The following will focus primarily on the progress made by the NCIHBH because of its breath and scope, although occasional studies will be referred to from the HFSC and APIYVPC where particularly relevant. In addition, an outcome summary will be provided toward the end of this chapter.

Methodologies and Statistical Analyses

Methodological design. Jack emphasizes getting the methodological design right first, or at least within practical limits. He does so because no amount of back-end statistical analyses, no matter how sophisticated, can always fully make up for a poorly planned methodology. One of his mantras is the importance of planning for and collecting longitudinal data, especially where repeated measures are involved. Jack's emphasis on longitudinal designs is reflected in nature of the data of our projects.

In addition, Jack emphasizes the advances in imputations to address incomplete data, such that longitudinal designs are even more useful (e.g., comparing differences in results between imputed vs. non-imputed data). In fact, Jack is the only researcher we know who gets positively excited about having "missing data."

By anticipating the analyses that are projected to be employed after the data are collected, Jack advises on the sample composition to assure the ability to make the required group comparisons. Just as one example, we were fortunate in having subsequently added new cohorts to the NCIHBH study, which allowed us to compare Native Hawaiian and non-Hawaiian adolescent groups.

Psychometrics. When studying minority populations, one of the perennial questions is whether newly developed and standardized scales that are used are applicable for the minority populations under study. Therefore, determining what constructs are actually being measured for minority populations must be first addressed.

To accomplish the goal of creating an epidemiologic map of Native Hawaiian adolescent mental health, the NCIHBH needed to develop an epidemiologic risk-protective factors survey battery that was reliable and valid with adolescents in Hawai'i. We obtained a start with the help of Dr Shore and Dr Manson of the University of Colorado, Denver. They had already developed and tested the Sequoia High School Health Survey (Ackerson, Wiegman-Dick, Manson, & Baron, 1990) with American Indian/Alaska Native adolescents. With their permission, we adapted this survey battery and developed the Hawaiian High Schools Health Survey (HHSHS; Andrade, Johnson, Edman, Danko, Nahulu, Makini, Yuen, Waldron, Yates, & McDermott, 1994). Jack provided invaluable guidance and training on investigating the reliability and validity of all the scales contained within the HHSHS (Hishinuma, Miyamoto, Nishimura, Nahulu, Andrade, Makini, Yuen, Johnson, Kim, Goebert, & Guerrero, 2000; McArdle, Johnson, Hishinuma, Miyamoto, & Andrade, 2001; Nishimura, Hishinuma, Miyamoto, Goebert, Johnson, Yuen, & Andrade, 2001).

Jack also provided guidance and training on the predictive-construct validity of the HHSHS. In the NCIHBH's most cited journal article, Prescott, McArdle, Hishinuma, Johnson, Miyamoto, Andrade, Edman, Makini, Nahulu, Yuen, and Carlton (1998) investigated the validity of the Center for Epidemiologic Studies-Depression (CES-D; Radloff, 1977) scale predicting Diagnostic Interview Schedule for Children (DISC; Shaffer, Schwab-Stone, Fisher, Cohen, Piacentini, Davies, Conners, & Regier, 1993) depression diagnoses. Subsequent examples included predicting DISC anxiety diagnoses (Hishinuma, Miyamoto, Nishimura, Goebert, Yuen, Makini, Andrade, Johnson, & Carlton, 2001) and predicting DISC substance use disorders (Nishimura et al., 2001).

Related to predictive validity was the objective to develop a short-form version of the HHSHS for research and clinical purposes. The HHSHS was between 17 and 22 pages in length, depending on the cohort year that it was used. Jack guided us on how to develop a short-form version, subsequently called the Hawai'i Adolescent Behavioral Survey (HABS; NHMHRDP, 1998), which was only seven pages. This also allowed us to later add more protective scales (e.g., family environment, coping skills) that were missing in previous versions. A subsequent version of the HABS was used in our 2001–2005 large-scale, longitudinal, epidemiologic study surveying over 1,000 students (i.e., surveyed students in the 8th grade and re-surveyed them in the 10th grade, and surveyed students in the 12th grade and resurveyed them in adulthood 2 years later; Pacific People Mental Health Research Support Program funded by NIMH).

One of the most important research questions posed by the NCIHBH was, "What is the role of culture in Native Hawaiian adolescent mental health?" Although "culture" could be indicated with an overly simplified traditional measure, such as Native Hawaiian ancestry or language use, the NCIHBH utilized a methodologically rigorous approach to develop and validate a new scale (i.e., Hawaiian Culture Scale – Adolescent Version) that measured different aspects of Native Hawaiian cultural identity (Andrade, Hishinuma, Miyamoto, Johnson, Nahulu, Yuen, Makini, Nishimura, McArdle, McDermott, Waldron, & Yates, 2000; Hishinuma, Andrade, Johnson, McArdle, Miyamoto, Nahulu, Makini, Yuen, Nishimura, McDermott, Waldron, Luke, & Yates, 2000). For example, focus groups of Native Hawaiian community elders, adults, and youth from working middle-class and professional middle-class groups, including cultural experts from each of the major Hawaiian islands, were first conducted to elucidate the constructs of Native Hawaiian cultural identity (i.e., face and content validity; Andrade et al., 2000). A quantitative scale was then developed and administered to a large sample of Native Hawaiian and non-Hawaiian adolescents. Utilizing exploratory and confirmatory analyses (Andrade et al., 2000), a seven-factor Hawaiian Culture Scale – Adolescent Version was found to be reliable (Cronbach alphas) and valid (i.e., concurrent, convergent, divergent, construct validity) for both Native Hawaiian and non-Hawaiian adolescents (Hishinuma, Andrade et al., 2000). To date, of the several scales measuring Native Hawaiian cultural identification, the Hawaiian Culture Scale – Adolescent Version utilized the largest sample to systematically test its psychometric properties.

Jack also applied longitudinal growth and change modeling to item response theory (IRT) using the 13 items of the CES-D Factor 1 (Negative Affect) from the NCIHBH's data set (McArdle, Petway, & Hishinuma, 2015). This study demonstrated that the only ethnicity-gender group to demonstrate any increase over time was non-Hawaiian males, who eventually converged with Native Hawaiian males.

Epidemiology. One of the major goals of the NCIHBH was to develop an epidemiologic map of Native Hawaiian adolescent mental health. A key traditional indicator of level of mental health is the prevalence of Diagnostic and Statistical Manual (DSM) diagnoses (e.g., American Psychiatric Association, 1987). Jack provided careful attention to this seminal study. With the use of weights, we found that Native Hawaiian adolescents had statistically higher levels of anxiety disorders than non-Hawaiian youth, with the highest level for Native Hawaiian girls. This study was followed by a more detailed investigation examining obsessive-compulsive disorder, which highlighted the risk for Polynesian groups (Guerrero, Hishinuma, Andrade, Bell, Kurahara, Lee, Turne, Andrus, Yuen, & Stokes, 2003).

We also compared the levels of psychiatric symptoms for the different ethnic groups. For example, Jack took the lead on examining the CES-D as a measure of depressive symptoms (McArdle et al., 2001). He demonstrated the advantages of an SEM approach (e.g., larger explained variance) over more traditional methods (e.g., analysis of variance), and found that Native Hawaiian adolescents had a higher level of depressive symptoms than non-Hawaiian youth. There were several additional studies that examined other psychiatric symptoms and compared the levels across the major ethnic groups in Hawai'i (e.g., for anxiety symptoms, Hishinuma et al., 2000).

Risk–protective and longitudinal–temporal models. The next step after epidemiologic studies is risk-protective models to determine possible causal pathways and potential prevention and intervention points. We explored different approaches, including more traditional exploratory methods (Hishinuma, Else, Chang, Goebert, Nishimura, Choi-Misailidis, & Andrade, 2006) and cumulative-risk models, (Goebert, Nahulu, Hishinuma, Bell, Yuen, Carlton, Andrade, Miyamoto, & Johnson, 2000). Early on, Jack introduced path analysis and structural equation modeling (SEM) to us, noting that the advantages included hierarchical analyses (e.g., A leads to B, and B leads to C) in one model, and latent variables based on manifest variables. This heavily impacted our approach for multiple projects, including for the NCIHBH and APIYVPC (Chung-Do, Goebert, Chang, Hamagami, & Hishinuma, 2015; Goebert, Chang, Chung-Do, Else, Hamagami, Helm, Kinkade, & Sugimoto-Matsuda, 2012; Miyamoto, Hishinuma, Nishimura, Nahulu, Andrade, Goebert, & Carlton, 2001).

Of particular innovation is Jack's expertise modeling longitudinal data that included repeated measures of the same variables across multiple time points. Such a design was the very nature of the NCIHBH's 1992–1996 cross-sequential study. We applied bivariate ("coupling") dynamic SEM to the depressive symptoms (CES-D) and self-reported grade-point average (GPA) (Hishinuma, Chang, McArdle, & Hamagami, 2012; McArdle, Hamagami, Chang, & Hishinuma, 2014). This model goes beyond the correlational nature of cross-sectional designs to be able to make conclusions about the temporal relationship between variables based on a longitudinal repeated measures design. Our findings suggested that depressive symptoms adversely impact GPA, and not the other way around. This same approach was utilized to determine the interplay among not two, but three repeated measures variables of hope, help-seeking, and suicide attempts using the NCIHBH data (Goebert, Hamagami, Hishinuma, Chung-Do, & Sugimoto-Matsuda, in press).

Multi-generational family-based models. Jack also highlighted that another distinct benefit of SEM is its ability to take advantage of data provided by different individuals who are somehow linked – for example, data from different individuals who are in the same family. This applied particularly to the HFSC where we had actual cognitive performance data from multiple family generations (i.e., parents & their children) (Onoye et al., 2014). In addition to finding that a "g-only" model did not fit well, the conclusion was made that cognitive differences were larger within families than between families for our ethnically diverse sample (McArdle, Hamagami et al., 2013).

Multi-group comparisons. Jack advocates the use of multi-group SEM instead of more traditional group interaction effects, because one can learn more about the differences between groups using SEM. Within this context, we have employed multi-group SEM to compare Native Hawaiian and non-Hawaiian adolescents on CES-D factors (McArdle et al., 2001), to compare the dynamic temporal relationships between CES-D and self-reported GPA (Hishinuma et al., 2012; McArdle et al., 2014), and to compare the dynamic temporal relationships amongst hope, help-seeking, and suicide attempts (Goebert et al., in press).

Program evaluation. The NCIHBH's initial aims were epidemiologic, and therefore there were no program evaluations. However, Jack's influence in the area of program evaluation is also evident for other projects. For example, Jack provided guidance on a program evaluation study for the APIYVPC that examined whether a Native Hawaiian 5th- and 6th-grade after-school program was effective. The evaluation methodology essentially entailed a longitudinal pre–post design with incomplete data (e.g., attrition), and the results were very supportive of the positive impact that the program had on the children and parents (Hishinuma, Chang, Sy, Greaney, Morris, Scronce, Rehuher, D, & Nishimura, 2009).

Culminating Studies. One particular study that has been cited previously in separate occurrences has been a prototype example of Jack's overall influence (Hishinumi et al., 2012; McArdle et al., 2014). Using the NCIHBH's longitudinal cross-sequential data, this study had several elements within this one investigation that were addressed using SEM: (1) incomplete data; (2) ordinal-scale dependent variable; (3) bivariate dynamic SEM; and (4) multi-group comparisons. This type of study is a culminating example of the methodological and statistical sophistication that was brought by Jack to the Department of Psychiatry.

Strategically Planning for the Long Term

A primary point to be made is that Jack's guidance and impact are always strategic and forward-thinking. This is evident not only in his recommendations on methodology even before data are collected (e.g., collect longitudinal data), but also during data analysis and dissemination (e.g., quality over quantity; establish the psychometric soundness first). The direct and indirect academic outcomes and products have been outstanding.

National Center on Indigenous Hawaiian Behavioral Health. The NCIHBH has published over 45 peer-reviewed journal articles – many cited previously – and in very prestigious journals: *Archives of Pediatrics and Adolescent Medicine* (10.3 impact); *Journal of the American Academy of Child and Adolescent Psychiatry* (7.3 impact); *Journal of Adolescent Health* (3.6 impact); *Structural Equation Modeling* (3.2 impact); *Developmental Psychology* (3.1 impact); *Assessment* (2.9 impact); *Psychological Assessment* (2.8 impact); *Alcohol and Alcoholism* (2.7 impact);

Social Psychiatry and Psychiatric Epidemiology (2.5 impact); *Journal of Anxiety Disorders* (2.4 impact); and *Journal of Substance Abuse* (2.0 impact).

At present, the NCIHBH is continuing to analyze its data and disseminate the findings through presentations and publications. In partnership with Kula No Na Po'e Hawai'i, for example, the NCIHBH has extramural funding from the US Department of Education to evaluate Native Hawaiian education activities in the Papakōlea Community. The NCIHBH's findings and publications have been instrumental in advancing the science and practice regarding Native Hawaiian mental health. For example, the epidemiologic results are being used as the cornerstone to the update of the *E Ola Mau A Mau Report*, which will be utilized to request funding from the US Congress to continually improve Native Hawaiian health and mental health.

Hawai'i Family Study of Cognition. The HFSC has published more than 50 peer-reviewed publications (http://blog.hawaii.edu/hfsc/). Although the majority were published prior to Jack's involvement with the HFSC, a revival of the HFSC was begun back in 2010. The goals of the revival were to: (1) preserve and systematically organize the archived data of the HFSC; (2) reanalyze the classic data with contemporary statistical methods that were not possible decades earlier; and (3) follow up with the HFSC and provide added-value to the data, including regarding cognitive aging for diverse ethnic groups. These efforts were supported by the National Institute on Aging (NIA), University of Southern California, and The Queens Medical Center.

Led by Dr Johnson and Jack, in collaboration with several of the original and later investigators, a new team of HFSC researchers was assembled to address the goals. Onoye et al. (2014) described the history of the HFSC and its archived data. The team also reanalyzed the classic data, but with contemporary statistical methods that were not possible decades earlier (McArdle, Hamagami et al., 2013; McArdle & Prindle, 2013; Zhou, Kadlec, & McArdle, 2013).

Finally, while several follow-ups of select groups from the original cohort occurred over the years since the original study (see Onoye et al., 2014), the 2010 revival attempted to leverage technological advances and the Internet to recontact and retest a longitudinal cohort, which included a large number of Asian/Pacific Islander families. The earliest studies of the 2010s determined feasibility for tracking and tracing, and garnered positive responses from a subgroup of the HFSC who were most likely to respond with updated contact and demographic information after being recontacted 30–40 years later (Bumanglag & Onoye, 2013; Lee & Onoye, 2014).

Based on a response rate of about 40% agreeing to participate in a follow-up study, a pilot project utilizing web-based cognitive testing and a survey of health-related questions was conducted with HFSC original parents, adult children (offspring), and volunteer grandchildren (Konishi & Onoye, 2014). One of the preliminary findings suggested that the middle-aged HFSC children experienced better current general health than their aging parents, but also higher levels of stress, possibly related to financial or family obligations, such as caregiving of their parents while still working. Additionally, cultural contexts and generational differences in web-based assessment needed to be explored further.

Other related studies involved interviewing a sample from the HFSC cohort to assess parent cognitive status or decline (Long & Onoye, 2014, 2015) and health-related quality of life of parents and children (Yatsushiro & Onoye, 2014). While preliminary, these studies showed that children could serve as informants of their parent cognitive status (Long & Onoye, 2014), that parent-report and children-report may vary when there are problems in the parents' memory and thinking (Long & Onoye, 2015), and that mental health was related to physical health (Yatsushiro & Onoye, 2014).

With the increasing burden of caregiving of aging parents becoming a national and local public health issue, HFSC families were also surveyed and interviewed in a study which found ethnocultural and family contexts to be important in later-life caregiving expectations, caregiver burden, and health-decision making (Lee, Thompson, Rehuher, & Onoye, 2016; Lee, Yatsushiro, & Onoye, 2015a, 2015b).

For all of these revival studies, Jack provided invaluable leadership and insight to guide the approach and methodology, thus contributing to our collaborative team in a way that made this research effort all the more meaningful.

Asian/Pacific Islander Youth Violence Prevention Center. As indicated before, Jack served as a Scientific Advisory Board member for the APIYVPC, as well as research advisor on a more frequent basis for individuals and research groups. As a Scientific Advisory Board member, he took the extra time to con-tinually help us improve the quality of our science at all stages (i.e., methodology, statistics), including our dissemination efforts (e.g., presentations to the Scientific Advisory Board and CDC Officials). The APIYVPC has published over 60 peer-reviewed journal articles, as well as several special issue journals and books on youth violence prevention.

At present, we continue to emphasize the importance of longitudinal obser-vational data and are involved with the evaluation of a youth-arrest diversion program in Hawai'i called Ho'opono Mamo. The goals of the program are to change arrests to citations and to decrease re-arrests, especially for Hawai'i's Native Hawaiian and Pacific Islander youth who are over-represented in this regard, by intervening with culturally responsive assessments and interventions. The over-all results have been positive showing a lower re-arrest rate for youth who went through the program as compared to a matched sample (Miao, Umemoto, Hish-inuma, & Smith, 2017). We are in the process of securing another extramural contract to evaluate the next phase of Ho'opono Mamo.

Other long-term impact. Implicit in the discussion above are the many clinicians, faculty, students, and staff who Jack has trained and/or mentored, and through the trainees and mentees, they in turn have trained and mentored even more junior researchers. Given the number of people who have been involved with the Department of Psychiatry's research since 1990, the number of researchers that Jack has directly or indirectly affected is likely over 200. Also implied in the previous discussion is Jack's impact on our extramural funding. Since 1990, the Research Division of the Department of Psychiatry has secured over $32 million in extramural funds. Jack has been involved with grants and contracts of at least a third of that amount.

Conclusion

Jack's positive impact on the Department of Psychiatry at the University of Hawai'i at Mānoa has been profound. He possesses a rare combination of skills which allows him to seamlessly blend into and become part of an organization's culture. For the Department of Psychiatry, he readily established trusting relationships and helped to assemble and be a part of a true team. He provided technical training and application in a manner that was understandable to those with no statistical background (i.e., down to earth), and he adapted the teaching and learning to be directly relevant, hands-on, and quality-driven. And he strategically planned for the long term. Some of the outcomes are obvious and readily observable (e.g., co-authored journal articles). However, we argue that Jack's "finger prints" are everywhere if you look hard enough.

FIGURE 16.1 Department of Psychiatry, University of Hawai'i at Mānoa, research faculty visiting John ("Jack") J. McArdle and Carol A. Prescott at their new home in Hawi, Hawai'i Island, January 12, 2017. Collectively, this group has over 135 years of experience in the Department of Psychiatry. From left to right: Jane M. M. Onoye, Deborah A. Goebert, Carol A. Prescott, Jack J. McArdle, Naleen N. Andrade, Earl S. Hishinuma, and Jeanelle J. Sugimoto-Matsuda. For additional photos, please go to: http://blog.hawaii.edu/dop/john-mcardle-chapter/.

References

Ackerson, L. M., Wiegman-Dick, R., Manson, S., & Baron, A. (1990). Properties of the inventory to diagnose depression in American Indian adolescents. *Journal of the American Academy of Child and Adolescent Psychiatry, 29*, 601–607.

American Psychiatric Association (1987). *Diagnostic and statistical manual of mental disorders III – revised (DSM-III-R).* Washington, DC: American Psychiatric Association.

Andrade, N. N. & Bell, C. K. (2011). The Hawaiians. In J. F. McDermott, Jr. & N. N. Andrade (Eds.), *People and cultures of Hawai'i: The evolution of culture and ethnicity* (pp. 1–31). Honolulu, HI: University of Hawai'i Press.

Andrade, N. N., Hishinuma, E. S., McDermott, Jr., J. F., Johnson, R. C., Goebert, D. A., Makini, Jr., G. K., Nahulu, L. B., Yuen, N. Y. C., McArdle, J. J., Bell, C. K., Carlton, B. S., Miyamoto, R. H., Nishimura, S. T., Else, I. R. N., Guerrero, A., Darmal, A., Yates, A., & Waldron, J. A. (2006). The National Center on Indigenous Hawaiian Behavioral Health study of prevalence of psychiatric disorders in Native Hawaiian adolescents. *Journal of the American Academy of Child and Adolescent Psychiatry, 45*(1), 26–36.

Andrade, N. N., Hishinuma, E. S., Miyamoto, R. H., Johnson, R. C., Nahulu, L. B., Yuen, N. Y. C., Makini, Jr., G. K., Nishimura, S. T., McArdle, J. J., McDermott, Jr., J. F., Waldron, J. A., & Yates, A. (2000). *Development and factor structure of the Hawaiian Culture Scale – Adolescent Version.* Unpublished manuscript, Department of Psychiatry, University of Hawai'i at Mānoa.

Andrade, N. N., Johnson, R. C., Edman, J., Danko, G. P., Nahulu, L. B., Makini, G. K., Yuen, N., Waldron, J. A., Yates, A., & McDermott, J. F. (1994). Non-traditional and traditional treatment of Hawaiian and Non-Hawaiian adolescents. *Hawai'i Medical Journal, 53*, 344–347. http://hjmph.org/53.12.htm

Blaisdell, K. (1989). Historical and cultural aspects of Native Hawaiian health. *Social Process in Hawai'i, 32*, 1–21.

Bumanglag, R. J. & Onoye, J. (2013, April). *Revival of the Hawai'i Family Study of Cognition: A 40-year follow up.* Poster presented at the annual John A. Burns School of Medicine Biomedical Sciences and Health Disparities Symposium, Honolulu, HI.

Chung-Do, J. J., Goebert, D. A., Chang, J. Y., Hamagami, F., & Hishinuma, E. S. (2015). Understanding the role of school connectedness and its association with violent attitudes and behaviors in an ethnically diverse school. *Journal of Interpersonal Violence, 32*(9), 1421–1446.

Defries, J. C., Ashton, G. C., Johnson, R. C., Kuse, A. R., McClearn, G. E., Mi, M. P., Rashad, M. N., Vandenberg, S. G., & Wilson, J. R. (1976). Parent-offspring resemblance for specific cognitive abilities in two ethnic groups. *Nature, 261*, 131–133.

Else, I. R. N. & Andrade, N. N. (2008). Examining suicide and suicidal-related behaviors among indigenous Pacific Islanders in the United States: A historical perspective. In F. Leong & M. Leach (Eds.), *Suicide among racial and ethnic minority groups: Theory, research, and practice* (pp. 143–172). New York: Routledge.

Goebert, D., Chang, J. Y., Chung-Do, J., Else, I. R. N., Hamagami, F., Helm, S., Kinkade, K., & Sugimoto-Matsuda, J. (2012). Social ecological determinants of youth violence among ethnically diverse Asian and Pacific Islander students. *Maternal and Child Health Journal, 16*(1), 188–196.

Goebert, D., Hamagami, F., Hishinuma, E., Chung-Do, J., & Sugimoto-Matsuda, J. (in press). Change pathways in indigenous and non-indigenous youth suicide. *Suicide and Life-Threatening Behavior.*

Goebert, D., Nahulu, L., Hishinuma, E., Bell, C., Yuen, N., Carlton, B., Andrade, N. N., Miyamoto, R., & Johnson, R. (2000). Cumulative effect of family environment on psychiatric symptomatology among multiethnic adolescents. *Journal of Adolescent Health, 27*(1), 34–42.

Guerrero, A. P. S. (2015). The University of Hawai'i John A. Burns School of Medicine Department of Psychiatry: Past, present, and future. *Hawai'i Journal of Medicine and*

Public Health, 74(2), 63–65. www.ncbi.nlm.nih.gov/pmc/articles/PMC4338569/pdf/hjmph7402_0063.pdf

Guerrero, A. P. S., Hishinuma, E. S., Andrade, N. N., Bell, C. K., Kurahara, D. K., Lee, T. G., Turner, H., Andrus, J., Yuen, N. Y. C., & Stokes, A. J. (2003). Demographic and clinical characteristics of adolescents in Hawai'i with obsessive-compulsive disorder. *Archives of Pediatrics and Adolescent Medicine, 157*(7), 665–670.

Hishinuma, E. S., Andrade, N. N., Johnson, R. C., McArdle, J. J., Miyamoto, R. H., Nahulu, L. B., Makini, Jr., G. K., Yuen, N. Y. C., Nishimura, S. T., McDermott, Jr., J. F., Waldron, J. A., Luke, K., & Yates, A. (2000). Psychometric properties of the Hawaiian Culture Scale—Adolescent version. *Psychological Assessment, 12*(2), 140–157.

Hishinuma, E. S., Chang, J. Y., McArdle, J. J., & Hamagami, F. (2012). Potential causal relationship between depressive symptoms and academic achievement in the Hawaiian High Schools Health Survey using contemporary longitudinal latent variable change models. *Developmental Psychology, 48*(5), 1327–1342.

Hishinuma, E. S., Chang, J. Y., Sy, A., Greaney, M. F., Morris, K. A., Scronce, A. C., Rehuher, D., & Nishimura, S. T. (2009). Hui Mālama O Ke Kai: A positive prevention-based youth development program based on Native Hawaiian values and activities. *Journal of Community Psychology, 37*(8), 987–1007.

Hishinuma, E. S., Else, I. R. N., Chang, J. Y., Goebert, D. A., Nishimura, S. T., Choi-Misailidis, S., & Andrade, N. N. (2006). Substance use as a robust correlate of school outcome measures for ethnically diverse adolescents of Asian/Pacific Islander ancestry. *School Psychology Quarterly, 21*(3), 286–322.

Hishinuma, E. S., Miyamoto, R. H., Nishimura, S. T., Goebert, D. A., Yuen, N. Y. C., Makini, Jr., G. K., Andrade, N. N., Johnson, R. C., & Carlton, B. S. (2001). Prediction of anxiety disorders using the State-Trait Anxiety Inventory for multi-ethnic adolescents. *Journal of Anxiety Disorders, 15*, 511–533.

Hishinuma, E. S., Miyamoto, R. H., Nishimura, S. T., & Nahulu, L. B. (2000). Differences in State-Trait Anxiety Inventory scores for ethnically diverse adolescents in Hawai'i. *Cultural Diversity and Ethnic Minority Psychology, 6*(1), 73–83.

Hishinuma, E. S., Miyamoto, R. H., Nishimura, S. T., Nahulu, L. B., Andrade, N. N., Makini, Jr., G. K., Yuen, N. Y. C., Johnson, R. C., Kim, S. P., Goebert, D. A., & Guerrero, A. P. S. (2000). Psychometric properties of the State-Trait Anxiety Inventory for Asian/Pacific-Islander adolescents. *Assessment, 7*(1), 17–36.

Konishi, M. & Onoye, J. (2014, April). *Differences in health and health behaviors of parents, children, and grandchildren of the Hawai'i Family Study of Cognition: A pilot study utilizing web-based assessment.* Poster presented at the annual John A. Burns School of Medicine Biomedical Sciences and Health Disparities Symposium, Honolulu, HI.

Lee, C. & Onoye, J. (2014, April). *Early cognitive and demographic factors for prediction of educational-occupational attainment, and healthcare utilization forty years later.* Poster presented at the annual University of Hawai'i Undergraduate Research Opportunities Program Symposium, Honolulu, HI.

Lee, M., Thompson, M., Rehuher, D., & Onoye, J. (2016, April). *Ethnocultural differences in later-life caregiving expectations, caregiver burden, family dynamics, and healthcare decision making factors.* Poster presented at the annual John A. Burns School of Medicine Biomedical Sciences and Health Disparities Symposium, Honolulu, HI.

Lee, M., Yatsushiro, K., & Onoye, J. (2015a, November). *Ethnic differences in caregiving expectation, burden, family dynamics and healthcare decision making.* Poster presented at the meeting of the Gerontological Society of America, Orlando, FL.

Lee, M., Yatsushiro, K., & Onoye, J. M. (2015b). Ethnic differences in caregiving expectation, burden, family dynamics, and healthcare decision making. *The Gerontologist, 55*(Suppl 2), 666–667.

Long, D. & Onoye, J. (2014, April). *Preliminary evaluation of the consistency of informant and parent report of cognitive function in a sample of elderly parents in the Hawai'i Family Study of Cognition.* Poster presented at the annual John A. Burns School of Medicine Biomedical Sciences and Health Disparities Symposium, Honolulu, HI.

Long, L. & Onoye, J. (2015, April). *Self-report and informant predictors of problems in memory and thinking in elderly parents of the HFSC.* Poster presented at the annual John A. Burns School of Medicine Biomedical Sciences and Health Disparities Symposium, Honolulu, HI.

Mayeda, D. T., Hishinuma, E. S., Nishimura, S. T., Garcia-Santiago, O., & Mark, G. Y. (2006). Asian/Pacific Islander Youth Violence Prevention Center: Interpersonal violence and deviant behaviors among youth in Hawai'i. *Journal of Adolescent Health, 39,* 276e1–276e11.

McArdle, J. J., Grimm, K. J., Hamagami, F., Bowles, R. P., & Meredith, W. (2009). Modeling life-span growth curves of cognition using longitudinal data with multiple samples and changing scales of measurement. *Psychological Methods, 14*(2), 126–149.

McArdle, J. J., Hamagami, F., Bautista, R., Onoye, J., Hishinuma, E. S., Prescott, C. A., Takeshita, J., Zonderman, A. B., & Johnson, R. C. (2013). Multilevel factor analyses of family data from the Hawai'i Family Study of Cognition. *Educational and Psychological Measurement, 74*(2), 292–342.

McArdle, J. J., Hamagami, F., Chang, J. Y., & Hishinuma, E. S. (2014). Longitudinal dynamic analyses of depression and academic achievement in the Hawaiian High Schools Health Survey using contemporary latent variable change models. *Structural Equation Modeling: A Multidisciplinary Journal, 21,* 608–629.

McArdle, J. J., Johnson, R. C., Hishinuma, E. S., Miyamoto, R. H., & Andrade, N. N. (2001). Structural equation modeling of group differences in CES-D ratings of Native Hawaiian and non-Hawaiian high school students. *Journal of Adolescent Research, 16*(2), 108–149.

McArdle, J. J. & Nesselroade, J. R. (Eds.). (2014). *Longitudinal data analysis using structural equation models.* Washington, DC: American Psychological Association.

McArdle, J. J., Petway, K. T., & Hishinuma, E. S. (2015). IRT for growth and change. In S. P. Reise & D. A. Revicki (Eds.), *Handbook of item response theory modeling: Applications to typical performance assessment* (pp. 435–456). New York: Routledge.

McArdle, J. & Prindle, J. J. (2013). Basic issues in the measurement of change. In K. F. Geisinger, B. A. Bracken, J. F. Carlson, J.-I. C. Hansen, N. R. Kuncel, Steven P. Reise, & M. C. Rodriguez (Eds.), *APA handbook of testing and assessment in psychology, Vol. 1: Test theory and testing and assessment in industrial and organizational psychology* (pp. 223–243). Washington, DC: American Psychological Association. http://dx.doi.org/10.1037/14047-000

McArdle, J. J. & Ritschard, G. (Eds.). (2014). *Contemporary issues in exploratory data mining in the behavioral sciences.* New York: Routledge.

McArdle, J. J. & Woodcock, R. W. (Eds.). (1998). *Human cognitive abilities in theory and practice.* Mahwah, NJ: Lawrence Erlbaum Associates.

McDermott, J. F. & Andrade, N. N. (Eds.). (2011). *People and cultures of Hawai'i: The evolution of culture and ethnicity.* Honolulu, HI: University of Hawai'i Press.

Merkin, R. (2015). The relationship between individualism/collectivism: Consultation and harmony needs. *Journal of Intercultural Communication, 39.* www.immi.se/intercultural/

Miao, T.-A., Umemoto, K., Hishinuma, E., & Smith, M. (2017). *Ho'opono Mamo: The Hawai'i Youth Diversion System Report, Year 1, March 16, 2015–March 15, 2016*. Honolulu, HI: University of Hawai'i at Mānoa.

Miyamoto, R. H., Hishinuma, E. S., Nishimura, S. T., Nahulu, L. B., Andrade, N. N., Goebert, D. A., & Carlton, B. S. (2001). Path models linking correlates of self-esteem in a multiethnic adolescent sample. *Personality and Individual Differences, 31*, 701–712.

Native Hawaiian Mental Health Research Development Program. (1998). *Development of the Hawai'i Adolescent Behavioral Survey (HABS)*. Honolulu, HI: Native Hawaiian Mental Health Research Development Program, Department of Psychiatry, University of Hawai'i at Mānoa.

Nishimura, S. T., Hishinuma, E. S., Miyamoto, R. H., Goebert, D. A., Johnson, R. C., Yuen, N. Y. C., & Andrade, N. N. (2001). Prediction of DISC substance abuse and dependency for ethnically diverse adolescents. *Journal of Substance Abuse, 13*, 597–607.

Onoye, J. M. M., Hishinuma, E. S., McArdle, J. J., Zonderman, A. B., Bumanglag, R. J., & Takeshita, J. (2014). Cohort profile: The Hawai'i Family Study of Cognition. *International Journal of Epidemiology, 43*(6), 1726–1735.

Prescott, C. A., McArdle, J. J., Hishinuma, E. S., Johnson, R. C., Miyamoto, R. H., Andrade, N. N., Edman, J. L., Makini Jr., G. K., Nahulu, L. B., Yuen, N. Y. C., & Carlton, B. S. (1998). Prediction of major depression and dysthymia from CES-D scores among ethnic minority adolescents. *Journal of the American Academy of Child and Adolescent Psychiatry, 37*(5), 495–503.

Radloff, L. S. (1977). The CES-D scale: A self-report depression scale for research in the general population. *Applied Psychological Measurement, 1*, 385–401.

Shaffer, D., Schwab-Stone, M., Fisher, P., Cohen, P., Piacentini, J., Davies, M., Conners, C. K., & Regier, D. (1993). The Diagnostic Interview Schedule for Children – rev. version (DISC-r): I. Preparation, field testing, interrater reliability, and acceptability. *Journal of the American Academy of Child and Adolescent Psychiatry, 32*(3), 643–650.

Singelis, T. A., Triandis, H. C., Bhawuk, D. P. S., & Gelfand, M. J. (1995). Horizontal and vertical dimensions of individualism-collectivism: A theoretical and measurement refinement. *Cross-Cultural Research, 29*, 240–275.

Staats, A. W. (1983). *Psychology's crisis of disunity: Philosophy and method for a unified science*. New York: Praeger Publishers.

Stannard, D. E. (1988). *Before the horror: The population of Hawai'i on the eve of western contact*. Honolulu, HI: University of Hawai'i Press.

Yatsushiro, K. & Onoye, J. (2014, April). *Health-related quality of life in an ethnically diverse sample of parents and children from the Hawai'i Family Study of Cognition*. Poster presented at the annual John A. Burns School of Medicine Biomedical Sciences and Health Disparities Symposium, Honolulu, HI.

Zhou, Y., Kadlec, K. M., & McArdle, J. (2013). Predicting mortality from demographics and specific cognitive abilities in the Hawai'i Family Study of Cognition. In J. McArdle & G. Ritschard (Eds.), *Contemporary issues in exploratory data mining in the behavioral sciences* (pp. 429–449). New York: Taylor & Frances.

INDEX

Page numbers in *italic* denote figures and in **bold** indicate tables.